D1599689

TEACHING
READING in
HIGH SCHOOL THIRD EDITION

Improving Reading in Content Areas

Robert Karlín

TEACHING READING in HIGH SCHOOL

THIRD EDITION

Improving Reading in Content Areas

BOBBS-MERRILL EDUCATIONAL PUBLISHING
Indianapolis

The Bobbs-Merrill Company, Inc.
4300 West 62nd Street
Indianapolis, Indiana 46268

Third Edition
Second Printing 1978
Designed by Viki Webb

Library of Congress Cataloging in Publication Data

Karlin, Robert.
  Teaching reading in high school.

  Bibliography: p.
  Includes index.
  1. Reading (Secondary education) I. Title.
LB1632.K3 1977   428.4   76-58523
ISBN 0-672-61402-2

to Andrea and Paul

CONTENTS

CHAPTER
3

PSYCHOLOGY
of TEACHING READING
43 in CONTENT AREAS

CHAPTER
4

IMPROVING
DIAGNOSTIC TEACHING
of READING
63 in CONTENT AREAS

GUIDING
READING in
109 CONTENT AREAS

CHAPTER
5

IMPROVING
WORD IDENTIFICATION SKILLS
135 in CONTENT AREAS

CHAPTER
6

PREFACE

Several years have passed since I wrote the preface to the first edition of *Teaching Reading in High School* in which I stated my views regarding the importance of teaching reading beyond the elementary grades and the need for upgrading existing high school reading instruction in content areas. In these intervening years technological developments have enabled us to put men on the moon, orbit space stations, devise sophisticated computer systems, and do much more. Research has permitted us to expand our knowledge of the universe and life itself. The future promises accomplishments that are bound to surpass even these.

Yet, the needs of youths to increase their reading power persists, perhaps *because* of what they now know and the decisions they must make. Scientific progress has not, as some sages predicted, erased print as one form of communication. Nor is it likely to do so. The importance of reading ability for all youth and quality programs to insure its development grows. This is hardly the time to exchange our objectives for lesser ones. In fact, we must do better than we have in the past. This is why I have revised this textbook for a second time in an effort to help teachers improve the quality of their reading instruction and thereby increase the reading powers of students.

Teaching Reading in High School: Improving Reading in Content Areas is designed for prospective and practicing secondary school teachers. Most teachers would describe it as a "practical" textbook in that its recommendations for teaching reading in content areas are specific and explicit. Methods of teaching reading in content areas should reflect a defensible rationale, and it is for this reason that an early chapter is devoted to the "Psychology of Reading and Learning," together with their applications. Moreover, a chapter on "Improving Diagnostic Teaching of Reading in Content Areas" precedes others which discuss and illustrate methods for helping students master content through improved reading strategies. My aim is to avoid "shotgun" instruction which fails to address itself to the reading requirements of students. I propose that instruction should focus on what students need in order to improve their reading ability.

The basic structure of the textbook has been altered in this revised edition, and its contents have been expanded and updated. Fourteen chapters have been condensed into eleven, and the order of the major topics is rearranged. These changes resulted from recommendations by professors and students who have used the book in classes on secondary school reading and by reviewers who studied the second edition and suggested changes to improve its usefulness.

Each chapter in this edition contains new information drawn from the results of recent research and many additional "how to" aids that will enable teachers to enhance the effectiveness of their reading programs. Included in the new material are ways to evaluate the difficulty of materials for reading instruction; strategies for teaching sentence and paragraph comprehension; methods for integrating reading instruction with the study of content, for individualizing instruction, and for overcoming reading difficulties in students of different cultural backgrounds. In addition, the standard reference sources at the end of each chapter, as well as the references in periodicals listed in Appendix A, have been brought up to date as have the lists of reading materials and reading tests in Appendixes B and C.

In summary, my views regarding the importance of teaching reading in content areas have not changed, nor have the premises on which the textbook rests. The best reading programs are conducted by teachers who understand what reading entails and how to promote reading efficiency. Some steps toward the goal "that all may read" have been taken, but many more remain. Good reading!

I wish to express appreciation to all who have suggested changes for improving this textbook and to the editorial staff of Bobbs-Merrill for their advice and encouragement. I also wish to acknowledge the invaluable assistance I received from my wife Edith who proofread the manuscript and facilitated its completion.

Robert Karlin

Queens College of the City University of New York

LIST of FIGURES

TEACHING
READING in
HIGH SCHOOL   THIRD EDITION

Improving Reading in Content Areas

CHAPTER 1

SOME ASPECTS of the READING PROBLEM in HIGH SCHOOL

Why should a book be written about teaching reading in high school? Don't students know how to read by the time they reach seventh grade? If they don't, is something wrong?

Such a book may strike the layman as absurd, but teachers see nothing amusing about the thousands of students in junior and senior high school who are not able to read as well as they should.

THE REASONS FOR WRITING THIS BOOK

Of course high school students can "read" — depending on what is meant by reading. Reading is a complex of skills that the individual uses to derive meaning from the printed page, and the ability to pronounce printed words ordinarily is not the best "reading" that a student is capable of doing. Yet that is about the best "reading" many of our high school students have achieved. Two students can read — in the vague sense of the word — but differ enormously in their ability to read. One is a skillful, efficient reader who, in accordance with his or her purposes, applies suitable reading strategies to master the content contained in materials of any subject area; the other is a word-for-word reader who pronounces each word, moving his lips slightly even when reading silently, and is unable to grasp the larger meaning of sentences and paragraphs. For one, reading is a tool for learning and a source of pleasure; for the other, reading fails to produce meaningful results and is a chore.

In addition to those high school students who can "read" only in the most literal sense are others who can barely recognize what the words say. They cannot recognize enough words to read with ease even the most elementary materials and do not have the skills needed to figure out what the words are. Greater numbers of these students will continue to attend high school, and we cannot afford to ignore them. While the high

1

school might not be able to raise the reading levels of all students to the point where they read well enough to complete a traditional academic program, it can help more students read better and thereby enable them to experience some success in the work they do.

During the 1950s, public schools were continually under attack by irresponsible persons who claimed that "modern" teaching methods — methods of teaching reading, in particular — produced a high number of illiterates. And in the seventies, other critics are saying that schools are not innovative enough and follow the same old methods that doom many students, particularly the poor of inner cities and isolated rural areas, to reading failure. As remedies, they urge that schools adopt performance criteria for teachers and be held responsible for students' failures. In addition, they favor giving parents the option of choosing the schools their children attend. Competition in the marketplace, they say, is bound to improve the quality of education. And because of the importance of reading in almost every field of learning, methods of teaching reading probably will continue to arouse controversy, despite the fact that investigations show our present school population is reading as well as or better than its predecessors. Yet schools, and more especially teachers, take no pride in pointing to "as well as" because they know that far too many young people in school today are not reading as well as they might.

Figure 1-1. Summary of Reading Status

29.7%		one year or more above grade level
17.1%		at about grade level
16.6%		one year or less *below* grade level
13.7%	were reading	from 1.1 to 2.0 years below grade level
10.7%		from 2.1 to 3.0 years below grade level
7.0%		from 3.1 to 4.0 years below grade level
3.9%		from 4.1 to 5.0 years below grade level
1.3%		from 5.1 years or over below grade level

Adapted from Bernard E. Donovan, *Survey of Reading Abilities of Pupils Entering the Academic High Schools in September 1955* (New York: Board of Education, 1955), p. 1.

Figure 1-2. Summary of Reading Status (in terms of mental ability)

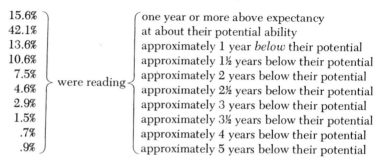

15.6%		one year or more above expectancy
42.1%		at about their potential ability
13.6%		approximately 1 year *below* their potential
10.6%		approximately 1½ years below their potential
7.5%	were reading	approximately 2 years below their potential
4.6%		approximately 2½ years below their potential
2.9%		approximately 3 years below their potential
1.5%		approximately 3½ years below their potential
.7%		approximately 4 years below their potential
.9%		approximately 5 years below their potential

Adapted from Donovan, 1955, p. 3.

Statistics make dull reading, but figures 1-1 and 1-2 are the sobering summaries that New York City faced when it surveyed the reading abilities of students entering the freshman and sophomore classes of its academic high schools. When reading grade scores were first tabulated, more than 10,000 out of 45,000 students were found to be reading two to five and more years below their respective grades. In other words, 23 percent of the freshman and sophomore students would not be able to read required high school textbooks. The facts in Figure 1-2, when reading grade scores were expressed in terms of mental ability, were more valid and even more depressing: 19,000 students or 42.3 percent were *reading below their potential ability*. These data tend to confirm the belief that reading is not a new problem for many high school boys and girls.

A more recent report issued by New York City underscores the need for providing reading instruction in many secondary schools.[1] In only 26 out of 168 junior high schools were half or more of their pupils reading at or above grade level. In the highest ranking school about 74 percent of the pupils were reading at or above grade level. In 76 junior high schools fewer than 20 percent of their pupils were reading at or above grade level. These data reveal how well some youth can read and highlight the need for offering reading instruction to most, if not all, of them.

New York and its schools may not be typical of the country as a whole, but the few surveys that have been reported show that a considerable number of boys and girls of high school age do not read as well as they should or could. In a "Report of the Study Group on Linguistic Communication" issued by a study group that was sponsored by the National Institute of Education, it is claimed that over twelve million people who are fourteen or more years old cannot read as well as the average fourth-grader.[2] The study group points out that seventh grade reading ability is required to perform jobs as machinist or cook. The report goes on to state that about 60 percent of the nation's thirteen-year-olds cannot follow directions in a relatively simple cookbook.

The reading summary of the National Assessment of Educational Progress reports, on a nationwide basis, the reading achievement of thirteen- and seventeen-year-olds, among others.[3] On measures involving word meanings, visual aids, written directions, reference materials, and fact getting, from 64 to 85 percent of those in both groups were judged successful. In reading for main ideas 51 percent of the thirteen-year-olds and 68 percent of the seventeen-year-olds were judged successful. Similar percentages are noted for drawing inferences and reading critically. Those responsible for the assessment acknowledge that, had they constructed the test items to represent more nearly the reading ability of those tested, the percentages would have been lower. Nevertheless, it is

1. *New York Times*, Dec. 24, 1974.
2. *American Education*, May 1974.
3. *Reading: Summary, National Assessment of Educational Progress, Report 02-R-00* (Denver, Colo.: Education Commission of the States, May 1972).

clear from the data that a significant percentage in both groups could not perform those reading tasks which they need to read books and other materials with understanding.

Students are individuals, not statistics, and the plight of these young people who are reading below their potentials is a matter of deep concern to schools and teachers. If this were not so, large numbers of secondary school teachers would not convene annually at the conferences of the International Reading Association and the National Council of Teachers of English to explore together their problems and possible solutions nor would they eagerly look forward to receiving publications on secondary school reading problems from these and other professional organizations. If the concern were not so great, the National Association of Secondary School Principals would not have surveyed the status of English language arts in school curriculums, the National Council of Teachers of English would not have assessed high school English programs, nor would such studies as that by James B. Conant have been undertaken. Basic to all such deliberations is the recognition that the ability to read is of prime importance to successful living as well as to success in school. Basic too is the recognition that, in our high schools, each teacher bears some responsibility to teach those reading skills that are pertinent to his subject area.

It would be erroneous to conclude that poor students and those with reading handicaps are the only ones who could profit from reading assistance. It might surprise teachers to learn that a considerable number of gifted students are weak in specified aspects of reading. Investigators have reported how they perceived reading difficulties in literature, mathematics, history, and chemistry. One group of gifted students said that they felt deficiencies in vocabulary and skimming. Where a school system organized an intensive reading program for gifted students, results confirmed the values of its efforts.[4] Investigations to determine the causes of poor reading among gifted students show that these causes are no different from those that relate to the poor reading of other students. If gifted students require help with reading, just imagine the needs of average students. This is why greater efforts have been made to offer reading instruction to all high school students.

The primary reason, then, for writing this book is to acquaint subject matter teachers with what others are doing to overcome student reading difficulties. It is addressed to teachers in both junior and senior high schools, especially those who have had little or no training in teaching reading. The emphasis here is on good teaching, not on any specific method of teaching reading, for the teacher will soon be aware that certain aspects of every subject matter lend themselves to practice in overcoming reading handicaps.

4. Melvin Michaels, "Subject Reading Improvement: A Neglected Teaching Responsibility," *Journal of Reading* 9 (Oct. 1965): 16-20; Cyril Woolcock, "Guiding the Reading of Superior Students in a Special High School," *Reading Teacher* 16 (May 1963): 448-451.

THE IMPORTANCE OF READING ABILITY

In a moving scene in the film *Viva Zapata!*, a Mexican revolutionary leader who is aware of his great power over men realizes that he lacks a power that to him is mysterious. Staring at a book, he puts his hand across his eyes, pounds the desk, and shouts with the frustration that has been felt by millions of illiterates throughout history. "I can't read!" While this scene is not likely to be reenacted in the classroom, the sensitive teacher may see that cry in the eyes of a student.

The relationship of reading ability to scholastic success is not open to dispute; teachers and students alike are aware of it. Although the ability to read may not be for everyone an end in itself, outside our schools the demands of this modern world underline the ability to read with skill. Daily living, jobs, and a satisfactory place in society depend somewhat on the ability to read, while an age of science, space, and propaganda calls for citizens who are able to read and think critically. And, although other activities often crowd it aside, reading for recreation, for pure pleasure, has untold value.

Reading and the Curriculum

High school curriculums often present reading problems that are difficult to solve. Reading achievement is necessary to success in school; when no provision is made for the poor readers to improve their reading skills, those students are eventually frustrated.

Ruth Penty did some interesting research in Battle Creek, Michigan, on the relationship between reading ability and successful performance in school. In her data, she reported that of the students in the lowest quarter measured by reading ability scores, 49.9 percent left school before the twelfth grade, while only 14.5 percent of those in the highest quarter left before completing senior year. More than three times as many poor readers as good readers dropped out, with the peak of the dropouts coming in tenth grade.

Statistics never tell the whole story, and behind that half of the lowest quarter in reading ability were the frustrated, listless, and finally bored faces of young people who, day after day, met nothing but failure when confronted by a book. There, too, was the embarrassment, often masked by bravado or childish defiance, that the poor reader feels when called upon to read or to answer a question based on material that he cannot read well. Penty followed up her initial interviews at the time of the dropout with second interviews six years later. In only 5 percent of the cases did the former students give the same reason for leaving school, and excerpts from these later interviews, when the truth came out, are worth quoting.

> I was discouraged. I was not getting any place in school. I thought the Marines was a better place to be. I had difficulty in reading. I couldn't remember what I read. I was often embarrassed in class.

> I didn't like school too well. I wanted to get married. I couldn't re-
> member what I read. I didn't like to go to classes and be around other
> kids who seemed to learn more easily than I did.
>
> I left school because I had to help support my mother and I was under
> the impression that I was inferior to the rest of the kids. I had trouble
> with reading, too. I couldn't keep my mind on it. I was afraid of being
> laughed at if I didn't know the answers. I would like to read better and
> still would.
>
> I was nervous at school. I felt all right when I started to work outside.
> I had trouble in getting the ideas from my reading. The words bothered
> me, too. I didn't like to recite in class. I would rather write my answers
> than give them before the class.
>
> We were always quarreling at home. I wasn't getting along in some
> subjects at school either. I wanted to get married. I think now that
> marriage isn't always rosy. It is better for kids to finish school first. I
> understand what I read if I am interested. English and history were hard
> for me. I didn't know some of the words so I couldn't understand them.[5]

The pathos of the simple, direct, often resigned statements by these
dropouts is a testament to and an indictment of an educational world they
never made. They should be food for thought for any teacher in whose
classroom are similar boys and girls marking time until the day comes
when they may leave school and all its unpleasantness. But these students
are not necessarily stupid, although some have more ability than others.
Quoting Penty again:

> A study of the disparity between reading ages and mental ages of the
> poor readers who dropped out of school and of the poor readers who
> remained in school but experienced difficulty in reading, revealed that
> a very large percentage of the young people in both groups had *poten-
> tial in reading ability* [italics added]. With proper help, these students
> could have shown marked improvement in reading ability, which would
> probably have contributed to better scholastic achievement and per-
> sonality.

While other factors, such as conditions in the home, socioeconomic
status, and intelligence account in part for low performance in school,
there is little doubt that poor reading is associated with school failures
and causes many students to drop out of school. Penty's conclusions are
supported by other investigators who reported that there were a significantly higher percentage of poor readers among school dropouts than
among students who remained in school and graduated.[6] Good readers
drop out of school too, but poor readers are much more likely to leave
school because of the failures they encounter.

How important is it for students to be able to read? It was not too

5. Ruth Penty, *Reading Ability and High School Drop-Outs* (New York:
Teachers College Press, 1956). Reprinted with permission.
6. Leonard R. Nachman and others, *Ohio Study of High School Dropouts,
1962-1963* (Columbus: Ohio State Dept. of Education, July 1964); P. Whitmore
and R. Chapman, *Dropout Incidence and Significance at Modesto High Schools,
1961-1964* (Modesto [Calif.] Public Schools, 1965).

long ago that Marshall McLuhan predicted the demise of printed materials in favor of other communication media. But even such a visionary as he has relied upon print to disseminate his ideas and has admitted that perhaps he overstated the case against type. Although films, records, radio, and television share some responsibility for imparting information, books remain the major vehicle by which our culture is passed along. The textbooks, reference books, and other printed sources of information that are used in junior and senior high school contain such stumbling blocks as technical and unfamiliar vocabularies, difficult concepts, and long and involved sentences and paragraphs with which the students must cope if they are to achieve understanding. And it is only by continuously developing reading skills through systematic instruction that students overcome such obstacles and realize accomplishment.

General reading ability, when it is achieved, is no guarantee of ability to read effectively the various types of material that high school experience demands of students. The research of both Ethel Maney and Elona Sochor has shown that there is small relationship between the ability to read narrative material and the ability to read science and social studies.[7] Both found that, when the influence of I. Q. was removed statistically, the relationships between "general reading ability and critical reading" were low and that one ability could not be predicated from the other. Similarly, Arthur Traxler of the Educational Records Bureau in New York City, in a summary of reading investigations,[8] concluded that

> When the various studies of the relationship between general reading ability and reading ability in different areas are considered as a group, it is apparent that there is a great deal in common between reading in a single field and reading in general and that improvement in general reading ability should have a favorable influence upon ability to read in a specified field. However, the correlations are by no means perfect, and it seems clear that in addition to training in general reading skill, there is a definite need for instruction in the reading skills peculiar to each field.

It should be obvious to the thoughtful teacher that each separate subject-matter area makes special demands on the student. Reading a word problem dealing with a proposition in geometry is considerably different from reading an exposition on planaria in biology or an analysis of Jefferson's conflict with Alexander Hamilton. While scholastic success depends on a variety of factors, students who cannot read in one subject-

---

7. Ethel Maney, "Literal and Critical Reading in Science," *Journal of Experimental Education* 27 (Sept. 1958): 57-64; Elona B. Sochor, "Literal and Critical Reading in Social Studies," *Journal of Experimental Education* 27 (Sept. 1958): 49-56.
8. Arthur Traxler and Agatha Townsend, *Another Five Years of Research in Reading*, Educational Records Bulletin No. 46 (New York: Educational Records Bureau, 1950), p. 21.

matter area have a definite handicap, but students who lack general reading ability stand almost no chance at all for achievement.

Reading Problems of Students

Let us examine this question of reading problems more closely. Why do so many typical high school students have trouble mastering content through reading information in various subject areas? How many of these same students are not achieving to their maximum extent? Is the explanation for their problems within the learners themselves, in the materials they read, or in the instruction they have received? I suspect we can make a good case for all of these explanations, and for their interaction.[9]

A majority of high school students lack a common ingredient which we identify as a sense of *organization*. They lack organization in almost everything they undertake, whether in meeting schedules or in study requirements. They find it so difficult to follow trends, to see relationships, to structure information. They fail to note organization in what they read, with the result that any records they keep lack organization too. As a result, they do not receive dividends in proportion to the energy they expend. They read long, understand little, and remember less. They have not learned how to assimilate the amounts of information we expect them to master. Failure to see organization in what they read and create organization for their own uses stymies their efforts to understand and remember.

A second and equally inhibiting condition that impedes their achievement is student failure to establish *purposes* for reading. Many students, because they are passive readers, find that subject-matter materials are more difficult to read than those that tell a story. Students who read for specified reasons are much more likely to be thinking as they read than if they read without an awareness of purpose. The active reader has a problem to solve, but the passive reader is just a receptacle into which information flows. Unless students are helped to establish purposes for study-type reading, they will experience only minimal benefits from their efforts, and they will show little mastery of content.

Most reading instruction has consisted of teaching students to read story-type narrative materials. This type of reading guidance carries over from primary to intermediate and upper grades when so often major emphasis is still upon learning to read and not on reading to learn, despite the fact that reading requirements change.

What are these new requirements? An ability to deal with reading materials that are more complex than materials previously encountered. Students are expected to explore wider fields by studying diverse content. They are expected to assimilate ideas in social studies, science, mathematics, and other subjects. The vocabulary in many of the books they read goes beyond the words they normally use and hear. The mate-

9. This section is adapted from an article by the author published in the November 1975 *High School Journal.*

rials often deal with new and unfamiliar concepts. Sentences are longer and more complex than students are accustomed to; they contain phrases and clauses which tend to hide their basic meaning — for example, "The intensity of light falling on a body is inversely proportional to the square of the distance from the light source." Paragraphs, too, are longer, and packed with specific information and detail. Not only do students have to cope with these new reading problems, they must also learn to perceive relationships among ideas and learn to evaluate the relative importance of information and to remember what is important. In short, reading materials that students are expected to read and comprehend make the leap that students cannot easily make without specific reading instruction directed to help overcome problems associated with the materials.

Moreover, students' reasons for reading informational materials are not the same as they are for reading narrative materials and, therefore, they have to read them differently. They study content to solve problems. They have to learn how to study so that they can solve these problems efficiently. They have to know how to establish purposes when none are given; they have to locate information from multiple sources; they must be able to select information from the larger body of data; they have to organize the information so that they may use and remember it; they need to extract information from aids that accompany printed text, interrupting and continuing the reading and seeing how each complements the other; they must vary the ways in which they read, for all purposes and content do not require the same pacing; they must follow directions carefully when required to do so. All these activities are functions of reading and studying, and it is no small wonder that many students who can read narrative materials with adequate understanding have real trouble meeting the demands that content mastery dictates.

In a report on the teaching of reading there appeared the following observation: "In the judgment of the Committee, the greatest progress in teaching reading during the next decade lies in an intelligent attack on reading problems that arise in the content fields. Satisfactory results can be attained only . . . as teachers from the kindergarten to the university recognize clearly their responsibility."[10] This statement was made over 40 years ago, and in my judgment is as relevant today as it was when first expressed. Why so? Is it because reading instruction in the content areas has been neglected or less clearly focused? Is it because there is a need for continuing instruction with progressively difficult materials? Is it because students fail to demonstrate proficiency in independent study? Perhaps the answers can be found in some of each.

Some time ago, a colleague's junior high school daughter was waiting in the office and picked up some publishers' brochures that advertised reading materials. She remained quiet for some minutes before exclaim-

10. William S. Gray, "A Decade of Progress," in *The Teaching of Reading: A Second Report*, Part 1, 36th Yearbook, National Society for the Study of Education, ed. William S. Gray (Bloomington, Ill.: Public School Publishing Co., 1937), p. 20.

ing, "I can't do these things!" By "things" she meant how to go about deciding what the major ideas of a chapter were, how to preview the contents of a chapter, how to scan for specific information, how to assess authenticity of ideas, and how to differentiate between relevant and irrelevant details. "Don't you ever spend time working on reading?" "No," she replied, "the teachers think we don't need any help."

Although many secondary schools offer reading instruction of one kind or another, we know that there are significant gaps in high school reading programs. While we observe both superior programs which attempt to reach all students and others that are narrowly conceived or available only to seriously disabled readers, we find a total lack of reading instruction elsewhere. The school administration in one large city has just decided to mount an effort to help prepare its students to cope with the reading demands they will face in college. It has finally realized that students, however capable, may be deficient in one or more reading skills.

So many of the reading skills that are supposed to be treated in elementary school are needed by high school students. Of course, older students have to learn to use these skills efficiently because of the nature of new reading demands and reading materials. Even if we were to assume that all of the necessary skills introduced at lower levels were mastered by all students, we would have to help them apply the skills with greater sophistication.

In addition, there are other skills with which lower grades do little, because younger pupils aren't ready to cope with them. They may be related to others previously taught, but now they must be treated deliberately. For example, we need to offer instruction in how to skim for general impressions (flexibility), recognize partial truths (evaluation), interpret cartoons (author's purpose), see relationships (generalization). Undoubtedly, some of your students can respond satisfactorily to such reading tasks when expected to do so. But there are so many others who cannot.

Reading and Daily Living

Stop for a moment and think about the print that bombards the average reader each day. Then think what it might be like to be a nonreader. You could not understand road signs or timetables. You would miss details of the news, what happened in sports or the stock market, what was on television. You could not read how to put together a new gadget or a dress pattern; you could not find a number in a telephone book. And you would face the embarrassment of asking a relative or a friend to read every piece of printed and written matter for you.

There is little need to elaborate on the daily reading activities of high school students during after-school hours, whether these involve reading mail, menus, or movie bills. The point is that these kinds of reading activities carry over into adult daily living where, at times, failure to read and understand can be inconvenient if not disastrous. Reading to follow directions is a skill called for in almost every high school class-room, yet most of us recall an unhappy moment when we failed to read well. A homemaker who used two cups of flour, sifted, instead of two cups of sifted flour made a heavy cake; another, who misread an insur-ance policy, possibly suffered more serious consequences.

An interesting but disconcerting sidelight on the relationship of reading to daily living are the findings of a survey conducted by Louis Harris and Associates for the National Reading Council. The Council was appointed by President Nixon in 1970 to seek ways of eliminating illiteracy throughout the country. The survey showed that of the sample population which consisted of persons over 16 years of age 34 percent could not complete a simplified Medicaid application, 11 percent a bank loan application, 8 percent a driver's license application, 7 percent a Social Security number application, and 3 percent a welfare application. Using inability to read well enough in order to complete these applica-tions as an index of functional illiteracy, the survey indicated that at least 13 percent of our population over 16 years of age lack adequate reading skills for day-to-day living. This estimate is in contrast to the federal government's figure of just over 8 percent, which is based upon the number of persons who completed the fifth grade of elementary school and not on how well they could read.

What is of far greater importance is the need to sort out from the mass of printed material that daily confronts us the fact from opinion, truth from half-truth, information from emotion. From all sides we are bombarded almost constantly with propaganda and slanted language, and the ability to think and read critically is demanded constantly in a world that makes such wide use of so many communications media.

No learning, whether it is through listening, reading, or any other source, is measured by ability to parrot what is heard, read, or experi-enced. Learning is measured by the ability to make intelligent use of experiences. Choosing wisely between one course of action or another, accepting or rejecting conflicting arguments or data, recognizing when you are not qualified to judge and knowing where to go to find some-thing or someone who is qualified to tell you — these are some of the goals of learning for the student who would wish to be educated. And the ability to read is part and parcel of this kind of learning.

Fortunately, critical reading is being taught with increasing fre-quency in today's high schools, and, consciously or unconsciously, teachers require students to do critical thinking in almost every subject area. They encourage students to read widely from a variety of sources; single textbooks are often no longer relied on for exclusive information. Newspapers, periodicals, and a variety of books are becoming available in increasing numbers in most schools, and high school students usually have ready access to these. The ability to read these materials and to read them critically must be developed if we are to have thoughtful adults in tomorrow's world.

Finally, just as reading skill is related to scholastic success, so the ability to read has bearing on personal satisfaction and the individual's adjustment to society. When a child learns to read and to study well, the nourishment he derives from the success he achieves feeds upon itself. He builds a concept of self that gratifies him. No one enjoys hating himself, but constant frustration in school from failure to learn to read and from other causes contributes to an increasing self-disgust. When this self-disgust festers within the problem student, he will find satisfaction where he can succeed and may seek avenues of support that are the opposite of the wholesome attitudes and behavior society would like to see in its young people.

Reading failure is certainly not the sole cause of delinquent behavior, but James E. Allen, Jr., former Assistant Secretary for Education in the Department of Health, Education and Welfare and former U.S. Commissioner of Education, has cited the inability to read as a potentially contributing factor to juvenile delinquency and has recommended suitable reading instruction for problem children. In some cases it does work. I have never forgotten a boy who was recommended to me for diagnostic and corrective reading treatment by the principal of his junior high school. The boy was a discipline problem in school and was on probation for breaking into a neighborhood store and selling merchandise he had stolen. The first day he swaggered into the university clinic, a sight to behold in his "weirdo" outfit. His I.Q. was 104, and he was not able to read better than a first grader. His bravado was a mask for his inability to read.

He remained at the clinic for nine months. His progress was slow, but he was aware that he was moving forward, and at the end of the period he could read a second-grade reader with some help. What was remarkable was his change in appearance and attitude. Although no one had mentioned it to him, the "uniform" had disappeared after about four months, and his friendliness amazed everyone. Of his own accord he asked to return to the clinic the next year — which made everyone's efforts in his behalf seem worthwhile.

Dr. Melitta Schmideberg[11] a psychiatrist, has cited statistics of the New York Training School for Boys that showed 30 percent of delinquent boys between the ages of twelve and fifteen were reading below second-grade level, and has made these observations about the nonreader:

> A nonreader feels his difference from other children; he is an outcast. His sense of inferiority creates bitterness, hopelessness, and often hostility.
> A child who cannot read usually sits in the back of the classroom, bored, apathetic, or restless; so he gets into mischief or plays hookey. Learning to read is a mental discipline, one of the primary socializing processes for a child. A nonreader who cannot read good books, go to Sunday school, or even sing with the others lacks all civilizing influences. He cannot make decent friends; if he plays hookey he drifts into

11. Melitta Schmideberg, "Reading Retardation and Delinquency," in *Tomorrow's Illiterates*, ed. Charles C. Walcutt (Boston: Little, Brown, 1961), pp. 135-136.

bad company and becomes delinquent. The fact that he is regarded by others as a dunce adds to his sense of inferiority and hostility.

Because of this chain of bad consequences that begins with falling behind, a reading retardation of even three months is serious and should be corrected before it gets worse; yet at present large numbers of children are allowed to pass through the schools relatively or completely illiterate.

Our schools, of course, cannot be held solely responsible for handicapped readers who arrive in junior and senior high school. In a home where no one reads, students are not encouraged to read. And all non-readers certainly do not turn into delinquents. Even in "illiterate" homes, most students have observed that people in better situations and better environments do read a lot. Such students may have the self-motivation to break the mold, and to do this despite the ridicule of being called a sissy, bookworm, and other choice epithets by their peers.

Homes that fail to provide responsive reading environments may be found in any economic bracket. In a privately circulated review of *Tomorrow's Illiterates and What Ivan Knows That Johnny Doesn't*, Arthur Gates has this to say:

> A home which is supplied with a television set, several radios, a phonograph, an automobile or two, and a host of mechanical gadgets and toys, but no shelves of books or magazines is not likely to house persons who care much about reading. If Johnny comes home each day to find a conspicuous array of good reading materials and his parents absorbed in reading and discussing what they have read, he will tend to share this happy home enterprise, and make it a permanent part of his pattern of living.

For high school students, then, the ability to read has effects far beyond scholastic realms, although some of these and their contributing causes lie well outside the province of the school.

Recreational Reading

If literacy is a practical necessity inside and outside the school, it is also a wellspring of pleasure for those who have the key that unlocks whole unknown worlds of adventure in print.

High school students (as well as adults and children) love to live vicariously — witness the popularity of television, movies, plays, and circuses. Any visual dramatization, whether movies, the stage, or television, makes the viewer identify, but it is radio and recordings and reading that call for greater creativity of the mind. Being able to feel and see in the mind's eye the moors, the seas, the hound of the Baskervilles, Scrooge, Holden Caulfield, King Arthur, or Archy the Cockroach involves the magic of vision that only the reader can create. In the end it is books that bring the quiet hours of relaxation and contentment when the reader scales the Himalayas with Hillary and Tensing, tracks down a criminal with Ellery Queen, or laughs for an hour with H. Allen Smith.

But what do high school students read? A poll of some 10,000 junior and senior high school students across the country showed that less than half of them had spent time the previous day reading a book. Some 80 percent had read a newspaper, and about 65 percent a magazine, but barely a half hour had gone to those. Secondary school students, if this sampling was representative, are not strong on outside reading. (They do, going by the same survey, spend time watching television, 10 percent of them as much as four to six hours a day.) But adults are not much different; statistics showed, lumping reliable surveys together, that 79 percent had not read a book within the past month, that only 31 percent had been reading a book during the past week, and that among representative elementary and secondary school teachers, only 18.4 percent had done any personal or general book reading in the past two months (42.2 percent had done no professional reading either).

Observers note a rather new development in the way teen-agers spend their free time. More of them are listening to rock music at the expense of watching television and doing other things, and radio stations are catering to this growing market by setting aside large blocks of time on their FM outlets to broadcast the music that appeals to teen-agers. Naturally, the more hours these young people are glued to their transistor radios (even when they "study") the less time they have for anything else. Reading continues to be a casualty among a large segment of adolescents.

If the development of reading as a leisure-time activity is desirable, then it would seem that some provision for its nourishment must be made in the high school curriculum. It is not enough to provide books and encourage more reading.

One other aspect of recreational reading deserves mention here. Vicarious experiences have sometimes been quite powerful and vivid. *Uncle Tom's Cabin* created images for readers that greatly influenced attitudes in the North toward slavery, and it is sometimes listed as one of the causes of the Civil War. Powerful writing, such as Thomas Paine's *Common Sense*, has stirred men to action, and one wonders how many children have tried to fly out the window after having had *Peter Pan* read to them. Sociologically, the *Hornbook* and the *New England Primer* did much to shape moral behavior, as did McGuffey *Readers*. Horatio Alger was a model for boys who wanted to move from rags to riches quickly. *Dennis the Menace* is another version of *Tom Sawyer, Huckleberry Finn, Peck's Bad Boy,* and *Penrod.*

A young person today is surrounded by a multitude of problems associated with approaching maturity. When he can identify with characters in similar situations, it helps him with the struggle, especially when he feels he has no one to whom he can turn for a sympathetic hearing and possible guidance. Anxieties may not disappear, but they may diminish in intensity. Sometimes his whole life may be influenced for the better by the characters and precepts he has found in literature. If there is a chance that this may happen, reading for pleasure needs every encouragement the schools and teachers can give it.

WHAT CAN BE DONE?

In this age of automation, the federal government has looked with alarm at the high number of unskilled workers that help cause unemployment figures to persist stubbornly above 7 percent of the labor force. It estimates that in this decade one-third of the 26 million who will join the potential labor force will lack high school diplomas. States and cities are equally concerned about dropouts and delinquents, and sociologists and others point to the slums where the percentage of dropouts and unskilled laborers is at its highest. On all sides there is genuine concern in this country for the achievements of today's millions of young people.

In the United States, as elsewhere, professional educators, political leaders, and interested observers are urging that the secondary school curriculum be strengthened by making it more relevant and responsive to the needs of students who live in a changing society and who must learn to cope with the new requirements of that society. A growing awareness is evident that less emphasis is needed on the minutiae of subjects and more on the important concepts underlying them. In addition, everyone agrees that students must be taught how to learn for themselves since the information explosion precludes the possibility of teaching them everything they ought to know. Even without the pressures of uncertainty about the years ahead, few persons would reject these proposals. More than ever before, the need for power in different areas of learning only reemphasizes the importance of reading ability. Its importance has been clearly recognized.

James B. Conant, in his influential and convincing report, recommended a reading program that is blended into the growth and development of the student in high school:

> A school should have the equipment for a developmental reading program. The program should be available on a voluntary basis for all the pupils in the school. The counselors and teachers of English should be asked to view this program sympathetically and to urge students to take advantage of the opportunity to increase reading speed and comprehension.[12]

Though a full reading program was not described in his recommendation, Conant also showed an acquaintance with the role that improvement in reading plays in helping the retarded student to succeed in high school. For the seriously retarded reader, he would make these provisions:

> Those in the ninth grade of the school who read at a level of the sixth grade or below should be given special consideration. These pupils should be instructed in English and the required social studies by special teachers who are interested in working with such

12. James B. Conant, *The American High School Today* (New York: McGraw-Hill, 1959), p. 67.

students and who are sympathetic to their problems. Remedial
reading should be part of the work, and special types of textbooks
should be provided. The elective programs of these pupils should
be directed toward simple vocational programs for boys, the dis-
tributive educational program, and the regular commercial program
for girls. These students should not be confused with mentally
retarded students. The education of the mentally retarded is a
special program which in some states is also handled in the regular
high school through special instruction and the use of special state
funds.[13]

Elsewhere, Conant has stated that vocational high schools should
not be the dumping grounds for poor pupils:

Some programs ought to be available in many schools for those
who, in spite of all efforts, are reading two or three grades below
their grade level. . . . There is an educational responsibility here
which rests on all who are involved in public high school work.[14]

The report of the Committee on Curriculum Planning and Development of the National Association of Secondary School Principals was
more specific in its recommendations:

Reading skills of an advanced nature should be taught as an
integral part of the literature program.
Developmental reading skills should be carefully taught.
Elective courses in "directed reading" are recommended to develop students' reading skills according to their abilities and purposes.
Remedial courses are recommended for students reading below
their potential.
Every school should organize a committee on reading to consider
and solve . . . problems. . . .[15]

This Committee also recommended that all teachers share some
responsibility for the language arts program and that each teacher should
assume the responsibility to teach linguistic skills pertinent to his subject.
A third report, English Teacher Preparation Study, "Guidelines for
English Teacher Preparation," based its recommendations upon earlier
studies of the education of English teachers. Two of its guidelines are of
particular interest:

The secondary school teacher of English should have an understanding of developmental reading, particularly at the junior and

13. Ibid., p. 55.
14. Address delivered before the American Vocational Association Convention,
Chicago, Dec. 7, 1959.
15. English Language Arts in the Comprehensive Secondary School (Washington, D. C.: National Association of Secondary School Principals, 1960), pp. 7, 8.

senior high school levels, and be able to utilize that understanding in his teaching.

He should have learned how to correlate the contents and skills of listening, speaking, reading, and writing with one another and with other subjects in the curriculum.[16]

These guidelines seem to place the major responsibility for conducting reading instruction in the hands of English teachers. How effectively the teachers could work with content other than literature is one issue the report fails to consider.

What effect have these reports had on high school reading? Have they produced any significant difference in the number and quality of high school reading programs?

One of the most comprehensive reports which offers some answers to these questions is based on a national study of high school English programs. James Squire and Roger Applebee conducted a survey of instructional practices in 168 schools whose English departments were highly regarded. This is one of the criteria they used to assess the quality of their programs:

The schools will provide comprehensive instruction in the skills of reading for all pupils, and, in addition, special instruction for pupils whose needs and abilities warrant more individualized procedures.[17]

They reported the distressing fact that little attention was given to teaching students *how* to read, let alone the teaching of reading itself. Three to 4 percent of the instructional time in the tenth grade and 2 percent in the twelfth grade were devoted to reading. In more than 1,600 classrooms, including those in which reading was supposed to be stressed, the teaching of reading was evident in only 10 percent of them. The reports of other investigators, who also surveyed high school reading programs, are no less disturbing.

One may wonder why recommendations about teaching reading in high school have not really been implemented. Squire and Applebee believe that they won't be until teachers see the difference between having students read and teaching students how to read. They say that unless English teachers recognize the need of students to improve their skills in comprehending different forms of literature, and assume leadership in seeking ways to develop these and basic reading skills, strong reading programs aren't likely to be established in high schools.

Very few prospective high school teachers whose preparation centers around specialized content receive any orientation in the teaching of reading. Some of the major professors voice reservations about the value of their "methods" courses, believing only in mastering subjects

16. *English Journal* 57 (April 1968): 535-536.
17. James R. Squire and Roger K. Applebee, *High School English Instruction Today* (New York: Appleton-Century-Crofts, 1968), p. 240.

and caring little about those students who cannot read well enough to do satisfactory work in their fields. Therefore, most prospective high school teachers do not know how to fuse reading instruction with their subject matter. Hence, they frequently adopt the same attitudes of their mentors regarding the "sink or swim" point of view. Teachers who retain these attitudes resist efforts by supervisors and curriculum specialists who offer in-service training programs in reading, particularly when the latter are not well qualified to show teachers how they can help students to read better. Moreover, even in schools where teachers express concern over student inability to read, they tend to shift to others the responsibility for doing something about it.

A Balanced High School Reading Program

Conant spoke of a "developmental reading program," and the Committee on Curriculum Planning and Development suggested that "developmental reading skills should be carefully taught." What specifically is meant by a "reading program" and, in particular, a "balanced reading program"?

The cornerstone of any good high school reading program is preventing reading failures rather than correcting reading problems. In a society that is committed to universal public education, every effort must be made to permit each student to develop to his fullest — a goal that may be realized once the student has ability to gain understanding and derive satisfaction from reading. A balanced reading instruction program has as its long-range goal the well-adjusted student who knows how and where to seek knowledge and information and may appreciate good literature for its own sake. A balanced reading program consists of experiences that contribute to developing diversified skills and positive attitudes, and its many facets encompass the entire curriculum. The degree to which it is successful depends on the cooperative efforts of the entire faculty and staff.

For years, teachers have been urged to help their students read the materials of the subjects they teach, and many have done so with varying degrees of success. On the other hand, some subject teachers, either because they don't know how to help their students, or because they believe it is not their responsibility, make reading assignments that students have trouble completing. Surely there are strategies teachers may adopt that will enable students to learn more than they might otherwise.

No one expects subject teachers to become reading experts and deal with all the reading difficulties every student might be experiencing. However, they can integrate reading guidance with content instruction, thereby helping students to achieve more and assume more responsibility for their own learning. Thus, one strand of a balanced and comprehensive program is the reading assistance that subject teachers provide in their own classrooms. The forms this assistance might take will be covered in subsequent chapters.

Some high schools schedule reading classes to which students are assigned or which they elect to take. These classes are taught by trained reading teachers who determine the general and specialized skills in which students are weak. The students who attend these classes do profit from individualized help, when instruction is tied to the reading they are required to do in subject classes. Other reading classes or guidance are available to students who have few reading problems but who wish to improve their reading ability. A balanced reading program offers these kinds of reading assistance.

A third strand in a balanced high school reading program is the instruction offered to seriously disabled readers who cannot read the subject materials because they find them too difficult. A major weakness that many of these students have is the inability to recognize many words, with the result that they cannot concentrate on meaning. They require individualized help in small groups or, when possible, on a one-to-one basis.

Thus, a balanced comprehensive reading program consists of a series of concerted efforts by both subject teachers and specialized personnel to improve the reading ability of all students. Instruction in reading is designed to help students to overcome weaknesses which interfere with their performance and to increase satisfaction from their reading and study, as well as to enable them to experience enjoyment from recreational reading and develop positive attitudes toward reading.

Reading Skills

Task-oriented teachers do not teach reading per se. Instead, they devote their attention to specific aspects of reading which can be stated in objective terms. Each of these components has been classified in different ways and the terminologies used for identification vary. It really doesn't matter what we call these developmental areas if we recognize that they are integral parts of a balanced reading instruction program. How well students read depends, to a great extent, on how well they have mastered the skills that make up reading ability. We might classify the skills and subskills as shown in Figure 1-3. Related to appreciation is the area of *reading interests.* While it is not completely accurate to think of developing and extending reading interests in the same way as we think of promoting reading skills, this is a logical and expected outcome of reading instruction. One of the behavioral measures that should be used to assess the success of any reading program is the amount and quality of independent reading students voluntarily undertake. Provisions for promoting recreational reading must be included in the plan of any balanced program; otherwise, the goal will not be realized.

Even though mature readers do not consciously separate the skills and subskills of reading, we have identified them for teaching purposes as determined by student needs. Nor are reading skills that discrete; they overlap and merge. For example, students who read for information use not only study skills but also different comprehension skills. Moreover,

Figure 1-3. Reading Skills

Word Recognition
  Acquisition of sight words
  Use of context clues
  Phonic analysis
  Structural analysis
  Use of the dictionary

Comprehension
  Understanding literal meaning
  Recognition of inferred meaning
  Evaluation of information and ideas

Word Meaning
  Use of context clues
  Structural analysis
  Use of the dictionary
  Recognition of multiple meanings
  Recognition of figurative language

Study Skills
  Location of information
  Selection of information
  Organization and retention of information
  Use of graphic and typographical aids
  Flexibility and rate of reading

Appreciation
  Recognizing forms of literature
  Recognizing the language of literature

there are times when a fine line separates literal comprehension from interpretation, or word recognition from word meaning. But unless we direct our attention to specific reading tasks, we cannot expect students to achieve in reading.

In a typical high school reading program, less attention will be paid to word recognition than to the other reading skills. Word recognition will not be the critical weakness of students who are progressing normally, although it is generally found among more severely handicapped readers and with them requires concentrated attention. Many secondary school students, however, lack or are weak in some of the higher level word-recognition skills, such as the ability to divide words into syllables or to use the pronunciation key of a dictionary. Flexibility involves speed of comprehension, and all students should be aware of the importance of varying their reading rates. However, teachers should note now that efforts to improve reading rate are reserved mainly for students who do not have serious reading problems. Too often, time is put in on increasing *rate* of reading when it should go to improving *quality* of understanding.

Specialists commonly classify reading instruction as developmental, corrective, and remedial. Each of these may be expanded as follows.

Developmental reading is provided for students who can profit from additional help although they are progressing satisfactorily. Learning to read is a continuous process, the complexities of which are not completely resolved at any one stage of development. Developmental-reading instruction is based on the concept of readiness for learning and the sequential treatment of reading skills. It begins in the primary grades and is pursued through the upper grades as the needs of the students dictate.

Corrective reading is remedial-reading instruction given within the framework of the regular class. In every classroom some students fail to learn what is being taught, and the teacher who sets out to overcome these difficulties found in conjunction with reading is giving corrective-reading instruction. Usually the learning problems are not severe and are readily overcome.

Remedial reading instruction is ordinarily reserved for special teachers who work with seriously handicapped readers operating on levels roughly two or more years below their capacities. These teachers are assigned students on either an individual or a group basis, and instruction may be given during or after the school day. Classroom teachers, however, have been successful in their efforts to help students with long histories of reading failures, and today more and more classroom teachers are taking courses in remedial reading solely to help problem students in their own classrooms.

Ordinarily, classroom teachers would not be expected to provide remedial-reading instruction, but one thesis of this book is that the guidelines for remedial-reading instruction are no different from those that support developmental-reading instruction. Teaching that is based on sound principles of learning is needed to prevent and to correct reading faults. If there is any difference between developmental and remedial instruction, it is a difference in degree and not kind. Developmental reading procedures probably have to be refined and intensified if they are to be successful with poor readers. The contention that good instruction has failed students with real reading problems and that other ways to teach them are needed is not based upon facts. Of course, students whose reading difficulties are associated with clearly identified organic problems may have to be treated quite differently from those whose reading weaknesses are due to other causes. But, even in this limited number of cases, there is little hard evidence to support methods that violate good teaching principles.

A balanced secondary school reading program has been described as one which provides for the reading requirements of all students. In a sense, all reading instruction is developmental, if by developmental we mean helping students to progress to personally higher levels of reading achievement. Subject teachers can make significant contributions to their students' reading development by helping them to apply reading skills as they study the content of their courses. Likewise, reading teachers can work with students on the general and content-oriented reading skills they need to improve. These cooperative efforts will have a positive effect on the reading growth of all students and their ability to learn.

SUMMARY

Studies on the achievement of high school students show that a considerable number of them are deficient in reading. Weakness in reading is known to be a factor in school failure and is frequently a principal reason why students drop out of school. Low reading achievement has also been shown to be associated with asocial behavior.

Surveys of high school programs emphasize the importance of reading ability and the need to offer reading instruction to all students. There is ample evidence to justify reading instruction for poor, average, and superior high school students. However, studies show that comparatively few high schools have implemented recommendations for the establishment of strong reading programs in which, on the basis of students' needs, attention is given to the fundamental areas of reading. The requirements of students are more likely to be met if all teachers accept some responsibility for teaching reading to those who can benefit from it.

Additional Readings

Discussion of the need for and scope of secondary reading programs are found in the following references:

A. Sterl Artley. *Trends and Practices in Secondary Reading.* IRA Research Fund Monograph. Newark, Del.: International Reading Association, 1968, pp. 3-10.

Robert C. Aukerman. *Reading in the Secondary School Classroom.* New York: McGraw-Hill, 1972, pp. 1-8.

Mildred A. Dawson, comp. *Developing High School Reading Programs.* Newark, Del.: International Reading Association, 1967, pp. 2-20.

Gerald G. Duffy, comp. ed. *Reading in the Middle School*, Perspectives in Reading No. 18. Newark, Del.: International Reading Association, 1975, pp. 2-6; 16-31.

Margaret J. Early, ed. *Reading Instruction in the Secondary School*, Perspectives in Reading No. 2. Newark, Del.: International Reading Association, 1964.

M. Agnella Gunn, ed. *What We Know About High School Reading.* Research Bulletin of the National Conference on Research in English. Champaign, Ill.: National Council of Teachers of English, 1969, pp. 1-18.

Robert Karlin. *Teaching Reading in High School, Selected Articles.* Indi-
    anapolis: Bobbs-Merrill, 1969, pp. 1-17.
H. Alan Robinson and Ellen L. Thomas, eds. *Fusing Reading Skills and
    Content.* Newark, Del.: International Reading Association, 1969,
    pp. 1-16.
Nila B. Smith, ed. *Current Issues in Reading,* Proceedings of the 13th
    Annual Convention, Vol. 13, Part 2. Newark, Del.: International
    Reading Association, 1969, pp. 419-443.

CHAPTER 2

CONDUCTING PROGRAMS for READING in CONTENT AREAS

Problems for Study and Discussion

1 *By what standards might secondary reading programs be evaluated?*
2 *What steps could a faculty take to plan and establish a reading program?*
3 *What is the role of the reading specialist in an all-school reading program? Of subject teachers?*
4 *Why is it said that "materials for reading instruction are no better than the teachers who use them?"*
5 *How can principals and superintendents help to insure the establishment of strong reading programs?*

CHARACTERISTICS OF READING PROGRAMS

An increasing number of secondary schools have organized reading programs, but surveys show that the majority merely offer special instruction for the poorest readers. Fewer schools conduct reading programs that reach students through subject classes. Explanations for diversity in reading programs can be traced to the ways schools view reading, the nature of their populations, and the attitudes and resources of their administrations and teaching staffs.

While reading programs need not be identical in scope or operation, those of high quality share certain characteristics.

1. *A good reading program reaches all the students who can benefit from reading instruction.* This is not to say that a reading program which reaches only part of the students is bad; however, programs which *do* implement this principle are more likely to have a favorable impact. It is a fact that learning to read is a continuous process, and even the very

best students can improve their reading ability in some areas. Schools should establish programs that meet the requirements of gifted readers, students of average reading ability, and poor readers.

2. *The entire faculty contributes to the reading program's effectiveness and operation.* Some teachers will resist the idea of teaching reading skills in their subject-matter area. They will feel that they are inadequately trained or that one more chore is being added to their already mounting duties. It takes a great deal of persuasion to convince some teachers that the entire school benefits when everyone on the faculty recognizes the reading problem and tries to do something concrete about it. All teachers do not have to be reading experts to become active participants in reading programs. They can learn how to apply specific strategies for helping students read in their content fields by observing reading teachers, joining study groups, attending conferences, doing independent reading, and taking in-service or university-sponsored courses.

One thing is certain: successful programs are those which classroom teachers, teacher-librarians, guidance counselors, supervisors, and administrators have helped plan and implement. They are not programs that rely on one department — usually the English department — or reading teachers to develop and conduct.

There are other ingredients that will help establish a comprehensive reading program. They are the knowledge and experience that a reading specialist brings to school faculties as they study, make plans, and put them into effect. The reading specialist can help channel the group's efforts. More will be said about this person.

3. *A sound reading program embraces all aspects of reading.* High school students benefit from guidance in applying comprehension and study skills to the materials they read and study. Some might also require instruction in some aspects of word recognition and word meaning skills. Students who are seriously deficient in reading concentrate on similar skills but at lower levels. All students engage in activities which promote wider reading.

4. *Attention is directed to specific reading needs.* The "shotgun" or incidental approach to the teaching of reading is avoided. Teachers use information about students' reading gained from testing, direct observation, and student conferences to plan suitable lessons. Naturally, any instruction which reading teachers offer is based upon having evaluated students' reading strengths and weaknesses. This information is then passed along to the subject teachers, who reinforce and extend those skills which promote greater understanding and efficiency in reading. They notice how well their students meet reading requirements, consult with them on what help they believe they need, and offer reading instruction that is integrated with content study.

5. *The reading program must be evaluated periodically and modified accordingly.* An empirical approach in viewing the reading program should be taken from the outset. Obviously a perfect program cannot be devised at the beginning. It should change according to the special problems that arise. If the program is allowed to drift aimlessly without such

examination, it will probably founder — eventually, if not immediately. If the program does not change the reading levels of students and fails to promote positive attitudes toward reading, reasons for this lack of progress must be sought. Each subject teacher can attest to the program's strengths and limitations, and everyone, including students and possibly parents, can review measures to improve it.

ORGANIZING A READING PROGRAM

A group of secondary school teachers once attended a meeting at which a reading program was thrust upon them. The superintendent had decided that his teachers should begin to teach reading immediately, for he had discovered that in his schools students were deficient in reading. (Either someone had pointed this out to him or reading improvement had just become fashionable.) The faculty had no advance notice of the purpose of the meeting; not even the guidance counselor knew why he was there. In a peremptory tone, the superintendent told the staff that the schools had a reading problem and that they had the job of solving it. When he had finished, there was a tomb-like silence; no faculty member commented, and the session ended abruptly. The schools had a reading program — like it or not. I was to have served as consultant, but I was soon aware that the superintendent had his own ideas and that these were the only ideas that would be considered. It was one of my least fruitful experiences. No one really bought the ideas of this martinet, even though the faculty went through the motions under condition of threat. In the end, the students were the ones who suffered.

The situation in another school system was totally different. Both the superintendent and his teachers were concerned about their students' performances in reading and together planned what to do about it. Each high school teacher submitted his views on the problem to a faculty committee and included questions he had about the teaching of reading. The elementary school teachers did the same. Then a joint committee studied the reports and questions and prepared brief summaries of each. Next, the two faculties met together to consider the summaries, under the chairmanship of a secondary school teacher who explained the group's purpose. When the problems and questions were discussed, the similar concerns of the elementary and the secondary teachers became apparent. Small committees composed of teachers from both faculties were appointed to study the areas identified in the summaries.

Both the superintendent and his assistant and the principals of the several schools in the system participated in the meetings and on the committees. When a second joint faculty meeting was called two months later and the small committee reports presented, the need for further study and consideration was felt. A steering committee, chaired by the assistant superintendent, decided to visit several communities that had all-school reading programs and to report the following September, since the school year was near its close. During these several meetings, I served as a resource person to whom the group could turn for guidance. My latest report from the school is that a reading program on a limited basis is under way and progress is being made toward a comprehensive program. Subject-matter teachers are interested in helping students read their textbooks more effectively, and one teacher is progressing well with two reading classes.

Of the two situations described, the latter is obviously the better way to institute a reading program. Imposing a program on a faculty does not work; it must grow out of the recognition that the need exists, and it takes work, imagination, cooperation, and energy to fashion a reading program that actually accomplishes something.

While there is no set formula for organizing a reading program, here are some practical suggestions that a school system might consider:

1. *Establish a reading committee consisting of representatives from all subject areas, pupil personnel services, administration, students, and the community.* This committee serves as the coordinator and facilitator of the school's efforts. It will identify needs, gather and disseminate information, formulate plans for study and evaluation, and initiate steps to establish the program. The reading committee is a permanent committee that monitors the program, invites recommendations, and facilitates its operation.

2. *Survey the reading status of the school population.* Some schools administer achievement tests to the entire student body each year. Though the results of these may give the investigator a comprehensive view of achievement, a better arrangement probably is to administer to the entire population a good reading test specifically chosen for this evaluation. Some tests can be scored mechanically, which eases the burden for everyone. Care should be taken when choosing the test; it should yield the information that will give a clear picture of the school's total reading ability, and it should be carefully administered so that the scores will be accurate.

A distribution of test scores should be prepared. This will reveal, in a general way, how well students read when compared to comparable students of similar age, and the degree to which reading is a problem in the school. Some information about performance in specified skill areas can be obtained by noting what percentage of students respond satisfactorily to different portions of the test. Such objective evidence could identify some major areas that need attention.

A questionnaire concerning students' reading habits and interests will show the extent to which reading plays a role in their leisure-time activities. It will also show to what extent their interests are being met by the materials provided by the school library and the textbooks and other materials used in classes.

3. *Identify the skills to be taught, the techniques to be followed, and the instructional materials to be used.* There is a vast amount of information in the literature of reading that can be tapped. The material should be studied and the ideas sifted so that all concerned know the conditions more likely to serve the interests of all the students. If a reading specialist is available to channel the group's efforts, the attack on the problem will probably reduce the possibility of misunderstanding and misapplication.

4. *Introduce the program.* If the program's goal is to meet the reading

need of all students, it probably should be established by stages. High school teachers who don't have any training in reading cannot be expected to assume a major role in integrating content and reading instruction. A reading consultant or reading teacher can work with some subject teachers who, in turn, will share with others what they have found helpful. In the meantime, teachers might take university courses in reading or participate in an in-service program directed by a member of the faculty or a reading expert from a university.

ADMINISTRATION OF THE READING PROGRAM BY THE READING CONSULTANT

Although establishing an effective reading program that affects the entire staff ideally should be the outgrowth of group cooperation between staff and administration, smooth and efficient program administration depends on leadership. Unless this leadership exists, the program may fail before it has a chance to prove its worth. Few school administrators know much about teaching reading, and most English teachers, while trained to teach literature, are not knowledgeable in teaching the fundamental skills of reading. Hence, the person to administer a reading program is a trained reading consultant.

Necessary Qualifications of the Reading Consultant

Several states at present issue special certificates in reading to secondary school teachers, and more states probably will follow their lead.[1] The International Reading Association has adopted *Minimum Standards for Reading Specialists*, which have added impetus to the trend of establishing criteria for specialists in reading. These standards are intended to serve as a guide for state departments of education that contemplate certification, colleges and universities that are establishing professional training programs in reading, school administrators in states that have no requirements, and teachers who wish to prepare for reading positions.

For special reading teachers the *Minimum Standards* specify at least three years of successful classroom teaching and completion of a planned program for a master's degree that includes a minimum of twelve semester hours in graduate level reading courses with at least one course in each of the following: (1) foundations or survey of reading; (2) diagnosis and correction of reading disabilities; and (3) clinical or laboratory practicum in reading. In addition, undergraduate or graduate level study should cover measurement and evaluation; child or adolescent psychology; personality, cognition, and learning; and literature for children or adolescents.

For reading clinicians, the preparation is the same as above plus advanced courses in diagnosis, correction, and clinical or laboratory practicum;

1. Arizona, Arkansas, Colorado, Connecticut, Delaware, District of Columbia, Florida, Georgia, Indiana, Iowa, Kansas, Kentucky, Maryland, Massachusetts, Minnesota, Missouri, Montana, Nevada, New Hampshire, New Jersey, New Mexico, New York, North Dakota, Ohio, Oklahoma, Pennsylvania, South Carolina, Utah, West Virginia, Wisconsin, Wyoming.

a course in individual testing; and appropriate field experiences under the direction of a qualified reading clinician.

For reading consultants and supervisors, the *Minimum Standards* call for completing a sixth year of graduate study. In addition to the above, these specialists should take work in curriculum development and supervision and engage in appropriate field experiences under qualified personnel.

Fulfilling these requirements does not guarantee reading depth. No list of courses can do this. The real measure of competency is the degree to which the consultant can translate knowledge into a dynamic force for improvement.

Dr. Laverne Strong[2] has suggested these criteria for a superintendent or a board of education when they are considering a reading consultant:

> Does the reading consultant have: A sound foundation in child growth and development? Specialized training in developmental and remedial reading? A thorough knowledge of the tests and procedures needed to diagnose reading difficulty? Successful clinical experience in working individually with a retarded reader? A knowledge of the over-all total school curriculum with an understanding of the contribution of reading to it? Successful experience in classroom teaching? The ability to work well with an individual and/or groups of teachers? The ability to plan with and give specific teaching suggestions to teachers? A knowledge of resource materials in all curricular fields? A broad knowledge of children's literature? The ability to interpret the reading program to parents and to community groups?

These criteria were prepared for elementary school personnel, but they are just as relevant for secondary reading specialists. There is a growing trend for specialists to assume responsibility for *system-wide* reading programs and therefore know about each level's requirements. Middle school and secondary school reading programs continue the work undertaken in the lower grades. Overall supervision of all these levels facilitates continuous development in reading. Recognizing the benefits of such arrangements, many state certifying agencies are now issuing reading certificates that are valid for both elementary and secondary schools.

The ability to work well, not only with students, but with colleagues and the community, should have high priority in any list of criteria. Reading consultants who supervise reading programs must be experts in human and public relations as well as in reading. When they are, they will not, as did one consultant of excellent professional background after a few weeks on the job, single out a teacher with over twenty years of experience to tell bluntly how bad his teaching of reading was. Since the entire faculty sided with the teacher when the story came out, the consultant was never able to overcome the results of this tactlessness and win teachers' confidence. Consultants must be able to build a solid foundation of human relations; before they presume to teach peers, they must have their respect. It is far better to lay

2. Laverne Strong, "The Role of the Reading Consultant in the Public Schools," *Reading Teacher* 13 (Dec. 1959): 129-133.

the groundwork as a human being than to proceed immediately to teaching others. Consultants must be familiar with the psychology of change. Conditions must be such that when they strive to promote innovations they encounter as little resistance as possible.

Resistance to change may be reduced by creating conditions that do not threaten others. Some of these conditions are a strong feeling of association among members of the group, the active participation of members of the group in making decisions, democratic leadership, and the right to be wrong without losing status. Good supervisors are aware how important it is for others to have positive images of them. Martinets may be right every time, but they often end up talking to themselves. Reading consultants, if they are wise, consult more than they teach. They are good listeners and respect the views of others. They are sensitive to the feelings of others and are kind, generous, and enthusiastic. In short, they possess qualities that each of us would seek in other teachers.

How schools view their reading programs will determine what responsibilities they expect reading consultants to assume. Teachers who try to incorporate reading guidance into their daily work will have different expectations from those who reject the idea that they have to improve the reading levels of students in their subject classes. Those who think of reading instruction as remedial will expect reading consultants and their staffs to carry on without them. They will expect consultants to offer help to students with serious reading problems and to others in scheduled reading classes. Teachers who believe they can promote growth in reading in their classes will seek help from the specialists in order to develop and improve strategies of teaching.[3]

Functions of the Reading Consultant

If we believe in the integration of reading instruction and subject-matter learning, the most important duty of reading specialists is to help classroom teachers accomplish their jobs. As they offer students opportunities to improve reading ability through special reading classes oriented to content, they work through the teachers to reach the students. It is in subject classes that the specialists can become truly effective and increase their usefulness.

Reading consultants serve teachers best if they are available when needed. This means that they will meet with individual teachers and groups of teachers who wish to discuss specific problems and seek ways of solving them. Teachers will be encouraged to form study groups, the outcomes of which they share with others. They will arrange observations so that teachers might catalog and evaluate reading strategies and, when requested, will plan content lessons with teachers, actually assuming responsibility for

3. Karl D. Hesse, Richard J. Smith, and Aileen Nettleton, "Content Teachers Consider the Role of the Reading Consultant," *Journal of Reading* 17 (Dec. 1973): 210-315. See also V. V. Garry, "Competencies That Count among Reading Specialists," *Journal of Reading* 17 (May 1974): 608-613.

teaching the lessons and discussing them afterwards. They will offer mini-workshops to highlight specific reading activities, concentrate on designated skills areas, and demonstrate how appropriate materials might be selected and used. They will invite reading specialists from other schools to meet with teachers and possibly arrange interschool visitations. These and other meaningful activities could serve as ongoing in-service training for any teacher.

Many schools lack professional libraries, and one step a reading consultants can take to remedy this condition is to subscribe to professional periodicals such as the *Journal of Reading, Reading Improvement,* and the *Journal of the Reading Specialist.* Also quite useful are the conference proceedings of the International Reading Association, the College Reading Association, and the National Reading Conference. Copies of particularly interesting and helpful articles can be sent to the teachers. In addition, the consultant can build a collection of reading textbooks and other publications. An excellent source of reading publications intended for secondary schools is the International Reading Association (800 Barksdale, Newark, Del. 19711) which publishes three professional journals, monographs, bibliographies, summaries, and other materials.

In addition to helping teachers become more knowledgeable about reading through publications, reading consultants could arrange to have some of them attend local, regional, or national reading conferences. Because of the growing interest in secondary reading, most programs include sections on reading improvement in the content fields and on the poor reader. Book publishers exhibit their wares at these meetings, and teachers have the opportunity to become familiar with a variety of materials they might be able to use in their work. Teachers who attend the conferences might report to the others what they have learned about latest developments in reading. These teachers, with the reading consultant, might serve also as liaison between the faculty and the community. By meeting with community groups, they can explain the school's reading program and enlist their support to help improve it.

Reading consultants should not spend much time working with students if schools have trained reading teachers. The latter will evaluate students' reading and conduct special classes of no more than twenty students of average and above-average reading ability. They will also offer individual and small-group instruction to those who require it and, hopefully, will have time in their programs to help subject teachers.

Occasionally, reading consultants will do diagnostic evaluations. Here, their expertise is required and they may possibly teach some of these students. However, such activities should not constitute the major part of their assignment. They should always be free to consult with teachers, students, administrators, parents, and community representatives, thereby assuming the responsibilities for which they have been trained and employed. To have them teach full time might benefit a few students, but they will reach many more students through the in-service activities they conduct for teachers. These teachers are the ones in a position to have a real impact on the reading development of all students.

A READING CENTER IN THE SCHOOL

Some middle and secondary schools set aside one large room or a suite of rooms that serves both as the center for reading instruction and as headquarters for the reading consultant and reading staff. There, conferences can be held with teachers and students. It may contain a professional library in reading for the staff, and it may also contain a wide variety of interesting reading for both students and teachers. Sometimes this center adjoins the school library so that there is a smooth flow from the center to the source of books.

The physical features of a reading center should be dictated by the nature of the reading program, but some general characteristics can be mentioned. Movable round or rectangular tables large enough for four persons are preferred. Tables and chairs thus can be arranged in different patterns to fit program requirements and the room's features. A bank of work spaces along one or more walls makes individual work easier. Work spaces can be achieved by using partitions. Open shelves for storing supplies and materials and for displaying books and magazines are common features. File cabinets should be available for tests and records and storage cabinets for such special equipment as tape recorders and projectors. A projection screen is desirable. Other usual equipment includes a bulletin board for announcements and displays and both fixed and movable chalkboards. And the reading center, of all places in the school, should have good lighting.

A comfortable reading corner with soft furniture and floor rug is a valuable adjunct to a reading center. Students and teachers should be encouraged to view the center as a place where they can come to relax with a book if they have free time. In this way the center, together with the library, will become the focal points of reading not only for students but also for teachers.

Figure 2-1 is the floor plan of a possible reading center. Its arrangement gives the room a feeling of spaciousness and affords flexibility in utilization of space. Individual work and group work are facilitated. An alternate plan might place the tables in horizontal rows across the room, which would accommodate more students.

Materials of Instruction

In an introductory statement about reading materials, a compiler for ERIC/RCS said the following:

> It is probably safe to assume that there does not exist one set of materials or one piece of hardware that will enable all secondary students to read to their fullest potential. However, knowledge of this fact does not lessen the burden of selecting reading materials for instructing secondary students.[4]

4. William H. Rupley, "ERIC/RCS," *Journal of Reading* 17 (Dec. 1973): 252. ERIC/RCS is the Clearinghouse on Reading and Communication Skills, one of the Educational Resources Information Centers sponsored by the National Council of Teachers of English in cooperation with the National Institute and the U.S. Dept. of Health, Education and Welfare.

Figure 2-1.   *Floor Plan of a Reading Center*

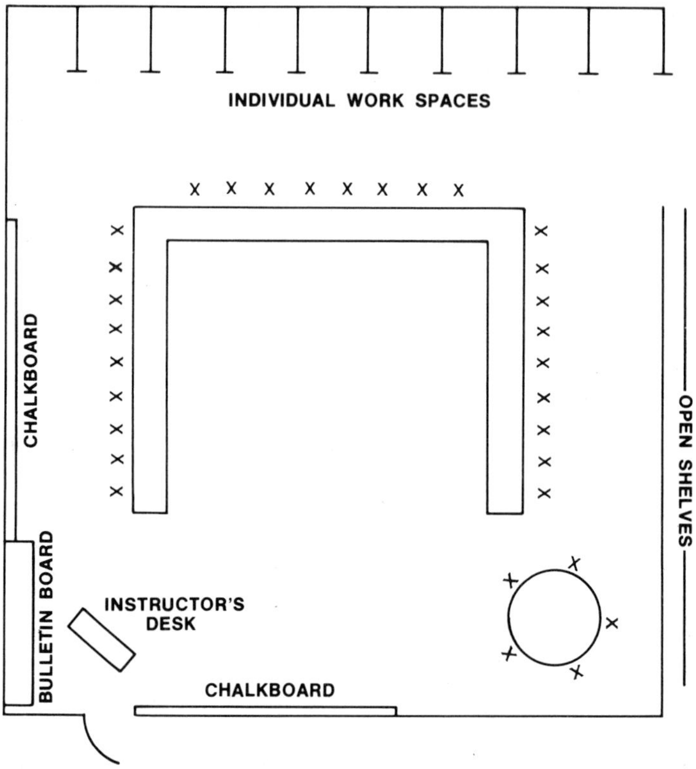

The best results in reading improvement may well be obtained by teachers who use the materials that students read: textbooks, reference books, newspapers, magazines, and so forth. By using such materials for reading instruction, rather than others not associated with the content that students normally read and study, teachers do not have to worry about students being unable to apply what they have been taught to the materials of their subjects. This is no less true of instruction conducted by reading teachers than it is for the guidance in reading offered by subject teachers. Of course, it is assumed that the content materials assigned for reading are not so far beyond students' ability to comprehend them that less difficult materials must be used.

Surveys of secondary reading programs show that commercially prepared reading "packages" make up the bulk of their instructional materials. These include textbooks, workbooks, boxed cards, and pamphlets, films, tapes, and cassettes. They are used to develop reading skills and provide practice in using the skills, and teachers have come to depend on them.

Can these materials be used in conjunction with other materials that students read? Of course they can, provided that teachers do not regard them as panaceas for curing reading ills. They must be selected carefully if they are to meet specified needs. *Caveat emptor* is still the byword when it comes to purchasing them. Some of the materials use passages drawn from standard texts and other sources to introduce given reading skills and provide practice in using them. The closer they represent what students read daily, the more helpful are they likely to become.

It is the reading specialists' responsibility to identify and obtain materials that will be useful for teaching reading. This important task cannot be left to chance. One very worthwhile project is to form a committee to evaluate materials. A cooperative effort such as this gives teachers an opportunity to become familiar with reading materials and gives them ideas on how to improve reading programs.

The ERIC/RCS statement contains some guidelines for selecting materials for a secondary reading program:

1. examine the usability of any particular item and try a sample with a few students before ordering it;
2. contact the school librarian for catalogs of published materials;
3. observe reading programs in operation to view the practicality of particular titles;
4. do no rely solely on publishers' descriptions for evaluations;
5. analyze and consider the intellectual levels, achievement levels, interests and cultural backgrounds of the school's students.

Another task the materials committee might undertake is to index the material contents according to their possible purposes. Folders containing materials on given skills might be placed in the reading center for teacher referral. This committee could prepare exercises modeled after those in the materials but whose excerpts are drawn from the materials of subject classes. The exercises could then be included in the folders.

Most reading materials are not self-instructional. In other words, they require students to perform but don't instruct them on *how* to perform. The latter is the teacher's responsibility; instruction should precede practice. This is vital if a reading program is to pay dividends.

Appendix C contains representative titles of reading materials intended for secondary school use. Two sources are *The Reading Materials Handbook* (Oshkosh, Wisc.: Academic Press, 1969) and the *Guide to Materials for Reading Instruction* (Bloomington, Ind.: ERIC/CRIER, 1971). In addition there are classified lists of materials such as those which appear periodically in the *Journal of Reading* (December 1972, January 1974, February 1975, February 1976, and subsequent issues).

POSSIBLE READING PROGRAMS

The ways in which secondary schools conduct reading programs vary from school to school, as illustrated by the examples that follow. However, whatever the school's size or finances, some type of reading program can be established. Each school system has its peculiar problems; to prescribe the same for all could create more difficulties than it would solve. Ideally, students will receive reading guidance in different settings and under conditions that are likely to promote learning — in subject classes, in reading classes, and in laboratories where individualized teaching, based upon identified needs, can occur.

The most important ingredients, however, regardless of arrangements, are willing teachers and able administrators. Large schools might have more resources and flexibility than small schools, but in any school wise planning and analysis, coupled with periodic evaluations, can lead to a good program.

A Campus School Program

In a campus school program, junior high school students are tested on standardized reading tests. Then they meet with teachers in the reading laboratory where they are encouraged to establish personal reading goals as they evaluate their reading strengths and weaknesses. Laboratory sessions are conducted over fifteen hours in blocks of six weeks, during which time all the students of combined classes in language arts and social studies attend the laboratory with their own classroom teachers.

The program is staffed by a reading specialist and graduate assistant. They supervise the students who are engaged in individual reading tasks which the supervisors correct; students also chart their own progress in reading. Students are encouraged to read library books so that they may apply the skills on which they work. Classroom teachers engage in reading activities of their own and become familiar with laboratory materials and procedures so that they might carry on follow-up activities in their classes.

At the end of the six-week block, students are tested again. Each student prepares a personal progress report. During a final conference with the laboratory staff, progress is noted, as are goals yet to be realized. Students may then return for additional six-week sessions; some students are encouraged to assist in the laboratory and receive additional help.

Two Big-City Programs

One school system has developmental and remedial reading programs in all its junior and senior high schools. Two or three full-time reading teachers are assigned to the faculty of every secondary school. In the beginning, teachers volunteered for these assignments; now, the positions are filled through a competitive, written examination.

All junior high school students are grouped by achievement levels. They receive reading instruction from subject-matter teachers several times each week. The program emphasizes study skills and reading habits. Special teachers of reading assist the classroom teachers.

The developmental reading classes contain no more than fifteen students of average or above-average ability. They meet five days a week. These students receive individualized help in small groups. In senior high school, the developmental reading class replaces the regular English class for one term.

Schools may refer students to a reading clinic run by full-time clinicians that studies the causes of reading failure. The administration uses the clinic not only as a source for individual reading instruction but also as a teacher-training center.

In an all-girl high school, the teachers of science, social studies, and English agreed that in each of their ninth-grade classes, the subject matter should be subordinated to the improvement of reading and writing skills. Each teacher assumed the responsibility for teaching skills appropriate to the subject. The English teacher used practice materials as well as literature books. The teachers of science and social studies collected selections of the kind students read in their subject areas. The development of vocabulary pertinent to each field was stressed.

A reading clinic was established by the English department. All ninth-year students received small-group instruction for a period of five weeks. Subject teachers realized that they needed training in reading. This need led to the establishment of an in-service program that included observations and demonstrations of reading lessons, and consultations with reading specialists.

A Right-to-Read Effort

The U.S. Office of Education, through the "Right-to-Read" program, has sponsored a nationwide campaign to insure that by the end of the 1970s no student leaves school without adequate reading ability. Millions of dollars have been appropriated and distributed to states and local communities to facilitate the upgrading of their reading programs. Another aspect of the Right-to-Read effort is identifying effective reading programs which could serve as models for other schools. Of twelve programs so identified, one was conducted by a junior high school whose goals were to foster positive attitudes toward reading, improve comprehension, and increase rates of reading.

All seventh-grade students were tested and their reading strengths and weaknesses analyzed. Teachers in social studies and English classes who were trained by resource teachers to apply reading techniques as they taught their subjects referred the poorest readers to a reading center. In addition, some students were tutored and their progress monitored by ninth-grade students and teacher assistants.

Classroom teachers were taught how to individualize their instruction according to the reading ability of their students. They received in-service training throughout the year and were assisted by teacher aides. Classrooms contained a variety of teacher-made and other materials including books, magazines, workbooks, audiovisual equipment, and diagnostic tests. It appears that classroom teachers were as involved in improving student reading and promoting good reading habits as they were teaching the content of their subjects.

A District-Wide Reading Program

Each of four high schools established reading laboratories whose activities were directed by reading specialists. All ninth-grade students spent eight weeks in the laboratory, working under the direction of the specialists or the English teachers who had voluntarily received training in reading. Other students attended the laboratory for shorter periods of time. The laboratory program sought to develop competence in word meaning, comprehension, and reading-study skills and techniques, as well as to promote interest in reading.

In order to prepare for the program, students visited the reading laboratory and learned about its objectives. All students were tested at the beginning and the end of each laboratory session and at the end of the school year. Students kept records of their progress and were encouraged to use the skills and study techniques they had learned in the laboratory.

At the end of the laboratory period, students spent one day each week in their English classes to help refine their reading and study skills. In addition, teachers sought to promote independent reading, and school librarians helped students select materials for both recreational and study reading.

When the reading laboratories began to operate, efforts were initiated to make reading a schoolwide concern. The reading committee in each school met with departments to determine ways of improving reading in subject areas. Laboratory teachers and librarians helped subject teachers identify and teach the skills and study techniques and select suitable materials. Special problems were referred to a counselor for study and recommendations.

A Three-Level Program

In this program, junior high school students are placed in one of three groups, according to their reading ability. Seventh and eighth graders attend combined English and social studies classes; the number of periods each of these meets per week depends on the reading composition of each class. Sections with the poorest readers meet more often than sections with students of average reading ability. In the ninth grade, there are English classes organized on the same three different reading-ability levels, and the classes with the poorer readers meet more often than the others.

Reading instruction is offered in these subject classes; teachers use content materials whenever possible. Instruction is differentiated according to student reading level requirements. Regardless of reading level, all students visit the library once a week, where teachers and librarians help them select books for recreational reading to be done there and at home. Vocabulary and spelling exercises are based on words drawn from the content materials that students read.

"Helping teachers" are available twice a week to help subject teachers who teach the two lowest reading ability groups. They have had more experience in teaching reading in subject classes than the teachers to whom they are assigned. At times, they work with smaller groups of students in the classroom, and, as subject teachers feel more secure, helping teachers may divide the class so that each teacher has fewer students to work with.

SPECIAL READING PROGRAMS

It is not very realistic to expect subject-matter teachers to work on reading with students who have severe reading problems. Most of these students have limited sight vocabularies and lack the skills they need to identify words. In addition, their vocabularies may be so restricted that they just can't cope with the ideas contained in the textbooks; and they also may lack the basic reading skills to comprehend literal statements. These are the students who are reading at levels several years below their age-peers and require concentrated attention that the typical content teacher cannot provide.

Included among these students are those who are slow learners, learners of average ability, and, in quite a few instances, bright learners. Additionally, there are a growing number of students who have been identified as "culturally different" learners. The latter, though usually of normal or superior intelligence, have been "turned off" by school with the result that many of them are among the poorest readers. It is important to recognize the responsibility that the high school has to all its students, and this includes provisions for helping them to overcome some of their reading difficulties and to progress in reading.

Each school should have specialized reading personnel to work with these students. They can be programmed for small group instruction — four to eight students make a good working group — with provisions for individual help when required. Or, if their reading problems are less severe, they may be placed in small reading improvement classes in lieu of regular English classes. Subject teachers might recommend for special treatments those students who can't do the assigned work in spite of efforts to adjust the reading demands and offer reading assistance. Schoolwide testing, followed by more intensive evaluation, will also identify others who need expert help.

Remedial vs. Developmental Instruction

Teachers usually consider remedial reading instruction to be quite different from developmental reading instruction. However, my position on this question is unequivocal: there are no basic differences between remedial and developmental reading. If any differences do exist, they are a matter of degree and not of kind. "Poor readers require the most highly skilled help teachers can provide. This means that developmental reading procedures probably have to be refined if they are to be successful with poor readers. For example, in a good learning climate some measurement and evaluation occur before instruction begins. Ordinarily they are not extensive, without any apparent losses to pupils. However, more detailed and specific information about the status of pupils with reading problems must be known if instruction to overcome them is to be truly effective. Good readers do not seem to be affected adversely by teaching procedures that fall somewhat short of the mark; poor readers are unable to compensate for any such deficiencies."[5] There should be no need to point out that most disabled readers do not suffer from physical or mental conditions which dictate unusual or unique treatments. Hardly any will not respond to meaningful, appropriate instruction which this textbook has explained and demonstrated.

5. Robert Karlin, *Teaching Elementary Reading: Principles and Strategies*, 2d ed. (New York: Harcourt Brace Jovanovich, 1975), p. 393.

THE SCHOOL ADMINISTRATOR AND THE READING PROGRAM

The principal of a school and the superintendent of a school system have many good reasons to support a good reading program. The major reason, perhaps, is that instruction and learning improvement is increased if a total reading program is part of the school system. Teachers will teach better if they teach the specific reading skills that their subjects require. Students will learn better if they read better.

What can school administrators do to help a reading program? They probably will know as little about reading instruction as untrained teachers, but through study and observation of other programs in action, they can gain insights that will help them to evaluate the efforts of their own schools. In addition, administrators must provide the leadership that will allow the reading program to operate. Once they clarify the responsibilities of the reading specialists, they will give whole-hearted support to those responsible for conducting the program by furthering its growth and development.

Ongoing in-service training will enhance any program's effectiveness. By showing that they believe in its importance, administrators can establish the proper conditions for the training. Teachers will give their time more freely if they believe that others are concerned about them and want to help them. Administrators have joined with teachers in learning about reading and shared their experiences with them. Participating in in-service activities demonstrates further their belief in the program; that they provide the necessary resources to implement it demonstrates concretely their support for it. Administrative faith in the purposes and personnel of the program, and active interest in its operation, can be a tremendous morale-building influence.

SUMMARY

An effective secondary-school reading program is an "all-school" program that benefits good, average, and poor readers. Subject teachers integrate reading and studying instruction with the content teaching. Reading classes taught by specialists offer instruction in basic reading skills and study skills. Students whose needs cannot be met completely in subject or reading classes receive help in reading through small group and individualized instruction. Promoting recreational reading is a program goal for all students.

Reading consultants and reading teachers assume responsibility for directing the program. They staff the reading center where teachers and students come for guidance and consultation. Through in-service courses and demonstrations, they help teachers learn how to assist students in reading and studying.

Although secondary schools have many reading needs in common, particular circumstances might require that they not all organize and conduct reading programs in the same way as do other schools. However the programs are established and operated, the faculty should be intimately involved in planning and decision-making, as well as evaluating outcomes. Administrators can show tangible evidence of their interest in having a successful program by sharing expertise, facilitating in-service training, providing the necessary budget, and enlisting community support for the program.

Additional Readings

A. Sterl Artley. *Trends and Practices in Secondary School Reading: A Review of the Literature*, ERIC/CRIER Reading Review Series. Newark, Del.: International Reading Association, 1968.

Lou E. Burmeister. *Reading Strategies for Secondary School Teachers.* Reading, Mass.: Addison-Wesley, 1974, pp. 278-291.

Thorsten R. Carlson, ed. *Administrators and Reading*, A Project of the International Reading Association. New York: Harcourt Brace Jovanovich, 1972, pp. 2-19; 242-263.

Mildred A. Dawson, comp. *Developing High School Reading Programs.* Newark, Del.: International Reading Association, 1967.

Gerald G. Duffy, comp. ed. *Reading in the Middle School*, Perspectives in Reading No. 18. Newark, Del.: International Reading Association, 1975, pp. 34-91.

Margaret Early, ed. *Reading Instruction in Secondary Schools*, Perspectives in Reading No. 2. Newark, Del.: International Reading Association, 1964.

Joseph S. Nemeth, ed. *Reading Rx: Better Teachers, Better Supervisors, Better Programs.* Newark, Del.: International Reading Association, 1975.

Arthur V. Olson and Wilbur S. Ames, eds. *Teaching Reading Skills in Secondary Schools: Readings.* Scranton, Pa.: International Textbook Co., 1970, pp. 3-26; 35-52; 423-443.

Wayne Otto and Richard J. Smith. *Administering the School Reading Program.* Boston: Houghton Mifflin, 1970, pp. 5-39; 143-207.

H. Alan Robinson and Sidney J. Rauch. *Guiding the Reading Program.* Chicago: Science Research Associates, 1965.

READING
AREAS

Discussion

1 *How might the reading act be described?*
2 *What is the difference between the reading act and the reading process?*
3 *What factors are believed to facilitate word perception?*
4 *Why is reading called a "psycholinguistic guessing game?" What elements are common to theories of reading that are based upon the knowledge of language?*
5 *Identify learning principles that might be translated into effective strategies for teaching reading.*

THE NATURE OF READING

What do we mean when we refer to "reading"? Although the question might seem to be simple, there isn't complete agreement on its answer. Some psychologists and linguists think of reading as a discrimination act or a decoding process — that is, one that involves merely the recognition of words. According to this explanation, thinking begins when reading stops. This view of reading could be compared to what beginning students of a foreign language might be doing as they pronounce words without comprehending them.

Other explanations include meaning as an integral part of the reading act. One refers to identifying words and acquiring meaning from them. Another describes reading as reconstructing messages that appear in written form. Both imply that reading is a thinking act. However reading is defined, it seems evident that it involves idea-acquisition. This is why reading instruction continues after decoding skills have been learned.

43

The meaning of reading might be extended to include reaction to and integration of ideas. A natural consequence of receiving ideas is reflecting upon them. Their acceptance or rejection could alter thinking and modes of behavior. In fact, ideas gained through reading, combined with previous experiences, might produce new insights which contribute to a person's total development. This broad view of reading is reflected in this text.

Word Perception and Reading

The whole subject of word perception has challenged the best efforts of theoreticians and practitioners alike, and some knowledge of its operation is now known. Studies have been made of the relationship of word perception to reading, and their findings have implications for both the teaching and the learning of reading.

Psychologists have investigated the phases of perception that relate to reading and, by a variety of experimental methods, have attempted to discover what really takes place from the moment a person is exposed to a word to the time he reacts to it. After all, word perception, the first step in reading, is not complete until the word symbol has evoked an adequate response in relation to meaning. This experimentation has led to the conclusion that, just as there are steps in the complete reading act, there are fundamental stages in the act of perceiving.[1]

In the first stage, the perceiver has the feeling or awareness that something is present even though it cannot be discerned. In the second stage, the perceiver realizes that what is seen is related to some kind of symbol or word. In this stage, certain parts stand out more than others. This differentiation leads to fuller recognition. The third stage in perception involves identification and understanding of meaning. In reading, the three stages seem to be telescoped and become one, for the reader is unaware of the stages.

Some psychologists include a fourth step, which is *naming*. They suggest that perception is related to speech and language and is almost an essential of accurate and complete perception. Some evidence supports the conclusion that naming does facilitate reproducing visual images and that some speech occurs even during silent reading.

Young children have been known to have the ability to perceive shapes without representational meaning. This ability seems to increase with maturity, and three-year-olds have been taught to recognize words — not that such learning is important or necessary at this stage of development. Investigators whose procedures required identification and reproduction of different shapes have concluded that mature perceivers ignore most details but note general forms. They report that attention to details decreases with maturity. Students of perception have observed that these findings are in harmony with the Gestalt point of view.

What a child sees as he learns to recognize words has been a matter of debate for some time. Do beginning readers see what adult readers do?

1. M. D. Vernon, *A Further Study of Visual Perception* (Cambridge: At the University Press, 1954).

Research findings are far from conclusive. We do know that skilled readers do not have to see a word clearly to identify it — that is, they do not have to identify each aspect of a word. Rapid exposure of words by means of tachistoscopic devices has shown that perceiving general shape or outline is sufficient for the skilled reader to identify the words.

Some studies have shown that the distinguishing characteristics that words possess enhance perception. These characteristics usually are letters that have ascenders or descenders: for example, *d, h, p, y*. Experience with beginning or older disabled readers has demonstrated that words containing these distinguishing characteristics are easier to identify than those whose letters are regular. It is possible that these ascenders and descenders do strengthen further the general shape of words.

Other research has indicated that the reader needs only to see the upper portions of words in order to identify them. When merely the lower half of the words is exposed it is almost impossible to read them. Moreover, the reader does not have to see every twist and turn of letters to identify words. Experiments in which portions of letters in words were omitted have shown that these words may be identified readily. It is possible that the skilled reader sees only parts of words rather than entire words. There also seems to be some agreement that the beginning and final portions of words are of greater concern to the reader than the medial ones.

Efforts have also been made to find out whether children perceive words in much the same way as adults do. Better readers among children tended to see words as units rather than as parts or as individual letters. Several investigators found that beginning readers frequently substituted words of the same general shape and length for the words being read. Others reported that young readers put an emphasis on beginning letters, with the result of confusion between words with the same beginning.[2] Still others noted confusion between words whose letters were similar — for example, *of* and *for*. These errors seemed to occur most often while learning was still incomplete. Psychologists explain this difficulty in terms of *interference*, which will be discussed later in this chapter. Especially during the early stages of learning, one stimulus similar in appearance to a second is likely to evoke a response appropriate to the latter. Thus, teachers find that such words as *through* and *thought* are read and written as though they were interchangeable.

Young children can learn to recognize individual letters in words. although certain ones are especially troublesome: *b* and *d, p* and *q, j* and *y*, for example. For any reader, identification is facilitated not only by the structure of a word but also by the context in which it appears. But attention to minute detail is not characteristic of young children; they find it difficult to perceive and recall these details, although some children may use one or more letters for purposes of identification.

2. Substituting one word for another while reading continuous text is a common error with which all teachers are familiar. A classic example is the reading by a W.C.T.U. member of *pupil prohibition* for *pupil promotion* — *promotion* and *prohibition* are not identical, but they do contain similar elements. In this instance, the factor of set may also have interfered with accurate perception of the word.

It would appear, then, that children do duplicate the processes of adult perception, but at a much less mature level. Their emphasis seems to be on wholeness rather than on individuality. Although perception studies multiply as new knowledge is sought, teachers may conclude, if only conditionally, that structure is natural to learning. The implication of this concept will be considered later in this chapter.

Although the brain-damaged student is not typically the concern of the classroom teacher, results of studies of such cases add something to the understanding of perception and reading. Persons who have suffered brain damage before, during, or after birth are common victims of perceptual aberrations. They do not seem able to differentiate one word from another or remember words even after many exposures to them. Some specialists have hypothesized that damage to parts of the nervous system changes the natural way perception occurs so that details now become more dominant than wholes. Consequently, they argue, methods and materials of instruction have to be different from those used with learners who perceive words naturally. They would recommend that training to allow discrimination of individual letters *precede* efforts to introduce whole words, and that the introduction of sentences be delayed until whole words are recognized.

Theories and Models of Reading

Efforts to explain the reading processes — that is, underlying conditions or structures that account for the ways in which words are perceived and ideas are understood through the print medium — have generated some theories, which, if demonstrated, could influence reading instruction. The state of present knowledge is far from precise, but some students of reading have proposed limited or fuller explanations, each of which attracts its share of adherents. Some explanations concentrate heavily on word perception, while others are more concerned with comprehension.

Theorists have tried to explain how words are perceived, or under what conditions word recognition is facilitated.[3] Smith and Carrigan suggest that a favorable chemical balance of acetylcholine and cholinesterase allows nerve impulses to pass from the eye to brain cells, and that this transmission results in word recognition. Lack of chemical balance blocks the transmission of nerve impulses and interferes with an individual's ability to recognize words. Delacato attributes successful word recognition to neuro-

3. Vernon (1954); Harry Levin and Joanna P. Williams, eds., *Basic Studies on Reading* (New York: Basic Books, 1970); Donald E. P. Smith and Patricia M. Carrigan, *The Nature of Reading Disability* (New York: Harcourt Brace Jovanovich, 1959); Carl H. Delacato, *The Treatment of Speech and Reading Problems* and *The Diagnosis and Treatment of Speech and Reading Problems* (Springfield, Ill.: Charles C. Thomas, 1959, 1963); John J. Geyer, "Models of Perceptual Processes in Reading," in *Theoretical Models and Processes of Reading*, ed. Harry Singer and Robert B. Ruddell (Newark Del.: International Reading Association, 1970), pp. 47-94; A. W. Staats, *Learning, Language, and Cognition* (New York: Holt, Rinehart and Winston, 1968); and Eleanor J. Gibson, "Trends in Perceptual Development: Implications for the Reading Process," in Singer and Ruddell (1976), pp. 186-216.

logical maturity and the establishment of cerebral dominance (use of the left hand and eye or right hand and eye). Lack of maturity or failure to establish dominance causes interference with word perception. Both models attempt to explain what facilitates the recognition of words after learners have been exposed to them.

Both Staats and Gibson believe that children become aware of the graphic features of letters, and this facilitates the recognition of words. This ability, as well as the ability to recognize letter-sound correspondences, can be developed through training. Gibson places greater emphasis upon the learners' ability to obtain information from the sound, meaning, and grammatical systems of language. The better they are able to do this, the more efficient will be their reading.

Geyer hypothesizes that during reading each letter space in words is processed at a rate of about 8 milliseconds and probably converted into sounds. The letter-sounds are organized into words which are then delivered to a storage system where each is integrated internally. If no covert response is made to the word, it is "lost" after about a second; after a response is made, the word is transferred to a second system with limited storage capacity where it can remain several seconds until it is recognized through oral or silent reading.

There are a number of language-related explanations of the reading process.[4] Essentially, each stresses the fact that knowledge of the language makes it possible to read with understanding. Goodman calls reading a "psycholinguistic guessing game" in which readers use *graphic* cues within words (letters and other parts), *semantic* cues (meaning), and *syntactic* cues (grammar). Readers use graphic cues only to the extent that semantic and syntactic cues do not enable them to comprehend adequately. They guess and predict meaning through these cues. Smith explains that *redundancy* (duplicated information) through cue recognition is actually anticipated by readers. This, in turn, makes comprehension possible. Good readers rely less on graphic cues than on other cues. Ruddell, as do Goodman and Fleming and Smith, bases his explanation of the reading process on the concept of deep structure in language or its grammar. Within the reader's memory system are the "rules" that govern language. The sentence structures are processed according to the rules and the transformed structures integrated with the semantic components in the memory system to convey meaning.

Holmes developed a theory of reading power based upon sets of skills and subskills expressed in hierarchic levels.[5] According to Holmes, interaction among these skills and subskills during reading helps reassemble and process information stored in the brain. When this interaction occurs smoothly, comprehension occurs. He identified knowledge of word meaning, understanding verbal analogies, and listening comprehension as important

4. Kenneth S. Goodman and James T. Fleming, eds., *Psycholinguistics and the Teaching of Reading* (Newark, Del.: International Reading Association, 1969); Frank Smith, *Psycholinguistics and Reading* (New York: Holt, Rinehart and Winston, 1973); and Singer and Ruddell (1970).
5. Jack A. Holmes, "Basic Assumptions Underlying the Substrata-Factor Theory," *Reading Research Quarterly* 1 (Fall 1965): 4-28.

contributors to reading comprehension.

It can be seen that some of these reading theories and models attempt to explain the ways in which processes of reading occur, while others focus on the processes themselves. Moreover, it appears that language models offer some promise of yielding information that can help determine the ways in which reading might be taught.

On the other hand, some observers have been highly critical of Smith and Carrigan's, Delacato's, and Holmes's presentations. Hypotheses about language and its relationship to reading have generated some research, part of which seems to help explain some of the forces that operate during reading. Of course, conclusions based upon this research are tentative. It is unlikely that all reading behaviors can be explained by a single theory or model, just as other kinds of learning cannot be explained by one formulation.

It has been suggested that if reading is indeed a psycholinguistic process, then semantic and syntactic constraints will play dominant roles in the way in which comprehension occurs. If this is true, less emphasis should be placed on the phonological system and more upon the other systems. Thus, if students were not fluent readers, materials which contain meaning and grammatical cues could be used. They would be taught to use their knowledge of language to obtain intended meanings even though they do not readily recognize all the words. To a large extent, this is what happens when students are taught how to use context clues for word identification and word meaning purposes.

THE NATURE OF LEARNING

One of the foundation stones on which this book rests is the belief that teaching is a science as well as an art. Teachers are both artisans and artists — artisans in the sense of processing knowledge of a craft, and artists in the sense of possessing creativity of thought — who can guide the learning of children at various stages of development.[6]

Teaching is a profession that requires preparation. While they vary from state to state, most training programs include one or more courses in psychology. The contribution that psychology can make to teaching is stated clearly in a university report issued some time ago:[7]

> Psychology should, and eventually will, supply a major part of the scientific foundation for the slowly evolving art of education. Dependable knowledge of the aptitudes and capacities of the pupil, and more important, his interests and enthusiasms, are incomparably more important for effective education of the individual from birth to maturity than are

6. I first expressed this view in a paper entitled "Preparation of Teachers for Reading" read before the 5th annual conference of the International Reading Association, New York City, May 6, 1960.
7. *The Place of Psychology in an Ideal University, Report of the University Commission to Advise on the Future of Psychology at Harvard* (Cambridge, Mass.: Harvard Univ. Press, 1947), p. 14.

the so-called "subjects" now taught in our schools from nursery to university. Until we apply what we know of the psychology of learning to the individual, we shall be evading the essential issue, whether the evasion be via a free elective system or the mass exposure of all students in common to the same curriculum.

Efforts to apply psychology to the teaching of reading do not — as some writers suggest when they reject the idea that teaching is both art and science — necessarily lead to the dehumanizing of learners. The science of learning and, as we shall see later, the science of teaching regard the motivations, feelings, and attitudes of pupils as concomitants of cognitive behaviors and elements to be accounted for in the promotion of learning. The learner is central in the search for more effective teaching strategies, a fact that some past. The next section suggests ents, and the same patterns will ces that are offered throughout

Learning and Reading

otings that are set in the psychol-
have studied the principles of
but a review of these principles
teaching of reading. They are the
on and provide the rationale of

of no one way to teach reading.
erent routes, some of which are
which are filled with stumbling
e noted that children learn under
learn in spite of instruction; to
n development is unknown. The
which learning is likely to occur.
y to the creation of such a climate
is taught is no exception.
is of learning. One that fits a plan
ation of a student's behavior to
en a student is confronted with a
ect response, he may try several
ble than another and, as learning
ones and follows those that are
He is changing his behavior as

earning, take the student who is seeking the correct pronunciation and specific meaning of a word but who is unable to use a dictionary. He realizes the importance of arriving at the solution to his problem and therefore seeks out the dictionary. He opens it and begins to turn page after page to locate the word. Something tells him that he should look elsewhere, so he grasps many pages at once and begins the search again. Obviously, he has made many responses, many of which are unrefined. Ultimately he may locate the word, but he is then faced with the problems of unlocking its pronunciation and selecting its appropriate meaning. Once again, his responses are undifferentiated because he does not know how to use the pronunciation guide and he does not realize that words may have multiple meanings. After learning has occurred, the same student discards improper responses and adopts better ones. He now uses the words at the top and bottom of the dictionary pages to guide him in his search, which is no longer randomly dictated. He finds the word quickly and easily and uses the pronunciation key if he is unfamiliar with the diacritical marks. He no longer takes the first meaning but chooses the one that is appropriate to his text. He has learned to use the dictionary the way in which it was intended to be used; he has changed his pattern of behavior from undisciplined responses to selective responses. Learning has occurred.

Theories of Learning

In a limited amount of space it is difficult to outline even briefly all the learning theories that have been seriously considered. Within any single school of thought there may be a number of smaller schools that vary in the way they view the learning process. For our purposes, it may be sufficient merely to indicate the predominant approaches to learning and to associate some important principles with each.[8]

The reader should be aware of the fact that learning theories contain many similarities as well as some major differences. A language peculiar to each theory is adopted, and, at times, what appears to be a real difference in viewpoint is actually a semantic difference. Some differences may be real in that the characteristics of the theories differ to the extent that emphasis upon them varies.

Followers of *Gestalt* theory explain learning in terms of the way in which all the factors that are involved in the solution of a problem are perceived. The memory of present or past experiences will affect and possibly alter the learner's behavior. Learning is tied to the way in which the total situation is viewed. Learning is dependent upon the ability to restructure the field; this new organization occurs with insight, although trial-and-error learning may be a contributing influence. Gestalt theorists seem to be more concerned about explaining perception than learning. Of course, it is difficult to separate the two. Koffka, Wertheimer, Köhler, and Lewin are regarded as the fathers of Gestalt theory.

The *stimulus-response* schools of psychology are numerous. They include the theories of Thorndike, Guthrie, Hull, Skinner, and others. Thorndike's well-known law of effect is tied closely to trial-and-error learning. According to this theory, a response made as a result of a stimulus is strengthened if the response produces satisfying results. Thorndike's laws of readiness and exercise (the strengthening or weakening of responses through

8. E. R. Hilgard and G. Bower, *Theories of Learning*, 3d ed. (New York: Appleton-Century-Crofts, 1966).

practice or lack of it) are further explanations of the way in which learning occurs.

Guthrie espouses stimulus-response learning too but adds a new dimension: conditioning. Guthrie's law of learning states that when a combination of stimuli accompanying a movement recurs, the movement is likely to follow. This principle is a modification of Pavlov's conditioned response, the prime example of which is the dog who salivates when the light is flashed even though food is no longer offered. Guthrie emphasizes the movements that the organism makes rather than its correct responses. He places less emphasis upon motives as producers of responses than Thorndike does and more upon cues that affect the responses.

Skinner distinguishes between responses that are made to known stimuli and responses whose stimuli are unknown. He believes that the responses of the latter type are characteristic of most human behavior. These responses may be strengthened through reinforcement, that is, through presentation of satisfying stimuli, such as food and water. Skinner actually charted the number of reinforcements needed to produce varying responses of animals. Motivation, practice, and transfer are also part of his learning design.

Skinner has applied his ideas concerning reinforcement to human learning. His teaching machine and step-by-step, or programmed, learning have been adopted by universities and other institutions to teach a variety of subjects and skills. Skinner has published a programmed textbook in psychology that attempts to insure learning by guiding the learner to make correct responses and by providing immediate reinforcement to these responses. The subject knows at once if his response is correct or incorrect. If the response is correct, he proceeds to the next item. If the subject makes an incorrect response, he receives further instruction.

A number of programmed materials, particularly for teaching word recognition and some comprehension skills and word meaning, have been developed by several publishers.[9] The results of experimentation with some of these materials suggest that they are more effective with below average and slow learners than with gifted learners. It is possible that the former benefit from carefully sequenced, fractioned presentations not ordinarily provided by many teachers. Those who learn more easily do not appear to be adversely affected by grosser presentations. In fact, there are indications that they are bored by the repetition provided by programmed materials. Few of them take into account differences among learners who are required to complete each small section or frame even though they know the information offered by it or vary the presentations when the learners fail to respond correctly to any item. These are some weaknesses that producers of programmed reading materials have yet to overcome.

A third school of learning theory has been labled *purposivism*. Tolman is one of its leading proponents. His theory of expectancy asserts that re-

9. *Programmed Vocabulary* (Appleton-Century-Crofts); *Steps to Better Reading* (Harcourt Brace Jovanovich); *Words* (Science Research Associates); *Building Reading Power* (Charles E. Merrill); and *Reading Comprehension, Series E-F* (California Test Bureau).

sponses to stimuli are not automatic but that prior knowledge of them and what they produce leads to the response. He believes that motives or need are incidental to learning—that they regulate performance but not the learning of it.

Other explanations of learning include the functionalism of Dewey, Woodworth, and others and the psychoanalytical theories of Freud and his followers. Both groups place great emphasis upon the role of motivation, although their explanations of it vary.

All these theories are far from being firmly established. Each has its proponents and its critics. The ideas of one are found in another. Most of the experimentation that has been conducted in learning has involved animals and not humans, and it may be unrealistic to explain human learning from what is suspected about animal learning. It may be equally unrealistic to try to explain every kind of learning by an all-encompassing theory.

Hilgard and others caution us not to expect too much from learning theorists. The latter are dealing with hypothetical concepts rather than with practical matters. They agree on what occurs but disagree on how and why it occurs. The time is bound to come when experimentation and study will reveal more about the true nature of learning. In the meantime, it is possible to take from each school of learning some supportable ideas that can be translated into useful practices. Some of these generalizations may be grouped under motivation, guidance and meaning, interference, and transfer and application.

Before making suggestions as to how each of these concepts can be applied to the teaching of reading, it may be useful to consider the basic question of the relationship of learning theories to teaching reading.

There is no doubt that the psychology of learning has had an impact on reading methodology. A number of the ideas of various schools of learning theories has been adopted by the profession. The Gestalt point of view of wholeness and form and its notions of insightful learning have left deep impressions upon those educators who have been seeking superior ways of teaching children how to read. Associative learning, which is related to the stimulus-response school of learning, has also played an important role in influencing reading methodology. The emphasis that purposivists and others give to motivational influences can almost be recognized in teaching methods. Nevertheless, there are serious differences of opinion about the way in which reading should be taught. These differences are expressions of the acceptance or rejection of basic views about learning. In some instances, these differences do not reflect any particular view of learning.

Controversies in methods of teaching reading exist in a number of areas. The argument regarding the whole-word or letter approach in introducing beginning reading has been noted earlier. Some students of reading have raised questions about present methods of developing perceptual skills in reading. The use of graded materials for developing reading skills has been rejected by those who favor an individualized program of instruction through different kinds of reading materials. The large-scale use of practice exercises in prepared workbooks has been criticized. There is some doubt about the effectiveness of present methods of developing skills of comprehension. Debate goes on over the merits of concentrating on more efficient eye movements or improving understanding ability as the means of increasing reading speeds.

None of these differences has been settled completely, and it is unlikely that all will be resolved in this or the next decade. Learning theorists and their educational interpreters have provided some clues about the nature of learning. Some aspects have been demonstrated in the laboratory as well as the classroom. Additional experimentation may yield new insights into the ways in which humans learn. It is possible that explanations for some learning tasks may vary with the individuals concerned.

It has been suggested, for example, that all learners do not have equal ability to process information through the same sensory pathways. According to this belief, some students are more predisposed to primarily aural presentations, while others may learn better through primarily visual presentations. Still others may require some physical participation (such as writing) to achieve optimum learning. The evidence on this question is not conclusive and suggests that students should be exposed to procedures that reflect different learning styles.

In summation, our knowledge of the ways in which learning occurs is incomplete, and explanations of conditions that lead to learning vary. Therefore, it seems reasonable to take the principles upon which there is some general agreement and use them as "building blocks" of teaching strategies. This implies that there is no single effective method for teaching reading and that different methods may be equally effective. Moreover, teachers can anticipate superior results from eclectic rather than narrow presentations.

Motivation and Learning

Although data support the view that some learning may occur without evidence of a desire to learn, teachers may assume that students are impelled to learn for reasons originating within and without. Learners have basic needs, such as satisfying hunger and thirst, and learners have secondary needs, such as enjoying success and approval. It is with these secondary needs that the teacher is most likely to be concerned, although primary needs may enter into the learning situation. No teacher would deliberately use deprivation of food and water as an instrument of motivation, but hunger and thirst could be factors that influence learning. Yet teachers at times may misuse the student's secondary needs, although most would agree that students have more impelling reasons for striving than a *mere* nod from the teacher.

Upon what motivations, then, should the classroom teacher concentrate? Naturally, emphasis should be on those that are likely to be factors in learning and that are bound to be more lasting. No one doubts the efficacy of punishment, physical or mental, in getting results, but this type of motivation, needless to say, is not acceptable to most teachers and may not be recommended for use in school settings. Furthermore, punishment may *interfere* with learning.

Goals

All too frequently the goals of the teacher are not the goals of the learner. If real learning is to occur, *the teacher's goals must be accepted by the student.* In other words, the student must understand that he has a need for learning what is being presented, this need preferably arising from a problem that he seeks to solve. This is not to suggest that some knowledge or skills are unworthy of being learned for their own sake. Actually, such a motive would be of a high order. What is being stressed here is the great value in using the student's rather than the teacher's felt need to learn.

Teachers know how useful an outline can be in helping them remember. They also know the value of being able to use a library card catalog to locate source material. Unfortunately, this knowledge is not conveyed to all students simply by informing them that some time in the future they may have to prepare a talk that cannot be read or must seek out information from an unknown source. A surer way to arouse student interest is for the teacher to point up the need to solve an acceptable problem. Is there any better opportunity to teach students than the time when they *have* to learn in order to achieve their goal!

Purpose

A second major motivation is purpose. Experimentation and experience show that when learners know what is expected of them, better results may be anticipated than when they do not know what to seek or why they perform. As one writer said, "a teacher would have to be stupid, if not altogether perverse, not to use a motive as simple as this."[10]

Aimless reading assignments suffer from a lack of purpose. The exercise that calls for no more than reading the "next ten pages" does not give students any direction or goal. All they know is that they must read those ten pages. They should know why they are reading — for example, to learn about the parliamentary system of England in order to compare it with the governmental system of the United States. In addition, they will benefit from signposts as they read. These could take the form of questions directly related to the main purpose for reading: How is the Prime Minister selected? How are English laws made? Questions such as these serve to keep readers "on track" and offer specific purposes for reading segments of the material. When the reading is completed, students have information they need to satisfy the main purpose for which they read about the English parliamentary system: to compare the political systems of England and the United States.

Recognition of Growth

Another source of motivation is the recognition of growth, no matter how small, when it occurs. To do this, a student must know what he can do now, what he cannot do now, and what he can expect to do. The student is not competing with other students in his class or with achievement

10. J. M. Stevens, *Educational Psychology*, rev. ed. (New York: Holt, Rinehart and Winston, 1956), p. 299.

standards of a sample population. If there is an improvement in performance, growth has occurred.

When teaching reading to high school students, teachers should be certain that each student knows precisely the reading areas in which he is strong and those in which he is weak. Diagnostic evaluations will yield such information. Relying on standardized tests to measure growth is not completely satisfactory, since these are gross measures and do not reveal day-to-day learnings. Informal tests are better suited to this purpose. (The advantages and drawbacks of tests will be discussed in the next chapter.) If a student is able to pronounce *cauterize* as a result of learning the sound of *au* (something he did not know last week) and verifies his pronunciation in the dictionary, he knows he has progressed.

Intrinsic Versus Extrinsic Motivation

Motivation from within is preferred to motivation from extraneous factors. Teachers should use the former whenever they can. However, it has not always been possible to rely on intrinsic motives, and, as a result, too many teachers have used devices such as prizes and certificates to encourage performance excellence. The satisfaction that students gain from learning serves to promote new desires to learn.

The pleasure one derives from reading is sufficient in itself. A reward for reading accomplishments — mastering skills or reading a minimum number of books — detracts, and its effect is not permanent. On the other hand, the sense of accomplishment from increasing one's reading ability and extending horizons by reading can be a powerful force for continuing efforts to improve in and grow through reading.

Success

Experiments show that schools may be conditioning a student for failure if they permit him to fail repeatedly. Students will not strive if the situation appears hopeless. Some expectation of success is necessary.

Reading materials may be too difficult for some students. While teachers should provide some measure of challenge, they should realize that too many obstacles tend to frustrate the student. Appropriate books must be provided if learning is to take place. To require students to perform in areas in which they are weak is not only unrealistic; it is damaging. Students must learn to deal with failure, and this they do through accomplishment. Good teachers will provide each student with opportunities to succeed.

Guidance in Learning

The primary function of every teacher is to stimulate and guide learning. In this book, acceptance of this responsibility is taken for granted. Now that the elements of motivation have been considered, we turn first to the consideration of what constitutes proper guidance and then to the related concern of how learning may be made meaningful.

Students may be able to learn through the process of trial and error. Much learning does occur in this fashion, and the old idea of sink-or-swim originated in the belief that one learns by his own mistakes. Teachers — like parents — would like to believe that such is always the case, but in too many instances error leads to error. The important consideration for the teacher is not that trial and error may lead to learning but that this kind of learning is inefficient and its products may not be good.

Guiding learning is much more efficient than trial-and-error learning. Ultimately, a student may arrive at a suitable solution to a problem without an assist from anyone, but the cost to him in time and effort cannot be justified. After all, if the student is to fend for himself, what reason is there for him to attend classes? He may as well stay home where he can struggle in privacy. Classes are conducted for the very reason of giving some direction to students' efforts.

Teachers use practice exercises in the hope of strengthening learning, but no exercise should be assigned for independent work until after the student has acquired some ability to do it. If practice elicits incorrect responses, then this practice is actually interfering with learning. Before asking students to find topic sentences independently, for example, teachers should work out many such exercises with them. It is a good plan for the students to check each response as soon as it has been made rather than to wait until all responses have been completed. Independent work may be assigned after students have demonstrated that they are able to perform satisfactorily.

These suggestions also apply to homework. Students who fail to complete their homework because they cannot make the required responses are not participating in fruitful learning experience. Teachers should assign homework that they believe the students are capable of doing.

In recent years, some educational psychologists have made a distinction between theories of learning and theories of teaching. According to Gage, knowledge of conditions favorable to learning does not necessarily lead to processes that promote learning.[11] He argues that teachers have to know how to control and manipulate their own behavior so that they promote conditions favorable to learning. Just as all learning cannot be explained by a single theory, so all teaching cannot be based upon a unitary proposition. For example, the ways in which the structure of an outline might be taught do not always fit the requirements for learning what goes into the outline. The demands of cognitive restructuring are not the same as those that entail model following. Until more research yields definite information about the nature of teaching, teachers may have to continue inferring from learning principles the behaviors they might subscribe to in order to promote learning.

Meaning in Learning

That meaningful learning is preferred to meaningless or rote learning is another assumption of this book. Experience has demonstrated that learning which is mechanical is not lasting unless it is being used constantly.

11. N. L. Gage, "Theories of Teaching," in *Theories of Learning and Instruction,* 63rd Yearbook, National Society for the Study of Education, Part 1, ed. Ernest R. Hilgard (Chicago: Univ. of Chicago Press, 1964), pp. 268-285.

Learning with understanding does not require sheer memorization or frequent repetition. Meaningful learning contains the element of motivation. It provides the answers to the questions "how" and "why," which are lacking in rote learning. Learning that is meaningful actually is easier to master.

How may learning be made meaningful? One way is to *use the learner's own experiences.* Readiness for undertaking a given task is increased if the learner can draw upon known experience to help him understand the new situation. Before reading a selection, the student should be able to relate what he already knows to what he is to cover. The fact that a student has experienced changes of air pressure in flight is assurance that some understanding is being brought to the air pressure topic under study. The student becomes an active rather than a passive learner.

The wise teacher will *provide experiences* to clarify meaning. Using words to help explain other words is not enough. The story has been told of some Africans who, on the eve of their country's liberation, asked whether they would have to go to the post office for independence or wait for it to be delivered. Students read about democracy but too few of them really grasp its qualities. Better understanding of this abstract concept will come not from talking about but from living democracy.

Both empirical findings and results of carefully controlled experiments indicate that many tasks are learned best if they contain a *framework* or *structure.* This helps bring together details that otherwise might be seen as unrelated. For example, it is better for the teacher to introduce the class to new words in sentences than merely to list words on the chalkboard. Context adds unity, and unity enhances meaning.

Complimenting structure is *wholeness.* Though the student may not be able to learn every task as a whole because of its length or difficulty, the teacher should try to help students obtain an overview of the problem before they deal with components. Depending on the subject matter, more understanding may be expected if a chapter is surveyed before it is read carefully. Most textbooks today include an introductory and a summary statement for each section. Students should be encouraged to read these before plunging into the complicated mass of details. Subheadings and sideheads within the chapter serve a similar purpose. They prepare the reader for what lies ahead.

Basic to meaningful learning is *hierarchy.* Some lessons are more difficult than others and their mastery depends upon prior understanding. Teachers possess the formula for assisting their students to deal with intricate matters:

1. Proceed from the known to the unknown.
2. Proceed from the concrete to the abstract.
3. Proceed from the simple to the difficult.

Many reading skills are complex and consist of smaller skills, as later chapters will detail. They are part of a continuum and may be presented in order of difficulty. Locational and organizational reading skills, among others, may be broken down into simpler ones and taught in turn. Students in both junior and senior high school benefit from this type of guidance.

Programmed lessons for teaching machines is based on this concept of learning, and therein lies one of its benefits.

Principles or generalizations can be learned deductively or inductively. In the first instance, teachers present the idea and then help students understand it by providing suitable experiences, explanations, and illustrations. In the second, students participate in a number of experiences that are designed to help them discover and formulate the idea for themselves.

Psychologists do not agree on which kind of learning is more meaningful, but it appears that aided self-discovery leads to more lasting and better learning. Teachers may help students develop inductive strategies in word identification, comprehension, and reading-study skills. For example, instead of telling students the meaning of a prefix and providing words which contain it, the prefix may be introduced as part of a word in a sentence and then paired with the known root word in the same sentence. Several such paired words in sentences will reveal the meaning of the prefix.

Interference and Learning

Every teacher knows that teacher attitudes and what a teacher does or does not do may influence the quantity and quality of student learning. All things being equal, better results may be expected in classrooms where teachers are friendly and not overcritical of students. Excessive harshness or punishment can produce resentments that make teaching ineffective, but this is an extreme kind of interference. Moreover, verbal behavior of teachers could promote or interfere with learning. More learning seems to occur in classrooms where teachers ask questions that help students clarify their own ideas and solve problems than in classrooms where teachers do most of the talking and telling.

What many teachers fail to realize is that situations for interference in learning are ever present in teaching. Perhaps the most common situation is inherent in the materials themselves, or in the methodology. Here, interference results when similar stimuli, intended to evoke dissimilar responses, are presented at a time when learning is not complete.

One example is teaching word-identification skills. It is not a good idea to introduce the long and short sounds of a vowel in the same lesson if both are unknown. As far as the learner is concerned, the *o* in *shock* and the *o* in *holy* are identical. The fact that the *o* in *holy* is long because of the influences of accent and syllabication is immaterial. Teach the long vowel sound first. After learning occurs to the extent where it can be correctly applied, attend to the short vowel sound. Confusion is avoided by withholding similar stimuli that control different responses.

Learning interference may also happen when multiple word meanings are being taught. The meaning of a word in one context need not be the same as the meaning of the same word in another setting. It is highly desirable that students study the different meanings of a word, but not when the context is constant. Presenting several meanings simultaneously can create a learning problem. After the meaning of the word in the given context is learned, introduce the same word in another context that clearly shows a change in meaning.

Transfer and Application in Learning

While learning for learning's sake is a good axiom for many teachers and students, the people who support our schools and the educators who operate them are agreed that children should acquire skills and understandings that they may use outside of school. Reading has purposes beyond utilitarian, but its value as a means by which information is obtained is unquestioned. Of course, we want students to apply reading skills to all types of materials and not merely those they use in school.

Transfer of learning from one situation to another happens when the learner perceives that two situations contain similar elements and operate in like fashions. A common example of similar elements in different situations is alphabetization — in the dictionary, in an index, an encyclopedia, a library card catalog, a telephone directory, and elsewhere. Students who are able to find a word in the dictionary should be able to locate a subject in an encyclopedia. The two situations are not identical, but they do contain similar elements.

Students who have participated in meaningful learning experiences are better prepared to use what they have learned. However, the certainty that transfer will occur is increased by *teaching for transfer*. Students who are given practice in applying what they have learned in one field to other fields of learning, who are urged to generalize as they work with details, and who are required to seek out aspects of present situations that are relevant elsewhere are bound to perform better than students who do not have the benefits of such teaching. If students are learning alphabetization as a part of making up or studying an index, the teacher will do well to refer to another alphabetized source (such as the telephone directory) and to provide practice in locating names in both. To draw conclusions from a set of facts in history is similar but not identical to drawing conclusions from an experiment in science. Opportunities for doing both are recommended.

Learning is incomplete until it has been put to use. The suggestion has been made that one measure of learning is the extent to which the learner is able to make use of what he has learned — a suggestion containing an element of practicality that few would reject. A student may be able to identify the personality traits of one character in a story but not be able to compare satisfactorily these traits with those of another character. Opportunities for participating in a variety of activities in which learning is applied should be present in every classroom. More and better learning is the product of this kind of teaching.

SUMMARY

The reading act consists of word perception, comprehension of ideas, critical evaluation, and integration. These stages occur in sequence and are mutually dependent.

Visual perception involves recognizing words together with their meanings. Although research results are not definite, it is believed that while the reader does not see every element in words, the characteristics of words facilitate recognition. Children and adults tend to deal with words as wholes, although some attention may be paid to details. Persons who have suffered brain damage often concentrate upon details instead of wholes. Auditory and verbal imagery is believed to contribute to the meaning of printed symbols.

A number of word recognition and comprehension models that attempt to explain how each occurs have been proposed. Relationships have been sought between body chemistry, the nervous system, and ability to recognize words, but none seems sufficiently strong to warrant much confidence in explanations of the controls of recognition. Models of comprehension have sought to identify its components, conditions underlying its performance, and the dynamics that lead to its fulfillment.

Various psycholinguistic explanations of the reading process identify language cues — phonological, semantic, and syntactic — as way in which readers acquire meaning. The reader's knowledge of the rules of language makes possible the transformation of surface meaning to actual meaning. A different explanation of reading comprehension stresses the interaction of abilities and subabilities which processes information stored in the brain. If the interaction progresses smoothly, comprehension occurs. There is greater agreement on what constitutes comprehension than on how it occurs.

The psychology of learning has implications for the teaching of reading. The needs and goals of the learner, together with the ability to achieve success and recognize growth, are important motivations that can affect reading performance. Learning should not be left to chance: teachers should guide learning so as to insure some degree of success. Reading skills are learned more efficiently through instruction than by trial and error. Meaningful learning is preferred to mechanical or rote learning. Reading may be taught meaningfully by providing experiences to clarify ideas and concepts, providing a structure through context, emphasizing wholes, and presenting lessons in order of difficulty. Interference with learning may be reduced by following these principles. Learning is incomplete until students are able to apply the skills they have been taught — a major objective of reading instruction.

Additional Readings

For more complete discussions of the nature of reading see the following references:

Kenneth S. Goodman and Olive S. Niles. *Reading Process and Program.* Champaign, Ill.: National Council of Teachers of English, 1970, pp. 1-38.

Doris V. Gunderson, comp. *Language and Reading.* Washington, D. C.: Center for Applied Linguistics, 1970, pp. 26-71, 107-119,136-162.

Helen M. Robinson, ed. *Innovation and Change in Reading Instruction,* 67th Yearbook of the National Society for the Study of Education, Part 2. Chicago: Univ. of Chicago Press, 1968, pp. 7-29, 261-272.

Harry Singer and Robert B. Ruddell, eds. *Theoretical Models and Processes of Reading,* 2d ed. Newark, Del.: International Reading Association, 1976.

Frank Smith. *Psycholinguistics and Reading.* New York: Holt, Rinehart and Winston, 1973.

Helen K. Smith, ed. *Perception and Reading,* Proceedings of the 12th Annual Convention, Vol. 12, Part 4. Newark, Del.: International Reading Association, 1968, pp. 1-16, 44-53, 77-82.

Nila B. Smith, ed. *Current Issues in Reading,* Proceedings of the 13th Annual Convention, Vol. 13, Part 2. Newark, Del.: International Reading Association, 1969, pp. 85-106.

Discussions of theories and principles of learning and their applications to teaching will be found in:

Morris L. Bigge. *Learning Theories for Teachers.* New York: Harper and Row, 1964.

J. S. Bruner. *Toward a Theory of Instruction.* Cambridge, Mass.: Harvard Univ. Press, 1966.

Emerald V. Dechant. *Improving the Teaching of Reading,* 2d ed. Englewood Cliffs, N. J.: Prentice-Hall, 1970, pp. 516-581.

Charles Galloway. *Psychology for Learning and Teaching.* New York: McGraw-Hill, 1976.

CHAPTER 4

IMPROVING DIAGNOSTIC TEACHING of READING in CONTENT AREAS

Problems for Study and Discussion

1   What is diagnostic teaching of reading?

2   How are norm-referenced reading tests different from criterion-referenced reading tests?

3   What are the values and limitations of standardized reading tests? What cautions should be observed in selecting them and interpreting their results?

4   For what main purpose are informal reading inventories and cloze tests used? How are they prepared?

5   Explain how a skills inventory is prepared.

A comprehensive reading program is one that develops the basic skills students need in order to read, that teaches them how they can use reading as a tool for learning, and that fosters an appreciation of literature and interest in reading.[1] These characteristics become the objectives of instruction and, at the same time, serve as guidelines for evaluating the progress that students make in reading.

Reading is not a simple skill, nor even a single skill. Students do not master reading in a few years, just as they do not master any other complex activity in a short time. They learn some reading skills and develop some attitudes toward reading as they move from one stage of development to another. What they may be able to accomplish at one point in their reading

1. This section is adapted from an article by the author entitled "Evaluation for Diagnostic Teaching," pp. 8-13 in *Assessment Problems in Reading*, ed. Walter H. MacGinitie (Newark, Del.: International Reading Association, 1973).

development will not be good enough at another. This fact explains why some can cope with early reading demands but not later ones. It also underscores the importance of continuously evaluating students reading. Orderly reading experiences, based upon such evaluation, is one way of describing the diagnostic teaching of reading.

BEHAVIORAL OBJECTIVES AND DIAGNOSTIC TEACHING

The aim of diagnostic teaching of reading is to identify areas in which student reading is progressing satisfactorily and also pinpoint other areas to which increased attention should be given. To fulfill these requirements, the broad objectives of reading instruction must be translated into learning tasks or behavioral objectives. Then, teachers can guide students in mastering them.

The basis for identifying learning tasks are the reading skills outlines in Chapter one, but with added specificity. Thus, teachers do not ask such broad questions as how fluently students read, how well they understand what they read, or how well they read for information. Instead, they realize that there are more basic questions for which they must seek answers to meet the requirements of diagnostic teaching: How well do students respond to different types of context clues as they seek the meaning of words? What pronunciation problems do they meet as they use the respellings in the dictionary? How well do they identify main ideas when they are stated and when they must be inferred?

The answers to these and other pertinent questions help teachers decide which growth areas need attention. Moreover, this evaluation helps suggest what types of instructional materials will be needed and what their levels of difficulty should be.

Some reading specialists would evaluate students' reading performances in still more precise terms. They might state a reading objective this way: *Given a nine-sentence paragraph whose main idea is stated in the third sentence, students are able to identify the sentence containing the main idea.*

Such a behavioral objective could also be stated as a question: "How well do students identify . . .?" When carried to extremes, however, this practice could lead to a fracturing of the teaching-learning act and make reading a mechanical, joyless task. Diagnostic teaching requires precise evaluation if students are to achieve important objectives, but precision carried to extremes will not serve teachers or learners. Surely a student who knows *how* to identify the sentence containing the main idea of a paragraph ought to be able to do so in a seven or nine sentence paragraph no matter *where* in the paragraph the main idea is stated.

Diagnostic teaching benefits students who are making satisfactory progress in reading. Teachers can anticipate superior results as they work with students if there is a positive relationship between the problems and the remedies. Inherent in this concept is the idea that evaluation is an ongoing activity as instruction continues. Although teachers formulate plans from information they acquire about students, they know that as they teach new data will be received. It is not unusual to have to modify practices to satisfy current student needs; teachers may occasionally have to discard plans developed from initial evaluations about their students' reading.

It should be understood that no test, whether teacher or commercially prepared, can yield as much valid information about student reading as can the teacher who is observing student behaviors during reading assignments and class response. The conditions associated with test-taking are not exactly representative of conditions which students must fulfill as they read different types of materials for a variety of purposes.

By observing students individually and in groups and analyzing what they accomplish, teachers may determine how efficiently each student performs reading tasks. Also noted will be what obstacles, if any, interfere with their reading efforts. Signs such as yawning, excessive lip movements, and inattention could be indicators of inability to manage the material because of its difficulty. Rapidly turning pages or "window gazing" might suggest that reading purposes have not been established. Teachers should sit down with students at the time and discuss with them why they falter and how they might proceed. Quite possibly, students will be able to explain their problems, whatever they might be, so that teachers can either provide on-the-spot help or plan some appropriate lessons to overcome the problems. Students should be asked to note any reading difficulties experienced as they do assignments. This information, together with that obtained through observation and from test data, will enable teachers to develop skill profiles that become the basis for future instruction.

It may now be recognized, then, that the best way to assess student reading needs is to study how they perform in actual reading situations. With that in mind, let us examine reading tests and how they might be utilized to facilitate diagnostic teaching.

VALUES OF READING TESTS

Teachers have been administering tests to students for centuries, and the forms that tests have taken have been as varied as the teaching itself. Until modern theories entered the picture, reading tests usually consisted of passages that the student read orally, and performance was judged on the number of words pronounced correctly. Today, reading is considered to be a complex of skills; in varying degrees, reading tests are tapping skills that less than fifty years ago were ignored.

Teachers require different kinds of information to meet the reading needs of all students and the conditions of diagnostic teaching. Essentially, they want to know in a general way how well students read now, what their specific strengths and weaknesses are, and the kind and amount of progress they are making.

Present Reading Status

Although secondary schools are extending their curriculums to include a wide range of subjects and are introducing varied sources of information, textbooks and reference books retain their places of importance. Teachers continue to depend on them, and students rely on them to yield knowledge on which they may base judgments. The critical question for the teacher then is, can students for whom given textbooks are intended read them with sufficient comprehension?

Today's authors of high school textbooks usually make every effort to grade their vocabularies and sentence structure as well as the difficulty of content. Assuming that the books have been graded carefully, the typical twelfth-grade student will find a twelfth-grade history book more difficult than one on the same subject prepared for eighth grade. Both discuss the concept of the democratic process, but the teacher knows that the latter text is more readable by the less-proficient reader. Just because a textbook has been prepared for the typical student in a specific grade is no guarantee that *all* students in that grade can cope with it.

A suitable reading test can help teachers to determine whether students can be expected to read the book with adequate comprehension if given help to do so, or if it will be too difficult regardless of the assistance provided. It also will identify students who might be able to read and study higher-level sources of information.

There is growing interest in finding out just how well our youth read and to what extent groups of students are achieving in reading. Since levels of achievement based upon standardized reading test scores are presumed to reflect the reading performances of representative student groups, schools may determine how well their students are reading in comparison with comparable students elsewhere. General interest in the achievement of our youth has prompted educators to undertake the National Assessment Project, one of whose purposes it is to determine how well younger and older students read. Nine, thirteen, and seventeen year olds have taken or will take reading tests devised for this purpose, possibly with the view to encouraging schools to study the results and adopt appropriate measures to remedy inadequacies in programs if they appear warranted. Testing on local, state, and national levels could reveal substantial differences in reading progress among similar populations within and among schools. If such were the case, it would be useful to seek reasons why marked differences exist.

Reading Progress and Specific Reading Needs

As was pointed out in Chapter One, reading programs have one common characteristic: emphasis is on the reader rather than on preconceived notions of what he must learn and do. Consequently, whether they are gifted, normally developing, or disabled readers, students need to evaluate their progress in reading achievement. And teachers need to judge how effective their teaching methods are. The data obtained from appropriate reading tests will enable the student to chart his successes and failures, and they will permit the teacher to ascertain whether a reexamination of teaching procedures is needed.

If a specific reading skill has been taught — for example, how to find the main idea of a paragraph — it is not enough for the student to *feel* that he has mastered this skill; he should *know* whether his performance is satisfactory or unsatisfactory. A reading test that adequately measures this ability and that is administered at a suitable time will tell both student and teacher whether growth has occurred.

Appropriate reading tests identify areas of strength and weakness and pinpoint for teacher and student what remains to be learned. Again, it is not enough to know that a student's critical weakness is the area of the study skills. Since there are several study skills, the teacher must establish which ones require attention. Once the skills have been identified, efforts to limit the scope of instruction to aspects that interfere with performance should be made. For example, a student may not be able to use the index of an encyclopedia efficiently. The teacher cannot assume that the student is ignorant of all the skills upon which the mature reader draws when locating desired information. A reading test will help the teacher find out what this student knows and does not know about an index. In other words, the stage for learning is being set: *the level of readiness that the student has reached* will be the starting place for new learning experiences. The student will not have to be bored with work on what he already knows, and the teacher will be able to make the most of his own time and efforts.

Suitable reading tests can serve another useful purpose: they can help teachers establish behavioral objectives that educators believe are important for reading. Examining test items can reveal what skills are needed to perform the reading act successfully. These may be stated as objectives for students to achieve and become the focus of the instructional program. For example, some reading tests require students to know the meaning of words as used in special contexts rather than in isolation. Such test items are a signal that students must learn to think of words as having multiple meanings that are determined by the context instead of familiar single meanings. Thus, the teacher is alerted to the importance of context as one element in developing vocabulary and can plan suitable lessons to establish proper attitudes toward word meanings and help develop new meanings for common words.

A word of caution: While teachers may devise their own reading tests and obtain others that are commercially produced, none will yield needed information if used indiscriminately. The best test will seem poor if it is expected to serve a purpose for which it was never intended. There are different kinds of reading tests; teachers should not only be familiar with them but also recognize their strengths and limitations and know how to interpret their results.

In summary, reading evaluation should not be haphazard or desultory. It must be an integral part of any school program. The following principles, as suggested by Walter Hill, may serve as guides for establishing and conducting a high school testing program in reading: (1) reflect the general and specific objectives of the reading program; (2) be a planned, sequential, and continuous program; (3) become the focus of the instructional program; (4) reflect the combined efforts of all school personnel — classroom, specialized, and administrative; (5) utilize various procedures for measuring and observing reading performance; (6) stress data that can be used effectively for instruction; (7) have as its main objective the improvement of student performance.[2]

TYPES OF READING TESTS

The National Assessment Project evaluates reading ability by evaluating student responses to items that are believed to measure specific, important reading skills — for example, drawing inferences, using reference materials to locate information, interpreting charts, and so forth. The purpose of administering such tests is to determine if a student or a group of students has mastered each of the measured skills. A teacher might construct a test to determine if students can recognize root words in words containing prefixes and suffixes or a test to assess their ability to recognize cause and effect relationships. In both instances, the primary purpose is to find out to what extent students have mastered specified reading skills; therefore, some students will be able to respond correctly to all the test items, others to fewer ones, and perhaps some to none at all. Tests that mainly seek information of these kinds are called *criterion-referenced* tests.

On the other hand, there are reading tests that also contain items intended to measure reading skills — perhaps the same ones appearing on criterion-referenced tests and presented in similar forms — but their primary purpose is different. These tests are designed to *compare* the performances of individuals and groups and rank them on the skills being measured. Thus, on such tests students are not expected to answer all items correctly. (If they did, they could not be ranked, since the test does not discriminate adequately among performances.) Standards (norms) based on peer performance are established; these are used to compare the reading performances of one's own group of students with the peer group. Hence, tests of this kind, such as the typical standardized reading test, are called *norm-referenced* tests.

✓ STANDARDIZED READING TESTS

Standardized reading tests are intended to show, in a general way, how well students achieve in reading. They are administered and scored according to specified procedures. Presumably, the test items have been chosen experimentally, and the test adequately samples the skills they claim to measure. Directions for administering and scoring the tests and interpreting the results are supplied in manuals that accompany these tests. Information about the way in which the tests were developed and the purposes for which they might be used are normally mentioned.

In addition to providing some information about the reading ability of students, standardized tests make possible a comparison of student reading performances within a class or school and with similar students of other

2. Walter Hill, "Evaluating Secondary Reading," in *Measurement and Evaluation in Reading*, ed. Roger Farr (New York: Harcourt Brace Jovanovich, 1970), p. 134.

schools. All students must master certain reading skills but, as every teacher knows, they do not all master them to the same extent nor within prescribed time limits. The results of suitable reading tests provide some indications of how well students are progressing toward objectives on which there is general agreement.

If students' test scores show that their reading achievement is considerably below that of their peers, explanations for their seemingly poor performance should be sought. Perhaps they have not been taught what others consider important, or some students are different from those with whom they are being compared. Whatever the answer, comparing test scores may well lead to more careful study of students and evaluation of instructional objectives and outcomes.

Reading Norms

Standardized reading tests have norms or standards against which to measure student progress on specified reading tasks. The norms are based on the average performance of students in given grades who participated in developing the tests. (These students are supposed to be representative of comparable students elsewhere.) Norms are commonly expressed as percentile ranks, stanines, or grade equivalents.

Figure 4-1 shows a portion of the table that accompanies a standardized reading test intended for high schools. The number of correct responses on each part have first been converted into standard scores by using a different table; now, percentile ranks and stanines can be obtained. For example, a student in the eleventh grade whose standard score on Test 1 Vocabulary is 184 has a percentile rank of 76. This means that on this portion of the test the student has equaled or surpassed the performances of 76 percent of the students involved in the development of the test. The same standard score of 184 on Test 1 Vocabulary is in stanine 6 which is another way of expressing how well the student compares to those who were used to prepare the test. Scores are divided into nine stanines, the lowest scores falling in stanines 1-3, the average scores in stanines 4-6, and the highest scores in stanines 7-9.

Figure 4-2 represents a portion of the grade-placement norms of another high school reading test. If some students were to obtain a raw score of 21 on the vocabulary section of this test, the grade placement would be equivalent to 10.5. This means that they had equaled the performance of the average student in the standard population who completed five months of the tenth grade. A raw score of 27 in reading comprehension equals a grade placement of 11.2, which is the accomplishment in reading comprehension of the average student who has completed two months of the eleventh grade. When the two raw scores are added, their sum equals 48, which is the total reading score. This total score is equivalent to a grade placement of 10.9 which represents the performance of the average student — who has completed nine months of the tenth grade. (These grade equivalent scores have been extrapolated from scores obtained by the standard population in a given month of the school year.) Thus, teachers may compare the perform-

Figure 4-1. Percentile Ranks and Stanines Corresponding to ISRT Standard Scores for All Grade 11 Students in the Level 3 Standardization Sample.

STANDARD SCORES

Stanine	%-ile Rank	Test 1 Vocabulary	Test 2 Reading Comp.	Tests 1 + 2 Reading Power	Test 3 Reading Efficiency	%-ile Rank
9	99+	Above 231	Above 235	Above 230	Above 229	99+
	99	221-231	226-235	221-230	217-229	99
	98	215-220	220-225	216-220	211-216	98
	97	212-214	216-219	212-215	207-210	97
	96	209-211	212-215	209-211	203-206	96
8	95	206-208	209-211	207-208	200-202	95
	94	204-205	207-208	205-206	198-199	94
	93	202-203	205-206	203-204	196-197	93
	92	201	203-204	201-202	194-195	92
	91	199-200	201-202	199-200	193	91
	90	198	199-200	198	191-192	90
	89	196-197	198	196-197	190	89
7	88	195	196-197	195	188-189	88
	87	194	195	194	187	87
	86	193	194	192-193	186	86
	85	192	192-193	191	185	85
	84	191	191	190	184	84
	83	190	190	189	183	83
	82	189	189	188	182	82
	81	188	188	187	181	81
	80	187	187	186	180	80
	79		186	185	179	79
	78	186	185		178	78
	77	185	184	184	177	77
6	76	184	183	183	176	76
	75	183	182	182	175	75
	74			181	174	74
	73	182	181		173	73
	72	181	180	180	172	72
	71	180	179	179		71
	70		178	178	171	70
	69	179			170	69
	68	178	177	177	169	68
	67	177	176	176	168	67
	66		175	175		66
	65	176			167	65
	64	175	174	174	166	64
	63		173	173	165	63
	62	174		172		62
	61	173	172		164	61
	60		171	171	163	60

Adapted from the "Manual of Directions, Level 3," *Iowa Silent Reading Tests.* Copyright © 1973 by Harcourt Brace Jovanovich, Inc. Reproduced with the permission of the Psychological Corp.

Figure 4-2.   Grade Equivalent Scores for a High School Reading Test

GE	READING		
	VOCAB	COMPR	TOTAL
9.6			
9.7		22	40
9.8			41
9.9	19		
10.0		23	42
10.1			43
10.2	20		
10.3		24	44
10.4			45
10.5	21		
10.6		25	46
10.7			47
10.8			
10.9	22	26	48
11.0			
11.1			49
11.2		27	
11.3	23		50
11.4			
11.5		28	51
11.6			52
11.7	24		
11.8			
11.9			53
12.0		29	
12.1			54
12.2	25		
12.3			
12.4			55
12.5		30	
12.6	26		56
12.7			57
12.8		31	
12.9	27		58
13.0		32	59
13.1	28		60
13.2			61
13.3	29	33	62
13.4			
13.5			63
13.6	30-40	34-45	64-85

Adapted from Ernest W. Tiegs and Willis W. Clark, "Raw Scores to Grade Equivalent," Table 5 in *California Reading Test Level 5* (1971). Reproduced with the permission of the California Test Bureau/McGraw-Hill Library.

ance of their students with the performances of comparable students, since the standard population of a well-constructed test is supposed to represent a typical cross-section of a given group of students.

Selection of Reading Tests

It is doubtful that any standardized reading test will ever measure all the skills that superior readers master. Most standardized, silent reading tests try to assess general reading ability, although some evaluate more discrete reading skills. Among the more general aspects of reading that standardized tests measure are vocabulary meaning and paragraph comprehension. Figure 4-3 represents a sample from the vocabulary section of a reading test intended for high school students in grades 9-12. The second part of the same test (Figure 4-4) is designed to measure how well students read for main ideas, draw inferences, and discern author's purpose.

Students have to recognize that a word's meaning depends on the context in which it appears. To measure how well they recognize changes in the meaning of words, some tests require students to identify word meanings as they apply to fixed contexts. Figure 4-5 represents such an exercise. Notice the use of a typographical signal (a star) to alert examinees to the line in which the specified word occurs.

Some silent reading tests measure ability to read content material. The paragraphs used in these tests parallel or actually reproduce material found in science and social studies textbooks. The test items measure ability to determine the main idea of single paragraphs, understand stated facts, and draw conclusions from the information presented.

Figure 4-3. Vocabulary Section in a Reading Test

PART I: VOCABULARLY (*15 minutes*)

Directions: In each question select the word or phrase that most nearly means the same thing as the word in darker type. Then mark the letter for that word or phrase next to the number of the question on your answer sheet. See the example below.

Example

E 1   **boast**

A   sew   B   suffer   C   brag   D   lift

The letter C for "brag" has been marked opposite E 1
at the top of your answer sheet.

1 abate	2 dupe	3 clan
A refund	E render unconscious	A illegal meeting
B return	F spy on	B banging noise
C stop	G defeat another's plans	C tribe with common ancestor
D diminish	H deceive	D place where reunion is held

From *Cooperative English Tests.* Copyright © 1960 by Educational Testing Service. All rights reserved. Published by Addison-Wesley. Reprinted with permission.

Figure 4-4.   Paragraph Comprehension in a Reading Test

The next day the Mexicans kept up a heavy fire of artillery, the Texans replying occasionally. The day after that, Saturday, March fifth, the bombardment eased off in the afternoon and by ten o'clock at night it had stopped altogether. Travis suspected a ruse and posted all his men, who loaded their rifles and guns and began their twelfth night of vigil. Since the siege had begun there had been no reliefs. The entire command had been continuously on duty. Beef and cornbread had been served on the walls. This was the sole ration. There was no coffee, which would have helped to keep the men awake, and sleep was an enemy more dreaded than the Mexicans. For days men had been dozing in snatches at their guns during the thunder of bombardment. Now the roar had ceased. The defenders of the Alamo leaned against their guns and slept.

Which of the following did the men need most?
A Guns
B Food
C Courage
D Sleep

In sentence 3, what sort of "ruse" did Travis probably suspect?
E The Mexicans were secretly retreating.
F The Mexicans were preparing a surprise attack.
G The Mexicans were saving their ammunition.
H The Mexicans were resting.

The last sentence in this paragraph was intended to make the reader
A happy that the men had time to sleep.
B puzzled at why the Mexicans had stopped shooting.
C afraid of what might happen while they sleep.
D pleased that the long battle had turned out so well.

From *Cooperative English Tests.* Copyright © 1960 by Educational Testing Service. All rights reserved. Published by Addison-Wesley. Reprinted with permission.

A few standardized reading tests include a section on locational skills, such as using an index and selecting appropriate references. Some measure related skills, such as alphabetizing and limited aspects of outlining. A teacher may obtain more extensive information about a student's ability in the study skills by administering tests specifically designed to measure some of these skills as well as such others as reading maps, graphs, and tables. Figure 4-6 represents sample portions from one such test.

Publishers sometimes differentiate between reading tests which survey broad aspects of reading and other reading tests, which tend to cover major skills and their components. They refer to the latter as diagnostic tests which yield information about students' reading and indicate areas to which attention might be directed. Figure 4-7 represents a profile of an "average" reader and shows how well the student did on literal and inferential reading (comprehension), word meaning and word parts (vocabulary), phonic and structural analysis (decoding), skimming, scanning, and rapid reading (rate). The main difference between a survey or achievement test and a diagnostic test seems to revolve around the issue of the number of skills and subskills that a test measures. No standardized reading test is completely diagnostic since none assesses major reading skills with great precision.

In addition to these standardized reading tests, *oral* reading tests can be used to assess accuracy and fluency of paragraph reading. Teachers have no way of knowing whether students actually recognize all the words in silent reading tests unless they require them to read orally. Many older students try to cope with reading materials containing words they cannot pronounce and which they guess with varying degrees of success. How well they succeed depends on the degree to which they understand what they *can* read, plus using grammatical and meaning cues. The paragraphs in these tests are graded in difficulty so that examinees start with paragraphs

Figure 4-5. Vocabulary in Context Section in an Advanced Reading Test

Reading

WHAT TO DO: *Read* each story. Then read each question about the story. *Pick* the best answer to the question. *Mark* the letter for that answer in your booklet or on your answer sheet if you have one. Some questions ask the meaning of a word in the story. These words can be found in the lines which have a star (★) beside them. *Now* read the sample. Question A has been marked for you. See if you can answer Question B.

SAMPLE: In Disneyland, California, there is a street called Main Street, U.S.A. Over one shop on Main Street there is a big sign. It tells us that this is a lock shop. Inside the shop there are all kinds of ★ locks, but they are not for sale. Visitors see **great** locks and tiny locks. Some of the locks are new and others are hundreds of years old. This shop is a lock museum.

A The locks in the lock shop are —
    all old   all small
    never sold   never cleaned

B In this story, the word **great** means —
    nice   famous
    good   large

From *Metropolitan Achievement Tests.* Copyright © 1970 by Harcourt Brace Jovanovich, Inc. Reproduced with the permission of the Psychological Corp.

Figure 4-6. A Study-Skill Test

Use the chart below to answer questions 82-85.

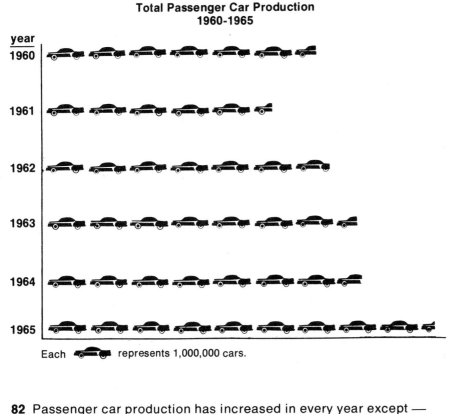

**Total Passenger Car Production
1960-1965**

Each 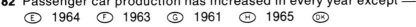 represents 1,000,000 cars.

82 Passenger car production has increased in every year except —
　ⓔ 1964　ⓕ 1963　ⓖ 1961　ⓗ 1965　(DK)

83 The number of cars produced appeared very close for —
　ⓐ 1962 and 1963　　ⓒ 1963 and 1964
　ⓑ 1960 and 1961　　ⓓ 1960 and 1964
　　　　　　　(DK)

84 In 1965, about 3.5 million more cars were produced than in —
　ⓔ 1961　　　　ⓖ 1963
　ⓕ 1960　　　　ⓗ any other year
　　　　　　(DK)

85 In this pictogram, one fourth of a car stands for how many new cars?
　ⓐ .4 million　　　ⓒ ¼ of all
　ⓑ 4 million　　　ⓓ 250 thousand
　　　　　　(DK)

Figure 4-7.   Profile for Ann H.

TEST	Test 1 Reading Comprehension		Test 2 Word Meaning	Test 3 Word Parts	Test 4 Phonetic Analysis	Test 5 Structural Analysis	Test 6 Scanning and Skimming	Test 7 Fast Reading	TOTAL SCORES			
	Literal	Inferential							Comprehension Test 1	Vocabulary Tests 2 + 3	Decoding Tests 4 + 5	Rate Tests 6 + 7
RAW SCORE	23	23	18	19	23	13	24	7	46	37	36	31

STANINE

9	9	9	9	9	9	9	9	9	9	9	9
8	8	8	8	8	8	8	8	8	8	8	8
(7)	7	7	7	7	7	(7)	7	(7)	7	7	7
6	(6)	(6)	(6)	(6)	6	6	6	6	(6)	6	(6)
5	5	5	5	5	5	5	5	5	5	(5)	5
4	4	4	4	4	(4)	4	(4)	4	4	4	4
3	3	3	3	3	3	3	3	3	3	3	3
2	2	2	2	2	2	2	2	2	2	2	2
1	1	1	1	1	1	1	1	1	1	1	1

From the manual for administering and interpreting the *Stanford Diagnostic Reading Test.* Copyright © 1974 by Harcourt Brace Jovanovich, Inc. Reproduced with the permission of the Psychological Corp.

that they can read easily and then they progress to higher levels. They continue to read successive passages until they make more errors than are allowed by the tests.

Naturally, such oral reading tests must be administered individually to allow the examiner to time the reading of each passage and record any errors a student might make. As the student reads each passage, the examiner notes (on his own copy) the types of errors that are made: word substitutions; whole or partial mispronunciations; omitted words or parts of words; inserted words; repetitions; words not pronounced. Each type of error is recorded in shorthand. For example, words or portions of words that are omitted are circled; words not pronounced are underscored. After reading each passage, the student answers questions about it. The score for each passage takes into account elapsed reading time, number of errors, and number of correct answers to questions. Test norms for oral reading tests are established in the same way as are norms for silent reading tests. Figure 4-8 contains an excerpt from one oral reading test, while Figure 4-9 shows what kinds of information are recorded on a summary sheet for another test.

Since reading tests vary in what they measure, a school must determine in advance which test or series of tests is best suited to its purpose. Research has demonstrated that although general reading ability and specific reading ability *tend* to go together, the latter cannot be predicted from the former. A student may score well above the norm for his or her grade in reading for comprehension but far below the norm when drawing conclusions from what he has read. Or he may have no difficulties with narrative prose but find science content a real problem.

Figure 4-8. An Oral Reading Test

Scientific discovery and advancing technology are continuously altering the world in which Mary and Dick will work as adults. Inven-
tions undreamed of a decade ago have become realities but these
in their turn will become obsolete. If Dick, for example, prepares for
the field of automobile maintenance, he will employ tools and procedures which — in their efficiency and precision — will make his
father's current equipment appear quite crude. Should Mary become
a stenographer, the improvement in the entire communication process will radically affect her responsibilities and the demands on her
skills. Shorthand is now employed less frequently than before, and
although typing may always be indispensable its use will vary with
the rapid advance in dictating equipment. Mary's supervisor can, by
touching a button, secure data from a central location several miles
away. Telephone conversations can be processed almost instan-
taneously. Records are kept on microfilm rather than in the cumbersome files which were formerly used. Throughout the world of work,
and indeed throughout life, machines will continue to increase enormously the accuracy, volume, and speed of work which is accomplished.

TIME _____ Seconds

1. How is the business world being affected by science and technology?
2. How will tools of today compare to those of the future?
3. How has the use of shorthand been affected?
4. What advantage do microfilmed records have over traditional filing
   systems?
5. What continued effect will machines have on the world of work?

ERROR RECORD	Number
Substitutions	
Mispronunciations	
Words pronounced by examiner	
Disregard of punctuation	
Insertions	
Hesitations	
Repetitions	
Omissions	
Total Errors	

From John V. and Eunice C. Gilmore, *Gilmore Oral Reading Test*, Form C. Copyright © 1968 by Harcourt Brace Jovanovich, Inc. Reproduced with the permission
of the Psychological Corp.

Figure 4-9.   Examiner's Record Booklet for the Gray Oral Reading Test

EXAMINER'S RECORD BOOKLET

for the

GRAY ORAL READING TEST

FORM A

Name __*Bill R.*__   Grade __*10*__ Age __*15.6*__

School __*Windhurst High*__   Teacher __*Smith*__ Sex __*M*__

City __*Windhurst*__   State _____

Examiner __*R. Jones*__   Date __*October 18, 1962*__

SUMMARY

Pas-sage Number	No. of Errors	Time (in Seconds)	Pas-sage Scores	Compre-hension
1.	—	—	9	—
2.	—	—	9	—
3.	—	—	9	—
4.	—	—	9	—
5.	0	16	9	4
6.	1	17	8	4
7.	2	34	3	4
8.	2	62	2	1
9.	3	74	1	1
10.	7	108	0	0
11.	7	—	0	0
12.	22			
13.				
Total Passage Scores			59	
Grade Equivalent			8.7	

TYPES OF ERRORS

1.	Aid	0
2.	Gross Mispronunciation	2
3.	Partial Mispronunciation	14
4.	Omission	1
5.	Insertion	1
6.	Substitution	0
7.	Repetition	4
8.	Inversion	0
		22

OBSERVATIONS
(Check statement and circle each part)

_____ Word-by-word reading
__✓__ Poor phrasing
_____ Lack of expression
_____ Monotonous tone
_____ Pitch too high or low; voice too loud, too soft, or strained
_____ Poor enunciation
__✓__ Disregard of punctuation
__✓__ Overuse of phonics
_____ Little or no method of word analysis
__✓__ Unawareness of errors
_____ Head movement
_____ Finger pointing
_____ Loss of place

COMMENTS: *Read passages through 7 with ease then began to sound unfamiliar words losing meaning.*

From William S. Gray, figure 13 in *Gray Oral Reading Tests Manual of Directions,* ed. Helen M. Robinson (Indianapolis: Bobbs-Merrill, 1967), p. 21.

Used by permission.

If schools wish to determine how well their students perform on certain aspects of reading, they must select tests which measure those aspects, because all reading tests do not cover the same reading skills. Most publishers will supply sample tests to schools so that the tests can be judged by knowledgeable staffs.

The manuals that accompany these tests should contain information about standardization procedures. One question that the school needs to have answered is, how reliable are the test scores? Reliability refers to the extent to which repeated administrations of the test will yield the same scores. If internal consistency is poor, the same students might respond differently to test items on successive trials.

A second question which is equally important is this: How *valid* are the test items? Do the test items actually measure what they purport to measure? Are the test items representative of the skills that represent reading ability? Teachers could be misled into believing, for example, that a given group of students can read inferentially on the basis of its responses to test items that are supposed to measure this ability. Close examination of test items might reveal that examinees are not really required to go beyond what some passages actually contain. Furthermore, tests might fail to include items which sample skills that most reading experts accept as components of reading ability. In such cases, teachers will have a false or incomplete assessment of their students' reading ability.

A third question involves grade and percentile norms: How *representative* is the population on which these norms are based? If the sample population truly does not represent typical populations, the results cannot be used with confidence. Norms based on the performances of limited samples, say poor students, will be inflated, and comparisons with the performances of better students will be very misleading. The latter will appear to be much better readers than they actually are. No valid comparison of test results can be made if the sample population is greatly different from the population the school will test.

Experience has shown that reading tests primarily designed for secondary school use may not be appropriate for *all* secondary school students. Students who have serious reading weaknesses will not be able to demonstrate what they can do on reading tests intended for the grade levels in which they may be placed; many of the test items will be too difficult. It is advisable to administer elementary-level reading tests to those high school students who are known to be very weak readers. The results from such tests will be fairer statements of the reading ability of such disabled readers than those from high-school-level tests. While it would not be proper to accept the grade-placement score or percentile rank as valid, a study of responses to test items could indicate an approximation of how well the students can read and what some of their reading needs are.

Each standardized reading test must be judged on its own merits and appropriateness for supplying the information needed about students' reading ability. Many standardized reading tests have been described and evaluated by reading and measurement specialists, and their reviews have been published in the *Mental Measurements Yearbook, Reading Tests and Reviews I and II*, and *Reading Tests for Secondary Grades: A Review and Evaluation* (see the additional readings listed at the end of the chapter for complete citations). Teachers ought to consult these publications in deciding which standardized reading tests will suit their purposes. A list of representative reading tests will be found in Appendix B.

Use of Standardized Tests

Carefully evaluating some standardized reading test results might yield valuable clues to the nature of students' reading problems. Should a number of students do poorly on a vocabulary section, perhaps more attention ought to be paid in future reading lessons to specific word meanings. Where understanding is being measured, studying the kinds of questions the student has missed could reveal whether the difficulties are matters of literal comprehension or deeper meanings.

Some standardized tests list in detail the skills that are being measured. They provide a guide to reading difficulties that may be readily identified by teachers for future remedial treatment. One such analysis is presented in Figure 4-10. Each of the test items is numbered and classified according to the reading areas being tested. If, for example, a student missed most of the items under "making inferences," the teacher could assume a weakness into which he should look further. Of course, such evaluations are valid only if there are an adequate number of test items which actually assess the skills it is claimed they assess. If test publishers do not offer an analysis of test items, it is possible to examine and categorize them according to skills.

For students with no serious reading problems, test scores represent an *approximate* measure of the level of materials they might be expected to read with adequate comprehension. Should students achieve test scores equivalent to or higher than their grade level or about the fiftieth percentile, the chances are that they will be able to cope with the books intended for their grade. Moreover, standardized reading tests provide an objective means of determining, in a general way, how well groups of students read. They enable teachers to combine objective evidence about students' reading performances with their subjective judgments.

As we have noted earlier, standardized reading tests make it possible for schools to compare their students with similar students around the country. If the results were to vary significantly, they could be an indication that the formers' reading programs are weak and require revision or at least study. Good standardized reading tests might serve as models for the kinds of learning activities schools should include in their reading programs. In addition, they can be used to appraise over time the effectiveness of reading programs in improving the reading ability of students.

The results of standardized reading tests might be used to group students for initial instruction. If schools were to establish reading classes for good and poor readers, the scores could be the basis for assigning students to them. Adjustments would be made after teachers acquired more information

Figure 4-10. A Test That Analyzes Reading Difficulties

DIAGNOSTIC ANALYSIS OF LEARNING DIFFICULTIES

1. Reading Vocabulary

A. MATHEMATICS:
    1-22 .... Basic vocabulary

B. SCIENCE:
    23-45 .... Basic vocabulary

C. SOCIAL SCIENCE:
    46-67 .... Basic vocabulary

D. GENERAL:
    68-90 .... Basic vocabulary

2. Reading Comprehension

E. FOLLOWING SPECIFIC DIRECTIONS:
    91, 92, 95, 99, 100 .... Directions in mathematical situations
    93, 94, 96, 97, 98 .... Reading definitions & following directions

F. REFERENCE SKILLS:
    101, 102, 103, 104, 105, 106 ..... Vocabulary
    107, 108, 109 ...... Use of index
    110, 111, 112, 113 .... Selecting references
    114, 115 .... Report outline

G. INTERPRETATION OF MEANINGS:
    116, 125 .... Selecting topic or central idea
    119, 120, 122, 123, 126, 127, 128, 129, 133, 137, 141, 143, 144 .... Understanding directly stated facts
    117, 118, 121, 124, 130, 131, 132, 134, 135, 136, 138, 139, 140, 142, 145 .... Making inferences

From Ernest W. Tiegs and Willis W. Clark, *California Reading Test*, Advanced, All Forms (1950). Reproduced with the permission of the California Test Bureau/ McGraw-Hill Library.

about their reading performances. Test scores also could be used by teachers who wished to group students for the purpose of differentiating reading instruction or reading assignments within their own classrooms.

Limitations of Standardized Reading Tests

Standardized reading tests have considerable value, but they also have important weaknesses of which teachers should be aware. Many standardized reading tests are *narrow in scope*. They attempt to measure only a few of the skills that have been judged important by reading specialists. Most tests include a section on vocabulary, but few attempt to measure the ability to deal with multiple meanings as determined by the context in which the words appear. Tests tend to place too great an emphasis on the ability to understand what is stated directly, and too few test items are devoted to making generalizations or drawing conclusion. Critical reading skills are almost entirely neglected in reading tests. (Is it possible that infrequently including appropriate items in these tests reflects the lack of emphasis put on these skills in the classroom?) Likewise, study skills receive scant consideration in most standardized tests. While there are some that measure a few of these skills, typical reading tests rarely mention them.

A second weakness of many standardized reading tests is their *failure to measure small units of growth*. Progress, no matter how small, is important to both students and teachers. For example, a student may be weak in using a complex index. Since the skill encompasses a variety of smaller skills that must be taught in sequence, it becomes necessary to test for these individual skills. A test that provides for the assessment of gross abilities is obviously unsuited for the task.

A third weakness is the *difficulty of interpreting incorrect responses*. Because the typical high school reading test is read silently, teachers do not know whether the student failed to know the *meaning* of a given word or whether he merely was unable to *read* the word. To answer such questions, teachers must probe deeper than test scores. Since most standardized tests provide multiple-choice answers, it is possible to assume without checking that students *know* the correct answers and do not make intelligent guesses. Quite frequently it is possible to eliminate some of the choices because of their obvious unsuitability. In this connection, there is evidence that some students can select the proper answer from among several without even reading certain passages!

Another weakness might not be as obvious as others. A reading test is merely a representation of all that we call reading. The reading process is very complex — witness the attempts to establish reading models that explain it. While reading specialists analyze the reading act and identify its components for instructional purposes, they know that reading performance is not segmented in that way. Thus, no reading test has as yet been devised that reveals just what is occurring as students read over extended periods of time. Furthermore, a reading test fails to duplicate typical reading situations. Students in school are required to read *pages* of continuous material; tests contain isolated *bits* to which we require them to respond. At best, a standardized reading test merely approximates in its roughest form the act of reading and its requirements.

Finally, *the grade-placement score attained on most standardized reading tests by a poor reader fails to represent even in a general way his actual reading ability.* In some cases this is no less true for the reader who is progressing satisfactorily, but the discrepancy between his test score and actual reading performance may be expected to be much smaller than that of the poor reader. In the latter's case, the grade-placement score more closely approximates the frustration level of the reader and not the level at which instruction should be offered.

One of the best ways to obtain information about how well students can read is to observe them under actual study conditions and evaluate the results of their efforts. As they work on assignments that require specific reading tasks, such as answering questions or preparing a report, teachers may detect gross problems, such as the inability to read materials with adequate comprehension which prevents them from completing their tasks. The simple procedure of asking students who seem to have trouble "to tell in your own words what you read" will confirm how much they understood. Noting that they need inordinate amounts of time to locate answers to specific questions could signal inability in scanning techniques. Indiscriminate placement of information in an attempt to prepare an outline might mean that students do not understand the basic concepts of outlining or how to identify important ideas or discriminate between them and significant details. Such observations and evaluations would be followed by informal tests to verify what teachers believe are problem areas for students.

INFORMAL READING TESTS

Teacher-made or informal reading tests are criterion-referenced in that they are not intended to compare the performances of one group of students with those of another, as do standardized reading tests. Even though informal tests are not expected to meet the standards claimed by publishers of reading tests, they may equal and surpass them. This is because informal tests are limited in scope and designed to assess specific behaviors of a given group of students. The extent to which the results of informal tests are valid (actually measure what they seek to measure) and reliable (similar results are obtained if the test is repeated) will depend upon teachers' ability to prepare them.

INFORMAL READING INVENTORY

Students should not be expected to master content from materials that they cannot read with adequate comprehension. Too many are expected to read books that require ability far beyond their levels of achievement. Since it is a well-established fact that the ability to read material intended for a given grade level often cannot be determined from the results of a standardized reading test, teachers are using informal reading inventories to match materials with students.

Levels of Performance

An informal reading inventory (IRI) may be used to determine the level of difficulty experienced by students as they read a given set of materials. The results may be used to identify four reading levels: independent, instructional, frustration, and expectancy.

When students read materials at their *independent* level, fluency and comprehension are high, and they experience little or no difficulty. Students reading at their *instructional* level do not read as well as when they are functioning at the independent level, but their fluency and comprehension is sufficiently high so that, in general, they can cope with the material. If students read materials at their *frustration* level, their comprehension is poor and the material is difficult for them. The *expectancy* level is the highest level at which students can comprehend materials when they are read to them.

Materials intended to be read for enjoyment should be read at one's independent level. Materials whose contents students are expected to study and master should be read at their instructional or independent level. If students are reading a textbook at their instructional level, they might require help to increase their comprehension. The teaching of reading skills should be done with materials at least at students' instructional level. The frustration level represents the level at which materials become too difficult for students to benefit from reading or receiving reading instruction in them. If students have serious word recognition difficulties, the expectancy level indicates how well they could understand material if it were not for the interference from word recognition weaknesses.

An informal reading inventory assesses students' ability to recognize words and fluency in reading (word recognition), their ability to understand what is stated directly (literal comprehension), their ability to draw inferences from what is stated (inferential comprehension), and their knowledge of word meaning (vocabulary). Figure 4-11 lists the suggested criteria for determining informal reading achievement levels on the basis of performance in each of the aforementioned skills areas.[3] If students can achieve the minimum standards of accuracy in the four skills areas for instructional level, then the material in which these standards were achieved can be used for instruction. It is possible that some students might not be able to achieve all the minimum standards but still be able to use the material because of their efforts and increased teacher assistance. These standards are intended as guides for placement in materials and not as rigid rules from which deviation is not possible. Teachers can make necessary adjustments to easier or more difficult materials as they observe students and evaluate the products of their efforts.

3. Some reading specialists suggest standards somewhat more demanding than these. For example, the recommended word recognition criterion for instructional level might be 90 to 95 percent accuracy instead of from 80 to 90 percent. However, teachers report that students who meet the lower standards are able to function with preparation and some assistance.

Figure 4-11. Standard Levels (%) of Informal Reading Achievement by Skills Area

Level	Skills Area			
	Word Recognition	Literal Comprehension	Inferential Comprehension	Vocabulary
Independent	99-100	90-100	90	100
Instructional	80-90	60-70	50-60	70-80
Frustration	Below 70	Below 60	Below 50	Below 70
Expectancy	Same as instructional level			

Administration of the Informal Reading Inventory

An informal reading inventory consists of two parts: oral and silent reading. Therefore, two representative passages of moderate length, one about 300 words for oral reading and a second about 400-500 words for silent reading, are selected from the book to be studied. It is a good idea to select one continuous passage and divide it into two parts (each should begin and end at a natural point in the selection) so that students are prepared for the part to be read silently. For the part to be read silently, prepare five questions to measure literal comprehension and five questions to measure inferential comprehension. Select five or more words in context from the more advanced vocabulary of the passage, to assess their knowledge of word meaning. The excerpt intended for silent reading, together with the questions and vocabulary items, may be reproduced with spaces for responses or just the questions and vocabulary items without the excerpt. Copies of the other passage for oral reading will also be required.

The following passage is an excerpt drawn from a narrative selection. It is of the type that students might read in a literature book.[4] Assume that the first part of the larger excerpt has been read orally by the students and they will be reading this passage silently. Representative sets of literal and inferential questions and vocabulary items to which students will respond follow the passage.

> He asked me to do him a favor. If he failed and fell, I might still make it, since I was longer-legged; would I give certain messages to his family in that event? I nodded.
> "Then listen carefully. Try to remember my exact words," he told me. "Tell Mother that I love her dearly. Tell her I think she is the most wonderful person in the world. Tell her not to worry — that I did not suffer, that God willed it so. Tell Sister that I have been a mean little devil but I had no malice toward her. Tell Dad I was brave and died unafraid. Tell him I have always been very proud of him, that some day I had planned to be a doctor, too. Tell Mother, Sister, and Dad I prayed for them."

4. Abridged from pp. 317-319 of *Of Men and Mountains* by William O. Douglas. Copyright 1950 by William O. Douglas. Reprinted with the permission of Harper & Row, Publishers, Inc., and the Lantz Office.

Every word burned into me. My heart was sick, my lips quivered. I pressed my face against the rock so that Doug could not see.

All was silent. A pebble fell from the ledge on which I was squeezed. I counted seconds before it hit below with a faint faraway, tinkling sound. Would Doug drop through the same space? Would I follow? When you fall eight hundred feet, do you die before you hit the bottom? Closing my eyes, I asked God to help Doug up the wall.

In a second Doug said in a cheery voice, "Well, here goes."

A false bravado took hold of us. I said he could do it. He said he would. He wiped first one hand, then the other on his trousers. He placed both palms against the wall, bent his knees slowly, paused a split second, and jumped straight up. It was not much of a jump — only six inches or so. But that jump by one pressed against a cliff eight hundred feet in the air had daredevil proportions. I held my breath; my heart pounded. The suspense was over at once. Doug made the jump, and in a second was hanging by two hands from a strong, wide ledge. There was no toe hold; he would have to hoist himself by his arms alone. He did just that. His body went slowly up as if pulled by some unseen winch. Soon he had the weight of his body above the ledge and was resting on the palms of his hands. He then put his left knee on the ledge, rolled over on his side, and chuckled as he said. "Nothing to it."

A greater disappointment followed. Doug's exploration showed he was in a final cul-de-sac. There was no way up. There was not even a higher ledge he could reach by jumping. We were now faced with the nightmare of going down the sheer rock wall. We could not go down frontwards because the ledges were too narrow and the wall too steep. We needed our toes, not our heels, on the rock; and we needed to have our stomachs pressed tightly against it. Then we could perhaps feel our way. But as every rock expert knows, descent of a cliff without ropes is often much more difficult than ascent.

That difficulty was impressed upon us by the first move. Doug had to leave the ledge he had reached by jumping. He dared not slide blindly to the skimpy ledge he had just left. I must help him. I must move up the wall and stand closer to him. Though I could not possibly hold his weight, I must exert sufficient pressure to slow up his descent and to direct his toe onto the narrow ledge from which he had just jumped.

I was hanging to the rock like a fly, twelve feet or more to Doug's left. So I inched my way toward him, first dropping to a lower ledge and then climbing to a higher one, using such toe holds as the rock afforded and edging my way crabwise.

Literal Comprehension Questions:
1. What was Bill thinking as Doug prepared to jump?
2. How high did Doug have to jump?
3. What was the boys' big disappointment?
4. How was Doug to get down off the ledge?
5. How did Bill get closer to Doug?

Inferential Comprehension Questions:
1. Why didn't Bill want Doug to see his face?
2. What was Bill doing while Doug prepared to jump?
3. Why did Doug try to sound cheerful?

4. Why were toes more important than heels in going down the rock?
5. How did Bill feel as he clung to the face of the cliff?

Vocabulary:
1. I had no <u>malice</u> toward her.
2. Every word <u>burned</u> into me.
3. A false <u>bravado</u> took hold of us.
4. So I <u>inched</u> my way toward him. . . .
5. His body went slowly up as if pulled by some unseen <u>winch</u>.

Notice that the word to be defined or explained is underscored and appears in the same context as in the selection. In some instances, it is necessary to provide the entire sentence in which the word appears in order for students to determine how the word is used.

The following excerpt represents the typical content of a biology textbook intended for average and better-than-average high school students.[5] It is more difficult than the previous selection because of its subject matter, concept load, and compactness of style. The first paragraph or two could be used to check oral reading and the entire passage for literal comprehension, inferential interpretation, and vocabulary. Note that fewer questions are provided for this selection than the literature selection but that more vocabulary is included. If students do not understand what many words in the passage mean, they will not be able to master its content.

Creatures of the depths. The diversity of organisms usually decreases as the depths increases. Number of individuals also decreases with depth, because life below the photosynthetic zone depends on food drifting down from above. And in general, the greater the depth, the less the food supply. With increasing depth there are also changes in the general characteristics of the organisms, although the limits of the zones in which different organisms occur are not sharp.

The peculiar deep-sea creatures shown in Figure 9-28 are usually 500m or more below the surface during the daytime. They may come nearer the surface at night or at times when the cold waters of the depths well up toward the surface. Apparently, their vertical distribution is controlled by light and temperature as well as by water pressure.

In the eternal night of the depths of the sea, most animals have become either black or dark red and have developed increasingly sensitive eyes. In the unending darkness of caves and underground streams, however, animals tend to become white and blind. This difference is associated with another factor — *bioluminescence.* In the depths of the oceans, many animals have the ability to produce light in their bodies. But bioluminescence is not found in the blackness of caves.

This curious difference may be a biological accident. Perhaps cave animals lack bioluminescence simply because no bioluminescent animal (except a New Zealand glowworm) ever got started on the path of

5. Marston Bates and others, *High School Biology,* BSCS Green Version (Chicago: Rand McNally, 1963), pp. 280-281. Reprinted with the permission of the Biological Sciences Curriculum Study.

cave evolution. Most permanent cave dwellers live in fresh water, and as far as we know there is no bioluminescence in any fresh-water animals. But the surface waters of the seas contain many kinds of bioluminescent organisms. If surface organisms evolved special adaptations for living in the depths, we can see the bioluminescence might be retained or developed further. This, of course, does not explain why bioluminescence is common among marine animals, rare among land animals (present in fireflies and a few other things), and absent among freshwater animals.

Bioluminescence among deep-sea animals may serve one or more of several different functions: as a lure for prey, as an aid to escape, as a mark of recognition. The angler fish dangles a light in front of its mouth; apparently this lures unwary victims closer. Deep-sea shrimp and one kind of squid give off clouds of luminescent secretion when disturbed. Patterns of luminescence on the body may serve as marks of recognition in the depths, just as color patterns do among many organisms in the world of light. In some cases the lights may serve to illuminate the field of vision. At least this seems the most likely explanation for the development in some species of large light organs in front of each eye.

Most of the deep-sea fish are small, minnow-sized creatures with fantastic shapes, enormous mouths, and fragile skeletons.

There is a tendency toward long, slender forms not only among fishes but also among invertebrates: crabs with spidery legs; shrimp with long, delicate antennae; starfish with thin, whiplike "arms." These last — the brittle stars — have been found on the bottom at great depths.

Literal Questions:
1. Why are there fewer living things at great ocean depths than close to the water's surface?
2. What factors account for differences in the characteristics of ocean creatures?
3. What characteristics do deep-water animals appear to have in common?
4. In what special way do salt-water and fresh-water animals differ?

Inferential Questions:
1. What conclusion might be drawn from the information the text provides about the ability of animals to produce light?
2. What might explain the fact that most deep-sea creatures are small with long slender forms?
3. True or false? Scientists have much to learn about the true nature of many sea creatures.

Vocabulary
1. *diversity* of organisms
2. *limits* of the zones in which different organisms occur are not *sharp*
3. *eternal* night of the depths of the sea
4. if surface organisms *evolved* special *adaptations*
5. *unwary* victims
6. *lure* for prey
7. there is a *tendency* toward
8. *fragile* skeletons

It is wise to test only a few students at a time. Have one student read orally the first excerpt. As the student reads the passage, note on another copy any errors made. The following shorthand system might be used to note main types of errors:

unknown words: *daredevil* proportions
                    (many)
substitutions: among marine animals
omissions: these difference(s) are (not) great
           big
insertions: made the ∧ jump

Do not correct the student, but tell him any word if he asks for help or stops reading. Note any hesitations, failure to use punctuation, word-by-word reading, repeating of words, reading in a monotone voice, or other indications of difficulty. If the student makes many errors in the first few sentences, have him stop the oral reading, read the second passage silently, and write out the answers to the questions and vocabulary items. (Students whose writing and spelling ability are poor might answer the questions orally.)

The oral reading should take about five minutes or less and the silent reading and the completion of the test items from ten to fifteen. Since students will be reading silently while one is reading orally, it is possible to complete several inventories within a regular period. If teachers prepare in advance the materials used for testing, students can be checked quickly. It would be helpful for a group of teachers who plan to use the same materials to prepare inventories that they may share and use more than once with different groups of students. Screening of students could be done at the end of the school year, in preparation for the new year, or at the beginning of the school year. In either case, adjustments in materials might be required once teaching has begun.

If, on the basis of inventory results, a given book or other material prove too difficult for some students, then other materials that they *can* read should be sought. There is variation in the difficulty of materials intended for a subject class, that is, one earth science textbook for ninth grade might be much more difficult for typical ninth-graders than another earth science textbook for the same grade. How well students do on another informal inventory based on the new material would determine its instructional usefulness.

Since teachers will have a record of any word recognition errors and responses to questions involving literal and inferential comprehension and vocabulary, the informal reading inventory can serve as an initial diagnostic tool of student reading. Perhaps one student consistently misses words that contain the same vowel sound, for example, e.g., "*cheat*" and "*reason*," or another fails to recognize words that contain familiar root words such as "garden" in "gardener" or "select" in "selection." This information could indicate the type of help in recognizing words that each student needs.

Other students might not do well on questions involving drawing conclusions or seeing cause and effect relationships. Further checking of these comprehension skills could reveal areas to which teachers ought to attend. The study of responses to vocabulary might show that some students fail to use context clues which the passage contains. This information then becomes the basis for planning lessons in how to use the context for determining word meaning.

To summarize, if the students achieve close to 100 percent accuracy in word recognition, literal and inferential comprehension, and vocabulary on the informal reading inventory, they should have little or no difficulty reading the material. Of course, this assumes that the inventory is based on a representative passage and assesses the skills areas with some precision. If they achieve somewhat less in these areas, they are probably reading at their instructional level, and the material is suitable for instruction. However, if they score well below 80 percent in word recognition, below 60 percent in literal comprehension, below 50 percent in inferential comprehension, and below 70 percent in vocabulary, the chances are that the material is too difficult and they should not be expected to struggle through it.

WORD LISTS

To determine student instructional levels for word recognition groupings, teachers may want to quickly evaluate their students' abilities to recognize words. To do this, teachers could administer the *San Diego Quick Assessment*[6] which consists of eleven lists of graded words drawn from basal reader glossaries and the Thorndike list. Students simply pronounce the ten words assigned to each grade level, progressing from one level to the next until they miss three or more words at any level. According to the compilers of this graded list, the highest list on which a student misses no more than one of the ten words is the level at which he can read independently. Two errors indicate his instructional level, and three or more errors identify the level at which material will be too difficult for him to read.

The words for grades 7-11 are given below:

7. amber	8. capacious	9. conscientious
dominion	limitation	isolation
sundry	pretext	molecule
capillary	intrigue	ritual
impetuous	delusion	momentous
blight	immaculate	vulnerable
wrest	ascent	kinship
enumerate	acrid	conservatism
daunted	binocular	jaunty
condescend	embankment	inventive

10. zany	11. galore
jerkin	rotunda
nausea	capitalism
gratuitous	prevaricate
linear	risible
legality	superannuate
aspen	luxuriate
amnesty	piebald
barometer	crunch

6. Margaret La Pray and Ramon Ross, "The Graded Word List: Quick Gauge of Reading Ability," *Journal of Reading* 12 (Jan. 1969): 305-307.

Teachers might prepare comparable lists of representative words. These lists will be drawn from the literature and other content books that students will be required to read. A fairer estimate of their ability to read these materials would include not only the pronunciation of these words but also a definition or explanation of their meaning. The criteria for instructional level used with the San Diego list could be followed with teacher-prepared lists.

CLOZE PROCEDURE

In recent years, investigators have shown much interest in a procedure known as *cloze*.[7] The origin of the term is found in *closure* which refers to the tendency that people show in viewing structures as wholes. Simply stated, *cloze* is a means of determining how well the reader understands what a writer says. It is another informal means of testing student comprehension. It helps determine how appropriate the material (on which cloze exercises are based) is for instructional purposes.

It is not difficult to prepare a cloze test. Select three or four representative passages of about 200-250 words each from the students' textbook or other materials they will be expected to read. Delete every fifth word beginning with the second sentence. Have students read each passage silently and fill in the missing words. They should write these words on another paper so that the passages may be used more than once.

Below is a cloze exercise of a passage taken from a social studies textbook.[8] The blank spaces are numbered so that students will not be confused and assign wrong words to them.

Weaknesses of the League. The League of Nations was not, of course, a perfect organization. It had several serious __(1)__. For one thing, taking __(2)__ against an aggressor was __(3)__ impossible for a number __(4)__ reasons. First the term, "aggressor" __(5)__ not defined. Second, the __(6)__ could only recommend that __(7)__ take action, and no __(8)__ could be compelled to __(9)__ upon these recommendations. Third, __(10)__ member of the council could __(11)__ the wishes of the __(12)__ members because all important __(13)__ of the Council had __(14)__ be reached by unanimous __(15)__. In brief, the work __(16)__ the League depended upon __(17)__ willingness of its members __(18)__ cooperate.

Another basic weakness __(19)__ the League was its __(20)__ of existing political boundaries. __(21)__ the map of the __(22)__ was redrawn, some peoples __(23)__ themselves living in the __(24)__ of their choice, but __(25)__ did not. Those who __(26)__ not had no way __(27)__ secure further changes in __(28)__ national boundaries.

7. John R. Bormuth, "The Cloze Readability Procedure," *Elementary English* 45 (April 1968): 429-436.
8. Lewis P. Todd and Merle Curti, *Rise of the American Nation*, 2d ed. (New York: Harcourt Brace and World, 1966), pp. 634-635. Copyright © 1966 by Harcourt Brace Jovanovich and reproduced with their permission.

A third __(29)__ was the League's failure __(30)__ provide adequate machinery for __(31)__ to economic problems __(32)__ might lead to war. __(33)__ rivalries and tariff barriers __(34)__ existed, as did imperialism, __(35)__ the League was not __(36)__ to do much more __(37)__ study such problems. Finally, __(38)__ League was in no __(39)__ to tackle the problem __(40)__ armaments.*

*The correct words are (1) weaknesses (2) action (3) almost (4) of (5) was (6) Council (7) nations (8) member (9) act (10) any (11) block (12) other (13) decisions (14) to (15) vote (16) of (17) the (18) to (19) of (20) guarantee (21) when (22) world (23) found (24) country (25) others (26) did (27) to (28) their (29) weaknesses (30) to (31) recommending (32) that (33) Trade (34) still (35) yet (36) equipped (37) than (38) the (39) position (40) of.

Note that the passage has enough independent content to stand by itself. If passages are drawn from the beginning of a topic, this problem is minimized. It is better to use a longer passage that covers a theme than a shorter one that fails to produce closure. Note that the blank spaces are of the same length regardless of the length of the deleted words.

If the rules for scoring the cloze passage are followed strictly, no word different from the one that is missing is considered correct. Synonyms are not counted as correct words. The total number of correct words from all the passages are averaged to obtain the score.

Let's assume that a student read three passages with a total of 123 deleted words. The student successfully filled in 52 words for an average score of 42.2 percent (52/123). On the cloze test, a score of 44 percent is equivalent to 75 percent on literal and inferential comprehension, while a score of 57 percent is equivalent to 100 percent comprehension. Thus, the score of 42.2 percent is just under 75 percent in comprehension and meets the criteria for instructional reading level. A score of close to 57 percent represents the independent reading level. Scores significantly below 44 percent represent the frustration level.

An alternate procedure is to delete every tenth word instead of every fifth word. A comparison of the following cloze exercise (which is a portion of the same passage that was used for the informal reading inventory) with the preceding cloze exercise shows that since the latter contains more context between deleted words, it might be somewhat easier to fill in the missing words. On the other hand, there might be no real difference if the concepts in one are more difficult to understand than in the other.

Creatures of the depths. The diversity of organisms usually _____ as the depth increases. Number of individuals also decreases _____ depth, because life below the photosynthetic zone depends on _____ drifting down from above. And in general, the greater _____ depth, the less the food supply. With increasing depth _____ are also changes in the general characteristics of the _____, although the limits of the zones in which different _____ occur are not sharp.

The peculiar deep-sea creatures shown _____ Figure 9.28 are usually 500m or more below the _____ during the daytime. They may

come nearer the surface _____ night or at times when the cold waters
of _____ depths well up toward the surface. Apparently, their vertical
_____ is controlled by light and temperature as well as _____ water
pressure.

In the eternal night of the depths _____ the sea, most animals have
become either black or _____ red and have developed increasingly
sensitive eyes. In the _____ darkness of caves and underground
streams, however, animals tend _____ become white and blind. This
difference is associated with _____ factor — *bioluminescence.* In the
depths of the oceans, many _____ have the ability to produce light in
their bodies. _____ bioluminescence is not found in the blackness of
caves.

Another variation in using cloze exercises to determine instructional
and independent levels is to accept synonyms for deleted words. If this practice were followed, it would be necessary to apply more stringent standards
in assessing the results. The average score of 44 percent for instructional
level might be raised to about 48 percent, while the average score for independent level might become 60 percent.

READABILITY FORMULAS

There have been many efforts to determine the relative difficulty of
printed materials and, thus, their appropriateness for students whose reading
grade levels are known. Readability formulas have been proposed as tools
for matching materials to students. Among formulas used with secondary
school materials are the Dale-Chall Readability Formulas, the SMOG Formula, and the Fry Readability Graph.[9]

The Dale-Chall Formula is based on the assumption that the length of
sentences (the number of words they contain), the length of words (the number of syllables they have), and word frequency or familiarity (as determined
by word lists) account for the factors that affect difficulty. The SMOG Formula takes into account the number of words containing three or more syllables in a ten-sentence sample, and the Fry Readability Graph involves the
number of syllables and sentences in a 100-word sample.

The Fry Readability Graph is very simple to use and provides as good
an assessment as other formulas. Figure 4-12 contains instructions and an
illustration of its use for assessing some material's level of difficulty.

Perhaps the most that can be said for readability formulas is that they
provide a very rough measure of the relative difficulty of sets of materials.
The grade-placement scores which the formulas yield should not be taken
too seriously since there is enough evidence to suggest that they frequently
overestimate or underestimate difficulty as indicated by grade placement. It
has been pointed out that the conceptual difficulty and idea organization of

9. Information about how to use these and other readability formulas can be found
in John Pescosolido and Charles Gervase, *Reading Expectancy and Readability*
(Dubuque, Iowa: Kendall/Hunt Publishing, 1971).

Figure 4-12.   Fry Readability Graph

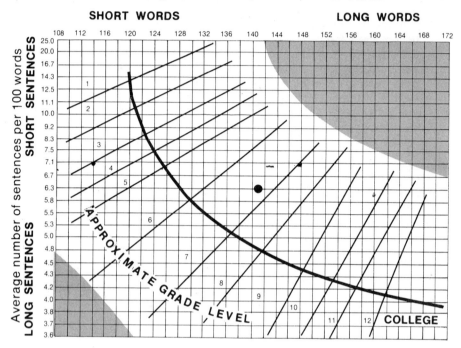

DIRECTIONS: Randomly select 3 one hundred passages from a book or an article. Plot average number of syllables and average number of sentences per 100 words on graph to determine the grade level of the material. Choose more passages per book if great variability is observed and conclude that the book has uneven readability. Few books will fall in gray area but when they do grade level scores are invalid.

EXAMPLE:	SYLLABLES	SENTENCES
1st Hundred Words	124	6.6
2nd Hundred Words	141	5.5
3rd Hundred Words	158	6.8
AVERAGE	141	6.3

READABILITY 7th GRADE   (see dot plotted on graph)

From Edward Fry, *Reading Instruction for Classroom and Clinic* (New York: Mc-Graw-Hill, 1972), p. 232. Reproduced with the permission of the publisher.

materials plus the interest and motivation of readers are ignored by the formulas and that these factors account for some of the variability in the difficulty of materials. John Bormuth suggested that language features, other than word and sentence length, influence readability: multiplicity of word meanings, their abstractness, and morphological complexity; and the grammatical complexity of sentences as measured by the number of grammatical facts they contain, the distance between words or phrases and their modifiers, and transformational complexity which refers to the problem of converting a sentence to its kernel sentences.[10]

In summary, teachers might use readability formulas to compare the relative difficulty of materials — that is, which are more or less difficult to read than others — with the full knowledge that they are tenuous. They could try out the materials on groups of students, whose reading status is known, to determine how closely the results coincide with the reading performances and evaluations of these students.

INFORMAL DIAGNOSTIC TESTS

The informal reading tests that have been described help teachers determine whether prospective reading materials are suitable for instructional purposes. Other teacher-prepared tests can reveal how well students perform reading tasks associated with study requirements. Any materials used for assessing reading skills should be at student instructional levels; if the materials are very difficult for them, they will experience interference and will not be able to demonstrate what they can do.

A survey test of reading skills may be administered to a group of students. Each survey test might cover a few skill areas and be completed in a short time. The results may indicate that some students are deficient in one or more skills; their performance on additional exercises covering these skills would enable teachers to pinpoint specific weaknesses.

Below is a series of representative exercises that could be used as models for preparing test items from any source. Notice that the test items for the skills areas sample different levels of performance within each area.

Using Book Parts
> *Directions:* Your world-history textbook contains a Table of Contents, a list of Maps and Charts, and an Index. In which of these sections would you look for answers to the following questions or problems? Write your answers in the spaces following each question.
>
> 1. When was Sir Thomas More's *Utopia* published? _____
>
> 2. What major problems does the world face today? _____

10. John Bormuth, "New Developments in Reading Research," *Elementary English* 44 (Dec. 1967): 840-845.

3. How extensive was the Roman Empire at the height of its power? _____
4. What was the Marshall Plan? _____
5. What social and economic changes took place in twentieth-century Europe? _____
_____

6. Trace the trade routes followed by merchants in the Middle Ages. _____
_____

Using a Table of Contents
Directions: Use the Contents of your chemistry book to determine in which chapter you would expect to find information about each of the following topics. Write the number of the chapter in the spaces after each topic.

1. Radioactivity in the atmosphere _____
2. Properties of hydrogen _____
3. How to write chemical formulas _____
4. The building of chemical models _____
5. The nature of synthetics _____

Using an Index
Directions: Use the index in your general office practice book to answer the following questions. Write your answers in the spaces provided after each question.

1. On what page will you find an illustration of a sales record?
_____
2. On how many different pages will you find information about alphabetic filing? _____
3. On what pages will you find information about route slips for interoffice communication? _____

Directions: Find the answers to the following questions. Write your answer in the spaces provided after each question.

1. What different systems of filing do offices use? _____
_____
2. What are the qualifications for someone who wishes to work in a bookkeeping unit? _____
_____

3. What is the difference between first and second and third class mail? _____
_____

4. Why should a cashier keep a voucher for each payment of petty cash? _____
_____

Using Context Clues

Write the meaning of the underlined words in the spaces after each passage.

A. In arithmetic, you learned a good deal about how to use numbers. In algebra, your initial aim will be to discover some of the <u>properties</u> of the numbers of arithmetic. By the word "property" is meant a distinguishing trait or an essential quality. You use this word when you say, "Sweetness is a property of sugar; hardness is a property of diamonds."[11]

properties means _____

_____

B. Specifying Sets:

To specify any set of numbers or other objects, you must identify the members, or elements, of the <u>set</u>. Sometimes you can specify a set by listing the names of its members within brackets [ ]. For example,

[2, 5, — 1]

(read "the set whose members are 2, 5, — 1") shows a roster (list) of the set *consisting* of the three real numbers 2, 5, and — 1. You can see at a glance that 5 *belongs to* (is a member of) this set, but that —5 does not belong to the set.[12]

set means _____

_____

C. The presence of ice crystals in a cloud may determine whether or not the cloud <u>precipitates</u> its moisture. Different kinds of precipitation are formed in different ways. The size of precipitation particles, shown in Figure 8-11, and whether they are liquid water or ice, are important clues to their formation.

The maximum diameter of raindrops striking the earth is about 6 millimeters, about the size of a medium-sized pea. Raindrops larger than this can form in the atmosphere, but they are quickly broken up by air resistance as they fall. The largest drops fall from cumuliform clouds.[13]

precipitates means _____

_____

D. Like the rest of literature, novels <u>reflect</u> life in all its variety. Every kind of mystery and adventure, every kind of humorous or serious problem or outlook on life is mirrored in some novel. *Twenty Thousand Leagues Under the Sea* and *The Three Muska-*

---

11. Mary P. Dolciani and others, *Modern Algebra* (1962), p. 1. Reprinted with the permission of Houghton Mifflin Co.
12. Mary P. Dolciani and others, *Modern School Mathematics, Algebra I* (1967), pp. 16-17. Reprinted with the permission of Houghton Mifflin Co.
13. *Investigating the Earth*, Earth Science Curriculum Project of the American Geological Institute (1967), p. 190. Reprinted with the permission of Houghton Mifflin Co.

teers portray excitement and conquest and energy; *Les Miserables* looks at serious problems of living; *Vanity Fair* deals with maturity. All of life finds some expression in the novel, and for every interest there is a novel. What one reader may find dull will fascinate someone else.[14]

reflect means _____

_____

Reading for Main Ideas
    Directions: In the space following each passage write its topic.

A. Many experiments have been carried out to discover what effect alcohol has on a person's work. One experiment with a group of typesetters showed that even 1 ounce of alcohol a day was enough to reduce the amount of work done by 10 percent. Another experiment showed the effect of alcohol on accuracy and judgment, which are very important in many kinds of work. The person to be tested was seated at a table with each hand on a push button. If a white light appeared, he pressed one push button. But if a red light appeared, he pressed the other one. The experiment showed that if a person drinks a small amount of alcohol, at first he will press the push buttons faster than if no alcohol is taken. However, he will press the wrong push button much more often. Quick and thoughtless judgments caused by drinking make his work inaccurate.[15]

The topic of this passage is _____

_____

B. If you wish to know the total weight of your chemistry class, you would add together the weights of all the individuals in the class. Similarly, if we wish to find the formula weight of any substance for which the formula is given, we must add together the atomic weights of all the atoms present, as represented by the formula. Let us use the formula of cane sugar, $C_{12}H_{22}O_{11}$, as an example.

Number of atoms	Atomic weight	Total weight
12 of C	12	$12 \times 12 = 144$
22 of H	1	$22 \times 1 = 22$
11 of O	16	$11 \times 16 = 176$

formula weight (molecular weight) $= 342$

14. Walter Loban, Dorothy Holmstrom, and Luella B. Cook, *Adventures in Appreciation* (1958), pp. 612-613. Copyright © 1958 by Harcourt Brace Jovanovich, Inc., and reprinted with their permission.
15. Wilbur Beauchamp, John Mayfield, and Joe West, *Science Problems*, pp. 338-339. Copyright © 1957 by Scott, Foresman and Co., and reprinted with their permission.

The formula for calcium hydroxide is $Ca(OH)_2$. The subscript 2 following the parentheses indicates that there are two hydroxide radicals, *OH,* with each calcium atom in calcium hydroxide.[16]

Number of atoms	Atomic weight	Total weight
1 of Ca	40.	$1 \times 40. = 40.$
2 of O	16	$2 \times 16 = 32$
2 of H	1	$2 \times 1 = 2$
		formula weight $= 74$

The topic of this passage is _____

Directions: Write the main idea of each passage.

C. But the central government under the Constitution was given power to make laws that applied directly to all citizens. The unrestricted possession of this power could easily lead to abuse. Therefore, the framers of the Federal Constitution put certain limits on the power of the central government. Contrary to popular opinion, the original Constitution did provide certain safeguards for the fundamental rights of individuals. The most important of these concern *habeas corpus,* bills of attainder, *ex-post-facto* laws, and treason, all of which are dealt with in Article 1, Section 9, of the Constitution.[17]

The main idea of this passage is _____

D. The radio, like the automobile and the motion picture, was an important instrument in bringing Americans closer together. Differences in speech, attitudes, and manners became less striking, since the same radio artists and the same programs were heard in every home of the nation. The radio also became important in political affairs. Candidates could reach much larger audiences and with less effort, and the voters could more easily acquaint themselves with both sides of the issues. A good radio voice became a political asset to a candidate and the newspapers tended to lose some of their importance in controlling political opinions. President Franklin D. Roosevelt used the radio with great success. He not only found it helpful in his political campaigns, but he also made periodic "fireside chats" in which he explained his administration's program to the people. The radio became a useful instrument to American business. The radio industry contributed much to the nation's economic life, and the broadcasting studios served as important outlets for commercial

16. H. Clark Metcalfe and others, *Modern Chemistry* (1974), p. 126. Reprinted with the permission of Holt, Rinehart and Winston.
17. George G. Bruntz, *Understanding Our Government*, p. 358. Copyright © 1955 by Ginn and Company (Xerox Corp.), and used with their permission.

advertising. The radio "commercial," in fact, became almost as important a feature on the air as the program itself.[18]

The main idea of this passage is _____

_____

Recognizing Pronoun Referents

Directions: **Indicate to what the underlined pronoun in each passage refers. Write your answer in the spaces after each passage.**

A. The "muckrakers." In addition to leaders in public office, and to such dedicated private citizens as Jane Adams, the Progressive movement included large numbers of scholars, journalists, preachers, and novelists. Theodore Roosevelt applied the name "muckrakers" to the writers who exposed in clear, graphic terms the evils and corruption they found in politics and the business world. Although Roosevelt used the term in a disparaging manner, the writers accepted it with pride, and it came into popular use.[19]

they refers to_____

it refers to_____

B. During the years between 1865 and 1900, the United States grew by leaps and bounds. By the opening years of the 1900's, the United States had become the leading industrial nation in the world. Smoking factory chimneys, the rumble of steam-driven and electric machinery, and long trains of freight cars pulling into and out of congested urban centers were symbols of the Industrial Revolution.

Particularly in the Northeast and Middle West, and to a lesser extent elsewhere in the nation, industrialism was transforming the lives of the people. Raw materials from America's vast reservoir of natural resources poured into the mills and factories. Finished products in ever-growing quantities poured from the factories.

Mass production led to specialization. Financiers raised the capital to build the railroads and the factories. Manufacturers developed more efficient methods of producing goods. Merchants developed new methods of advertising and selling. Many workers — clerks, stenographers, managers, factory workers, and others — manned the new industrial plants. New methods of business organization were developed, and great corporations and combinations of corporations increasingly replaced the earlier family-owned businesses.

---

18. Fremont Wirth, *United States History*, rev. ed. (1957), pp. 680-681. Reprinted with the permission of the American Book Co.
19. Lewis P. Todd and Merle Curti, *Rise of the American Nation*, 2d ed., p. 522. Copyright © 1966 by Harcourt Brace Jovanovich and reproduced with their permission.

Throughout America a new spirit of fierce competition drove men at a faster and faster pace. <u>It</u> was an exciting and a productive period in the nation's history. But some of the changes created problems for many people. Much of the nation's history since 1865 is concerned with the efforts of Americans to adjust their ways of life to the new forces of growing industrialism.[20]

<u>It</u> refers to_____

C. **What caused the Great Depression?** There is no simple way to explain what caused the Great Depression. Economists agree that there were many causes, but they disagree about which was the most important.

President Hoover insisted that the major cause of the depression was the world-wide economic disorder that followed World War I. Many economists agreed with Hoover. They pointed to the vast destruction of property during the war and the world-wide dislocation of trade during and after the war.

Other economists argued that America's high tariff policies helped to stifle world trade and hurt American business. High tariffs, they claimed, prevented other countries from selling their goods in the United States. <u>This</u> in turn prevented them from securing the dollars that they needed to buy American products.[21]

<u>This</u> refers to_____

Drawing Conclusions

A. Which of these conclusions or generalizations about city life appears to be valid?

1. The cities' problems are partially due to the size of their populations.
2. Nothing can be done to alleviate or eliminate many of the conditions from which big cities suffer.

Drawbacks of City Life. Crowds. Why then do many Americans say they would rather not live in a city? One important reason is the crowding of so many people into a small area. Thousands of people are jammed into trains and buses during the morning and evening rush hours every working day. Crowds fill the sidewalks at lunch time, the theaters and sports stadiums in the evenings, and the parks and beaches in warm weather. The streets are crowded with traffic, often moving so slowly that it is faster to walk than to ride. Yet even with the crowds, a person can feel very lonely in the city because he is surrounded by strangers.

Pollution. A comedian recently said of city life, "If the water we drink doesn't kill us, then the air we breathe will." He was talking about the increasing pollution that threatens many of our cities.

20. Ibid., p. 468. Copyright © 1966 by Harcourt Brace Jovanovich and reproduced with their permission.
21. Ibid., p. 628. Copyright © 1966 by Harcourt Brace Jovanovich and reproduced with their permission.

The waters around them have become more and more polluted because of the growing amounts of waste matter from factories and homes. In some cities it has already become hard to get enough good drinking water or to find a safe place to swim. A recent study showed one of the Great Lakes to be so polluted that its plant and animal life was dying out.

Air pollution is still another serious problem. Many industrial cities already suffer from smog (a smoky fog) whenever the winds die down for a few days. Smog is caused by the tons of waste matter that gasoline-burning motors, coal- or oil-burning furnaces, and certain industrial plants pour into the air every day. Smog dirties everything in the city. It irritates the eyes, throat, and lungs. In certain kinds of weather some of its chemicals turn into acids that eat away even the stone and metal walls of buildings. So it is hardly surprising that it has been proved harmful to human beings. A great smog that blanketed London in 1952 was blamed for the death of more than four thousand people. Some American cities have already had smogs almost as deadly. Unfortunately, we can expect more and worse smogs as the number of automobiles, trucks, buses, and factories continues to increase.

Other Problems. Because they are so large and complex, modern cities have other difficult problems. A heavy snowstorm, a strike in an important industry, or some other unusual event can stop normal activities for days at a time. Juvenile delinquency and crime rates are high, especially in slums. With many people living close together, disease epidemics are a constant threat. To deal with these problems, cities have to set up a large police force, a public health service, and other very costly facilities.[22]

Conclusion _____

_____

B. What conclusion might be drawn from this passage about buying on credit?

Buying on credit has been debated for and against by economists, bankers, business people, and consumers; but no clear-cut conclusions have been reached. Those in favor of the system of personal credits by which consumers can buy on the installment plan point out that this system has made it possible for many, many more people to buy products; and in turn, has made it possible for manufacturers to sell at lower prices. Thus, purchasing on time has led to a higher standard of living throughout the country. More people have more consumer goods than ever before in the history of the world. There seems to be no question but that credit buying has brought comfort, satisfaction, and happiness to millions of families in the United States.

Those who do not favor credit buying point out that these millions of families have all paid higher prices than if they had paid

22. Sidney Schwartz and John R. O'Connor, *Exploring Our Nation's History* (1969), pp. 642-643. Reprinted with the permission of the Globe Book Company.

cash. Interest charges on installment buying are often very high. Economists sometimes argue that money paid for interest charges is poor management from the standpoint of the consumer.

It is also true that thousands of families have lost considerable money through failure to complete the payment of installments. When installments are not paid, the dealer who sold the product may have the right to repossess it without refunding the whole amount paid in by the buyer. Thus the buyer loses both the product and the money he has already paid for it.[23]

Conclusion _____

Recognizing Facts and Opinions
Directions: Indicate after each statement whether it is a fact or an opinion.

1. The average annual rainfall in the eastern portion of the United States is forty inches. _____

2. The American Colonies were more a liability than an asset to England. _____

3. Voters are more likely to be influenced by a male candidate's appearance than by his special qualifications for office. _____
   _____

4. Two of the great medical accomplishments of the twentieth century was the discovery of penicillin and the development of a polio vaccine. _____

Preparing Outlines
Directions: Read pages 420-425 in your social studies book and complete the following outline.

Causes of the American Revolution
I. Political
   A. Lack of representation in Parliament
   B. _____
II. _____
   A. Taxation of imports from other countries
   B. _____
   C. _____

Directions: Outline the section on *The Sun,* pages 163-167 of your earth science book. There are three main topics, and each has some subtopics.

Directions: Outline the section on the *Structure of the United Nations,* pages 466-471 of your world history book.

23. Irene E. McDermott and Florence W. Nicholas, *Living for Young Moderns* (1956), p. 208. Reprinted with the permission of J. B. Lippincott, Publisher.

Using the Dictionary
> *Directions:*   Use the dictionary to determine the pronunciation of the following words. Be ready to pronounce them.

quay	ptomaine
requiem	synod
abalone	caveat
flaccid	schism

> *Directions:*   Use the dictionary to determine the pronunciation of the following respelled words. Be ready to pronounce them.

(griz′lē)	(sam′o͝o-rī)
(lär-jes′)	(od′ə-tē)
(prə-fán′)	(Kôr′dən)
(rōg)	(āpē-er′ē)

It should be apparent that any inventory may be prepared for any subject and skills area. Word recognition, comprehension, and study skills may be sampled broadly or in depth; tests of these kinds become diagnostic tools for determining how well students can read and how much they can gain from independent study. Information obtained from a skills inventory may be verified by observing students as they read and study activities and from evaluating their own performances. Thus, any instruction that teachers offer will reflect actual student needs rather than the contents of a predetermined program.

MISCUE ANALYSIS

An analysis of oral reading errors, or *miscues*, can reveal what strategies readers follow to process and comprehend written language. The system of evaluating miscues on the basis of the graphic, syntactic, and semantic information in printed material is called *miscue analysis.*[24]

During miscue analysis, the teacher records miscues as the student orally reads material somewhat more difficult than that intended for instruction. The miscues are then analyzed according to the following questions:

1. Is the miscue the result of variation in dialect?
2. Is there a graphic similarity between the miscue and the actual word?
3. How similar do the miscue and actual word sound?
4. Do the miscue and actual word have the same grammatical function?
5. Is the miscue corrected?
6. Is the miscue grammatically and semantically acceptable?
7. Does the miscue produce a change in meaning?

24. Yetta Goodman and Carolyn L. Burke, *Reading Miscue Inventory Manual: Procedure for Diagnosis and Evaluation* (New York: Macmillan, 1972).

Miscues that are the result of variation in the reader's dialect are not counted as errors. Miscues that are synonyms for the actual word or do not change the meaning indicate that the reader is using semantic and syntactic information and comprehends the material. If the miscue resembles the actual word but is grammatically or semantically unacceptable, it could indicate problems in comprehension or word analysis. Miscues that are corrected suggest that the reader comprehends the material.

The analysis might show weaknesses in using grammatical or semantic information. If this were the case, it would be necessary to prepare passages that make them aware of their language competence and own knowledge. By having them respond to passages with deleted words — for example, "*The _____ sun shining on the windshield blinded the driver,*" — they can be helped to realize what type of word belongs in that position. Miscues that are gross deviations from actual words in graphic and auditory similarity and are unacceptable grammatically or semantically could require lessons in word-attack as well as using language information.

CUMULATIVE RECORDS

Standardized tests and informal reading inventories are particularly valuable for the information they reveal about groups of students and individuals. We have seen how the information from one type of test supplements the results of another. Another important source of information can also be of great help to teachers. That source is the cumulative record folder kept for each student.

In many school systems, this folder follows the student from the time he enters kindergarten or first grade to the time he graduates from high school. Each teacher keeps a record of the child's reading progress, test scores, special problems, interests, and other useful data about his health, general development, and achievement. The folder also contains records of significant incidents that may have had some bearing upon his success in school. As the child progresses through the grades, a rather complete picture of him emerges.

Cumulative records are useful instruments. They can help teachers become acquainted with their students before classes actually start. They may be used to classify students tentatively and help place them if achievement level grouping is contemplated. They may indicate that specialized help is required for some and thus make possible advanced planning for providing such help. The different uses to which they can be put makes these cumulative folders valuable diagnostic tools.

It is assumed, of course, that the folders contain helpful and accurate information. One should remember that so-called objective results are not always completely free from bias and that judgment and observations are often highly subjective. There is the danger, too, that a teacher can be strongly influenced by the information they contain and as a result fail to draw independent conclusions about students. The writer remembers one seventh-grader about whom such caution was necessary. Joseph had a cumulative folder that was an inch thick. Every teacher in the school knew of him and was familiar with the record. In fact, several openly declared, on the basis of the information in the folder, that they would be unhappy if he were assigned to their classes. There was no doubt that Joseph was a child with academic and personal problems, but his past record served to remove any chances he had for a fresh start. How much better it would have been had these teachers and their supervisors analyzed the data about Joseph and planned a program that was suited to his abilities. Instead, to him the new year only meant continuing failure and rejection.

Let us not despair. Many Josephs are receiving every consideration from teachers and other school personnel. Progress with these children is being realized in widely scattered communities throughout the United States. Regrettably, limitations of knowledge, time, and money prevent us from accomplishing more.

SUMMARY

Diagnostic teaching is the means by which students may be helped to achieve in reading to the extent they are able. Evaluating students' reading ability is an ongoing activity; teachers must modify their plans as they acquire new data.

The best sources of information about students' reading are their actual performances in reading-study activities. Observing how they acquire and use information from books and other materials and evaluating results of their reading will yield valuable data about students' reading strengths and weaknesses. Such data may be supplemented by the results obtained from standardized and informal reading tests. Informal reading inventories and other teacher-prepared tests are better tools than are standardized tests for determining the "fit" between students and materials. The former also enable teachers to pinpoint with greater precision what the reading requirements of students are. However, standardized reading tests may be used to assess the general reading achievement of students, and their results could serve to identify limited areas to which attention should be given.

Additional Readings

The following publications contain comprehensive treatments of the measurement and evaluation of reading:

Mary C. Austin, Clifford L. Bush, and Mildred H. Huebner. *Reading Evaluation: Appraisal Technique for School and Classroom*. New York: Ronald Press, 1961.

William E. Blanton, Roger Farr, and J. Jaap Tuinman, eds. *Measuring Reading Performance*. Newark, Del.: International Reading Association, 1974.

Roger Farr. *Measurement and Evaluation of Reading*. New York: Harcourt Brace Jovanovich, 1970.

———. *Reading: What Can be Measured?* ERIC/CRIER Reading Review Series. Newark, Del.: International Reading Association, 1969.

Ruth Strang. *Diagnostic Teaching of Reading,* 2d ed. New York: McGraw-Hill, 1969.

Information about the preparation and administration of informal reading tests will be found in the following publications:

Marjorie S. Johnson and Roy Kress. *Informal Reading Inventories,* Reading Aids Series. Newark, Del.: International Reading Association, 1965.

David Shepherd. *Comprehensive High School Reading Methods.* Columbus, Ohio: Charles E. Merrill, 1973.

Ruth G. Viox. *Evaluating Reading and Study Skills in the Secondary Classroom.* Newark, Del.: International Reading Association, 1968.

For a comprehensive description and evaluation of standardized reading tests, see the following publications:

William Blanton, Roger Farr and J. Jaap Tuinman, eds. *Reading Tests for the Secondary Grade: A Review and Evaluation.* Newark, Del.: International Reading Association, 1972.

Oscar K. Buros, ed. *Seventh Mental Measurements Yearbook.* Highland Park, N.J.: Gryphon Press, 1972.

_____, ed. *Reading Tests and Reviews* I, II. Highland Park, N.J.: Gryphon Press, 1968, 1975.

CHAPTER 5

GUIDING READING in the CONTENT AREAS

Problems for Study and Discussion

1 *Why are informational materials generally more difficult to read than narrative materials?*
2 *What types of preparatory activities might all subject teachers adopt to facilitate students' reading?*
3 *Prepare a directed reading activity for some content in your subject area. What factors should be taken into account when considering variations in the plan?*
4 *How might a process guide facilitate comprehension? A content guide?*
5 *What strategies might teachers help students adopt for independent study of informational materials?*

Ideally, each teacher of content subjects should provide intensive instruction in overcoming difficulties in comprehending and interpreting information found in textbooks and supplementary materials. Hygiene teachers, for example, would provide a comprehensive reading program as it affected their own subject matter, and the same would be true for teachers of industrial arts, science, history, home economics, mathematics, or any specialized field. However, most schools that have reading programs offer intensive reading instruction through the language arts department, on the assumption that other teachers do not know how or do not have the time to teach reading. Such programs can be effective in overcoming specific reading weaknesses, but even when such programs exist, content teachers should not assume that they cannot assist their students with textbooks and other reading. One of their aims is to help students master content, and one way to achieve this is to teach content through reading. The old slogan "Every teacher is a teacher of reading" can take on new meaning when the teaching of reading is effectively applied to learning.

READING STRATEGIES FOR TEACHING CONTENT

Most students find that subject-matter textbooks are more difficult to read than books that tell a story, because they are passive readers of texts, they are unfamiliar with the language, and their reading is complicated by the author's style of expression. Put another way, students lack purpose in reading content, and their reading of science, mathematics, history, and other subjects is interfered with by technical vocabulary and concept load. Moreover, they have difficulties with the ways information and ideas are expressed. It is in these areas that the content teacher can provide real reading help.

Teachers want students to master the content of their subjects. One of the ways to achieve this objective is to help students to complete reading assignments in and out of school. This assistance may take different forms but will include opportunities for students to strengthen and apply word, comprehension, and reading-study skills that they use in acquiring information. The most helpful feature of guidance will be its integration with subject learning.

Surveying Content Materials

Students should learn how books they will be using are organized and what special features they contain. They will be able to use these materials more efficiently if they study their organization and parts, and they will gain an overview of their contents, a knowledge of which will prepare them for reading and studying.

A first step is to become aware of a book's contents. The titles on covers and title pages intended for high school use are superimposed on illustrations which suggest areas the content covers. For example, one science textbook contains on the cover a series of photos of land surfaces and sky taken from space.[1] On the title page are other photos of natural phenomena. On the cover of an American history textbook is a bust of Washington, and on the title page is a scene of a covered wagon on a dirt path and one of the early railroad trains traveling through an uninhabited part of the country.[2] Students might speculate about a book's contents from the title and illustrations and then verify their ideas by examining the table of contents.

Next, students may obtain information about the book's organization from the table of contents and any features the book might contain. Many books are divided into sections or units with related chapters under each; other tables of contents not only provide this breakdown but also include the

1. *Investigating the Earth*, Earth Science Curriculum Project (Boston: Houghton Mifflin, 1967).
2. Lewis P. Todd and Merle Curti, *Rise of the American Nation*, 2d ed. (New York: Harcourt, Brace and World, 1966).

major subheads in each chapter. Special features, such as a list of maps and charts, boxed excerpts of historical documents, or a pronunciation guide, will be indicated. These and other contents should be discussed so that students understand why the author included them and how they could be used.

The organization of the book will be understood better if students examine a few chapters and their parts to determine if they are designed uniformly (this is usually the case). Any unusual typographical features such as marginal notations or colored type faces should be noted and their purposes understood. Some books provide an introduction or summary, together with questions to guide the reader and check his comprehension. Why they are included and how they could be used to advantage should be known too. Finally, many authors speak directly to students through a preface that explains why the book was written and what might be gained from reading it. All this background information enables students to approach the material with greater preparation and precision and consequently makes them better able to deal with the content.

Providing a Purpose in Reading

Reading with a purpose is more efficient than reading without one, for the power of motives to influence learning is considerable. Students who read with a purpose are thinking about what they read instead of merely receiving information that they are supposed to digest. The active reader has a problem to solve; the passive reader is a receptacle for facts.

Students who read actively discover that the way in which they read is governed by their purpose in reading. If they are reading technical material with which they are unfamiliar and which they must discuss at a later date, they may have to reread certain passages and reduce their reading rate. If they are seeking the causes of the American Revolution, they will not approach their history text in the same way they do when scanning its pages for the name of the victorious general at the Battle of the Marne. In each instance, the type of material, together with the purpose for reading, determine the technique for reading.

Purposes for reading in content fields will not have to be completely teacher-inspired if students have been participating in a variety of activities that are stimulating and thought-provoking. Teachers who are experimenting with the problem approach to learning find that motives for reading content flow naturally from such an organizational pattern. A group of students considering social problems facing the United States today may wish to trace the origins of these problems and the progress toward their solutions. Immediately a variety of questions arise from the original problems:

1. Who were some of the people who pioneered social legislation in the United States?
2. How do federal, state, and local governments cooperate to eliminate slums in large cities and small communities?
3. Why did federal and state governments enact minimum-wage laws?

These and other questions that are formulated by class and teacher provide reasons for the students to read their content materials with purpose.

And such an approach is a far cry from the one that requires students "to read the next chapter for tomorrow and be ready to answer questions" with no reason given.

Reading science textbooks becomes more meaningful if answers to problems are sought. How many of us have looked with awe as an airplane taxied down the runway, rose swiftly, and disappeared into the distance? The marvel of flight can be explained in simple terms but how many pupils truly understand its underlying principles? A trip to an airport or the viewing of a film can generate questions such as these:

1. Why do airplanes require long take-offs?
2. What function does the propeller perform?
3. Why are wings of airplanes curved?
4. Does a jet airplane operate on the same principles as a propeller-driven airplane?

Students who are interested in finding answers to such questions have a purpose for reading. They may find that their textbook answers only some of their questions and that they must turn to other sources. They may realize also that they do not fully understand some of the principles and need to have these clarified. Class discussion, demonstration, and experimentation are natural outgrowths of this kind of reading.

Students may establish their own purposes for reading content by making special note of the headings and subheadings and converting them into questions. These heads will also suggest ideas that are related to the topic with which they deal and with which they may have some familiarity, and these may be stated in the form of questions.

Below are examples of headings with some questions (in parentheses) each suggests. The first (A) is drawn from a mathematics textbook and the second (B) from an English textbook containing a chapter on the elements of basic sentence structure.

Students should examine the headings in their own texts and reference sources and discuss what questions and ideas they trigger. When they do independent reading, these procedures will serve as a means by which they can establish their own purposes for reading.

A[3]

1. Numbers and Numerals
   (Are these terms synonymous?)
2. The Real Numbers; the Number Line
   (What is a real number? Why are numbers called real? Is a number line like a time line?)
3. Comparing Numbers; Statements
   (How may numbers be compared? Under what circumstances might numbers be compared? Is a math statement similar to a sentence?)

3. Mary P. Dolciani and others, *Modern School Mathematics, Algebra 1* (1967), pp. 1, 5. Reprinted with the permission of Houghton Mifflin Co.

B[4]
1. What Grammar Is
   (What is grammar?)
2. Basic Sentence Structure
   (Of what does a basic sentence consist?)
3. A Noun Phrase
   (What is a noun phrase? Are all noun phrases alike? How is a noun phrase different from other phrases?)

Regardless of the subject, students are expected to read and retain facts and ideas. Even with daily assignments in the textbook, teachers should provide some guides to reading. These may be questions or outlines that are prepared before reading. Students need to know whether they must concentrate on important details, broad ideas, or both; questions and outlines offer them guides to the way in which they are to approach the content.

Teaching Technical Vocabulary

One of the major responsibilities of subject-matter teachers is to acquaint students with the specialized and technical vocabulary associated with their field, and the responsibility is just as great for the home economics teacher as it is for the science or social studies teacher. A large number of vocabulary studies have shown that inability to deal with the meaning of words is a major cause of students' failure to understand what they read in literature, mathematics, science, and social studies.[5]

The vocabulary of mathematics includes such words as *hypotenuse, quadratic, ratio, power, base, root, axis, exponent, complement,* and *factor.* It is not difficult to understand what problems these words can present, for several of them have special meanings that students ordinarily do not associate with them. Students may know the meaning of "balance of *power*" or "*exponent* of jazz," but now they must learn new meanings for these two words. The comprehension of mere mathematical definitions is a formidable task; the development of mathematical concepts requires even greater insights.

Science vocabulary is ever increasing in size and complexity. Words such as *radioactivity, athodyd, neutrons, parity,* and *betatron* are newer additions to the list of those words of less-recent origin, such as *convection, oxidation, metamorphic,* and *chromosomes,* with which high school students have to cope. While students are likely to have heard or read these words many times, few of them really understand the ideas they represent. Textbook authors have recognized the vocabulary problems that science presents

4. John S. Hand and others, *Power in English: Experiences in Language* (1972), pp. 222, 224, 226. Reprinted with the permission of Laidlaw Brothers, a division of Doubleday & Company, Inc.
5. Mary C. Serra, "The Concept Burden of Instructional Materials," *Elementary School Journal* 53 (May 1953): 508-512; George Mallinson and others, "The Reading Difficulty of Some Recent Textbooks for Science," *School Science and Mathematics* 57 (May 1957): 364-366; Milton D. Jacobson, "Reading Difficulties of Physics and Chemistry Textbooks in Use in Minnesota," doctoral diss., Univ. of Minnesota, 1961; Russell G. Stauffer, "A Vocabulary Study Comparing Reading, Arithmetic, Health and Science Texts," *Reading Teacher* 20 (Nov. 1966): 141-147.

and frequently define difficult and complex terms within the text itself. But teachers must not assume that meaning difficulties are completely resolved in this way.

Teachers of other content subjects are faced with similar vocabulary problems. Home economics teachers have students who cannot successfully follow a recipe because it either contains words that are new or uses words in ways that are different from those students know. History teachers have students who do not comprehend the meaning of many concrete words and who are confused by the large number of abstract words that take on new connotations as times change. Teachers of any subject can compile a long list of terms whose meanings are either only partly familiar or completely unknown to their students.

Any time a teacher spends clarifying meanings is bound to increase students' responsiveness to the information about which they are reading. Specialized vocabulary should be introduced in a meaningful context; using examples and illustrations will enhance their understanding of those unfamiliar words. If teachers did nothing more than teach this vocabulary *before* students read the pages that contained them, their comprehension of the material would be increased significantly.

Clarifying Concepts

Clarifying concepts is a major responsibility of the subject-matter teachers who present them. In this area of reading instruction, the content teacher is better prepared to deal with abstract ideas than is the teacher who is responsible for improving general reading ability. While the latter might present such concepts as *balance of trade* and *gold content of the dollar*, he would not ordinarily possess the knowledge to make these concepts as clear as would the economics teacher who, through training and experience, deals continually with these abstract ideas.

Textbook writers often explain the concepts that fill their books and may add meaning to words through pictures, diagrams, and examples. Again, teachers should not assume that concepts so treated are understood; many students will need more help than their text contains. These concepts should be studied *before* reading is undertaken. A few writers suggest that the teacher take several days to develop understanding of difficult concepts. If, after the initial reading, further clarification is made, less time may be needed, but in the end the nature of the material and the sophistication of the group will dictate how much time will be needed. When a text is overloaded with unknown concepts, perhaps the teacher can substitute a less-difficult book on the same topic. However it is done, efforts to build student understanding will pay high dividends in increased comprehension and interpretation.

Experience is another way to make concepts more meaningful, and students who have had first-hand experiences with ideas are more likely to understand them than those who have to depend on words. Certainly students who have lived on farms and cultivated acreage have a much clearer idea of the amount of land the Homestead Act provided settlers than students who have spent their lives in apartment houses. Similarly, city dwellers are better able to appreciate the marvels of underground rapid transit or the wonders of a skyline.

Teachers can enrich their students' background by providing real experiences for them, and opportunities exist for every content area. Concrete forms have served as excellent models for mathematical concepts, while classroom living has strengthened students' appreciation of social and political concepts. No amount of words can convey what occurs in some of the more complicated processes in science and industry. Take, for example, the refining of gasoline. It is no mean task to help students understand what takes place from the time the petroleum reaches the refinery to the time gasoline is ready for distribution. Some students actually have seen this process through the medium of perfectly scaled mechanical models that permit observers to trace the flow of oil through pipes and equipment, while a running commentary explains what is occurring. Most schools are not so situated that students may be taken to such a display, but those that are certainly are not taking full advantage of community resources if they ignore its existence. First-hand experiences are preferred, generally, to vicarious ones, but motion picture films can be used with students who do not have access to actual demonstrations. Even photographs and diagrams are superior to mere words as conveyors of these ideas. Teachers should use any pertinent means that will broaden and extend student experiences in order to make complex concepts more meaningful.

Surveying Chapter Content

Surveying a book to assess its organization and features can be useful, similar to studying its table of contents. Likewise, surveying a single chapter will provide an overview of its contents and facilitate the reader's comprehension of it. The procedure for surveying a chapter is a simple one and consists of a few steps:

1. Read the introduction and relate its contents to what is already known about it.
2. Study the major headings and subheadings to determine what areas of the main topic will be covered.
3. Examine any pictorial aids for additional information about the topic.
4. Read any summary and relate its contents to what has been learned about the topic.

Naturally, not every book will contain an introduction and summary statement, but many will. In some books the introductory material is not labeled as such but precedes the first major heading; in others it may be found in the preliminary material before each unit consisting of two or more chapters.

The examples of an introduction, major headings, and chapter summary shown in Figure 5-1 demonstrate how much can be learned about a topic by surveying a chapter.

Figure 5-1.   Preliminary Chapter Survey

CHAPTER

27   The "Square Deal" Stimulates Reform

1897–1909

THE FORTUNES of nations as well as of individuals sometimes change with bewildering rapidity. But men have no certain way of foreseeing when change will come or of predicting its directions.

The administration of President McKinley, from 1897 to 1901, is a case in point.

Who on McKinley's inauguration day could have foreseen that within a little more than a year the nation would be at war with Spain in a conflict called the Spanish-American War, and that before McKinley's four years in office were over the United States would become a great colonial power with possessions in the Pacific and the Caribbean? (You will read about these striking international developments in Unit Nine.)

And who, looking at the solid triumph of big business in the election of 1896, would have dared to predict that within six years a new reform movement, the Progressive movement, would begin to sweep the country and a progressive President and Congress would draw up new rules for the conduct of business?

The reform movements of the early 1900's were really a continuation, on a broader front, of earlier efforts to preserve and strengthen democracy in the new industrial age. As you will see, however, the progressives also tackled other problems, including the increasingly serious issue of the conservation of the nation's natural resources.

AS THE STORY DEVELOPS

1. The Progressive movement brings reforms to government.
2. Theodore Roosevelt promotes a "square deal" for all people.
3. Theodore Roosevelt stimulates conservation of natural resources.

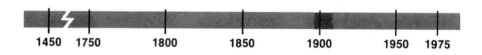

| 1450 | 1750 | 1800 | 1850 | 1900 | 1950 | 1975 |

TRACING THE MAIN IDEAS

The victory of the Republicans in the election of 1896 broke the strength of the Populist movement. With the triumph of the Republicans and with the returning of prosperity, many people concluded that the reform movement had lost its force.

But the reform movement was not dead. On the contrary, during the opening years of the 1900's it gained new life in the Progressive movement. Guided by the progressives, including President Theodore Roosevelt, the relationship of government and business began to change. In earlier times—until, say, the 1880's—the government's role had been, in general, that of a referee who stood on the side lines and was called in only when one of the players disobeyed the rules. Now, in the twentieth century, the government was beginning to take a more active part, to accept more responsibility for regulating the activities of business in the interest of the public welfare. For this changing conception of the role of government in the new industrial age, both Republicans and Democrats were responsible.

As you will see in the next chapter, the reforms started under President Roosevelt were continued under the Republican administration of President Taft and, to an even greater degree, under the Democratic administration of President Wilson.

From Lewis P. Todd and Merle Curti, *Rise of the American Nation*, 2d ed. (New York: Harcourt, Brace and World, 1966), pp. 520, 534. Copyright ©1966 and reprinted with the permission of Harcourt Brace Jovanovich, Inc. In this textbook the major headings are listed at the end of the introduction and repeated as titles of the different sections of the chapter.

Additional information about the "Square Deal" is given in sub-headings such as "The Australian Ballot," "Woman Suffrage," "Direct Election of Senators," "Roosevelt as 'trust buster,'" "Laws protecting public health," "Natural resources are wasted," and "The Newlands Reclamation Act." Moreover, the chapter contains cartoons (one shows Theodore Roosevelt placing one foot on a bear, labeled "Bad Trusts," that he had shot) and photographs which fill in some of the details of the topics and subtopics. Some students might be able to contribute more information about the topic which could be related to what they know about present conditions in government and business. Students certainly will be better prepared to read with understanding about this period in American history than if they plunged into the chapter without this preliminary survey of it.

It isn't enough to inform students that they should survey a chapter before reading it, or indicate how to proceed with a survey. Teacher and students should survey a chapter together and discuss what they have learned from it. With some groups it may be necessary to survey a few chapters from one or more books before students learn the procedure and appreciate its value.

TEACHING CONTENT THROUGH READING

For some students, the textbooks they use are on the borderline between their instructional and frustration levels. For other students, the materials as a rule do not pose major problems since they are appropriate for instructional purposes; nevertheless, some do encounter occasional difficulties when portions of the books contain vocabulary and concepts with which they are unfamiliar and do not adequately understand. In classes where textbook study is stressed, it is important that all students acquire basic information from them. In classes that rely on multiple sources where students study selected problems, teachers will want to be certain that all have mastered this basic information.

One of the ways teachers may help students learn from books is to guide the reading as a *directed reading lesson*. This directed reading lesson, of selected portions of the book, may be approached in the following phases:

1. Preparing for reading
   a. Relating student experiences to the purpose(s) for reading the content.
   b. Introducing vocabulary for pronunciation and/or meaning
   c. Clarifying concepts
   d. Establishing purpose(s) for reading
2. Silent reading
3. Discussing content and developing skills
   a. Checking comprehension
   b. Verifying information
4. Application

The readiness concept has been applied to beginning, or primary reading, but its influences may be felt at each instructional level. No student can fully profit from any instruction if he is not ready to participate in it. Just as he is not able to master principles of algebra without a knowledge of arithmetic fundamentals, so he is not ready to respond satisfactorily to concepts if he lacks prior experiences with them or fails to see any relationship between new learning and what he already knows.

The first phase of the directed reading lesson, then, is *readiness*, or preparing to study the content to be learned. The experiences of the readers are related to the content that is to be covered and their purpose(s) for reading it. Students are encouraged to discuss and share what they know about the topic, and the teacher may give students the benefit of his experiences. This background information serves the purpose of intimately involving the students with the content and preparing them for what is to follow. Presenting unfamiliar vocabulary and clarifying difficult concepts make reading less burdensome and more meaningful than it would be without such advance treatment. The readiness stage is completed when a major purpose for reading is set by guiding questions. If the lesson is forty-five minutes long, approximately five to ten minutes should be devoted to readiness. Some specialists suggest that longer periods of time should be spent preparing students for reading and, if necessary, that the actual reading be done outside class.

The second phase of the directed lesson is *silent reading*. (Oral reading is reserved for audience situations and is preceded by some preparation.) During this reading the teacher is able to confer briefly with those students who need additional help with vocabulary or concepts. The actual time spent reading is not great since lengthy assignments are reserved for out-of-class reading.

The third stage is *discussing* the material in terms of the larger and smaller purposes. This is the time when the teacher discovers to what extent the students have grasped the principles underlying the factual details and what he must do to help students master them. If the discussion reveals that students have misunderstood some sections of the text or misinterpreted information, then these sections should be reread silently or orally. Another reason for rereading portions of the text is to clarify issues or confirm judgments. A point may be proved by reading a few sentences only; one student might read them aloud while the others listen.

During this phase of directed reading, word, comprehension or study skills might be reinforced if students would benefit from their treatment. Perhaps a group of students needs practice determining the meaning of words from their parts, and there are compound or other words in the material whose parts do carry meaning. Students can identify the parts and decide what these words mean. Another group of students might need some help in recognizing and using context clues, and students could seek clues and use them to explain the meaning of some words in the passages. The material might contain a few paragraphs with unstated main ideas and these could be reread to determine what they are.

These kinds of reading activities serve to meet students' specific needs and offer practice in using skills they have been taught. Some teachers have introduced a skill for the first time during this phase of the directed reading lesson since there is no more appropriate time than when students are involved in an assignment and the instruction is tied to the content they are studying.

The final stage of the lesson consists of *using the information* gained from reading. What form application will take depends on the nature of the content and the aim of the lesson. A chart may be drawn, comparisons made, models constructed, scripts written, or plays acted. If knowledge integration is accepted as the ultimate goal of the reading process, the teacher will impress on students the need to use what they have learned. If any justification for teaching knowledge application is needed, what has been said in earlier chapters applies: Transfer of learning is facilitated by teaching for transfer and by noting elements that are common to different settings.

There is another way to treat the lesson. It is to combine the survey techniques indicated earlier with the steps that have been enumerated. This process includes not only using the headings to establish purposes for reading, but also directing attention to introductions and illustrations to obtain some general impressions about the content and establish a set for reading it. An outline of a lesson that combines the two techniques follows the developmental lesson in social studies. Its format is somewhat different from the latter although it combines all the essential elements of the directed lesson.

Directed Reading in Science

By no stretch of the imagination does textbook reading constitute the total science program or replace experimentation and the inductive thinking that grows out of discovery. But textbook reading does provide the basis for common understandings and leads to laboratory experiences that are the heart of any sound science program.

An outline of a lesson that combines the techniques of reading and science is presented here to show how a teacher might approach a science textbook. The lesson is based on content found in most general science texts. It is offered merely as a suggestion; two teachers may use different paths within identical frameworks to reach similar goals.

LESSON: How Airplanes Fly

1. *Preparation for Reading*

   Relating experiences of students to content and purpose(s) for reading
   Students: Discuss take-offs and landings observed on visit to airport; those who have flown are encouraged to describe aircraft and flight briefly; teacher may relate personal experiences.
   Teacher: Introduces model airplane and demonstrates what happens when it is released; seeks explanation from class.

Students: Respond to demonstration on the basis of previous experiences.

Introducing vocabulary and clarifying concepts
Teacher: Writes technical vocabulary and some concepts on chalkboard; these are presented as natural outgrowth of discussion; meanings are clarified through the use of model, diagrams, demonstrations, questions.

a. The *fuselage* is the body of the airplane.
b. The air *whirls in eddies* around the wings.
c. The *ailerons, rudder,* and *elevators* control the flight of the craft.
d. *Streams of air* flow over and under the wings.
e. *Thrust* is produced by the propeller.

Setting the purpose for reading
Students and Teacher: Raise questions to be answered.

MAJOR PURPOSE: *How does an airplane fly?*
SUBSIDIARY PURPOSES (related to major purpose):
What forces must be overcome if the airplane is to become airborne?
Why are the top surfaces of wings curved?
What happens to the air as it passes over and under the wings?
How is the flight of airplanes controlled?

2. *Silent Reading* (based on major and subsidiary purposes)

Teacher: Assists students who need help in vocabulary or who have questions about the material.

3. *Discussion* (in terms of purposes for reading)

Students and Teacher: Discuss ideas obtained from reading.
Students: Demonstrate what happens as air moves rapidly; formulate principles governing action.

Rereading (for a new purpose)
Students: One student reads aloud section that shows what happens when rapidly moving air moves over the top of an airplane wing while second student demonstrates.

Skill Development (based on need or appropriateness of material)

Students and Teacher: Identify cause and effect relationships as they relate to principles of flight; skim a passage to determine how level flight is maintained.

4. *Application*

Students: List principles underlying flight and read to compare method of creating thrust in jet-driven planes with that of propeller-driven planes.

Directed Reading in Social Studies

Some social studies teachers follow the *unit* approach, whereby groups of students select topics for which they do extensive reading in a variety of sources. The basic textbook may be read by all students in order to secure a common background for the larger area into which the topics fit. Other teachers continue to follow a program in which the textbook is the main source of information. In either case, some guidance is generally required for textbook reading. The framework into which this guidance fits may be the same as for science or another content.

What follows here is an outline of a lesson ordinarily covered in a senior high school American history course. The first part of the lesson prepares the students for reading. Students are asked to recall what they already know about the topic, and discussion usually reveals the extent to which they can relate their experiences to the new problems and helps to develop a "set" for reading. American history textbooks may use terminology that is unknown to students and is not explained in the text. When the meanings of such terms are clarified before reading, chances are that student understanding of the content will be greatly increased. Since the students are helping to develop the purposes for reading, they have a stake in the outcome that is likely to assure highly motivated reading.

The first reading and the discussion that follows are based on the major and smaller purposes. About ten minutes of a forty-five-minute period is devoted to reading and more time to considering the factual information and its implications. Complete mastery of a given amount of material cannot be expected after one short reading; discussion should reveal the areas in which more attention is needed. A second reading of portions of the text is recommended where gaps in understanding are evident or new ideas are contained. As with the directed reading lesson in science, promoting skill development can be integrated with the discussion of the content. Even if students do not seem to require special help in using word-identification, comprehension, or study skills, practicing them will sharpen their abilities and enable them to apply the skills in materials which do challenge their best efforts to comprehend the content.

The final stage of the lesson consists of using what has been gained and applying it in other settings. No single form of application is recommended over another. The purposes of the group and the nature of the content help to determine its suitability.

LESSON: Government Regulation of Business

1. *Preparation for Reading*

   Relating experiences of students to content and purpose(s) for reading
   Students and Teacher: Discuss need for school and local regulations that control actions of individuals; recent occurrences in which government interfered with business operations are brought up.

   Vocabulary and concept clarification

Teacher: Selects from text words and ideas that require some explanation or expansion:
   a. big business versus small business
   b. "trust-busting"
   c. combinations in restraint of trade
   d. "muckrakers"

Setting the purpose for reading
Students and Teacher; Prepare questions for reading.
   a. (MAJOR PURPOSE): How has the federal government attempted to control the activities of business?
   b. (SUBSIDIARY PURPOSES related to major purpose):
   Under what broad powers does the federal government regulate business?
   Why was it necessary to pass laws that regulated certain business activities?
   What laws were passed to protect the health of the people?
   What laws were enacted to eliminate unfair business practices?

2. *Silent Reading* (for specific purposes)

   Students: Refer to questions that have been placed on chalkboard and read to find answers.
   Teacher: Provides help in reading to any student who requires it: how to pronounce words; discover word meaning: select pertinent ideas and details.

3. *Discussion*

   Students and Teacher: Discuss factual content, draw inferences, and react to ideas.

   Rereading (for different purposes)
   Students: Skim and scan material to find out:
   a. attitudes of Theodore Roosevelt and Warren Harding toward business
   b. the meaning of "interlocking directorates"
   c. attitude of the cartoonist toward government interference in business.

   Additional Skill Development
   Students and teacher: Complete partial outline of content

4. *Application*

   Students: List pros and cons of government regulation of business; team interviews with local business representatives to discover how latter feel about government regulation of business and how they are affected by it.

Directed Lesson Plus Survey

Purpose: To find out how New York endeavors to make better citizens of its people.

1. *Relating experiences to purpose*
   Why do we need good citizens?
   How do parents help make better citizens of their children?
   How do schools help make better citizens of children?
   How do community groups. . . .?

2. *Survey introduction*
   Read the introduction to determine the meaning of "New York Conserves Human . . . Resources."

3. *Reading heading:* "New York Takes Pride in Its System of Education"
   What kind of information might we expect to read about?
   What information do the *photos* in the section suggest?

   Concepts and vocabulary:
   a *Board of Regents*
   an *institution of higher education*
   The State Education Department *regulates professions* such as medicine and engineering. (context clue)
   Centralized schools have taken the place of one-room schools. (context clue)
   Read this section to find out how New York endeavors to make better citizens through education.

4. *Discussion of Content*

5. *Survey next section:* "New York Safeguards the Health of Its Citizens"
   Concepts and vocabulary: None
   Read to find out how New York endeavors to make better citizens through its health program.

6. *Survey following section:* New York Helps People in Trouble"
   How does New York help people in trouble? Does this help to make better citizens?

7. *Discussion of Content*

   Skill development: Reread headings to summarize how the state helps its people to become better citizens.

8. *Application*
   Find out what state services are available in the community and area. Discuss with parents and others how they feel about paying taxes to help make better citizens of all the people.

Directed Reading in English

The basic structure of the directed reading lesson may be followed for reading in any subject, if the material warrants it. In the sample lesson outlined below, the four phases are included but they are not treated in exactly the same way as in the previous sample lessons. The material on which the lesson is based does not contain vocabulary whose pronunciation or meaning is likely to be unknown. Therefore, there is no provision in the lesson for dealing with these words. Also note that there are no subsidiary purposes to guide the students' reading, since the text is limited to an explanation of a single topic. Moreover, no provision for rereading selected portions is included: rereading is useful if students fail to understand or need to verify information. These variations underscore the importance of adjusting any procedure to fit the learning requirements of students.

LESSON: Understanding Surface and Deep Structure

1. *Preparation for Reading*

Relating experiences of students to the purpose for reading
Student and Teacher: Give examples of language usage in which one or more words express a complete idea.

Clarification of concepts
Teacher: Selects and discusses any that might not be understood.
a. structure of a sentence

Setting the purpose for reading
Teacher: Read this section to learn the difference between the surface structure of a sentence and the deep structure of the same sentence.

2. *Silent Reading*

3. *Discussion*

Students and Teacher: Discuss difference between surface and deep structures; analyze sentences to determine whether they express surface or deep structures.

Skill development
Students and Teacher: From information gained through reading and discussion they draw an appropriate conclusion about the structural characteristics of sentences.

4. *Application*

Students: Collect sample sentences from other sources that express surface structures and convert them to deep structures.

Directed Reading in Physical and Health Education

Physical and health education teachers might appear to be those least likely to need to help students with textbook and outside readings. However, more and more of them are enrolling in courses intended for teachers who have never had an undergraduate course in the teaching of reading. Several have confided to me that they have become involved with the problem of reading for purely selfish reasons — in order to help students maintain their eligibility to play football or basketball. These same teachers have come to realize that, aside from this motivation for learning how to deal with some aspects of reading, they too, like other teachers, must face these problems as they assign students readings in health and personal hygiene.

The same kinds of problems found in social studies and science books are met in materials prepared for hygiene classes. In one twelve-page chapter on food such terms as the following appear: *vitamin-B complex, calorimeter, oxidation, deficiency disease, carotene, roughage, respiratory infections, international units, hulls of grain, nutrient, milligrams, pellagra, and thyroxine.* How many of these terms are really understood by typical high school students? Some are explained briefly in the text, but others are used merely to discuss the nature and problems of diet. It is necessary to deal with them as concretely as possible if students are to acquire more than just vague notions about them.

Much information is packed into those twelve pages. Is all this important information? Obviously, some ideas should be stressed over others. Students who know in advance the purposes for which they are to read the chapter not only are more motivated to read but also know how they must read to achieve their purposes. One section may be of much greater importance than another and may thus require a less-hurried reading. Others, because of their complexity, may demand several readings. Even though students have been prepared to read the chapter, discussion of the content may reveal misunderstandings that can be removed by further reading. Some hygiene teachers may be doing these very things without realizing that they are teaching reading. Let's follow the reading outline prepared by one hygiene teacher for a lesson about food.

1. *Preparation for Reading*
   Relating experiences of students to content and purpose(s) for reading
   Students and Teacher: Each lists the foods and the quantities eaten for breakfast, lunch, and dinner during the previous day; several are compared and tentatively rated by the group.

   Vocabulary and concept clarification
   Students and Teacher; Complex terms are pulled from previous discussion and textbook and presented in context:
   a. The number of *calories* required daily by individuals varies with their age, weight, sex, and the amount and type of work they do.
   b. The *oxidation* that occurs within the body may be compared to the burning of fuel.
   c. Many vitamins are *synthesized* in the laboratory.
   d. Deficiencies of vitamin K may affect the *coagulation* of the blood.

   Purpose for reading
   a. (MAJOR PURPOSE): To determine whether our personal diets meet bodily needs.

b. (SUBSIDIARY PURPOSES):
   1. Of what elements do foods consist?
   2. Of what value are these elements?
   3. Which foods contain these elements?
   4. What are our own personal daily requirements for each of them?

2. *Silent Reading*
   Students: Read section to find information that will permit them to evaluate their own diets; questions serve as guides to their reading.
   Teacher: Circulates among students and provides help with pronunciation, word meanings, and the like, as needed.

3. *Discussion*
   Students and Teacher: Ideas contained in section are clarified and expanded; questions are raised in terms of the group's purposes for reading.

   Rereading
   Students: Refer to calorie and elements charts to establish daily nutritional needs; each student composes his own diet with these requirements.
   Skill development: Teacher lists *effects* of diet deficiencies; students supply *causes*.

4. *Application*
   Students and Teacher: Plan a weekly menu of foods they prefer that meet their bodily needs; comparisons to be drawn.

Directed Reading in Industrial Education

Industrial arts teachers have the same kinds of opportunities to help students as they study topics associated with wood, metal, plastic, electricity, and leather. In fact, in senior high schools they often find that some of their students do not read nearly as well as do typical students in other classes. In schools where special tracks are established for students of different abilities, it is not uncommon to place the less academically talented student in a program that provides many shop experiences. We are all familiar with systems that have vocational schools to teach various trades. Many students in these schools are weak in reading, and any help they receive in reading textbooks and other sources of information will pay dividends in increased understanding and interest.

Here are some excerpts on wood finishing that have been selected from a textbook intended for classroom use.[6] Many students would have difficulty understanding exactly what they meant without some explanation and demonstration:

> . . . and swan neck or concave scrapers are suitable for convex or concave surfaces.

6. Louis Newkirk, *General Shop for Everyone* (Boston: D. C. Heath, 1959), p. 78.

The cutting edge of the scraper is turned or burred so that it resembles a small hook extending across the cutting edge.
. . . it produces fine downy shavings. . . .

Industrial arts teachers can prepare students for reading in their field
much in the same way as do other subject-matter teachers. They can pull out
of the text vocabulary whose meaning students are not likely to know and
ideas that require clarification. They can guide students by giving them a
reading goal to achieve as well as by directing their reading step by step.
They can help individual students overcome some word-identification and
meaning difficulties and provide opportunities for discussing the material in
terms of the group's purpose for reading. They can arrange demonstrations
for which rereading of selected passages may be necessary. Finally, they can
provide opportunities that allow students to apply what they read. The four
steps in a directed reading lesson — preparation, reading, discussion, and
application — can be adapted by teachers of sheetmetal, woodworking, and
other shops to make material meaningful.

Study Guides

We have seen how directed reading lessons help students overcome
some of the difficulties they meet in reading content. Reading guides provide
another form of assistance. One guide helps students to focus attention on
reading skills; the second type helps them to identify information that must
be mastered.

A *process* guide suggests to students how they might read some content to acquire information. Once the purpose for reading has been established, students could undertake to satisfy it. Those who have reading
weaknesses might not be able to cope with some of their difficulties unless
they receive more help from the teacher. The process guide provides this
help by pinpointing the skills needed to overcome difficulties as well as suggesting solutions. Such a guide for some science content follows.[7]

Process Guide

Creatures of the depths. The diversity of organisms *Note cause*
usually decreases as the depths increases. Number of *effect*
individuals also decreases with depth, because life
below the photosynthetic zone depends on food drifting
down from above. And in general, the greater the
depth, the less the food supply. With increasing depth *What does*
there are also changes in the general characteristics of *also signal?*
the organisms, although the limits of the zones in which
different organisms occur are not sharp.

The peculiar deep-sea creatures shown in Figure
9.28 are usually 500m or more below the surface
during the daytime. They may come nearer the sur-

7. Marston Bates and others, *High School Biology*, BSCS Green Version (Chicago:
Rand McNally, 1963), pp. 280-281. Reprinted with the permission of the Biological
Sciences Curriculum Study.

face at night or at times when the cold waters of the depths well up toward the surface. Apparently, their vertical distribution is controlled by light and temperature as well as by water pressure.

Is this statement a generalization?

In the eternal night of the depths of the sea, most animals have become either black or dark red and have developed increasingly sensitive eyes. In the unending darkness of caves and underground streams, however, animals tend to become white and blind. This difference is associated with another factor — *bioluminescence.* In the depths of the oceans, many animals have the ability to produce light in their bodies. But bioluminescence is not found in the blackness of caves.

Note contrast

Where is the context clue?

This curious difference may be a biological accident. Perhaps cave animals lack bioluminescence simply because no bioluminescent animal (except a New Zealand glow-worm) ever got started on the path of cave evolution. Most permanent cave dwellers live in fresh water, and as far as we know there is no bioluminescence in any fresh-water animals. But the surface waters of the seas contain many kinds of bioluminescent organisms. If surface organisms evolved special adaptations for living in the depths, we can see that bioluminescence might be retained or developed further. This of course, does not explain why bioluminescence is common among marine animals, rare among land animals (present in fireflies and a few other things), and absent among freshwater animals.

Bioluminescence among deep-sea animals may serve one or more of several different functions: as a lure for prey, as an aid to escape, as a mark of recognition. The angler fish dangles a light in front of its mouth; apparently this lures unwary victims closer. Deep-sea shrimp and one kind of squid give off clouds of luminescent secretion when disturbed. Patterns of luminescence on the body may serve as marks of recognition in the depths, just as color patterns do among many organisms in the world of light. In some cases the lights may serve to illuminate the field of vision. At least this seems the most likely explanation for the development in some species of large light organs in front of each eye.

Main idea?

Details

Most of the deep-sea fish are small, minnow-sized creatures with fantastic shapes, enormous mouths, and fragile skeletons.

There is a tendency toward long, slender forms not only among fishes but also among invertebrates: crabs with spidery legs; shrimp with long, delicate antennae; starfish with thin, whiplike "arms." These last — the brittle stars — have been found on the bottom at great depths.

tend ency

The guides to reading appear in the margin. Note how each item in the guide lines up with the text of the passage. In some cases, there are questions that direct the student's attention to the way in which he should read (What does *also* signal? Main idea?) At other times the guide tells the student information to use (Note contrast. Details.) This guide covers several skills areas: paragraph structure, inferences, selection and evaluation, and context clues. A guide that pays special attention to fewer areas or just to one can be prepared in the same way. If a passage stressed comparisons and contrasts, then a guide to highlight these elements could be developed for students who needed this kind of help.

Below is a sample process guide that directs student attention to one specific skill which, in this case, is recognizing words which signal time order or a sequential presentation of ideas. The content is drawn from an English textbook.[8]

Not Too Big, Not Too Heavy

    This is a chapter about writing reports. If you look up the origin of the word *report,* you'll find that it means to "carry back." Later on, near the end of this chapter, you're going to be asked to write a report. What you'll do is investigate a particular subject and "carry back" what you've found. You'll do some reading in several sources — books, magazines, encyclopedias, that sort of thing — and take notes. Then you'll assemble these notes into a composition for someone else to read.

What words or phrases in the para- graph suggest time order?

    A report contains mainly "second-hand" knowledge. It's not about something that happened directly to you. Usually it's about something that lies outside of your experience. And because your report does not deal in personal experiences, the language you use is imper- sonal and somewhat formal.

    Actually, the writing is one of the last steps you take in putting together a report. One of the first steps is deciding what to write about. Usually, you will be given a general *subject* to report on — space exploration, fashions in dress, the search for a cancer cure, pop music, political reforms, the automobile of the future, whatever. Your subject might even be a person — someone who's done important things or led an inter- esting life.

What words in this sen- tence pre- pare you for a new idea?

    Once you've got your subject, your search for a *topic* can get under way. Mainly, this involves scaling down your subject to a manageable size. Say for example, that you are asked to write a report on the subject "political reforms" for a social studies class. Such a subject is too big and too heavy for a report of 500 to 700 words. But if you explore this subject a bit, you'll

More time words.

8. John S. Hand and others, *Power in English: Experiences in Language* (1972), pp. 28-29. Reprinted with the permission of Laidlaw Brothers, a division of Dou- bleday & Company, Inc.

find within it smaller subjects or topics. For instance, inside the subject "political reforms," there are topics like these:

1. extending the terms of congressmen from two to six years
2. redrawing the boundaries of the states
3. changing the residence requirements of voters

Any of these might make a suitable topic for a report.

Your next step would be to form a *controlling idea* for your report. That is, you make a statement about your topic. Say, for instance, you find that many people believe congressmen should be elected for the same length of time as senators. You might write a sentence like the following:

Another idea?

Many people believe that the terms for the members of the House are too short and should be extended.

This is your controlling idea. But, remember, as you put your report together, you may wish to rephrase this idea.

Process guides should not be needed for all the passages in a book, just as directed reading lessons are not ordinarily prepared for reading every section. Teachers and students could identify parts that appear to be more difficult than others and either duplicate them with the guides in the margin or just duplicate the guide items on strips of paper that can be placed alongside the text.

The *content* guide suggests what information the student should concentrate on and might indicate where needed information will be found. In effect, the guide establishes subsidiary purposes for reading. In addition, it may indicate reading assignments based upon students' abilities — that is, require one level of responses for poor readers and another level of responses for better readers. Since students would be required to respond to the items in the guide, it could replace some of the discussion that follows the reading.

The content guide may take different forms. The one that follows suggests to students that they read about several land biomes in their biology textbook and contrast them on the basis of their climate, vegetation, and animal life.[9]

BIOMES	CLIMATE	VEGETATION	ANIMAL LIFE
1. Tundra			
2. Taiga			
3. Middle-Latitude Deciduous Forest			
4. Tropical Rain Forest			

9. This guide is based on pp. 217-227 of Bates and others, *High School Biology* (1963).

This type of guide requires students to think about the information in a specified way, that is, how these land masses are different, instead of learning about each separately and not relating one set of information to another. Not only does the guide provide direction to students' reading, it also aids their learning by helping them to organize what they study.

The following content guide is taken from a U.S. history text:[10]

*1. What were some of the problems of the postwar period? (p. 745)
**2. Why did the Congress feel obliged to pass the "GI Bill of Rights"?
*3. What events led to the passage of the Taft-Hartley Act? What were its major provisions? (p. 746)
**4. Why did organized labor feel that the Taft-Hartley Act discriminated against it?
**5. Explain the essential difference between the views of the Democrats and Republicans in the 1948 election.
*6. What were some accomplishments of the "Fair Deal" administration? (p. 748)
*7. How did the government react to a possible threat to internal security? (p. 749)
**8. What constitutional guarantees might be violated by efforts to insure internal security?

*to be answered by all students
**optional questions

Item matching, sentence completion, and true-false responses may be used in addition to questions to direct students' reading.

Reading for Independent Study

In the first sections of this chapter, ways to help students read more efficiently and with greater comprehension were explained. These techniques included establishing purposes by converting headings into questions and surveying content to gain a general impression of what a chapter is about. These procedures can be combined with others to make it possible for students to comprehend and remember more of what they read. The strategy is called Survey Q3R, of which there are several variations but no major differences.[11]

The first part of the strategy is the *survey*. This corresponds to the chapter survey which was explained earlier and includes reading any introductions, summaries, major headings, and illustrations and reflecting upon the information gained.

Now for the next phase. Most students cannot retain all the important information in a chapter if they read it through without pausing. It is better that they read one section at a time and master its content before moving into the next section. Therefore, the Q refers to the conversion of the first major heading into one or more questions; the 3R means to *read, recite,* and

---

10. This guide is based on pp. 745-750 of Todd and Curti, *Rise of the American Nation*, 2d ed. (1966).
11. Francis P. Robinson, *Effective Study* (New York: Harper and Row, 1961).

review the content in the first section. Many sections contain *subheadings* and key sentences which state the main idea; these could also be converted into questions to guide the reader.

For example, the key sentence, "Wind and water cause soil erosion," can be converted into one or more questions, such as "What is soil erosion?" "Under what conditions do wind and water cause soil erosion?" If the material lacks these aids to reading, students can begin to read and gain insight into the kinds of questions for which the author provides answers. But they must look for them.

Students read to answer the questions they formulated. As they read, they should think about the information to be certain they comprehend it. They might have to read some parts more slowly than others, or read them more than once if they have difficulty understanding the content. Throughout the reading they must search for answers; this will keep them alert and involved.

The second R means *recite*. Recitation might include answering questions orally or telling what has been read, indicating the major points. Some students might prefer to write the answers or prepare an outline or a summary of the content. They should check themselves to determine whether or not they grasped the main points, filling in wherever they failed to include necessary information. If they own the books they can indicate main ideas and significant details by underlining the former and bracketing the latter, or making notations in the margins that distinguish between them.

The process of survey, question, read, and recite is repeated for each section of the chapter. However, unless students have more than one exposure to the content, they are bound to forget some of the important material for which they will be held responsible. Periodically, then, they need to fulfill the requirements of the third R, which is to *review*. They can do this by looking over the major headings and subheadings, referring to notes they have made, checking notations, and so forth. Reviews should be made as often as necessary, and this will vary from student to student.

Teachers and students should go through the entire process step by step. Students may also need to spend several sessions together studying a section of a chapter before they understand the purposes and procedures of Survey Q3R and come to realize that it may well be a better method of studying than the one they have been following. Of course, increased dividends from their study will convince them more than any amount of telling or persuasion.

SUMMARY

Many students who have no real trouble reading narrative materials do have difficulty understanding expository materials of comparable complexity. This difference in reading ease may be explained by the nature of content and the elements of which it is composed. Each subject area has a vocabulary of its own, and the extent to which this is mastered influences the students' ability to draw meaning from the content. Dozens of abstract concepts fill the pages in each textbook chapter, and the students' lack of familiarity with such concepts interferes with their comprehension of the material. Purpose in reading (or its absence) is another factor that affects outcomes in reading.

Each content teacher can help his students overcome many of the problems associated with reading textbooks and other sources of information. He can follow the outline of the directed lesson to assure readiness for reading, help students with difficulties, discuss and clarify complex ideas obtained through reading, reinforce skills that contribute to increased comprehension, and help students use newly acquired information in constructive ways. He can teach students to establish their own purposes for reading and how to study effectively as well as provide process guides which show students how to apply reading skills to solve content difficulties and content guides which direct students' attention to important and relevant information. Teachers do not have to be reading specialists to help students master the content of their subjects with increased confidence and greater success.

Additional Readings

For additional information about strategies for reading and studying in the content fields see the following:

William S. Gray, ed. *Improving Reading in All Curriculum Areas.* Supplementary Educational Monographs No. 76. Chicago: University of Chicago Press, 1952.

Harold L. Herber. *Teaching Reading in Content Areas.* Englewood Cliffs, N. J.: Prentice-Hall, 1970.

James L. Laffey, ed. *Reading in the Content Areas.* Newark, Del.: International Reading Association, 1972, pp. 31-74; 95-126; 153-176; 191-210.

Ralph C. Preston and others. *Guiding the Social Studies Reading of High School Students,* Bulletin No. 34. Washington, D.C.: National Council for the Social Studies, 1963.

H. Alan Robinson. *Teaching Reading and Study Strategies: The Content Areas.* Boston: Allyn and Bacon, 1975, pp. 40-56.

H. Alan Robinson and Sidney J. Rauch, eds. *Corrective Reading in the High School Classroom.* Perspectives in Reading No. 6. Newark, Del.: International Reading Association, 1966, pp. 75-113.

David L. Shepherd. *Comprehensive High School Reading Methods.* Columbus, Ohio: Charles E. Merrill, 1973, pp. 127-139.

Judith Thelen. *Improving Reading in Science.* Newark, Del.: International Reading Association, 1976.

Ellen Lamar Thomas and H. Alan Robinson. *Improving Reading in Every Class,* abridged ed. Boston: Allyn and Bacon, 1972, pp. 45-104.

CHAPTER 6

IMPROVING WORD IDENTIFICATION SKILLS in CONTENT AREAS

Problems for Study and Discussion

1   *What constitutes a comprehensive word-attack skills program?*
2   *Why should students be taught to apply word-identification techniques in combination?*
3   *What advantages does instruction in analytic phonics have over synthetic phonics?*
4   *Outline a complete lesson for teaching a phonic element.*
5   *Why might structural analysis be considered a more efficient means of analyzing words than phonic analysis?*
6   *In order of sequence, list the dictionary skills required for pronouncing words.*

Before any meaning can be derived from or attributed to a word, the reader must be able to identify it. This is to say that the word *raw* in the sentence "I like raw carrots" is read as *raw* and not *red* or any other word. Meaning is attached to the word symbol, but this word symbol must first be recognized by the reader.

Students whose reading ability is comparable to typical third-graders probably can read the sentence about raw carrots without much trouble. But there is no question that some high school students cannot recognize several words in the following passage, taken from a textbook intended for high school seniors:

> These revelations of *corruption* in high places *stimulated* a wide-spread demand for *reform*. Among the many reform *movements* of these years, none *aroused* greater interest than the *proposal* to *appoint* men to public jobs on the basis of merit. Under the "spoils system," which Andrew Jackson helped to establish (page 263), *government* jobs were handed out to political *favorites*. Under the *proposed* "merit system,"

the men who received the highest grades in competitive *examinations* would get the jobs, whether they were Republicans or Democrats.[1]

For some reason, these students have failed to develop a large enough "sight" vocabulary — that is, words that can be recognized quickly and easily without having to be examined carefully. The passage does contain a number of words which readers who have a working knowledge of word-identification skills will be able to analyze and identify without difficulty. For example, mere recognition of familiar word parts in the italicized words could result in their quick identification. Once the words have been pronounced, students may be able to associate the appropriate meanings with them. But the first step is recognizing the words.

WORD IDENTIFICATION SKILLS

Readers build a sight vocabulary gradually. Regardless of the ways in which words are introduced, the ultimate goal of any word-skills program is to enable students to recognize many words without having to analyze them carefully. Sight vocabularies begin to develop during the early years, in many instances even before entrance into kindergarten or first grade, through repeated exposures to words. By the time most achieving students reach the upper grades, they can easily recognize several hundred and possibly a few thousand words.

Mature readers have several recognition techniques at their command if they fail to recognize a word. They may not have to call on them often, since their stock of sight words is large, but everyone of us occasionally meets a word for the first time and must stop to determine what it is. The mature reader will call upon a combination of recognition techniques instead of relying on a single one. For example, to identify *philanthropists* in the sentence, "Many philanthropists have bequeathed large sums of money for medical research," one could use knowledge of syllabication and letter-sound association to identify the word.

Whether teachers are dealing with typical readers who have minor problems or with disabled readers whose primary weakness is inability to recognize many words, word-identification skills instruction will increase reading efficiency. A comprehensive word-identification program develops abilities in several areas and equips readers to use them. Word-identification instruction techniques should be based upon the reader's requirements. The techniques could include one or more of the following:

1. Using context clues
2. Using phonic analysis
3. Using structural analysis
4. Using the dictionary
5. Recognizing sight words

1. Lewis P. Todd and Merle Curti, *Rise of the American Nation*, 2d ed. (New York: Harcourt, Brace and World, 1966), p. 420. Copyright © 1966 by Harcourt Brace Jovanovich, Inc., and reprinted with their permission.

Two aspects of word recognition have been omitted intentionally: picture clues and configuration clues. Books for beginning readers have one or more illustrations on every page, and these *picture clues* follow the stories very closely. If the text is telling about a cat who is playing with a ball, a picture on the page will show the cat doing just that. Young readers should be instructed to look at the pictures as well as the words, since the former may aid in recalling words of which they are not sure. This practice is recommended for young readers to help them build a sight vocabulary, but *older* readers who are using picture clues are using a crutch that should be discarded as soon as possible. Reading materials designed for the higher grades simply are not illustrated like first and second grade books. Teachers who have worked with word-recognition cases of high school age know how frantic and useless are their efforts to use pictures as word-recognition aids. Picture clues should be used only with students who are reading on the very

l⸺⸺⸺   sic sight vocabulary.

personalizing growth in Chil   ration clues. The shape of words, their
                                   to help beginning readers recognize
                                   n that distinguishing characteristics in
                                   r — lead to his perception. But there is
                                   upon the total shape of words. Words
                                   d descenders do seem to be more rec-
                                   qual height. Compare, for example, the

                                        were

                                   basket   blue

                                   f helping the beginning reader see the
                                   l when the letters of words are regular

swimmer   reasons   people   purple

Besides, there is no research that demonstrates that readers perceive shapes of words in this way.

When working with students whose inability to recognize words is critical, concentrate on developing and using independent word-identification techniques. This could lead to building adequate sight vocabularies. These techniques — context clues, phonic and structural analysis, dictionaries, and building sight vocabularies — will be explained and illustrated later in the chapter.

USING CONTEXT CLUES

Native-born English speakers are often able to anticipate what will follow from what has already been said. It is not uncommon, during conversations, for the listener to supply, either mentally or verbally, words that have not yet been uttered. They are able to do this because of their knowledge of the language's grammar, that is; where what kinds of words belong within the sentence structure, and the semantic constraints or meaning of the utterances.

Readers also can use grammatical and semantic clues and their experiences to predict what words are likely to follow previous ones. Some contexts are sufficiently narrow as to leave little doubt about what word is to follow others. For example:

Most cats are afraid *of* dogs.

On the other hand, a number of different words could replace the italicized word in this context:

The lake was filled with *debris*.

However, the larger the context, the greater the likelihood that the number of different possibilities will be reduced. Even though students might never have heard the word *debris* and therefore couldn't supply it, they might be able to offer a suitable alternate such as *refuse* or *junk* from the clues the passage contained and essentially retain the meaning.

It is unlikely that many junior and senior high school students are not familiar with the concept of using context clues, although they might not apply it. For those who are not, it is a good idea to use oral exercises that require them to supply missing words for incomplete statements. At first, introduce a few for which they have to supply the word at the end of the sentence; after they understand what is involved, they should respond to statements in which words in other positions are missing. Have them indicate what clues in the statements helped them decide what word was missing.

EXAMPLE: It is easier to learn a foreign language in the country where it is spoken everywhere than in a typical American classroom where the language is rarely _____.

EXAMPLE: One of the objectives of the Apollo missions was to determine the physical _____ on astronauts as they performed different tasks on the moon.

In each case, more than one word may be supplied and students should decide which words are better "fits" than others.

From these examples, it is apparent that the meaning of a passage will often be retained, even though another word, which is not a synonym, has been substituted for the unknown word. However, the real meaning may be lost unless the reader uses other word-identification techniques with context clues to determine what the unknown word is. Therefore, teachers should encourage students to use whatever word-identification skills they can, together with context clues, to identify words.

The following lesson transcript requires a knowledge of letter-sound associations (in this case merely the beginning sound of a word) and the use of context clues to identify an unknown word. The purpose of the lesson has been explained, and the teacher has written this sentence on the chalkboard:

The doctor visited his _____ in the hospital.

Teacher: What word will complete this sentence?
Student: wife

Teacher: Any other word?
Student: assistant
Student: friend
Student: relative
Teacher: You can supply different words and all of them make sense. Here is one word no one has suggested. (Writes the word *patient* in the blank space.) Is it a word anyone has said?
Students: (No responses)
Teacher: What other words begin with the same letter?
Student: piece
Student: pass
Student: position
Teacher: (Writes the words and underlines the *p* in each.) Can you think of a word that begins with the same letter as piece, pass, position but makes sense in the sentence? Who would a doctor visit in the hospital?
Student: patient

Of course, students who have never heard or used the word *patient* wouldn't be able to supply it. But it isn't very likely that many high school students have never heard the word or don't understand what it means. The choice of words that teachers use to teach any skill will depend upon their students' ability to cope with them. The purpose of the lesson would not be met if students were able to recognize *patient* without having to use their knowledge of letter-sound associations and context clues.

Other types of sample lessons which combine knowledge and application of letter-sound associations (phonic analysis) and word parts (structural analysis) are indicated below.

USING INITIAL AND FINAL CONSONANT SOUNDS AND CONTEXT CLUES

1. The scout pitched the *tent* along the river's bank.
2. One effect of the energy *crunch* is a sharp increase in the price of oil, coal, and gas.

USING CONSONANT COMBINATIONS AND CONTEXT CLUES

1. The tiger tried to *claw* the new trainer.
2. In recent years the Congress has *strengthened* its control over the budget.

USING WORD PARTS AND CONTEXT CLUES

1. Nuclear bombs release *radioactive* particles into the atmosphere. (compound words)
2. Throughout history, warring nations have used the *block*ade to defeat the enemy. (root word)
3. Some stores offer *dis*counts to customers if purchases are for cash. (prefix)
4. Navigators can determine their position in the open sea by sighting on the stars with a sex/tant. (syllables)

In each of these lessons, it is assumed that students have sufficient command over whatever aspects of phonics or structural analysis are introduced to help them recognize unknown words. It is pointless, for example, to use words containing roots if students cannot identify roots, or to expect them to divide words into syllables if they don't know how. Moreover, all the words except the one intended for study should be known. If the other words are unfamiliar, they will interfere with the students' efforts to use the context and other clues. In every case, the context provides a definite clue to the unknown word; the phonic and structural elements suggest additional clues.

Students who need help using context clues require many exposures to passages that contain them. Provide many practice exercises as part of the instruction. Have the students explain what context and other clues they used to identify the unknown words. There will be additional opportunities to practice the skills as they read different materials. Alert them to the possibility that there could be words they don't know, and tell them to use context plus any other clues to determine what the words are. As part of any discussion that follows the reading of content, words unlikely to be part of their sight vocabularies and which might be identified from context and other clues can be discussed. Students might reread those sentences containing the words and indicate what clues enabled them to identify each one.

Single sentences have been suggested for use in developing students' ability to use context and phonic and/or structural clues to unlock unknown words. As with context clues that are used for discovering word meaning, it is desirable to introduce longer passages after students demonstrate that they can respond to the clues in shorter ones, for in typical materials the context clues may be found in sentences that precede and/or follow the unknown word(s).

There is one other point about recognizing context clues that should be noted. Context clues have been classified according to type — contrast, experience, mood, definition, explanation, typographical — but their recognition has much greater relevancy for discovering the meaning of words than for unlocking the pronunciation of words.

USING PHONIC ANALYSIS

Phonics refers to the sounds for which letters in words stand. When a reader uses phonics, he makes use of his knowledge of the sounds of letters and letter combinations to pronounce new words. One-syllable words as well as polysyllabic ones yield to phonic analysis, although there are elements in many words that do not. Approximately 84 percent of all words in our language, it has been estimated, are regular and can be analyzed through phonics. *Phonics* and *phonetics* are terms that teachers often confuse. They should distinguish between phonics, which refers to letter-sound relationships, or, as the linguists explain, phoneme-grapheme correspondences, and phonetics, which deals with the science of speech sounds that persons make in talking.

The debate over the usefulness of phonics instruction has subsided, although not completely. Through the years, poor reading has been said to be the product of programs in which no phonics was taught, in which too much phonics was taught, and in which poor methods of teaching phonics were followed. There isn't much hard evidence to support any of the explanations, but time and again proponents of one phonic system or another have suggested (if not actually proclaimed) that phonics is the only means by which words may be analyzed.

Schools have been and are teaching phonics as part of word-identification programs, but there isn't agreement on how it should be taught. Some, who accept a psycholinguistic explanation of the reading process, would offer limited phonics instruction to beginning readers and stress as early as possible the study of syntactic and semantic cues for identifying words. This position has some merit, but it does not justify not teaching students different ways of solving word problems.

High school reading programs should include phonic analysis instruction to the extent that students should be able to use it as a word-identification technique. Sample lesson and exercises in using context clues have shown that students should use their knowledge of phonics and word parts with meaning clues in order to identify unknown words. A surprisingly large number of high school students cannot use phonics in a way that permits them to pronounce new words quickly and efficiently or in combination with other techniques. For those students, an instructional program based upon demonstrated weaknesses will be of value.

Phonic Programs

There are numerous approaches to teaching phonics, and each has its advocates. In actual practice, however, teachers usually adopt a combination of methods in the hope that children will learn to use phonics more efficiently if they are exposed to just one method. Particularly teachers of older students take this approach, because their students probably have not learned to apply whatever phonics knowledge they have to word analysis. Many phonics materials are available in the form of workbook exercises, cards, games, record, and tapes, which support one or more approaches that are currently in use.[2]

Followers of the *synthetic* method recommend that the students be taught the sounds of individual letters and letter conbinations and then how to join these letters to form words.[3] Vowel sounds usually are introduced first, followed by consonant sounds; these are combined to form simple words, such as *c-a-t, r-a-t, r-u-t*. New words would be analyzed letter by

2. Gerald G. Duffy, comp. ed., *Reading in the Middle School* (Newark, Del.: International Reading Association, 1974), pp. 71-84, and "New Materials on the Market," *Journal of Reading* 17 (Jan. 1974): 306-313. See also "Reviews of Instructional Materials" in the *Journal of Reading* and "Critically Speaking" in *The Reading Teacher*.
3. For a brief description of several programs, see Arthur W. Heilman, "Phonic Emphasis Approaches," pp. 194-209 in *Teaching Word Recognition Skills*, comp. Mildred Dawson (Newark, Del.: International Reading Association, 1971).

letter, e.g., *r - u - n*, and the sounds joined or blended to form the word. One variation of this approach is to combine the consonant and vowel *ru* and add the sound of *n* to form the word. Another variation is to start with the sound of *r* and add *un* to form the word.

Proponents of the *family* approach urge that a host of phonograms or letter groupings be taught.[4] To these are added beginning sounds to form words. For example:

(b)ack	(b)ell
(h)ack	(d)ell
(j)ack	(f)ell
(l)ack	(j)ell
(n)ack	(s)ell
(p)ack	(t)ell
(r)ack	(w)ell
(s)ack	(y)ell
(t)ack	(sh)ell
(wh)ack	(sw)ell

A system somewhat related to word "families" is advocated by some linguists who have prepared instructional materials for beginning readers.[5] Basically they propose using words in lists and sentences that emphasize similar spelling-speech patterns. Thus, they and others introduce such words as *Nat, cat, fat, Nan, can, Dan, fan* to teach the letter-sound correspondence of *a* and formulate sentences with them:

Nan can fan Dan.
Nat is a fat cat.

High frequency words such as *a* in the second sentence are introduced in some materials even though they don't conform to the usual spelling-sound pattern which the children are expected to learn.

A third method holds that the basis of instruction in phonics rests in words that are known to the reader. This is called the *analytic* method. The learner is taught to take down words and make appropriate subsitutions in them to form the new word. For example:

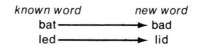

Variations in methodology will be found in all three phonic programs, and anyone who takes the time to examine the workbooks that accompany

4. Gerald C. Glass, "The Teaching of Word Analysis Through Perceptual Conditioning," pp. 227-230 in *Teaching Word Recognition Skills*, comp. Dawson.
5. Leonard Bloomfield and Clarence L. Barnhart, *Let's Read: A Linguistic Approach* (Detroit: Wayne State Univ. Press, 1961); Charles C. Fries, *Linguistics and Reading* (New York: Holt, Rinehart and Winston, 1963).

basal readers and specially designed phonics books will find differences among those prepared for the same phonics program.

Results of research in phonics teaching are mixed. Most of the investigations have been conducted in the lower grades, not with older populations, and have generally been characterized by looseness of design and lack of control over factors that could influence the outcomes. Some investigators have reported the superiority of one method over another, while others have not found any significant differences among them.[6] In a survey of more than fifty years of research on the value of phonics instruction, Jeanne Chall concluded that there was insufficient evidence to support one system for teaching phonics over other systems.[7]

Until the results of more and better research become known, any approach to teaching phonics that agrees with accepted principles of learning is to be preferred to one that does not. There is no question here of whether any learning can occur under a given set of conditions (as was said before, children often learn in spite of conditions surrounding their learning); teachers need to be most concerned with *optimum* learning climates, if maximum results are to be realized. Since older students are able to recognize a number of words at sight without having to analyze them, it seems wise to use what they know about words to teach them letter-sound correspondences and how to apply this knowledge to determine the pronunciation of unfamiliar words.

Teaching Phonics

By the time they reach high school, most students have some knowledge of letter sounds, even though they may not be able to attack a new word efficiently. If students are known to have difficulty using phonics, have them read orally to determine which words cause them trouble. Perhaps words that contain *e, oi, ew,* or *ea* prove to be difficult, or *sk,* which presents no problems so long as it comes at the beginning of a word, as in *skate,* may be troublesome when it appears at the end of a word, as in *brisk.*

Some students are able to identify letter sounds when they are isolated, but fail to know them when the letters appear in words. The teacher, therefore, is advised not to present a list of phonic elements to be sounded but, instead, to prepare an oral reading list of words with a specific phonic element. If a student fails to pronounce several of these words, chances are great that he would benefit from instruction in using that phonic element. Words containing one phonic element should be mixed with words that contain others. Such a list of words as the one that follows may help to reveal how well

6. Several of these studies have been published in the *Elementary School Journal,* three of which are Mabel Rudisill, "Interrelations of Functional Phonic Knowledge, Reading, Spelling and Mental Age," Feb. 1957, pp. 264-267; Paul Sparks and Leo Fay, "Evaluation of Two Methods of Teaching Reading," April 1957, pp. 386-390; and David Bear, "Phonics for First Grade: A Comparison of Two Methods," April 1959, pp. 394-402. Also, Emery Bliesmer and Betty Yarborough, "A Comparison of Ten Different Beginning Programs in First Grade," *Phi Delta Kappan* 47 (June 1965): 500-504.
7. Jeanne Chall, *Learning to Read: The Great Debate* (New York: McGraw-Hill, 1967).

students can analyze words containing specific phonic elements such as *ur*, *ai*,*ea*, *aw*, and *oi*. These lists should contain more than one word with a given phonic element.

1. churn	6. lurk	11. curdle
2. waist	7. swain	12. gaited
3. goiter	8. poilu	13. loiter
4. wean	9. mead	14. easel
5. fawn	10. dawdle	15. awl

Patterns of errors might be noticed as students read a book orally. Here is a record of several such errors: the first column contains nine misread words and the second column indicates what the student said. (A blank space indicates that the student made no attempt to pronounce the word.)

1. larder	longer	6. alarm	alone
2. flash	flesh	7. faction	fiction
3. personnel		8. partition	position
4. warrant	worry	9. ferment	
5. terse	tease		

Larder, warrant, alarm, and *partition* contain the same phonic element. The letter *e* followed by *r* appears in *personnel*, *terse*, and *ferment*, while the short *a* is found in *flash* and *faction*. Each of these phonic elements may be the cause of the reader's inability to read the respective words correctly. A list of different words which contain these phonic elements could be prepared and read by the student. If words were misread, it could mean that the student cannot associate the proper sound with the letter or letter combination or cannot apply that knowledge to new words.

Phonic elements are classified as consonants, consonant blends, vowels, digraphs, and diphthongs. Many beginning and final consonants represent one sound:

b as in *b*oy, *b*ad, *b*est, *b*etter
f as in *f*an, *f*or, *f*ist, *f*arm
m as in *m*other, *m*e, *m*ist, *m*ock
t as in be*t*, ten*t*, ha*t*
b as in ca*b*, hu*b*, sta*b*
n as in wo*n*, ca*n*, bi*n*

The consonants *c* and *g* may be hard as in

call	come	cattle	catch
gas	get	gone	girl

or soft as in

city	cent	ceiling	cite
gem	gist	George	germ

A consonant blend consists of two or three consonants, each of which retains its identity in a word. Some examples of consonant blends are

break	*drop*	*speak*	*close*
price	*stop*	*credit*	*swim*
skate	*flee*	*snow*	*frigid*
splash	*strange*	*screw*	*spring*

Vowels may be long[8] as in

agent   mind   me   hope   utensil

or vowels may be short as in

happen   swim   help   Tom   under

Some vowels are neither short nor long but assume a different sound when followed by *l* or *w:*

always   new   law

If *a, e, i, o,* and *u* are followed by *r,* each takes on a different sound:

tar   term   fir   torn   burn

Some consonants join to form a digraph or one sound:

show   ghost   gnaw   neck   photograph

Among the consonant diagraphs are some whose sounds vary:

child   choir   chic   the   thin

Vowels frequently join to form a digraph with a single sound:

toast   bleed   mean   automobile

but some vowel combinations may take on more than one sound:

book   soon   shoulder   touch

---

8. The terms *long* and *short* are used for convenience to differentiate between these common sounds. Some linguists point out quite rightly that the "length" of a sound depends upon the stress it receives in words. Thus the *a* in the word *jazz* would be considered to be a "short" vowel sound by reading teachers but "long" by linguists when the latter compare the sound of this *a* to the *a* in a word such as *back.*

Some vowels blend to produce almost one sound and are known as diphthongs:

oil   toy   out   buy

Students should know that there are some words in which phonic elements are pronounced differently from what is normally expected. Since the English language is irregular, one may not assume that a phonic element is to be pronounced the same way every time.

Teachers should be familiar with certain phonic generalizations. Although there are many exceptions to each of them, these generalizations may be applied to many situations and will aid the reader's efforts to pronounce unknown words. Some phonic generalizations have greater usefulness than others,[9] and the purpose for helping students to understand them is to point out the regularity that does exist in our language. What teachers should emphasize as they introduce any generalization about letter-sound relationships are the notions of its usefulness but lack of 100 percent utility and the need for flexibility in associating letters and sounds. No real problems teaching these generalizations will arise if students understand from the very beginning that shifts in pronunciation might be required to identify certain words. The problem is minimized further if students are expected to deal with words in context and are also aware of the structural or morphemic clues they contain. It is hardly likely that a student will persist in pronouncing the first vowel sound in the word *measurement* as a "long" *e*, particularly if it appears in a meaningful context and the student is aware of its root word.

Some basic principles of phonics are:

1. A single vowel at the beginning or in the middle of a one-syllable word is usually short. (Short syllables are known as *closed* syllables.)
   EXAMPLES: end, hot

2. A single vowel at the end of a one-syllable word (*open* syllable) is usually long.
   EXAMPLES: go, me

3. A single vowel that is followed by a final *e* in a one-syllable word is usually long.
   EXAMPLES: lake, time

4. In words that contain two vowels together, usually the first is long and the second is silent.
   EXAMPLES: chain, groan

5. When *a* is followed by *l, u,* or *w*, it is usually pronounced the same way.
   EXAMPLES: also, caught, awful

9. Mildred H. Bailey, "The Utility of Phonic Generalizations in Grades One Through Six," and Robert Emans, "The Usefulness of Phonic Generalizations Above the Primary Grades," *Reading Teacher* 20 (Feb. 1967): 413-418, 419-425.

6. **When *e*, *i*, or *u* is followed by *r*, each is usually pronounced the same way.**
   EXAMPLES: *fertile, sir, curd*

7. **When *a* is followed by *r*, it is neither long nor short.**
   EXAMPLES: *cart, argue*

8. **A vowel followed by two consonants and a final *e* is usually short.**
   EXAMPLES: *hinge, dance*

9. **When *c* or *g* is followed by *e*, *i*, or *y*, both are usually soft.**
   EXAMPLES: *cent, city, cycle*   *gem, gist, gym*

10. **Any vowel may have the schwa sound in an unstressed syllable.**
    EXAMPLES: *about, totem, button*

How may students be taught to use phonics? The phonics program suggested here translates modern principles of learning into school practices. It provides opportunities for teachers to base instruction on what is known and to make use of structural and contextual settings. In short, it provides for meaningful learning.

Regardless of the phonic element to be taught, there are four processes to be covered:

1. auditory discrimination
2. visual discrimination
3. word blending or building
4. contextual application.

The importance of including visual and auditory discrimination in a phonics lesson cannot be overemphasized. It is a sheer waste of time for a teacher to try to teach students to blend or build new words if they do not distinguish the sound being taught from other sounds. It is also important for students to associate the sound of the element with the way it appears in a word.

Each phonic lesson grows out of a contextual setting and ends with a contextual setting. The lesson's pattern of development moves in the following way:

context ⎯⎯⎯⎯⎯⟶ out of context ⎯⎯⎯⎯⎯⟶ context

At no time is the sound of the phonic element removed from its natural surroundings. Emphasis is placed upon its sound as it appears in different words.

Here is a word-by-word account of a phonics lesson a teacher might wish to use. Explanatory remarks appear in brackets.

LESSON: Use of the consonant blend *dr*.
Teacher: Here are sentences that contain two words which caused you people some trouble. [Sentences that contain these words are placed on the chalkboard.]

1. The players were <u>drenched</u> within five minutes after the rain began to fall.
2. All the oil was <u>drained</u> from the crankcase.

Each underlined word begins with a *d* followed by an *r*, and these two consonants join to form a blend — *dr*. We shall return to these sentences later. [The teacher places a list of words, each of which begins with *dr*, on the board. These words may be selected from passages that have been read and are part of the student's sight vocabulary.] Listen carefully to the beginning of each word as I pronounce it. [The teacher pronounces each word slowly with emphasis upon the *dr*. This phase of the lesson is called *auditory discrimination.*]

> drive
> drop
> draw
> drink
> dress

What characteristic do these words have in common:

Students: Each starts out the same way.

Teacher: Draw a box around the same letters that are found in each word.

[This phase of the lesson is known as *visual discrimination.* Care must be taken to associate the sound of the consonant blend with its letters. The visual stimulus is presented with the auditory stimulus.]

Students.
dr	ive
dr	op
dr	aw
dr	ink
dr	ess

Teacher: This time I am going to read words that are not on the chalkboard. Some have the same beginning consonant blend as in *drive, drop, draw, drink,* and *dress,* while others do not. Listen carefully and decide whether these new words begin like the others. [This part of the lesson provides additional opportunity to hear the consonant blend in words whose meanings are known to the students. It will enable the teacher to determine whether more work in auditory discrimination is needed. Words that do not contain the consonant blend *dr* should come toward the end of the list. Each word is to be read naturally.] Does *drizzle* contain the consonant blend *dr? Dry? Draft? Drug? Grip? Dramatic? Drape? Free? Breeze? Drum?*

Students: [Respond to each word.]

Teacher: Now make use of what you have learned. You know what the sound of the consonant blend *dr* in a word is. Here is a new list of words that you know. For each beginning consonant or consonant blend, substitute *dr* to form a new word. [The teacher will demonstrate what is to be done by the students. This part of the lesson is called *blending* or *word building.*] Here is the word *lip.* Remove the *l* and in its place substitute *dr.* What new word is formed? Yes, *drip.* Let's try another one together. Substitute *dr* for the *w* in *will;* and what new word is formed? *Drill.* Now do the same to each of these words. [Teacher draws a line through the beginning consonant, consonant blend, or consonant digraph of each word and substitutes the *dr.*]

~~h~~ead	~~pl~~astic	~~c~~ab	~~h~~edge	~~sh~~awl
dread	drastic	drab	dredge	drawl

Students: [The new words should be read orally by the students. It is desirable that each new word be one that they have heard before and understand.]

Teacher: You have built new words that contain the consonant blend *dr.* These sentences may be completed with one of the new words. Fill in the missing word. [Each lesson should end with *contextual* application. The true test of phonic knowledge is the ability to use it in a functional way. When the exercise is completed, each sentence will be read orally.]

1. Most Southerners speak with a familiar _____.
2. It is not unusual for young children to _____ the dark.
3. The dean threatened the culprits with _____ punishment if they did not change their behavior.
4. The walls were painted a _____ color.
5. The shallow channel was deepened by means of a _____.

Teacher: Here are the two original sentences that bothered you. Read them now.
1. The players were <u>drenched</u> within five minutes after the rain began to fall.
2. All the oil was <u>drained</u> from the crankcase.

[If the underlined words can be read, the teacher has some assurance that the lesson's objective was achieved. The true test remains — the identification in future readings of other words that contain *dr.* It is possible that some students may require additional help with this blend. The lesson may be concluded with the rereading of passages that were sources of difficulty.]

Other phonic elements may be taught in the same way or with some variation. Below are sample lessons for teaching other phonic elements.

LESSON: *c* followed by *e*

Put the book in its <u>place</u>.

1. *Auditory and Visual Discrimination* [Placed on chalkboard and read by teacher.]

> piece
> ice
> cent
> dance
> mice

2. *Additional Auditory Discrimination* [Words read by teacher.]

center	twice
glance	fleece
concern	show
census	child
chance	race

3. *Word Blending or Building* [Start with known words.]

cøde cøllar cønch cánter
cede cellar cinch center

4. *Contextual Application* [Read the sentences containing the new words.]

Some countries have been forced to cede part of their territory to another.

Farmers store potatoes, turnips, squash, carrots and similar vegetables in a root cellar.

Everyone believed that he was a cinch to win the tournament.

The artist was the center of attraction at the opening of her exhibit.

LESSON: short *i*

The jackal ate bits of fish which he found near the edge of the pond.

1. *Auditory and Visual Discrimination* [Placed on chalkboard and read by teacher.]

hit
big
river
swim
improve

2. *Additional Auditory Discrimination* [Words read by teacher.]

ginger	listen
picnic	wire
list	tell
chill	which
improve	prick

3. *Word Blending or Building* [Start with known words.]

áll dráfted húnt stráps
ill drifted hint strips

4. *Contextual Application* [Read sentences orally.]

The sailboat drifted with the wind.

The meat was cut into thin strips and broiled on a spit.

We had no hint of the surprise party.

Viruses can cause one to become ill for short periods of time.

Phonic generalizations may be taught in similar ways. From what they have observed about known words, students can learn to generalize about phoneme-grapheme relationships.

LESSON: Vowel sounds affected by final e.

1. *Auditory and Visual Discrimination* [These are known words which exemplify the generalization.]

plate	close
fuse	gene
ice	

2. *Word Building* [Add e to known words.]

cap	grim	cut	rot
cape	grime	cute	rote

3. *Contextual Application* [Use new words in sentences.]

4. *Statement of Generalization* [Help students state the generalization in their own words. Refer to Steps 1 and 2 if they have difficulty in seeing the relationship between spelling patterns and sounds.]

In each of these lessons, known sight words are presented for initial auditory and visual discrimination. For follow-up auditory practice, it is not essential that sight words be used; however, it is important that students recognize these words when they hear them. Furthermore, for optimum results, the new words that are developed through word blending or building should not be in the sight vocabulary. If students can recognize these words easily, there will be no reason for them to apply what they have learned about letter-sound relationships.

This system for teaching phonics is intended to help students learn to recognize visual clues, master letter-sound correspondences, and blend speech sounds to form syllables and words. The system does facilitate learning these skills since it focuses attention upon what students already know and reduces new learning to a minimum. However, once students have learned to associate letters and their corresponding sounds, they should be encouraged to scrutinize unfamiliar words for visual clues, associate them directly with their proper sounds, and blend the sounds to form syllables or words without searching for appropriate words to use in the substitution process.

This process can prove to be very cumbersome when attacking new words, particularly where more than one substitution is required to move from the known to the unknown word: trick ⟶ track ⟶ trap. The student not only has to think of similar words but also has to know how to spell them. There is no need for students to take this circuitous route to discovering how to pronounce words if they have mastered phoneme-grapheme relationships and learned to blend sounds smoothly.

Teachers may use a cue chart to help students remember some of the correspondences. The words they select for this purpose are readily identifiable by the students.

CUE CHART

Short Vowel Sounds	Vowel Digraphs	Consonant Digraphs
at	teach, bread	photo
bet	look, wood	show
tip	receive, eight	who, when
on	caught	child, character
us	coat	laugh

In addition, they might utilize exercises found in workbooks such as *Breaking the Sound Barrier* (Macmillan), *Speech to Print Phonics* (Harcourt Brace Jovanovich), and *New Phonic Skilltexts* (Charles E. Merrill) with students who need extra practice in auditory and visual discrimination of phonic elements.

USING STRUCTURAL ANALYSIS

That pupils must be trained to use a variety of techniques to unlock unknown words has been emphasized several times. These techniques are often combined. Knowledge of structural analysis (awareness of word parts) will facilitate the recognition of many words which contain prefixes, suffixes, and root words without further analysis or additional study being required. Structural analysis involves recognizing root words, affixes, and syllables.

Compound Words

A compound word consists of two distinct words that are joined to form one word. *Mailman, keepsake,* and *gentleman* are typical examples. Students who are weak in word-attack skills often find compound words troublesome. They fail to recognize the units of which such words are composed, even though they may be able to read each unit when it is presented separately. Students who are blocked by compound words need specific instruction if they are to learn to deal with them. Compound words that are part of their sight vocabulary are not the problem; unfamiliar compound words become sources of instruction.

The four processes comprising a lesson in phonics may be utilized in a lesson on compound words. Auditory and visual discrimination, word building, and contextual application join to form a meaningful experience in learning.

The suggested steps of a lesson in compound words follow.

LESSON: To learn compound words.
The *countryside* was ablaze with fall colors.

1. *Auditory and Visual Discrimination* [Taken from sight vocabulary.]

birthday	blackboard
grandfather	policeman
anything	homework
someone	outside

[The teacher introduces the lesson by referring to the contextual situation in which the unknown compound word appeared. A group of compound words that are known to the students is placed on the board and read by the teacher. He stresses each of the words within the compound word. Students are asked to identify the word components of the compound words by placing one line under the first part of the word and two lines under the second part, for example, birthday.]

2. *Additional Auditory Discrimination*

[A second group of compound words is then read to the students to make certain that they *hear* the components. Some students may confuse these parts with syllables.]

postman, everywhere, sunshine, downstairs, swallow, nearby, newsboy, peanuts, swimmer, airplane

3. *Word Building*

[The teacher chooses words that can be recognized by the students. These are placed in two columns. The students are to match a word in the first column with a word in the second column to form a compound

word. A line may be drawn from one word to the other, as, for example,
sun⸻►set.]

whole	set
sun	ship
book	lace
relation	some
neck	stone
lime	keepers

4. *Contextual Application*
[Sentences that contain the newly formed compound words may be prepared as an exercise. These should be read orally by the students. An alternate exercise would omit the compound word, the students supplying the omission.]

The expensive _____ was placed in the vault for safekeeping.

Farmers use _____ to reduce the acidity of the soil.

What is the _____ between temperature and altitude?

Milk is considered to be one of the most _____ foods that can be given to children.

The brilliant _____ was reflected in the pool.

Most competent _____ are known to possess legible handwriting.

[After these sentences are read the teacher should return to the sentence that contained the unknown compound word. Additional reading in books will provide opportunity for putting to use what the pupils have learned.]

Teachers might provide additional practice exercises to reinforce recognizing word parts in compound words. The following types of exercises using compound words which appear in students' materials might be used.

EXERCISE
Draw a line between the root words in the compound words. Be ready to pronounce the compound words.

livestock	gangplank	furthermore	intake
widespread	limestone	framework	outbound

EXERCISE
Below are sentences containing compound words. Analyze those you don't recognize for their word parts. Be ready to read the sentences.
1. Southern plantations employed overseers to supervise the slaves.
2. Landform maps reveal flat plains, high plateaus, central lowlands and mountain ranges.
3. Increases in wholesale prices generally produce increases in retail prices.

Be sure that students realize that the meaning of a compound word might be derived from its word parts, as in *shipwreck, shortchanged,* or *outcast.* At the same time, they should realize that both word parts might not contain the elements of their meaning, as in *withstood* (stood against), *overstep* (go beyond), or *nosegay* (a small bunch of flowers). They should seek confirming clues to the meaning of compound words in the context of the passage.

Root Words and Affixes

A root word is one to which a prefix or suffix has been added to form a new word. The underscored parts of the following words are their roots: <u>perform</u>ance, <u>difficult</u>y, re<u>create</u>, un<u>realistic</u>. The spelling of roots may change when suffixes are added to them: *variety* (vary), *requisition* (require), *efficiency* (efficient).

Recognizing roots within words reduces the need for students to apply phonic analysis and other word recognition techniques to discover their pronunciation. Encourage students to look for roots in unfamiliar words before they analyze them in other ways. The following activities involving auditory and visual discrimination will aid them to recognize roots as well as to establish the habit of searching for them in words.

1. Present words that contain easily recognizable roots. Have students indicate the roots.
   ending   turned   reasons   rewind
2. Present sentences which contain modified forms of root words. Have students indicate the original forms of the words.
   a. The farmer wearily (weary) trudged up the hill.
   b. Doctors often recommend blood analysis (analyze) when they are unable to diagnose a patient's illness.
   c. Divisive (divide) forces plunged the country into civil war.
3. Build new words from known roots.
   a. <u>prefer</u> + able = preferable
   b. <u>recognize</u> + tion = recognition
   c. dis + <u>believe</u> = disbelieve
   d. <u>rule</u> + er = ruler
   e. <u>consumer</u> + 's = consumer's
   f. un + <u>reward</u> + ing = unrewarding

A suffix that changes the number, tense, or degree of a word is called an *inflectional ending.* Examples of inflectional endings are

```
number: boy   = boys
tense:  blast = blasted
degree: green = greenest
```

Frequently, these endings are omitted by students who have some difficulty recognizing words. The teacher should provide help with the endings that are known to be obstacles to quick recognition. These suggestions should be helpful:

1. Start the lesson with the contextual setting.
   He decided to choose the lesser of two evils.
2. Provide for auditory and visual discrimination
talier	greener	higher
younger	quicker	sweeter
3. Build new words.
   soon + er = sooner
   bright + er = brighter
   short + er = shorter

4. Provide for contextual application.
   Labor unions are seeking a shorter work week.
   Some artists use brighter colors than others.
   It will happen sooner than you think.

Prefixes and other suffixes may be taught in the same way. When teaching suffixes, first introduce words which do not alter their spelling when the suffix is added, such as *personal, employment.* Then, introduce words such as *division* (divide) and *inspiration* (inspire), whose spellings and pronunciation change when the suffix is added. Words already in the listening or speaking vocabularies of students are not likely to be mispronounced because of accent shifts after a suffix is added.

Syllabication

Words of more than one syllable do not necessarily contain word parts such as root words and prefixes or suffixes. In such cases, students should divide the words into syllables before applying phonics to the words. It is so much more efficient to recognize the syllables than to analyze words letter by letter and then combine the sounds.

Teachers may assume that high school students know the difference between a consonant and a vowel, but many students will confuse a vowel with a *vowel sound.* The vowel in the word *tent* stands alone and contains the vowel sound, while the vowel sound in *team* is derived from the two vowels, *e* and *a.* In other words, students must be familiar with the ways in which vowels join to form a vowel sound. They must be familiar also with the ways in which the consonants combine to form a single sound as the *sh* in *show* or the *ph* in *photograph.* Practice in recognizing vowel sounds and consonant digraphs in words should be provided for those who need this type of instruction. Obviously, students who are weak in phonic analysis are not ready for syllabication. If they cannot blend consonant and vowel sounds, they may learn to recognize syllables visually but will not be able to pronounce them to form words.

Generally speaking, of course, it is desirable to help students discover rules or generalizations, rather than present them to be memorized. Accordingly, those rules that govern syllabication should be taught inductively. As with learning phonic principles, students should realize that principles of syllabication are not foolproof and that some have greater utility than others. If they divide a word incorrectly, they may mispronounce it and not recognize it as a word they know. On the other hand, if the word is one that they have heard used, they are bound to change the pronunciation so that it conforms to the context. Naturally, students should be encouraged to verify the pronunciation of a doubtful word by using the dictionary.

Some of the common principles of syllabication are:

1. If two consonants follow the first vowel sound, the word usually is divided between the consonants.
   EXAMPLES. but-ter, win-dow

2. If one consonant follows the first vowel sound, the consonant might end the first syllable or start the second syllable.
EXAMPLES: cov-er, wea-sel

3. If a word ends in le, the consonant which precedes le starts the last syllable.
EXAMPLES: a-ble, cou-ple

4. Prefixes and suffixes usually are syllables.
EXAMPLES: sub-merge, pre-dict-ed

To aid the teacher, sample lessons in syllabication are given here:

LESSON: Number of syllables

Every syllable contains a vowel sound, and the number of syllables in a word is determined by its number of *vowel sounds*. The teacher may present known words of one syllable and ask the students to underline the vowel sounds. When the teacher reads these words, the students *hear* that the words do not contain any pauses or stops. Some students may know the number of syllables in a word if they can hear it pronounced by syllables and can be led to see the relationship between what they hear and the number of vowel sounds they have underlined.

After they have generalized that a word of one vowel sound contains one syllable, words of two syllables may be presented, for example, *pollen, basket, children, reason.* Students should mark the vowel sounds, listen to them, as the words are read, and then decide how many syllables each contains. Words of three and four syllables may then be introduced. This procedure helps students to understand upon what basis the number of syllables in a word is determined.

LESSON: Words with two consonants that follow the first vowel sound.

Known words that contain this letter pattern should be written on the chalkboard:

annode	conclude
pollen	obtain
surround	halter
current	structure

1. Students should indicate the vowel sounds and the number of syllables in each word.
2. Draw a line between the two consonants that follow the first vowel sound to show how each word is divided into syllables.
3. Have the students examine the words to determine their letter patterns and state the principle that governs the words' syllabication.
4. Provide sentences containing similar words which are unfamiliar to the students and have them divide these words into syllables. Then have the students read the sentences.

Word syllabication reflecting *other* letter patterns may be taught in a similar way. The point to remember in planning any lesson on syllabication is that there is no reason to divide words into syllables that can be analyzed more readily by recognizing their root words, prefixes, and suffixes. Students should divide multisyllabic words into syllables when they cannot recognize other word parts and then use their phonic knowledge to pronounce them.

The context in which these words appear could contain enough clues so that it might not be necessary to divide multisyllabic words into all of their syllables before they can be identified.

As with any skill development, syllabication instruction should be integrated with the "normal" reading material students use and not taught independently. The sentences and words can be drawn from the materials students study, reinforcing the skill developed during silent and oral reading and discussions of the content. If, for example, a student is orally reading a passage to verify information and hesitates over a multisyllabic word, remind the student to examine the letter pattern and divide the word accordingly.

Knowing accent principles is helpful in pronouncing words which have been divided into syllables. Some of these generalizations are;

1. The root usually is accented in words that end in a suffix.
   EXAMPLES: tall´est, swift´ly
2. The syllable that precedes *le* usually is accented.
   EXAMPLES: bau´ble, a´ble
3. The last syllable of action words that begin with a prefix usually is accented.
   EXAMPLES: trans port´, re serve´
4. The last syllable in a root word is accented when double consonants precede the ending.
   EXAMPLES: propel´ lant, occur´ rence
5. Multisyllabic words have primary and secondary accents.
   EXAMPLES: book´keéper, leǵerdemain´

These principles may be taught by presenting known words for auditory and visual discrimination. Students are led to see and hear what these words have in common and thus become able to formulate the principle that governs the accent mark.

As with phonic generalizations, students should understand that they must be flexible in applying rules of syllabication and accent. If they are taught to apply them in actual reading rather than to words in lists, they will be more likely to recognize errors in dividing words or misplacing accents. As they grasp the meaning that the context offers, it will not be crucial that they remember the precise ways in which words are divided into syllables or accented. They will be uncertain about the correct pronunciation of a word only if it is one that they have never heard before. In that case, they ought to be encouraged to verify its pronunciation in the dictionary.

USING THE DICTIONARY

The dictionary, of course, is a storehouse of word meanings, but it has other functions, one of which is related to word identification. Ordinarily, students will not consult dictionaries until they have exhausted other techniques for independent word recognition. However, they may use dictionaries to determine or verify word pronunciation.

When using the dictionary for this purpose, students should:

1. open the dictionary to the section in which the word is located;
2. apply alphabetical knowledge to find the word;
3. use the guide words as aids to locate that word;
4. identify the root word from alternate forms of the word;
5. pronounce the word.

If they cannot follow this simple sequence easily — if, for example, they are unable to locate words quickly and efficiently — teachers must plan lessons to overcome these weaknesses. The suggestions that follow are for teachers whose students are not yet ready to use the dictionary for pronunciation help.

Steps before Pronunciation

The first series of exercises prepared by the teacher should develop the ability to open the dictionary to the approximate section in which the word is found. The dictionary may be divided into thirds or fourths and practice given in turning to the section that contains the word.

> **EXERCISE:** Opening the dictionary to the sections in which each of these words is located.
>
> agile   bestial   flail   hearth
>
> **EXERCISE:** Opening the dictionary to the sections in which each of these words is located.
>
> keynote   matron   parsimony   quorum
> raven   stave   usurp   yogurt
>
> **EXERCISE:** Opening the dictionary to the sections in which each of the following words is located.
>
> neophyte   base   ptomaine   tambour
> hilarious   adroit   yak   credence

The second series of exercises is for pupils who do not know the principles of alphabetization or cannot apply them efficiently. All students may not need practice in each aspect of alphabetization, but some will be weak in locating words through letter sequences, even though they can say the alphabet.

> **EXERCISE:** Inserting the missing letter in each sequence of letters.
>
> a_____c   e_____g   i_____k
> n_____p   v_____x   x_____z
>
> **EXERCISE:** Inserting the letter that precedes each of the letters.
>
> _c   _h   _j   _r   _w
>
> **EXERCISE:** Placing words in alphabetical order on the basis of their first letters.
>
> chasm   fagot   render
> action   haste   nasal
> bastion   gem   pensive
> dearth   zenith   tacit
> semblance   azure   choir
> hydrated   waif   lug

EXERCISE: Placing words in alphabetical order on the basis of their second letter.

additive	design	hazard
alternative	dais	hearse
flaccid	wheeze	myopic
fend	wane	mercator
fixate	woeful	monastery

EXERCISE: Placing words in alphabetical order on the basis of their third letter.

mute	goiter	meliorate
muster	gob	meander
prompt	hawser	sofa
pride	haunt	social
praise	hare	sophisticated

The third series of exercises is designed to help students use the guide words on dictionary pages to locate words quickly. After students realize that the first guide word introduces the first entry on a page and the second guide word represents the last entry on that page, they should practice determining whether entries are found between two guide words.

EXERCISE: Determining whether each of the following words may appear on this page of the dictionary.

aft   28   aid

ago	afraid	aim
ahead	add	after

EXERCISE: Determining on which page each of the following words may appear.

bind	**140**	**biology**
biophysics	**141**	**bird**
birth	**142**	**bit**

birch	bipod	birl
binge	bisque	binocular

The fourth type of exercise should train students to identify the root or base word that will be found in the dictionary. Students must understand that inflected word forms do not ordinarily appear as first entries in the dictionary.

EXERCISE: Determining the root word.

loneliest	promiscuously	parted
operating	haughtier	intensified

Pronunciation

The ability to pronounce words as they appear in the dictionary is based on three skills:

1. applying the pronunciation key
2. blending sounds
3. interpreting accent marks.

To use the pronunciation key found at the bottom of the pages of the dictionary, students should learn first that each symbol represents a single sound, e.g.,

best (bĕst)   main (mān)   make (māk)
city (sĭtĭ)   friendly (frĕndlĭ)   dusk (dŭsk)

The student then should be taught how to relate the diacritical marks to the words in the pronunciation guide. Emphasis should be on learning to select the appropriate sound rather than on memorizing what the diacritical marks represent. Teachers should carefully select the words used for teaching purposes so that pupils may relate them to the appropriate guide words without confusion. Beginning exercises may be based on one-syllable words, all of whose vowel sounds are represented in one section of the pronunciation guide. Advanced lessons may require pupils to use the entire guide as it appears in the dictionary.

> EXERCISE: Write in the blank space the key word that contains the same vowel sound as the given word.
> Key words: tăp, āte, cär, cåre
> wasp (wäsp) _____
> braze (brāz) _____
> crass (krăs) _____
>
> EXERCISE: Select the guide words that contain the same vowel sounds as the given words.
> crease _____
> chrome _____
> quay _____
> droll _____
> gilt _____
> irk _____
>
> EXERCISE: Select the word that contains the guide to the pronunciation of the vowel sound in words.
> likin (lēkĕn) _____   _____
> lignose (lĭgnōs) _____   _____
> oozy (o͞ozĭ) _____   _____
> ether (ēthĕr) _____   _____
>
> EXERCISE: Pronounce and identify the following words. Use the pronunciation key as a guide.
> (dēm) _____
> (ko͞o) _____
> (lĭnt) _____
> (māt) _____
> (ōp) _____
> (mŭk) _____

Skill in blending sounds will have been developed during phonic instruction. Students who have not learned this skill will be handicapped when using the pronunciation aids of the dictionary. Orderly learning processes dictate that dictionary work requiring this ability be delayed until blending skills are developed sufficiently to permit some measure of success.

Known words may be used to relate the accent mark to the stressed syllable. Two-syllable words should be introduced before longer words are studied. The concept of primary and secondary accents may be developed **through known words**. These, in turn, will be followed by words with unknown pronunciations. The performance of this final step — identifying an unfamiliar word — will depend upon the degree to which the other skills have been learned.

The dictionary skills associated with the meanings of words are treated in Chapter 7.

SIGHT WORDS

High school students who are not seriously disabled readers can recognize a large stock of words instantly, without resorting to any of the word-identification techniques that have been covered in this chapter. These same students are able to recall the pronunciation of a new word even when it appears in a context other than the one in which they first met it. Poorer readers may need help in building their sight vocabulary. This may best be accomplished by introducing them to new or troublesome words in contextual settings, providing short drills in recognizing these words out of context, and reintroducing the words in another context. Games or puzzles containing words that have first been presented in meaningful contexts can be used to help students with limited sight vocabularies. Card games such as rummy and war and other games such as bingo, dominoes, and Monopoly can be adapted to fit group or individual requirements by substituting words for numbers and playing them in the usual ways. Any activity that just focuses attention on isolated words should then be followed by exercises that require students to read these same words in context.

Some words are similar in appearance to other words and are confusing to poorer readers. It is advisable to treat each separately; as soon as one word is thoroughly learned the similar word may be taught. For example, if some students confuse words such as *through* and *thought*, have students read sentences in which the word *through* appears:

1. The bullet passed *through* two thicknesses of wood panels.
2. Investors hope to earn money *through* increases in stock prices.
3. The innocent prisoners were released from jail *through* their lawyers' efforts.
4. The explorers had to crawl *through* several passages before they found the cave's exit.

In each case, the context requires that the student read the word as *through* and not *thought*. After having learned to recognize *through* in a variety of contexts, the student should read the word *thought* in different contexts which leave no doubt as to what the word should be.

Directed reading lessons provide for the introduction of difficult or unfamiliar words as part of building reading readiness. This part of the lesson may be the most important one for some readers. Students who are not fluent readers because they fail to recognize many words readily will profit from additional instruction in developing an adequate stock of sight words. The number of such words will increase as students become proficient in using independent methods of word attack.

SUMMARY

Proficient readers use several techniques to identify a new word. They may use the clues in the context, seek out word parts, or apply their knowledge of phonics. The superior reader often uses these aids in combination. Methods of teaching that are in harmony with generally accepted principles of learning are recommended for instructing students in how to identify words. These principles emphasize learning based on student needs, using known words to teach word-analysis skills, presenting words in meaningful contexts, and applying word identification skills to daily reading. Remember that a major goal of any word-identification skills program is to help students build sight vocabularies, permitting them to recognize many words readily. Word-analysis instruction is one means of satisfying this purpose.

Additional Readings

The following publications are devoted exclusively to word recognition:

Mildred A. Dawson, comp. *Teaching Word Recognition Skills.* Newark, Del.: International Reading Association, 1971.
William S. Gray. *On Their Own in Reading,* 2d ed. Chicago: Scott, Foresman, 1960.

For specialized treatments of phonics and structural analysis see the following:

Anna D. Cordts. *Phonics for the Reading Teacher.* New York: Holt, Rinehart and Winston, 1965.
Arthur W. Heilman. *Phonics in Proper Perspective.* Columbus, Ohio: Charles E. Merrill, 1964.

Several textbooks on elementary reading offer comprehensive treatments of word recognition. Among them are:

Gerald G. Duffy and George B. Sherman. *Systematic Reading Instruction.* New York: Harper and Row, 1972.
Arthur Heilman. *Principles and Practices of Teaching Reading,* 3d ed. Columbus, Ohio: Charles E. Merrill, 1972.
Robert Karlin. *Teaching Elementary Reading: Principles and Strategies,* 2d ed. New York: Harcourt Brace Jovanovich, 1975.
George D. Spache and Evelyn B. Spache. *Reading in the Elementary School,* 3d ed. Boston: Allyn and Bacon, 1973.

Miles Tinker and Constance McCullough. *Teaching Elementary Reading,* 3d
    ed. Englewood Cliffs, N.J.,: Prentice-Hall, 1975.
Miles Zintz. *The Reading Process,* 2d ed. Dubuque, Iowa: William C. Brown
    Co., 1975.

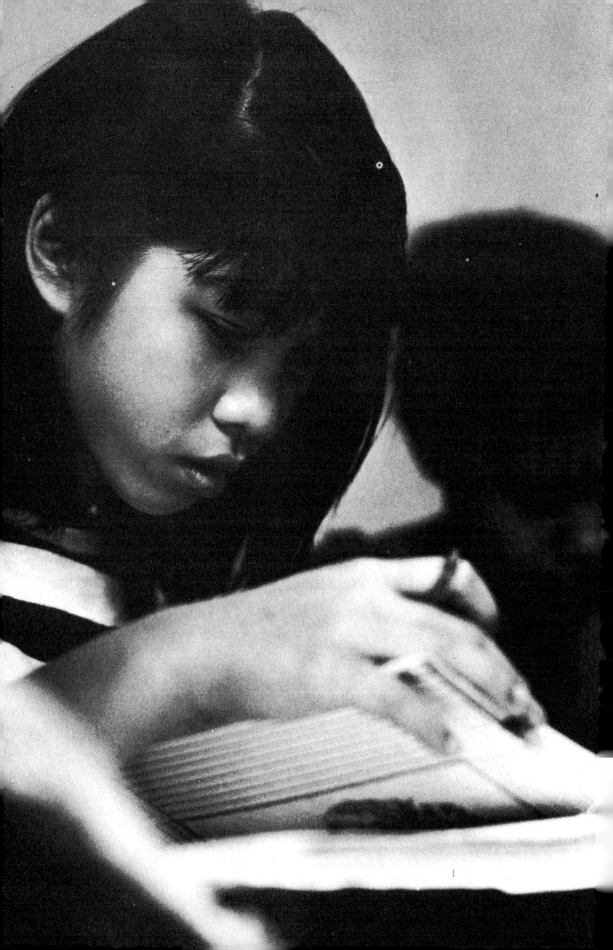

CHAPTER 7

IMPROVING COMPREHENSION
for READING
in CONTENT AREAS

Problems for Study and Discussion

1   *Explain the differences between the components of comprehension.*
2   *In what ways might vocabulary development be promoted?*
3   *How might sentence structures interfere with comprehension?*
4   *How does recognizing paragraph patterns contribute to comprehension?*
5   *How might teachers improve student ability to read inferentially?*
6   *Define critical reading. What types of exercises could teachers use to promote critical reading?*

ASPECTS OF COMPREHENSION

In contextual reading, there seems to be a relationship between word recognition and comprehension. Recognition triggers comprehension; comprehension facilitates recognition. Comprehending continuous text involves not only knowing what is stated directly and what is implied, but also reacting to the contents. In this book, critical reading is treated as a function of comprehension rather than apart from it, because the way in which readers react to printed ideas is one reflection of their understanding of them. Overcoming problems associated with individual words is also an aspect of comprehension, because thought units originate in words and in the ideas words convey.

When reading any passage, the reader must be able to grasp the meanings of words in relation to the surrounding vocabulary. For example, the meaning of a fairly simple phrase such as "the most promising road to fame" would be lost if the student were to think of the individual words *promising* and *road* in their usual sense of "pledging" and "highway," respectively. Such errors in understanding would interfere with the student's understanding of the selection in which they appeared. The experiences that the reader has had with verbal language, once the problem of individual word meanings is overcome, permit him to follow the written thoughts of the author. The idea that the author expresses directly in the sentence, "The most promising road to fame is politics," becomes meaningful insofar as the experiences of the reader allow. Naturally, this sentence would be one among others in a paragraph or series of paragraphs that serve to explain the author's views.

Any effort by the reader to go beyond what the author openly discusses, e.g., to read between the lines, would be considered interpretive reading (understanding what is implied). Perhaps the reader might reach the conclusion that the author is actually trying to discourage young people from entering politics, even though the author has not stated his views on this matter. Another reader might reach a different conclusion. In either case, both readers would be using the ideas that have been presented in order to "get the author's message." A final step, that of evaluating the logic of the author's presentation or the accuracy of his facts, would involve critical reading. The extent to which a reader might intelligently react to the author's views would depend upon the reader's understanding of them as well as upon his background of experiences, real or vicarious.

The degree of comprehension is likely to be influenced by two factors: the intelligence and the personal feelings of the reader. Evidence suggests that intelligence is intimately related to the ability to extract meaning from printed symbols — witness the difference in the reading performances of slow learners and high achievers. Hence, students of greater ability may be expected to better understand reading materials than do students of lesser capacity. But their feelings toward the ideas expressed may also influence understanding. Research on this hypothesis is not extensive, but there are indications that the reader's attitude toward content has some bearing on his comprehension of and reaction to reading material.[1] Teachers should help students become aware of their own beliefs and attitudes by calling attention to them, since such recognition may reduce the extent to which feelings influence understanding. More will be said about feelings in the last section of this chapter.

---

1. Patricia Kendall and Katherine Wolf, "The Analysis of Deviant Cases in Communications Research," pp. 152-159 in *Communications Research, 1948-1949*, ed. Paul F. Lazarsfeld and F. N. Stanton (New York: Harper & Bros., 1949), and Anne McKillop, *The Relationship Between the Reader's Attitude and Certain Types of Reading Response* (New York: Columbia Univ., Teachers College Bureau of Publications, 1952). See also Patrick J. Groff, "Children's Attitudes Toward Reading and Their Critical Reading Abilities in Four Content Type Areas," *Journal of Educational Research* 55 (April 1962): 313-319; C. Gratton Kemp, "Improvement of Critical Thinking in Relation to Open-Closed Belief Systems," *Journal of Experimental Education* 31 (March 1963): 321-323; and William Eller and Judith G. Wolfe, "Factors in Critical Reading, pp. 64-72 in *The Philosophical and Sociological Bases of Reading*, ed. Eric L. Thurston and Lawrence E. Hafner, 14th Yearbook of the National Reading Conference, 1965.

The fourth component which some students of reading ascribe to the reading act — that of integration or assimilation — is possibly the product of the first three and a natural outcome of thoughtful reading. The reader who has thoroughly understood and evaluated the thoughts and ideas of the author might change his behavior and attitudes as he fuses his past experiences with the newly acquired ones.

Whether or not this aspect is a distinguishable component of reading for meaning is debatable. The extent to which teachers can offer guidance in personal behavior is in question. It is possible to discuss logical outcomes of thoughtful reading, but modifications of behavior are not likely to occur unless the reader feels a need for altering typical responses that are based on past experiences. The position on this question taken here is that integration is a long-term process resulting from interactions of many different influences and that behaviors are not easily directed by mere exposures to alternate routes.

The subskills of reading comprehension have been identified. This has been done so that teachers do not view comprehension in a global way and assume that when they deal with one subskill they provide for the others. Surely there is a significant relationship among all the components of comprehension; mature readers do not consciously move from one comprehension level to another. But, when problems in comprehension do occur, it becomes necessary to determine what they are so that efforts to overcome them can be developed.

READING FOR LITERAL COMPREHENSION

Difficulties in understanding direct statements are not uncommon among high school students. Although many students are able to repeat what they read, some probing by the teacher may reveal shortcomings in their grasp of the literal, let alone the implied, meaning of what they have read. These shortcomings are tied to weaknesses associated with word meanings, concepts, and sentence and paragraph structure, and possibly are aggravated by the attitude and purposes of the reader. If one or more of these weaknesses is present, the student's ability to read for comprehension might be severely limited.

Word Meanings

Aside from technical words identified with special content subjects, all high school textbooks have a general vocabulary. Every teacher is familiar with the problems that even these words cause — meanings often are only vaguely known and sometimes generate ideas that have little or no relationship to the context in which the words appear. Facility of spoken language is a factor in reading vocabulary, although the reading vocabulary is likely to be larger than the oral one. Students are able to grasp in reading the meanings of words they never or rarely use in speaking. The size and depth of their vocabularies are products of all the years in which they have been exposed to spoken and printed language, and it would be misleading to suggest that word-meaning weaknesses can be overcome completely within a relatively short period of time.

The surest route to vocabulary building is wide reading. Along this road readers are sure to meet many new words which are repeated in similar and varied settings, and gradually they will add them to their reading vocabulary. Many of these new words ultimately become so familiar to readers that they will use them in speaking and writing. Teachers should encourage and facilitate recreational reading if only for this purpose.

Students should be encouraged to learn the meanings of unfamiliar words as they meet them in daily reading. This is a much more productive way to build vocabulary than to study isolated lists of words. Undoubtedly, you may have determined the meaning of an unknown word that appeared in material you were reading and then were not able to remember the meaning some pages later where the word was used again. To help students avoid this, urge them to keep a set of 3 x 5 cards handy whenever they read and to write each unfamiliar word on a card. (Or, if they own the book, they can underscore the word and record it later.)

It might not always be necessary for them to stop reading to check the meaning of a word. However, if they fail to understand the material as a result of not knowing the word, they should take the time to look it up. On one side of the card have them write the word. On the other side of the card, have them copy the context in which the word appeared (underline the word) and, below it, the appropriate meaning. See Figure 7-1.

Figure 7-1.   Vocabulary Building with 3 x 5 Cards

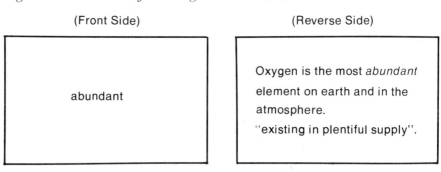

(Front Side)   (Reverse Side)

These words should be reviewed frequently until learned. If the meaning of a word cannot be recalled, a student may simply turn the card over to refresh his memory. Students may test each other and discard words after they have learned them. They should make an effort to use the new words in speech and in writing. Each appropriate usage will strengthen their knowledge until these words become as familiar as any others in their vocabularies.

While students are being encouraged to read widely, teachers can help them comprehend more by making them conscious of words and offering specific lessons in building and extending the meanings of words. Rachel Sutton reported her efforts to help build the reading vocabularies of thirty-six pupils of below-average intelligence. She spent four months with word exercises prepared from materials they were using in class, and individual word lists were maintained. The results on a standardized reading test showed that the group had made greater gains in reading achievement than would have been expected over the four-month period.[2] Isadora Miles spent thirty minutes each day over a semester, emphasizing the meaning, uses, kinds, and values of vocabulary with tenth-graders. She reported an average gain of two years in vocabulary growth. Two and one-half years later, when the experimental group was compared with a control group, the experimental group's average score was higher than that of the latter.[3]

The results of two other studies confirmed the value of devoting time to vocabulary development.[4] The first, which consisted of talks on word origins, study of words in context, and self-teaching and checking exercises, was conducted for only eight weeks. Nevertheless, the experimental group of seventh-graders showed a significant gain over other students who did not receive special vocabulary work. The second study involved two groups of high school seniors, one who spent twenty-seven weeks working on commercial vocabulary exercises as well as on the vocabulary in their literature reading, and the other who received no special work in vocabulary beyond that normally offered in class. The former group scored significantly better than the latter on a vocabulary test.

Not all vocabulary building is done by studying the meanings of words that appear in the reading materials. Students should still be able to use context clues and structural or morphemic clues within words to determine word meanings. Students can extend their vocabularies by experiencing the meanings of words in multiple settings, by studying synonyms and antonyms and figurative language, and by using the dictionary.

Context Clues

Context is as basic to word meaning as it is to word recognition. Superior readers recognize the meanings of unfamiliar words through the aid of context clues, and as a result of either teaching or the development of insight, they are able to spot the words that serve as keys to other words whose meanings are unknown. Whatever the reason, some students do not use context to ascertain the meanings of unfamiliar words. Teachers can prepare simple exercises that illustrate the ways in which context may be used to unlock the sense of these words.

The most simple type of contextual clue is the one in which there can be little doubt about the meaning of a word. Its exact meaning may not be revealed, but readers will have enough knowledge about it to permit them to proceed.

2. Rachel Sutton, "The Effects of Vocabulary Building on Reading Skills," *Elementary School Journal*, Oct. 1953, pp. 94-97.
3. Isadora Miles, "An Experiment in Vocabulary Building in a High School," *School and Society*, April 1945, pp. 285-286.
4. G. Eicholz and R. Barbe, "An Experiment in Vocabulary Development," *Educational Research Bulletin* 40 (Jan. 1961): 1-7, 28; J. Jackson and H. Dizney, "Intensive Vocabulary Training," *Journal of Developmental Reading* 6 (Summer 1963): 221-229.

EXAMPLE:
1. The deep-sea diver used a special searchlight to help him see in the *murky* waters.
2. The ballon *ascended* to a height of six hundred feet.
3. The fire was *extinguished* with a special kind of liquid foam.

There are clues in each of these sentences that point to the meaning of the italicized words. Students should be helped to realize what these clues are. Questions may be utilized to help bring them out:

Why would a deep-sea diver use a searchlight?
What would a ballon have to do to reach six hundred feet?
What might liquid foam do to a fire?

A second type of context clue is found when a definition is contained within the sentence. The definition may take different forms, but students should be able to recognize the definition, whatever its form.

EXAMPLE:
1. Some industries hire *apprentices who learn* as they work.
2. A cold front *or air mass* stretched across the entire northwestern section of the United States.
3. The artichoke, *a leafy vegetable,* is not grown widely in this country.
4. Cuneiform — *wedge-shaped writing* — was used in ancient Babylonia.
5. Lubricants, *such as oil and grease,* are used to reduce friction in moving parts of machinery.

Sentences which represent each of these types of contextual clues will be found within paragraphs. The paragraph below contains several clues that students can use to determine the meaning of primates.

The great apes of the Oriental realm are the orangutans, found in the swamp forests of Sumatra and Borneo, and the graceful gibbons, which swing rapidly from tree to tree in many areas — from the Himalayas to Java and nearby islands. Other *primates* are numerous in the realm. One species, the rhesus monkey of eastern India, is especially well known because so many are used in medical research.[5]

In this example, the second sentence provides the first clue. Teachers might ask students what *Other primates* refers to. The last sentence contains more clues; students should be asked to identify the word which is an example of primates.

The knowledge of language that students have can help them recognize word meanings. They may know a great deal about the *syntax* of the

5. Marston Bates and others, *High School Biology,* BSCS Green Version (Chicago: Rand McNally, 1963), p. 361. Reprinted with the permission of the Biological Sciences Curriculum Study.

language, even though they might not be able to verbalize this knowledge. Some attention to sentence structures can bring syntax into sharper focus and cause them to use these structures as best as possible. While the reader might not be able to determine the precise meaning of an unfamiliar word just from its position in a sentence, being aware of its function in the sentence will serve as a clue to its meaning. Moreover, even single sentences might contain other contextual clues that together will provide some idea about its meaning.

EXAMPLES:
1. The soldier had little time to *ponder* the message.

The position of *ponder* indicates some action on the part of the soldier. While its precise meaning is not clear from the sentence, the reader knows that it is tied to what the soldier might *do* with the message. The words *had little time* added to the function of *ponder* in the sentence do provide additional insight into its meaning.

2. Men who serve as laborers are more likely to eat *hearty* meals than those who spend their days behind desks.

The position of the word *hearty* suggests its function and relationship to the word *meals*. There can be no doubt that *hearty* describes what kind of meals the laborer enjoys. This knowledge, plus the other context clues contained in the sentence, combine to suggest an appropriate meaning for the word.

A third type of contextual clue uses contrasts (or *opposites*) to reveal word meanings. Contrasting ideas may be contained in a single sentence or a longer passage. In either case, clues in the form of punctuation or words signal the contrasted meanings.

EXAMPLE:
1. The value of most automobiles decreases as soon as they are sold; diamonds often *appreciate* with the passage of time.
   appreciate means: lose value; increase in value
2. Some cheeses remain flavorful for months, while butter becomes *rancid* after several days.
   rancid means: sweet; dark; spoiled
3. An overland journey from Paris to the kingdom of Nepal can be a *grueling* experience. On the other hand, the same trip by air is an effortless jaunt.
   What words signal an idea quite different from the meaning of *grueling*? Might grueling mean the same as "effortless"? Explain.

A number of details that, in combination, refer to a single idea constitute still another type of contextual clue to the meaning of an unknown word.

EXAMPLES:
1. The huge waves tossed the craft as though it were a toy. The hurricane winds tore through the sails and smashed the ropes. Jagged rocks ripped open its bottom. The vessel's *doom* was sealed.
   doom means: dock; fate; rudder
2. Activity at dockside increased as the ship edged into her berth. The roar of reversed engines filled the air and intermingled with shouts of men. The hawsers were secured and the cargo unloaded. Then all was quiet on the *quay* again.

List the details that help to identify the meaning of the italicized words.

It is important to realize that context clues might be situated some distance from the word in question. Therefore it is advisable to have students work with longer passages after they have learned to spot and interpret context clues in shorter ones. The following excerpt is an example of a selection whose context clues for one word, *diversity*, are scattered through several paragraphs.

EXAMPLE:
Creatures of the depths. The diversity of organisms usually decreases as the depth increases. Number of individuals also decreases with depth, because life below the photosynthetic zone depends on food drifting down from above. And in general, the greater the depth, the less the food supply. With increasing depth there are also changes in the general characteristics of the organisms, although the limits of the zones in which different organisms occur are not sharp.

The peculiar deep-sea creatures shown in Figure 9.28 are usually 500m or more below the surface during the daytime. They may come nearer the surface at night or at times when the cold waters of the depths well up toward the surface. Apparently, their vertical distribution is controlled by light and temperature as well as by water pressure.

In the eternal night of the depths of the sea, most animals have become either black or dark red and have developed increasingly sensitive eyes. In the unending darkness of caves and underground streams, however, animals tend to become white and blind. This difference is associated with another factor — *bioluminescence*. In the depths of the oceans, many animals have the ability to produce light in their bodies. But bioluminescence is not found in the blackness of caves.[6]

Clues: number of individuals also decreases; less the food supply; limits of the zones in which different organisms occur; their vertical distribution; most animals have become either black or dark red; many animals have the ability to produce light.

The following types of lessons, in which students explain relationships of clues to word-meaning, may be prepared with materials similar to those used in the examples.

6. Ibid., p. 280. Reprinted with the permission of the Biological Sciences Curriculum Study.

1. Identify a known word and supply context clues that support its meaning.
2. Identify a known word and seek context clues that support its meaning.
3. Provide clues to meaning of an unknown word and suggest alternate meanings.
4. Provide clues to meaning of an unknown word and have students determine possible meaning.
5. Have students seek clues to the meaning of an unfamiliar word.

Morphemic Structure

We have seen how the recognition of word parts facilitates their identification. In the same way, recognizing the meaning of these word parts can be a factor in word knowledge. The direct study of words in high school reading materials can be of great help to the student in increasing his comprehension and extending his reading vocabulary. Direct study of words can take several forms, but one that has proved helpful for some students is the study of *etymology*, or the origin and derivation of words. Many commonly used words have their origins in Latin and Greek roots and take on more meaning by the addition of prefixes and suffixes. Knowing the more typical roots, together with the context, can help students determine the meaning of words. Ernest Thompson[7] reported the results of a study in which students concentrated upon twenty prefixes and fourteen roots. They showed a mean gain of 20 percent over the pre-test vocabulary score.

However, complete dependency upon origin and derivation of words for meaning is unwise. Many English words contain identical elements but have dissimilar origins. Such anomalies are found in these two words:

*legi*slate: — from the Latin *lex, legis* (law)
*lege*nd: — from the Latin *legere* (to read)

On the other hand, a number of words may derive from a single source:

legal
legate
legation
legislate
legislature
legitimate

Once again, the importance of context cannot be underestimated even when origin of words is being studied. In the sentence

His handwriting was *illegible.*

the meaning of *illegible* is suggested by the context. Any association with *law* would be far-fetched. An acquaintanceship with both *legis* and *legere*

7. Ernest Thompson, "The Master Word Approach to Vocabulary Training," *Journal of Developmental Reading*, Autumn 1958, pp. 62-66.

would enable the reader to make an intelligent decision regarding its meaning. The dictionary would be the final arbiter if there were any doubts over the way in which the word should be used.

Some of the more prevalent prefixes, roots, and suffixes that may be stressed are presented here.

Prefixes	Meaning	Examples
a or an	not	asocial, analgesia
ab	from, away from	abstain, abduct
ante	before	antecedent, antedate
anti	against	antifreeze, antiaircraft
circum	around	circumference, circumscribe
com	with, together	commission, compilation
de	down from, reversing	detract, detour
dis	away	discharge, disconnect
ex	out of, former	exit, ex-president
hyper	overly	hyperactive, hyperexcitement
in	in or on, not	invest, invalid
inter	among, between	intertwine, intervene
mis	wrongly	misinformed, misconduct
per	through	persist, permeate
post	after	postpone, postdate
pre	before	prepare, precede
pro	for, forward	propose, proponent
re	back, again	reduce, reexamine
sub	under	submarine, subway
super	above, highest	superimpose, superintendent
trans	across	transport, transatlantic
un	not, back	undisciplined, untie

Root Stems		
cap, capt	take, head	capital, captain
ced, cess	go	precede, process
cred, credit	believe	credible, discredit
duc, duct	lead	induct, aqueduct
equ	equal, just	equation, equity
fac, fact	make, do	fact, factory
graph	write	typography, graphic
ject	throw	projectile, object
loqu, locut	speak	loquacious, elocution
mis, mit	send	mission, admit
mor, mort	die	moribund, mortician
nomin, nomen	name	nominate, nomenclature
port	carry	portable, support
pos	place	opposite, position
reg, rect	rule	regent, direct
spic, spect	look	suspicion, spectacle
tang, tact	touch	tangible, contact
ten	hold	tenet, tenable
tend, tens	stretch	tendency, tension
vert, vers	turn	convert, diverse

| vid, vis | see | video, visible |
| voc, vok | call | vocal, evoke |

Suffixes

able, ible, ble	capable of being	sociable, horrible
al	pertaining to	local, formal
ance, ence	relating to	resistance, permanence
ate	make	fixate, locate
er, or	one who	keeper, creator
ful	full of	hopeful, wonderful
hood	state of	adulthood, boyhood
ic	pertaining to	comic, scenic
ion	state of	action, pollution
ism	quality of	heroism, classicism

These common affixes and roots are not presented with the intention of having students memorize them. We have enough experience to know that such activity wastes their time and energies. In fact, only the most gifted students ever apply such knowledge gained through rote learning. Instead, teachers should call students' attention to their presence and function in meaningful contexts and help them see relationships that exist among words that contain common morphemic elements.[8]

The teacher should base practice in ascertaining the meanings of words through the study of word origins that high school students meet in their daily reading. It is advisable to have the students study these words in their contexts, which will provide additional clues to their meaning. Several types of exercises, that teachers may prepare, follow.

EXERCISE: Underline the root stem in each of the italicized words.
1. The soldiers completed their *mission* and returned to their own lines.
2. "Good will" is an *intangible* asset for which businessmen are willing to pay large sums of money.
3. Both major political parties seek *converts* to their points of view.

EXERCISE: Add an appropriate suffix to the italicized words in each sentence.
1. Mountain climbers make *hero* efforts to reach the summit.
2. The *form* presentation of awards was made in the president's office.
3. Government and industry are seeking ways to prevent the *pollute* of rivers and lakes.

EXERCISE: From the roots listed below, determine an appropriate word that will complete each sentence.
ject = throw   loqu, locut = speak   duc, duct = lead
1. The president of the student council made an _____ plea for a new library.

8. A morpheme is the smallest meaningful unit of speech. *Postpaid* contains two morphemes: *post* and *paid; mules* contains two morphemes: *mule* and *s; apple* is one morpheme.

2. An atmosphere that contains many distractions is not _____ to learning.
3. Actors who aspire to the stage must learn to _____ their voices to the farthest reaches of the theater.

Another type of exercise, in which students may determine the meaning of a word that contains an unknown morpheme and familiar root, is one in which sentences are paired with a third to reveal the word's meaning.

a. The company claimed that the strikers had made *unreasonable* demands for wage increases.
b. It is *unrealistic* to expect local governments to meet its citizen's needs without state and federal assistance.
c. We are *unable* to complete the task assigned to us. (Sentence containing known word.)

By analyzing the meaning of *unable*, students may decide what *unreasonable* and *unrealistic* mean, thereby fixing the meaning of the morpheme. New words containing the same morpheme may be built by the students and placed in context with the original word.

un + systematic = unsystematic
un + balanced = unbalanced

The plan was rejected because of its (systematic, unsystematic) treatment of possible outcomes.
The (balanced, unbalanced) budget is one in which expenditures exceed income.

Compound words contain two or more morphemes; quite often, it is possible to determine the meanings of these words from them. Contextual clues, combined with these morphemic clues can reveal their exact meaning. Students can study the elements of known words that appear in their materials in order to learn how to deal with unfamiliar words. It should be noted that in some cases only *one* of the morphemes provides a real clue to the word meaning. The following sentences contain compound words whose meanings can be determined from their morphemes even without contextual clues.

1. Some nomadic tribes move constantly from one area to another in search of new *grasslands* for their cattle.
2. The markings of *freshwater* trout are different from those caught in the sea.

In the next passage, the context clues make the meanings of the compound words quite clear.

As every fisherman knows, food in the *upland* streams is not entirely a matter of what grows in the water itself. Land organisms — most notably, insects — are constantly falling in and contributing to the diet of the stream inhabitants. Both living and dead organic material is washed into the stream with every rain. These materials from the land are an important part of the energy supply for the stream dwellers. Anything not used immediately, however, is washed down to the lower reaches of the stream system. Thus, in the *headwaters,* there is very little food for decomposer populations to work on.[9]

Other compound words contain morphemes whose meanings are less clear without adequate contextual clues:

1. The construction company did not have the *wherewithal* to complete the luxury apartment building.
2. *Kinfolk* expect to be treated differently from friends.

No effort should be made to teach compound words except those that students need to understand for their reading. However, in teaching them how to *analyze* these words for meaning, they learn how to approach other similar words that they will meet in subsequent reading.

Multinyms[10]

Another approach to direct word study is attention to the multiple meanings of words. Words change their meanings as the context changes. Completely depending upon single dictionary meanings will result in mistakes. Words appearing in textbooks and other sources can be studied in their original contexts or in other contexts. Unless contexts provide clues to the possible meaning of unfamiliar words, it is wise to combine lessons on multiple word meanings with the proper use of the dictionary. Students should be shown how to substitute the dictionary meanings for the unfamiliar word to determine which of its meanings fit the context. On occasion, it will be necessary to reword the dictionary meaning so that it makes sense in the sentence. In the first usage of *charge* in the first EXERCISE, it will be necessary to add *for* and delete *of* when substituting *responsible* for *in charge of;* in the second usage, *with* will be omitted: *accuse of* murder instead of *accuse* (with) murder.

EXERCISE: Select the appropriate meaning for the italicized words.
1. in *charge* of public relations   a. instruct
2. *charge* with murder   b. responsible
3. *charge* the jury   c. accuse of

EXERCISE: Select from the dictionary an appropriate meaning for each italicized word in the following phrases.
1. in *open* opposition _____
2. *open* negotiations _____
3. an *open* tennis tournament _____
4. an *open* date _____

9. Bates and others, *High School Biology* (1963), p. 262. Reprinted with the permission of Biological Sciences Curriculum Study.
10. The author coined this term to describe words whose meanings vary with the context.

EXERCISE: Select the sentence in which the meaning of the italicized word differs from the other two.
1. Do you have any *knowledge* of the accident?
2. *Knowledge* is power.
3. The pursuit of new *knowledge* is the scientists' main objective.

Synonyms and Antonyms

The study of words of similar meanings (synonyms) and of opposite meanings (antonyms) can contribute to the students' reading vocabularies. Exercises calling attention to similarities and differences in word meanings help to strengthen comprehension.

EXERCISE: Select from the list of words a synonym for each underlined word.
advance, pervaded, laboring, secure, adorned
1. Many animals <u>obtain</u> protection from their surroundings.
2. A strange odor <u>filled</u> the room.
3. Persons throughout the world are <u>striving</u> to promote peace.

EXERCISE: Use a dictionary to find words that may be substituted for the underlined word in each phrase.
1. an <u>inferior</u> quality of merchandise

_____

2. to <u>infer</u> from clues

_____

3. <u>contaminated</u> food

_____

EXERCISE: Select from the words in the right-hand column the antonym of the italicized words.

1. *imitation* leather	a. immaculate
2. a *filthy* sheet	b. genuine
3. an *impartial* observer	c. biased
	d. soiled
	e. unfavorable

EXERCISE: Indicate whether each word in the series is a synonym or antonym of the italicized word.
1. a *poor* location: choice, inferior, select
2. *hide* one's feelings: conceal, reveal, expose
3. a *mournful* tale: comical, amusing, melancholy

Figurative Language

Often, teachers must draw student attention to words and phrases whose meanings have been extended. Figurative language enhances the vividness of a scene and expresses ideas with a precision that might not otherwise be possible. The most common forms of figurative language are metaphors, similes, and hyperboles. Recognizing the use of comparison and exaggeration can contribute to meaningful reading for many students.

Just as students should not be given lists of words to study, however, they should also not have to memorize lists of figurative expressions that have no relationship to the materials they are reading. How the author uses words to convey special meanings should be considered when the words are encountered. Students might discuss such language usage in relation to what they already know. Because they use figurative language in their daily speech, familiar expressions can serve as samples for analyzing connotative meaning from literal meaning.

Unfamiliar word usages need to be studied in their contexts. Some students may not be able to recognize words that are not intended to be understood in their literal sense. Have these students explain the differences in word meaning between such paired sentences as the following. Note that one represents the unfamiliar usage encountered in reading.

1. Exercises can stretch your muscles.
2. I think I'll stretch my legs.

3. The sky is a deep blue.
4. Once in a blue moon rain falls on the desert.

Other activities, such as those suggested in the sample EXERCISES and accompanied by discussion, can promote recognizing and appreciating figurative language.

EXERCISE: Identify the figures of speech contained in each of the following sentences:
1. He stood ten feet tall.
2. The water sparkled like diamonds.
3. The headlines screamed, "Reagan Wins California Primary!"

EXERCISE: Explain the meaning of the following figures of speech:
1. A violin can be made to sing.
2. He is a Paul Bunyan.
3. The wine flowed like water.

Dictionary

If there is any reference book with which high school students should be thoroughly familiar it is the dictionary. Too few junior and senior high-school students know how to make efficient, let alone full, use of this invaluable tool. (Chapter 6 included several pages on the mechanics of dictionary use for word recognition.)

The dictionary is the most reliable source to which students can turn if word meanings are being sought or verified. In addition to pronunciations and definitions, many dictionaries give the etymology of words, with their derivatives, as well as synonyms and antonyms. Illustrative phrases and sentences further clarify word meanings. All these features contribute to better understanding of words.

Teachers should offer "dictionary instruction" to those students who need help in clarifying word meanings. They should teach them to substitute different meanings for the unknown word if more than one meaning is given, and then select the meaning that fits the context. For example, this sentence might appear in a social studies text:

The framers of the Constitution represented a diversity of interests.

The dictionary meanings for diversity are

1. a being unlike; difference
2. variety

If each meaning is substituted for *diversity,* it becomes apparent that the second definition is more appropriate than the first.

Some definitions will include examples of word usage. There are several meanings for *foundation:*

1. a base, as for a building which supports everything above it.
2. an underlying basis, as for a belief.
3. the act of founding.
4. an organization established to carry on or pay for some worthy purpose, as charity or research.

But if the word *foundation* appears in a context involving ideas or opinions, the examples will help students to select the correct meaning.

High school students may be able to define a word or even explain it, but because they are using words to describe other words, the teacher has no assurance that real understanding is present. Any reader brings meanings to words that serve as triggers to thought, because reconstructing experiences is one way in which words take on meaning. But students' understanding of concepts is often tenuous, with the result that their comprehension is incomplete or faulty. Vague understanding of ideas is a common weakness of high school students; one sound way for teachers to deal with this is to provide opportunities that broaden and enrich the backgrounds of experience.

The importance of meaningful experiences for reading and their influence upon understanding was understood by a layman[11] who examined the problems and hopes of Puerto Ricans in the United States. He pointed out that *cold* is a meaningless concept to these people; in their native land they rarely if ever *feel* cold. However, when they live in New York City they do experience cold weather and know what that means. It would have been fruitless to have tried to explain the concept of *cold* to these people; the concrete experience resolved the issue.

Direct experiences can add much meaning to words. These may include field trips and concrete objects. Even dramatizations can be used effectively to clarify abstract concepts. If first-hand experiences are not feasible, instructional materials, such as maps, pictures, films, and graphs, may be used. The thrust created by a jet engine cannot be described or explained

11. Christopher Rand, *The Puerto Ricans* (New York: Oxford Univ. Press, 1958).

by words. To be appreciated, it must be seen or, better still, felt; a trip to the airport is indicated. The notion of poverty, on the other hand, may be clarified effectively by pictures or films. It would not be too difficult to demonstrate "regal bearing" merely by walking across a room. There may be times when the teacher would find it desirable to use a combination of procedures. Whatever the means, enrichment through experiences is recommended.

Sentence and Paragraph Structure

The ability of high school students to comprehend the meaning of a sentence or a group of sentences depends on their ability to see the relationship between one part of a sentence and another and between one sentence and another. Students must understand the meanings of individual words and groups of words and be able to consolidate these into units of thought. This ability to see relationships between parts seems to be associated with a knowledge of grammar, although formal studies to test this hypothesis have reported negative or inconclusive findings.[12] Perhaps the grammar that is tested is expressed differently from the grammar they intuitively know. Native speakers do seem to know the syntax of their language even though they might be unable to verbalize this knowledge, since they normally construct different types of sentences with complex structures. It is possible some students do not use this knowledge when they read. Sentences are tied together by a unifying idea that may or may not be obscure.

Sentence Structure

Although single sentences are likely to be less of a problem than entire paragraphs, students may require some help in analyzing and comprehending them. Single sentences contain a central thought and details subordinate to it. The reader's job is to separate the subordinate information and expose the central thought. Students and teacher may work together on sentences containing these elements.

EXERCISE: Underline the parts that give the main topic of each sentence.
 1. Geologists, some of whom are young men, continue to seek new sources of uranium.
 2. There is often enough lumber in some sequoia trees, that grow very tall, to build more than one house.
 3. Although most hunters obey the game laws, some deer are taken out of season.

Ask students to decide which parts of the sentence could be omitted and still retain the essence of the sentence:

Geologists . . . continue to seek new sources of uranium.

---

12. Ingrid Strom, "Does Knowledge of Grammar Improve Reading?," *English Journal*, March 1956, pp. 129-133; Roy C. O'Donnell, "A Study of the Correlation Between Awareness of Structural Relationships in English and Ability in Reading Comprehension," *Journal of Experimental Education* 31 (March 1963): 313-316.

There is often enough lumber in some sequoia trees . . . to build more than one house.
 . . . some deer are taken out of season.

They could be led to see that in each case, punctuation sets off the subordinate information from the central information. Once they recognize the essential part of the sentence, they should read it in its complete form.

Some words, phrases, or clauses are added to the central thought in sentences in order to give the reader more specific information. Failure to pay attention to them may leave the reader with some incomplete ideas about the main topic. Students should be able to recognize these descriptive elements, and skill in identifying them may be built.

EXERCISE: **Underline the single word or group of words that give a more vivid picture of the central thought.**
1. Tortuous rivers flow through steaming jungles.
2. Tornadoes are different from cyclones in that they are accompanied by funnel-shaped clouds.
3. The cotyledon of leafy plants serves as a storehouse for plant food.

EXERCISE: **Select the numbered statement that contains the central thought of the following sentence.**
A simple majority of votes cast in the Electoral College is needed to elect the President of the United States.
1. The President of the United States is elected by members of the Electoral College.
2. Half the total number of votes plus one in the Electoral College is sufficient to elect the President of the United States.
3. The candidate who receives the highest number of votes in the Electoral College becomes the President of the United States.

A related activity is one in which students learn to *identify simple subjects and predicates* which carry the basic meaning of sentences. Recognizing of them may prove helpful to students who are confused by long and involved sentence structures. Teachers may first introduce sentences whose structures are clear and show how the subjects indicate the *who* or *what*, and how the predicates give information about the subjects. Later, more complex sentences may be analyzed in the same way to reveal their basic meaning. Students should identify whole subjects and predicates first, and then analyze the sentences for their simple subjects and predicates. What function the other words in the sentences have will be discussed to reveal their complete meaning:

Subject   Predicate
1. *Dogs* | *chase cats.*
2. *Paper money* | *lasts comparatively long.*
3. *The strong winds* | *increased to hurricane force.*
4. At certain times of the year
explorations into space | *must be curtailed* |
because of unsettled climatic conditions.

Another way to analyze a sentence is *to determine how many different ideas it contains.* Such analysis can be helpful for understanding complex sentences such as the following:

A fragment of jawbone that appears to push early man back to five and one-half million years ago has been discovered in Kenya by a group of Harvard scholars.

Ideas in the Sentence
1. A fragment of jawbone has been discovered.
2. The fragment appears to push early man back.
3. The fragment appears to push early man back to five and one-half million years ago.
4. The fragment was discovered in Kenya.
5. The fragment was discovered by a group of scholars.
6. The scholars are from Harvard.

At times, pronouns can be sources of confusion, particularly when writers are not careful in clarifying to what the pronouns refer. Students should be encouraged *to substitute possible referents for pronouns* when they are not certain about them. Both types of pronouns should be dealt with — those that refer to persons or things and others that refer to ideas. The following passages contain both types; students should be taught to formulate questions such as those after the passages[13] and then substitute their answers for the pronouns to determine whether they have the correct meaning.

1. The height of an object can be computed from the length of the shadow *it* casts. You will find *it* very helpful to draw pictures.
   a. What casts a shadow?
   b. What is very helpful?

2. On page 160 we mentioned that *it* is possible to compute sine and cosine of angle measures given to one-tenth of a degree using the table like *that* on page 160. *This* is done by the use of interpolation.
   a. What is possible?
   b. Like what on page 160?
   c. What is done by the use of interpolation?

An additional clue to sentence meaning is *punctuation.* This idea can be conveyed to students by using the same words in different kinds of sentences. Each carries a distinct meaning.

The train is late.
The train is late?
The train is late!

The comma is the most common form of punctuation mark. It not only suggests a juncture or pause in a sentence but also can carry its own

13. Eugene D. Nicholas and others, *Elementary Mathematics* 8 (New York: Holt, Rinehart and Winston, 1966), pp. 167, 184. Reprinted with the permission of the publisher.

meaning. Note how different meanings are suggested by the commas in these sentences:

1. The jet pilot, who formerly was an accountant, was selected to serve as back-up man for the test flight.
2. The menu for the banquet includes shrimp cocktail, onion soup, roast prime ribs of beef, and parfait.
3. As soon as the weather clears, all grounded flights will be scheduled to depart every three minutes.

Each comma in these sentences represents a different construction, and questions may be devised to help student comprehension.

a. What position did the jet pilot formerly hold? (apposition)
b. What foods will be served at the banquet? (enumeration)
c. When will grounded flights be allowed to take off? (subordination)

Other punctuation, such as the colon and semicolon, may be treated in similar ways to establish the relationship of ideas that are separated by them. Many examples of the different meanings that punctuation conveys will be found in students' books.

Some students pay no attention to the details in a sentence and, as a result, fail to grasp its full meaning. The following exercise can call attention to seemingly unimportant words that are central to the meaning. Qualifying words should be noted, for they can change the meaning of seemingly innocent statements.

EXERCISE: Decide whether the following statements are true or false.
1. All trees lose their leaves in winter.
2. Some banks pay higher rates of interest than others.
3. It is usually to the borrower's advantage to repay a loan as quickly as possible.

In sentences that students decide are true, have them substitute one word for another which will make the statements false, and in those that are false, have them substitute one word that will make them true.

1. Many trees lose their leaves in winter.
2. No banks pay higher interest rates than others.
3. It is never to the borrower's advantage to repay a loan as quickly as possible.

There are other types of sentence structures which might interfere with student comprehension. One type omits words which the reader is expected to supply. The following passage contains a number of places where words must be supplied to complete the meaning.

1. For centuries men have spun tales and stories from the fabric of their imagination. 2. Such stories are read and told today mainly for entertainment. 3. In earlier times, however, such stories had a greater im-

portance. 4. Primitive man saw the sun set and the sky grow dark. 5. He saw the moon and stars appear in the blackness above. 6. He saw many strange animals roaming the land around him. 7. He and his fellows saw the days grow short and cold with the coming of winter.[14]

In Sentence 1 the reader must supply missing words before "stories" *(For centuries men have spun)*. In Sentence 2 the reader must supply missing words before "told" *(Such stories are)*. In Sentence 4 the reader must supply missing words before "the sky" *(Primitive man saw)*. In Sentence 5 the reader must supply missing words before "stars" *(He saw the)*. In Sentence 7 the reader must supply missing words before "cold" *(He and his fellows saw the days grow)*. In passages such as this one, have students indicate at a given point what thoughts the author has not repeated. This activity could help those who have not realized that they must supply missing parts to complete the thought.

Sentence structures that are not commonly used in student speech seem to create more comprehension difficulties than those that are. The passive voice, for example, seems to be more troublesome to process than the active voice, because the reader expects the subject to be followed by the object. A teacher may present groups of sentences, such as those below, and have students indicate whether each sentence in the pair expresses the same idea.

> 1a. Inflation is caused by several factors, including excessive government spending and high interest rates.
> b. Several factors, including excessive government spending and high interest rates, cause inflation.
> 2a. Marine fossils have been found by scientists on mountain tops.
> b. Scientists have found marine fossils on mountain tops.

They might also convert passive sentences in the materials they are reading to active sentences.

There are other types of sentences that seem to be more difficult to comprehend than some. One is the sentence whose main clause is preceded by a subordinate clause:

> Although President Grant was not personally involved in scandals which occurred in his administration, the American people held him responsible.

The meaning of such sentences becomes clear if the reader reorders the clauses so that the main clause precedes the subordinate clause.

Sentences which begin with *it* can also be troublesome:

> It is not surprising that there is more than one theory to explain similarities among languages.

14. John S. Hand and others, *Power in English: Experiences in Language* (1972), p. 186. Reprinted with the permission of Laidlaw Brothers, a division of Doubleday & Company, Inc.

In sentences such as this, ask students to substitute the question *What is not surprising?* for *It is not surprising.* This will help them realize that the idea expressed by the rest of the sentence is that to which the introductory phrase refers.

Paragraph Structure

Paragraph reading is more complex than sentence reading. Paragraphs contain many more details and subordinate clauses to confuse the reader. In addition, they usually have a unifying or underlying idea of which the reader must be fully aware. Practice exercises that help students sort out the details and see the relationship among the sentences are useful devices for improving comprehension.

EXERCISE: Read the following paragraph and answer the questions below.

Plants, of course, have no lungs or other organs to pump air in and out of their bodies. The molecules of oxygen diffuse in through stomata, which are tiny pores in the leaves. The bark of trees and shrubs also has pores that let oxygen diffuse through the thick corky layers that protect the stem. These pores, called *lenticals,* are important to plants because they make it possible for the living cells beneath the cork to get oxygen.[15]

1. Plants breathe in the same way as animals. (True or False)
2. Tiny pores in the leaves, called _____, permit oxygen to enter.
3. Stomata in leaves and ___ in bark have a similar function in plants.

Some paragraphs contain words that alert the reader to what is coming. These signposts indicate that a statement or series of statements is to be made to enable the reader to follow the thought. The italicized words in each of the following sentences illustrate such signposts.

1. There are *three* possible explanations for this phenomenon.
2. *Some* examples of simple machines are found in the home.
3. *In the first place,* test results may not be reliable.
4. *Finally,* there is rarely complete agreement on the choice of presidential candidates.

Signposts tell the reader that similar ideas may be expected, while other signposts introduce different or new ideas. Such words as *another, moreover, also,* and *furthermore* indicate that more of the same kind of information is to follow. Such words as *however, on the other hand, nevertheless,* and *but* prepare the reader for a new or contrary idea. Practice in spotting these different clues will help students develop the habit of reading actively. Paragraphs and longer selections that contain these signposts may be found in textbooks and periodicals.

Knowing the function of a paragraph aids comprehension. If students recognize the use of paragraphs in a selection, they will pay more attention

15. Wilbur Beauchamp, John Mayfield, and Joe West, *Science Problems*, Book 3. Copyright 1946 by Scott, Foresman and Company. Reprinted with the permission of the publisher.

to those that are important and spend less time on those that are not.

Paragraphs are of several kinds. One is the *introductory* paragraph that merely introduces the reader to the subject and allows him to anticipate what is to follow. It is not uncommon to find several such paragraphs at the beginning of a selection. Another is the *illustrative* paragraph that contains examples of an idea that has been expressed. A third kind is called a *transitional* paragraph because it helps to bridge the gap from one idea to another. Such words as *however* and *but* often are found in these paragraphs. Last, there is the *summary* paragraph that restates and reinforces the essential ideas. The paragraphs that follow illustrate three of the various types of paragraphs just described.

INTRODUCTORY PARAGRAPH:

The study skills have been defined as skills that students use when they study. The act of studying implies not merely that reading of materials but the retention of required information. Students frequently complain that they are unable to remember what they read. One of the reasons for this weakness is their failure to organize their notes systematically. Another explanation is their inability to recognize the organizational plan that the writer has followed. Chapters in many textbooks are written from a predetermined outline, and this recognition by the reader will facilitate understanding and retention of what he reads.

ILLUSTRATIVE PARAGRAPH:

Even writers of highly regarded publications occasionally use words in such a way as to color the facts and influence the reader. A few years ago there appeared in one of the country's leading newspapers a front-page account of the efforts of an "ex-school teacher" to enact in a foreign country social legislation to which many persons were opposed. In this case, straight factual reporting did not require the revelation of the sponsor's previous profession. Its inclusion might accomplish a single purpose: the reader would associate the provisions of the bill with its sponsor who is cast in an unfavorable light and evaluate the proposed legislation not on its merits but by its advocate.

TRANSITIONAL PARAGRAPH:

Few educators argue the importance of teaching phonics to children. They agree that phonics is an important means of identifying words children do not recognize immediately. *However, most agree that is only one way to attack words and that several methods of dealing with new words should be taught.* These methods include context clues, structural analysis, and dictionary aids.

The final paragraphs in this chapter are examples of the manner in which paragraphs summarize.

Each of the aforementioned paragraphs serves a function in pulling together the ideas that authors wish to express. These paragraphs exemplify writing patterns that bind the content into a meaningful whole. There are other types of paragraphs that unify ideas that are closely related. The ways

in which the ideas are expressed to convey their association are *time order,
comparison-contrast, cause* and *effect, enumeration* and *topic.*

Students who perceive the structure that binds ideas will understand
and remember the ideas much better than if they view them merely as separate entities. Therefore, it is desirable to teach students to recognize the patterns authors use to give form to their ideas. In this way students will begin
to think about ideas in the same way as do the writers. Questions that direct
the former to see relationships may be used to underscore a given structure.
Note how, in the different examples that follow, the questions do not merely
highlight information but tie it together in the form that the author offers.
Longer passages may be more useful than shorter ones to teach students to
recognize the patterns, but individual paragraphs also contain them.

TIME ORDER

Before the nineteenth century, the relation of energy to plant growth
was not understood. Botanists were concerned with the materials used
by plants during growth. But because early investigations of plant
growth eventually led to the discovery of photosynthesis, it is necessary
to begin with them.

One of the first to use an experimental approach to plant growth was
Jan Baptista van Helmont. Here, translated, is his account of an experiment, published in 1648.

"That all vegetable (matter) immediately and materially arises from
the elements of water alone I learned from this experiment. . . ."

During the next two centuries research in chemistry as well as in biology revealed more about plant growth. Van Helmont would have had no
reason to suspect that the air was a source of material for his willow
tree. But toward the end of the eighteenth century, air became a new
center of interest for scientists.

In 1772 Joseph Priestley discovered that green plants have a most
remarkable effect upon air. . . .

Other investigators of the period were unsuccessful in repeating
Priestley's experiments. He himself failed when he tried again, six years
later. The reason for this failure became clear in 1779, when Jan Ingen-
Housz showed that plants act in the manner described by Priestley only
when they are exposed to sunlight. . . .

In 1782 Jean Senebier discovered that illuminated plants absorb
carbon dioxide. And in 1804 Nicolas de Saussure showed that the increase in plant weight after exposure to sunlight is greater than the
weight of the carbon dioxide taken in. . . .

By 1845 Julius Robert Mayer was able to bring the entire picture into
focus. He recognized that the essential steps in photosynthesis are the
absorption of energy in the form of light and the transformation of this
light energy. . . .[16]

1. Approximately how long did it take scientists to discover and understand the process of photosynthesis?
2. Upon whose earlier studies did Mayer base his experiments?

16. Bates and others, *High School Biology* (1963), pp. 413-414. Reprinted with
the permission of the Biological Sciences Curriculum Study.

COMPARISON-CONTRAST

The Nearctic Realm[17]

The plants and animals of North America are, in many cases, so like those of Europe and northern Asia that some biogeographers think these areas should be treated as a single realm. The American bison is the counterpart of the Old World wisent, which now lives only in European zoos and wildlife preserves. Our moose, with its broad antlers, is very closely related to the animal called the elk in Europe. Our elk, which ought better to be called the wapiti, is very similar to the European red deer, or stag — all of which makes for a nice confusion of common names. North American elms, oaks, spruces, and birches are very like those of Russia and Germany; and our maples, beeches, and azaleas have their counterparts in China, Japan, Iran, and Europe. The cause of these similarities is found in the past. Over long periods of geological time, a broad isthmus (a "bridge" of land) connected Alaska and Siberia; thus, in periods of mild climate, animals and plants could pass along this route in either direction, from one continent to the other.

Yet today the fauna and flora of these two northern realms are by no means identical. For example, the wild rats and mice of North America and those of the Old World belong to quite different groups. And the closest Old World relatives of our racoons are the pandas of the distant Chinese forests. Other animals native only to the Nearctic realm include cottontail rabbits, skunks, muskrats, and prairie dogs. The pronghorn, of the western United States, is also unique to this realm (see Figure 11.14). The Nearctic realm is far better supplied with species of poisonous snakes than is the Palearctic. In addition to the brightly banded coral snakes, which have spread northward from the Neotropical realm, there are the copperhead, the cottonmouth, and many kinds of rattlesnakes. Among birds, we share crows, jays, and chickadees with Europe; but for the most part, our birds are different — their closest relatives inhabit South America.

1. How do scientists explain the fact that counterparts of species living in North America are found also in Europe and Asia?
2. "Every species has its own distinctive pattern of distribution." Explain and give some examples of this generalization.

CAUSE AND EFFECT

Condensation of Water from the Atmosphere[18]

Moisture is constantly evaporating from bodies of water and moist surfaces on the earth. The air near the surface of the earth therefore contains water vapor. When the air is holding as much water vapor as it possibly can at a certain temperature, a very small drop in temperature causes the water vapor to condense. When there is very little water vapor in the air, the temperature will have to be lowered much more before it condenses. The temperature at which the vapor condenses is

17. Ibid., p. 353. Reprinted with the permission of the Biological Sciences Curriculum Study.
18. J. Darrell Barnard and Lon Edwards, *The New Basic Science* (Macmillan Science Series), pp. 266-267. Copyright © Macmillan Publishing Co., Inc., 1951, 1956, and reprinted with their permission.

called the dew point. When the temperature of the air is lowered to its dew point, water may form a cloud or fog or it may be returned to the surface of the earth in the form of dew, frost, snow, rain or hail. Water that falls to the earth as rain, as snow, or as hail is called precipitation.

Formation of fog, dew, and frost. The cooling of a large body of air near the surface of the earth to a temperature below its dew point may result in a fog. A fog is formed when the moisture in the air condenses into extremely small droplets and remains suspended in the air near the surface of the earth as a thick mist.

At night plants, other objects, and the ground itself often lose much of their heat, becoming cooler than the surrounding air. When the temperature of these objects drops below the dew point of the air, water vapor in the air immediately surrounding them condenses and is deposited on them as dew (see page 263). Dew is not formed, however, when there are winds blowing, for then the air does not remain in contact with a cooler object long enough to be cooled to its dew point. Vapor condenses only when the air is in contact with a colder object. When the dew point of the air is below 32° F, moisture in the air condenses directly from a gas to solid ice crystals as frost. Before frost will form on an object, the temperature of the object must also be below 32° F.

Clouds, rain, and snow. When rising moist air is cooled below its dew point, clouds are formed. The moisture condenses and may form either tiny droplets of water or ice crystals, depending upon the temperature. Rain may be formed in a cloud when the tiny particles of water combine or when warm moist air enters the cloud from below, and the water vapor in it condenses. If the temperature in the cloud is above freezing, the condensed moisture falls as rain; if the temperature in the cloud is below freezing, it falls as snow. Before snow will fall on the earth, air temperatures between the earth and the cloud must be cold enough so that snowflakes do not melt as they fall. The air below the cloud must also be moist enough so that the snowflakes or rain will not change back into water vapor.

Formation of hail. Hail is usually formed when large drops of water are carried from a lower to a higher part of a cloud that extends to very high levels where temperatures are below freezing. As each drop of water reaches the colder cloud levels, snow and frost are added to it. It then falls but soon stronger currents of air may carry it up again to freezing layers of the cloud where more snow and frost are added. Each time the growing hailstone falls and is returned to the colder part of the cloud, another layer of ice is added until it becomes too heavy to be suspended by updrafts of air and falls to the earth.

1. How do changes in the atmosphere's moisture content and temperature affect weather conditions?
2. How are clouds formed?

TOPICAL ORDER

Controlling Harmful Plants[19]

Protection from bacteria. One of the big problems in growing crops is protecting the crops from diseases known as rots and wilts caused by

19. Ibid., p. 393. Copyright © Macmillan Publishing Co., Inc., 1951, 1956, and reprinted with their permission.

harmful bacteria. The bacteria may enter the plant through natural open-
ings, such as the stomata, or through broken places in the outer covering
of the plant. They are also carried by insects from one plant to others
upon which the insects feed. Once harmful bacteria have entered the
plant, they may destroy plant tissue, thus causing parts of the plant to
rot. If the bacteria get into the water-conducting tubes, they obstruct the
flow of water through the plant, thus causing it to wilt. When bacteria
destroy plant cells to obtain food, the waste products, such as acids,
given off are poisonous to the plant. Once bacteria have entered the
plant, little can be done to control them. Generally the infected parts of
the plant must be removed and burned. Therefore plants subject to rots
and wilts should be protected from insects which would carry the harmful bacteria from diseased plants.

Protection from mildews, rusts, and smuts. Fungi, such as powdery
mildews, rusts, and smuts, cause great damage to farm crops. These
fungi differ from bacteria in that each individual fungus is made up of a
large number of cells, whereas bacteria are single-celled plants.

The powdery mildews cause many diseases among such plants as
rose and gooseberry, and apple, cherry, and ash trees. The mildews are
propagated by spores, which are microscopic in size and easily carried
from one plant to another through air. The spores of powdery mildew
generally start growing on the leaves, producing rootlike structures
which pierce the leaves and absorb food from leaf cells. The strands of
the fungus that grow over the surface of the leaf then produce millions of
spores which appear as a powdery substance on the leaves.

1. What kinds of organisms attack crops?
2. By what mechanisms do they harm the crops?

ENUMERATION

The Realms[20]

In studying the distribution of the land animals of the world, Wallace
recognized six different realms (Figure 11.12): the Nearctic (all of North
America except the southern end, where tropical animals are dominant);
the Palearctic (Europe and northern Asia, from the British Isles to Japan
and including Africa north of the Sahara); the Ethiopian (Africa south of
the Sahara); the Oriental (India, Malaya, the Philippines, and nearby
regions); the Australian (Australia and New Guinea); and the Neotropical (South and Central America). With some exceptions, the boundaries
of Wallace's realms correspond rather closely to the boundaries of the
continental land masses.

Now what kinds of barriers have operated to bring about this grouping
of plants and animals? Figure 11.13 is a rather unusual map of the world;
it is designed to show the location of the major barriers between the
realms. Four kinds of barriers are indicated.

1. Oceanic barriers, generally running north and south. These prevent
   the direct dispersal of plants and animals in eastward or westward
   directions — for example, from the Neotropical to the Ethiopian
   realm.

20. Bates and others, *High School Biology* (1963), p. 349. Reprinted with the permission of the Biological Sciences Curriculum Study.

2. A barrier of high mountains — the Himalayas and related chains — separating the Oriental and Palearctic realms.
3. A complex barrier, separating the Oriental and Australian realms. This barrier has effectively isolated the great island continent of Australia, and it can be crossed only by means of sweepstakes dispersal.
4. Partial barriers, involving filter routes that join four of the realms — the Isthmus of Panama, for example.

1. There are large areas in which distinctive groups of land animals are distributed. How are these areas classified?
2. What types of barriers tend to maintain animals within their natural realms?

Quite often, passages contain information that is related in more than one way. It is not uncommon for authors to combine patterns, particularly in longer passages. Cause and effect will be joined by topical order, enumeration with comparison-contrast, and so on. But one is apt to be highlighted more than another. If students identify more than a single pattern in a paragraph or longer passage, the teacher should have the students decide if they are equally stressed.

Students who learn to recognize these different paragraphs as they read have an additional aid to understanding. Practice exercises in identifying types of paragraphs may be prepared by the teacher from the materials found in textbooks and other sources. Students should learn to identify the "word signals" in a given passage. These are words which indicate the way in which the ideas in the passage are related. In the passage that illustrated time order, there were several signals: "Before the nineteenth century," "One of the first," "in 1648," "During the next two centuries," and so forth. The comparison-contrast passage contained such word signals as, "are . . . so like," "is closely related," "Yet . . . are by no means identical." "When" signalled the relationship in the cause and effect passage. Enumeration was indicated by phrases such as "six different realms" and "four kinds of barriers."

The ability to separate important ideas from their details is essential to comprehension. Most paragraphs are built around a central theme. Some main ideas are stated plainly while others must be inferred. At times, the main idea is found at the beginning of a paragraph; at other times it is in the middle or end of a paragraph. Students must be able to recognize it wherever it may be located. This is discussed at length in Chapter 8.

READING FOR INFERENTIAL COMPREHENSION

At the high school level, one important objective of reading instruction is increasing the students' abilities to extract deeper meaning from what is read. Authors do not spell out every single idea in narrative or expository writing but leave much for the reader to do. Superior readers naturally seek deeper or hidden meanings that are implicit in statements. They try to determine the author's purpose from what he says, since knowledge of his purpose will help them clarify what is left unsaid. Cause-and-effect relationships that are unstated are sought, generalizations are made, and conclusions are drawn.

Guidance in Interpretation

Teachers should not assume that all good readers extract information from between the lines. These students may be capable of drawing inferences, yet many will not have made interpretation an important part of the reading act. Less able readers are content to deal with explicit statements. Both categories of students can benefit from instruction that guides them in seeing the relationships contained in expressed ideas and that exposes the bases on which they may make inferences.

Teaching high school students to read for deeper meanings is not solely a matter of guidance. As in other kinds of reading, the influences of experiential background are felt. Students who have not read widely or who must depend upon concrete representations to obtain much meaning from abstract ideas may not be expected to perform in the manner of more sophisticated readers. Limited and narrow experiences will be reflected in the amount and kind of interpretative reading that will be realized.

Guidance in interpretative reading can take several forms, and one that has proved effective is the use of questions. Questions stimulate thinking, because they force the reader to make use of what he already knows — the information that is given — and read between the lines. When answers are discussed, analysis can reveal to students any errors in their thinking and suggest ways in which to deal with future reading tasks. One such type of exercise follows.

EXERCISE: Read these statements to determine the author's purpose.
1. The spoils system is in the American tradition.
2. A welfare state would dominate the life of every citizen in the nation.
3. Although the number of deaths due to injuries suffered in high school football games has decreased, many casualties are reported each year.
   a. Is the author in favor of the spoils system?
   b. How does the writer regard the welfare state?
   c. What recommendation(s) would the author make regarding high school football?

Students should identify the words in a passage that suggest to them how the author feels about the topic discussed and explain how they reasoned, to reach a judgment about the author's purpose.

Another way to teach students to recognize an author's purpose is to present two passages that contain the same basic information, but one of which is presented so as to suggest that the writer's intentions go beyond merely offering information.

EXERCISE: Which of the following passages express the author's viewpoint about treatment of the American Indian? What is the author's purpose in expressing this viewpoint?

a. And the Indians fought back to hold on to their lands and customs. As the area under their control became smaller, the harder the Indians struck back. But the whites fought hard too.
b. And the Indians fought back, struggling to hold onto their lands and their distinctive way of life. The smaller the area into which they were compressed, the more savagely the Indians struck back. But the savagery was not all on one side. The whites fought with broken promises as well as with guns.[21]

Questions may also be used by the teacher to direct student attention to parts of a piece of writing that reveal more than is actually stated. In effect, the reader is being shown what he must do to reach beneath the mere surface of the writing.

EXERCISE: Read the following paragraph and then answer the questions.
He strode into the room, looked about, and without uttering a word to anyone, stretched out on the sofa. Everyone seated at the table waited expectantly as though something would occur any moment. No one stirred. Suddenly, he lifted himself up on one elbow, waved his hand imperiously in the manner of a conductor readying his orchestra and began a monologue that continued for what seemed an eternity.
1. How would you describe the man who came into the room?
2. What attitude did those present have toward him?
3. Is the writer of this paragraph merely acting as a reporter or does he have some feelings about what is occurring?

Instead of using questions, the teacher may present the students with a series of possible conclusions and let them determine the validity of each. The teacher should make clear that more than one conclusion often may be drawn from a statement but that one may be more appropriate than another. Students often draw conclusions that are wholly unwarranted, and the importance of basing judgments on supporting evidence should be emphasized.

EXERCISE: Determine whether the numbered conclusions may be drawn from the statement.
Speeds in excess of 1,000 miles per hour are likely to be reached by passenger planes.
1. Passenger planes capable of flying at more than 1,000 miles per hour will become operational within three years.
2. Passenger planes will be capable of flying from New York to Los Angeles in less than four hours.
3. The cost of air transportation will decrease with the introduction of planes capable of flying at high rates of speed.

Instead of providing questions or drawing conclusions, the teacher may indicate clues in a paragraph and ask the students to draw inferences. A discussion of the kinds of ideas that may be inferred from these clues will

21. Lewis P. Todd and Merle Curti, *Rise of the American Nation*, 2d ed. (New York: Harcourt, Brace and World, 1966), p. 433. Copyright © 1966 by Harcourt Brace Jovanovich, Inc., and reprinted with their permission.

help students to understand what they need to think as they read and to use to the fullest whatever information is given. The paragraph that follows may be used in this way.

> **EXERCISE: Draw suitable inferences from the underlined words or phrases.**
> He strode into the room, looked about, and without uttering a word to anyone, stretched out on the sofa. Everyone seated at the table waited expectantly. No one stirred. Suddenly, he lifted himself up on one elbow, waved his hand imperiously in the manner of a conductor readying his orchestra and began a monologue that continued for what seemed an eternity.

Frequently, cause-and-effect relationships are introduced by such words as *when, for this reason,* and *as a result of.* In such cases, the author states the relationship. However, there are times when this relationship must be inferred, as in the following passage:

> The remains of dead plants and animals may be decomposed by microscopic organisms like bacteria. These microorganisms also respire and contribute carbon dioxide to the weathering environment. The dead plant and animal debris is eventually reduced to very fine particles that adhere to the surfaces of mineral grains.[22]

In reading passages that express cause-and-effect relationships that may be inferred, students might be taught to seek them by indicating the cause if given the effect, or vice versa.

> effect: decomposition of the remains of dead plants and animals.
> cause: _____
> cause: carbon dioxide from microorganisms.
> effect: _____

Later, they should be able to recognize what is the cause and what is the effect when the relationship is pointed out to them. Finally, they should be able to identify a relationship if one exists.

Interpretive reading involves not only reading between the lines to discover the author's purpose, draw conclusions, and see relationships, but also to anticipate what ground the author is likely to cover. Students should be taught to recognize words that are "signals" for what is coming and to raise questions or make comments which serve as continuous purposes as they read. In the passage that follows, the "signals" are underscored and the types of questions or comments they suggest follow in parentheses.

> **Continuity and change in foreign policy.** In its efforts to meet the nation's responsibilities (What efforts?) in a rapidly changing world, the Kennedy-Johnson administration followed in general the basic foreign

22. *Investigating the Earth,* Earth Science Curriculum Project of the American Geological Institute (1967), p. 273. Reprinted with the permission of Houghton Mifflin Co.

policy developed by the Truman and Eisenhower administrations. (What was that policy?) It continued to resist Communist aggression, to strengthen the nation's military defenses, to maintain America's lead in missiles, and to catch up with the Soviet Union in the conquest of outer space. (Some are related only to our foreign policy.) At the same time, (What else did it do?) the administration continued to support the United Nations, appointing Adlai Stevenson as ambassador to the world organization, and made a determined effort to reduce international tensions.

But there were new phases (What?) as well as continuity in foreign policy during the opening years of the 1960s. The Trade Expansion Act of 1962 (page 758) (I remember it.) was designed to increase the flow of world trade as well as to meet the growing competition of the Common Market countries of Western Europe. Consistent with its policy of encouraging the arts at home, (Here come some examples.) the Kennedy-Johnson administration sponsored programs to strengthen international cultural relations. As part of these programs, outstanding American musicians, theater groups, writers, and artists visited friendly, neutral, and Communist countries. By far the most imaginative innovation, (I think I know.) however, was the Peace Corps.[23]

Whichever form of guidance the teacher adopts, single sentences and paragraphs may be used to develop interpretative reading. But whatever material is presented, students must be helped to "see" how suitable inferences are drawn.

CRITICAL READING

The reader deals with printed language much in the same way that a listener deals with spoken language, and once the added element of visual symbols has been mastered, the orderly processes of thinking are activated. Hence, many writers have described the reading process as a thinking process. If this is so, then critical reading may be considered as critical thinking. Critical thinking has been compared with the method of science in that it is a series of steps that must be made before reaching a conclusion. Another definition considers critical thinking as "the process of examining . . . verbal materials in the light of related objective evidence, comparing . . . the statement with some norm or standard, and concluding or acting upon the judgment then made."[24]

Problems in Critical Reading

The teaching of critical reading is an important part of any secondary school reading program. If any justification were needed for the stress put upon it, schools need only point to the contributions critical reading makes

23. Todd and Curti, *Rise of the American Nation,* (1966) p. 792. Copyright © 1966 by Harcourt Brace Jovanovich, Inc., and reprinted with their permission.
24. David Russell, *Children's Thinking* (Boston: Ginn and Co., 1956), p. 285.

to the development of the individual and people as a whole. In the society to which each of us is dedicated — a democratic society — desirable attitudes and values must be fostered, and one way of accomplishing this is to encourage decision making based upon critical evaluation of information presented as truth.

Teaching critical reading (thinking) runs into two problems. The first of these is the influence of teaching upon the learner. Children pattern their thinking and behavior upon models in whom they have confidence, usually their parents and other adults with whom they feel kinship. Teachers may well find that some high school students are not sufficiently mature to cope with situations in which doubts are cast upon their models' reliability. In an accepting classroom climate, these students will be helped to deal with conflict and may in time be ready to take a second look at their assumptions that are being questioned.

The second teaching problem arises from the issue of the kinds of attitudes the school shall foster and who has ultimate responsiblilty for deciding what these shall be. In homes where complete submissiveness to authority is demanded, ideas presented and pronouncements made must be accepted without reservations. It is quite possible that children who have been encouraged to read and think critically might not know how to deal with restrictive conditions at home. In situations such as these, an explanation to parents of the program's objectives could reduce conflicts arising from children's reactions to parental dictates and views.

Many high school students need help in improving their ability to read and think critically. This is not to suggest that all students are uncritical, but even for those who do make evaluative judgments, data indicate that additional growth can be promoted. One investigator[25] taught a large number of high school students and found that they improved their ability to recognize disagreements in the accounts of different writers on the same subject. A second investigator[26] reported significant gains in students' ability to analyze statements of propaganda and evaluate arguments. Other investigators[27] reported similar findings for different kinds of populations. The results of these studies indicate clearly the positive effects of instruction on the critical reading abilities of students.

What are some of the factors associated with high school students' ability to do critical reading? *One*, of course, is intelligence, with the students of

25. Sylvia Kay, "Critical Reading: Its Importance and Development," *English Journal*, Sept. 1946, pp. 380-385.
26. Edward Glaser, *An Experiment in the Development of Critical Thinking*, Teachers College Contributions to Education No. 843 (New York: Columbia University, Teachers College, Bureau of Publications, 1941).
27. C. Gratton Kemp, "Improvement of Critical Thinking in Relation to Open-Closed Belief Systems," *Journal of Experimental Education* 31 (March 1963): 321-323; Howard Livingston, "An Investigation of the Effect of Instruction in General Semantics on Critical Reading Ability," *California Journal of Educational Research* 16 (March 1965): 93-96; Willavene Wolf and Bernice D. Ellinger, "Teaching Critical Reading: An Observational Study," pp. 434-445 in *Critical Reading*, ed. Martha L. King, Bernice D. Ellinger, and Willavene Wolf (Philadelphia: J. B. Lippincott, 1967).

normal or superior intellectual ability being expected to achieve to a higher degree than slower learners. But the latter, by all means, should be encouraged to react to ideas. Although intelligence and the ability to read critically appear to go together, high performance on an intelligence test is not a guarantee of equally high performance in critical thinking. When a student is faced with a situation that calls for careful evaluation, there is no assurance that he will respond appropriately, and this fact has prompted educators to point to the importance of instruction that provides encouragement of critical thinking.

A *second* factor is experiential background. Critical thinking involves comparison with a known standard. "In general, the more a child knows about the circumstances surrounding a problem, the better his solution will be. Knowledge does not necessarily mean good thinking, but high-order thinking is dependent upon knowledge."[28] Knowledge is identified with concepts, and vague and tenuous concepts may not be used as models for comparison. Many of the ideas with which students deal in high school are abstract, and real experiences help to add substance to them. As the teacher knows, the background of experience will vary from student to student.

The *third* factor that may affect the student's ability to do critical reading is his attitude toward the content. It has been said that the reader who does not think critically is at the mercy of the writer, and the converse is just as true: the writer is defenseless before the uncritical reader. Prejudices toward or against persons, ideas, or topics have been shown to interfere with the reader's evaluation of printed matter.

Finally, the nature of the individual may be a factor in his response to persuasive writing. Some psychologists have been categorizing patterns of behavior and identifying persons who are likely to be swayed or bound to resist.

Scope in Teaching Critical Reading

Basic to any good teaching is the concept of sequential learning, which carries with it the concept of readiness for learning. Yet teachers in high schools cannot assume that students are ready to learn or are prepared to profit from instruction planned for them. Individual differences are great by the time students reach high school, and as other chapters in this book have stressed, these differences must be taken into consideration. Teaching critical reading may have to begin with very simple lessons before it can proceed to complex ones.

Although no systematic studies have determined in what order the critical reading skills should be taught, teacher experiences suggest a hierarchy. Studies have examined different aspects of the ability to do critical reading in terms of the known versus the unknown, the simple versus the complex, the concrete versus the abstract, and have reached the significant conclusion that the student's experiences and his ability to draw on them control the level of critical reading that he can achieve.

28. Russell, *Children's Thinking* (1956), p. 336.

Critical thinking associated with critical reading begins in the primary grades, where children evaluate pictures in their books for accuracy and appropriateness and decide whether or not characters in stories acted as they would. Skill in selecting suitable sources of information is fostered in the lower grades, and ability to recognize the reliability of a source of information is built up from gross to finer discriminations. Children learn to discriminate between fanciful tales and factual reports, to compare the worth of books, and to express preferences on the basis of some standards. All these skills require discriminatory thinking.

In the middle and upper grades, students are encouraged to read widely among expository material in textbooks, magazines, and newspapers. Solutions to problems that the curriculum presents will demand that students begin to use care in selecting and evaluating information from these kinds of sources. To determine the adequacy and accuracy of what purports to be a factual statement is an ability that calls for rather mature insights in a high school student. If the teacher has any doubt that his students cannot distinguish between fact and opinion, an exercise such as the following may be useful.

EXERCISE: Determine whether each of the following statements is a fact or an opinion.
1. The Treaty of Versailles placed an intolerable burden upon the people of Germany.
2. Senate filibusters will continue to prevent the passage of controversial legislation.
3. Experimental aircraft have flown at three times the speed of sound.
4. It is claimed that children are natural mimics.

How might students determine whether each of these statements express facts or opinions? One way is to decide whether the statement can be proved. Students should discuss where proofs might be obtained (encyclopedias, textbooks, diaries, historical documents, articles, and so forth). Some statements are easier to prove than others. For example, Statement 1 *might* be a fact but difficult to prove. On the other hand, Statement 3 would be easily proved or disproved.

Some words signal opinions, as in Statement 4. Other words such as *think, believe, could, might, seem,* and *probably* introduce opinions. It is quite common to read official statements that contain words such as *might* and *could* but really are intended to leave the impression that the statements are factual. To ignore them or fail to recognize their meaning will not serve society's purposes.

Many students, like many adults, have the attitude that any statement that appears in print must be accurate. They must be taught to evaluate what they read in terms of the author's possible bias, qualifications, and personal opinion. Magazine and newspaper articles, especially, demand critical review. Students should be given ample opportunities to evaluate the authenticity and accuracy of information as to its source.

EXERCISE: Who is best qualified to make this statement?
The total effects of radiation from atomic wastes are not completely known.
  a. newspaper reporter
  b. nuclear physicist
  c. electrical engineer

EXERCISE: Who is qualified to make each of the following statements?
  1. Viruses cause the common cold.
  2. Periodic depressions are not inevitable.
  3. Some form of exercise is recommended for the aged.

EXERCISE: Which sources are likely to give the most accurate information about frontier life in the eighteenth century?
  a. historical novel
  b. autobiography of a pioneer
  c. history textbook
  d. encyclopedia

It is important that the student be aware of the purposes and motives of a writer — is he presenting factual material or sharpening an axe? The reader is in a better position to question if he recognizes the author's intent. He will not then view as one and the same a statement by the president of some organization known to have a vested interest and one by an impartial observer. Teachers may take paragraphs from a variety of sources and ask the students to analyze them with a view to identifying their origin and intent.

Along with this ability to sense the author's purpose goes the ability to discern and evaluate propagandist or persuasive statements. Although we may not take issue with efforts to indoctrinate, we can reject deceptions or distortions of information. The techniques of propaganda have been analyzed and are well known.[29] One to which the high school teacher should give special attention is the propagandist's device of citing quotations that have been removed from a larger context to mislead the reader into believing what he ordinarily would not accept. A second technique is the truthful but incomplete statement. Others include the testimonial, the band wagon, the "common touch," and the glittering generality. Students not only need to be alerted to these devices but also must have opportunities to respond to them. Possession of the ability to identify a propagandist or persuasive technique does not guarantee its use during independent reading. Students should study examples of each and point them out wherever they exist.

Most teachers are familiar with Samuel Hayakawa's study of the use of language and its influences.[30] There is no question that words can generate feelings, and the sophisticates have responded intelligently: in economics, depressions have become recessions; in ladies' wear, half sizes are now B sizes! Even writers for highly regarded factual publications occasionally use words to color facts and influence readers.

29. Clyde Miller, *What Everybody Should Know about Propaganda, How and Why It Works*, 4th ed., rev. (New York: Commission for Propaganda Analysis, Methodist Federation for Social Action, 1952).
30. S. I. Hayakawa, *Language in Thought and Action* (New York: Harcourt, Brace, 1949).

High school students must learn to separate words that have the power to produce feelings from those that merely serve to identify referents. By the simple act of interspersing words that are known to evoke emotional responses among factual words, a writer can cause reactions that he seeks to create. This is one thing in the field of fiction, and something quite different in other forms of writing. Attention should be drawn to textbooks or other printed material if these contain words that generate feelings, and discussion of them should be encouraged. A thinking attitude toward printed symbols is likely to contribute to positive results in comprehension and interpretation.

EXERCISE: Which of the paired sentences is designed to influence the reader?

A raise of ten dollars a week was recommended for civil-service workers whose annual salaries did not equal $5,000.

Modest raises of ten dollars were recommended for civil-service workers who earned less than $100 a week.

There is a shocking increase in the number of crimes committed by boys and girls under the age of eighteen.

The number of cases in which boys and girls under the age of eighteen violated the law increased from 1,052 to 1,895.

The student's ability to develop into an expert critical reader is always complicated by his own values. Few educators would deny that it is important for the teacher to deal with moral questions which fall within the reader's level of maturity, but this is not always possible. Before high school students are really able to answer the question "Was it the right thing to do?" as they study the westward movement and the ultimate placement of Indians on reservations, they need to have accumulated more facts than opinions so that they are sufficiently informed to weigh the issues.

Allied with the ability to base value judgments on facts is the ability to withhold judgment until as many facts as possible have been accumulated. It is tempting to base conclusions on minimal amounts of information — witness the tenuous decisions reached by some adults — and students should be encouraged to ask themselves, "Have I sufficient information on which to base an opinion?" The importance of this kind of learning cannot be overstressed.

SUMMARY

Reading for meaning involves literal comprehension, inferential comprehension, and critical reading. Literal comprehension refers to the ability to understand what is stated directly and inferential comprehension to understand what can be inferred. Critical reading is the act of evaluating information and ideas.

Instruction in reading for literal comprehension consists of vocabulary and concept development and helping students to understand sentence and paragraph structures. Inferential comprehension involves the ability to recognize author's purpose, draw conclusions, see relationships, and anticipate outcomes. Lessons to promote these abilities should be offered to students who will benefit from them. Instruction in critical reading should include ways to separate facts from opinions, accurate from misleading information, and information from emotion.

The comprehension of all students may be improved by directing their attention to specified aspects instead of treating comprehension as a unitary ability. The materials students read are likely to pose problems in comprehension, and these should serve as a basis of instruction.

Additional Readings

Two anthologies consist of articles on theoretical considerations and practical applications for teaching literal, inferential, and critical reading:

Mildred A. Dawson, comp. *Developing Comprehension Including Critical Reading*. Newark, Del.: International Reading Association, 1968.

Martha L. King, Bernice D. Ellinger, and Willavene Wolf, eds. *Critical Reading*. Philadelphia: J. B. Lippincott, 1967.

Several other publications deal with reading and thinking skills. They provide background information on which lessons in comprehension can be based.

John Dawkins. *Syntax and Readability*. Newark, Del.: International Reading Association, 1975.

Edgar Dale and Joseph O'Rourke. *Techniques of Teaching Vocabulary*. Palo Alto, Calif.: Field Educational Publications, 1971.

Gerald G. Duffy, comp. ed. *Reading in the Middle School*. Newark, Del.: International Reading Association, 1974, pp. 130-174.

Christian Gerhard. *Making Sense: Reading Comprehension Improved Through Categorizing*. Newark, Del.: International Reading Association, 1975.

Marjorie S. Johnson and Roy A. Kress eds. *Reading and Thinking*. Proceedings of the 22nd Annual Reading Institute, Temple University, 1966.

James F. Kerfoot, ed. *Reading and the Cognitive Processes*. Highlights of the 1966 Pre-Convention Institutes. Newark, Del.: International Reading Association, 1967.

Russell G. Stauffer, comp. *Dimensions of Critical Reading*. Proceedings of the Annual Education and Reading Conferences, University of Delaware, 1964.

CHAPTER 8

IMPROVING READING-STUDY SKILLS in CONTENT AREAS

Problems for Study and Discussion

1   *State in behavioral terms the skills and subskills needed for study.*
2   *What principles might all subject teachers follow as they plan lessons for teaching the study skills?*
3   *Outline a series of lessons for teaching students to recognize main ideas.*
4   *What measures could students adopt to help them remember important information? How might teachers develop lessons for this purpose?*
5   *What skills are required for using indexes and other sources to locate information?*
6   *Assume students fail to follow directions in your subject area. Plan a series of lessons to overcome this weakness.*
7   *Of what value are illustrative materials and how might students use them?*
8   *Why is flexibility in reading a more valid concept than speed in reading?*

READING AND THE STUDY SKILLS

Even though high school students are required to study many hours each week — to read to understand and remember content in textbooks and other materials — few students have been trained to use the skills that will help them study. I remember a panel discussion in which several alert high school students from a privileged community participated. In reply to a question from the audience, each discussed the way in which he did his assignments. One student said he underlined the main ideas; another said she took notes; and a third indicated he outlined whole chapters. In answer to a second question, "Were you taught how to pick out main ideas of paragraphs or to outline chapters?" the unanimous response was "No. I guess our teachers thought we already knew how."

While teachers in the past have too often assumed that high school students were acquainted with study skills, schools today are aware that students are weakest in this aspect of reading and are trying to do something about the problem. In their reading programs, elementary schools are paying increased attention to developing study skills as a contribution to reading ability, and some high schools have special classes for students seeking to enter college. Others are requiring attendance in reading classes on the basis of test scores and teacher recommendations, and a few provide instruction in study skills to all students through regular classroom programs. But until the effects of any or all of these solutions are felt in the higher grades, each high school teacher should take it upon himself to strengthen and extend students' mastery of the study skills.

Reading *content* is different from reading *stories*. These differences are found in the terseness of writing, numerous ideas, and unfamiliar concepts which are common to subject matter but often lacking in narration. Students need to master study skills to read the former efficiently and retain information so that they can apply the ideas they have gained. Mastering study skills allows students to obtain information and solve problems through their own efforts.

There is no general agreement about what skills ought to be included in the study skills. Obviously, all the word recognition and comprehension skills which are treated in previous chapters are used by students as they study. But, in addition to these, are those skills that enable students to undertake independent study. Stated in behavioral terms, students have to learn to *locate information, select and evaluate information, organize and retain information, understand graphic aids, follow directions*, and *develop reading flexibility*. Omitted from this list are the *survey* skills which permit students to learn about the content and organization of materials and establish purposes for reading them and the Survey Q3R method of studying, both of which are explained and illustrated in Chapter 5.

All of these skills can be used in reading any content, but some of them have greater applicability to one subject area than another. Students will be required to select pertinent information whether they read science, social studies, or mathematics, but they are more likely to follow directions in science than in social studies — to study maps in social studies, but read diagrams in science. Moreover, these study skills are related and dependent on each other. For example, a student's ability to summarize the views expressed by an editorial writer (organization) depends on his ability to recognize important ideas (selection and evaluation) in the writing. Each of these skills, together with suggestions for developing ability in them, will be considered separately.

The checklist below may help some teachers find out those study skills in which students are deficient. The checklist may be used also as an outline around which instruction can be planned.

CHECKLIST OF STUDY SKILLS

Study Skills

I. *Selection and Evaluation*

    Can the student do the following?

        a. recognize the significance of the content
        b. recognize important details
        c. identify unrelated details
        d. find the main idea of a paragraph
        e. find the main idea of larger selections
        f. locate topic sentences
        g. locate answers to specific questions
        h. develop independent purposes for reading
        i. realize the author's purpose
        j. determine the accuracy and relevancy of information

II. *Organization*

    Can the student do the following?

        a. take notes
        b. determine relationship between paragraphs
        c. outline single paragraphs
        d. outline sections of a chapter
        e. outline an entire chapter
        f. summarize single paragraphs
        g. summarize larger units of material

III. *Location of Information*

    Can the student do the following?

        a. find information through a table of contents
        b. locate information through the index
        c. use a library card catalog to locate materials
        d. use the *Reader's Guide to Periodical Literature* to locate sources of information
        e. use an almanac to obtain data
        f. understand and use various appendixes
        g. use glossaries
        h. use encyclopedias to locate information

IV. *Following Directions*

    Can the student do the following?

        a. see the relation between the purposes and the directions
        b. follow one-step directions
        c. follow steps in sequence

V. *Graphic Aids*
   Can the student do the following?
   a. understand the significance of pictorial aids
   b. read and interpret graphs
   c. read and interpret tables
   d. read and interpret charts
   e. read and interpret maps
   f. read and interpret cartoons
   g. read and interpret diagrams
   h. read and interpret pictures

VI. *Flexibility in Reading*
   Can the student do the following?
   a. adjust reading rates to purpose for reading
   b. adjust reading rates to difficulty of materials
   c. scan for specific information
   d. skim for general impressions and important ideas

There are some guidelines for teaching study skills which all teachers might follow as they plan instruction for students who require it. Planned programs of instruction have been found to lead to results far superior to those of hit-or-miss instruction, because with study skills it is not enough to require students to do a task; they must be shown *how* to do it. Practice is part of learning, but practice without direction is unrewarding. Therefore, high school teachers who find it necessary to help their students master study skills may wish to follow these five suggestions when setting up a program.

1. *Use selections from materials for which the students are held responsible.* If students fail to follow directions when performing science experiments, then science materials should be used in teaching that study skill. If history students do not understand bar graphs and charts in their textbooks, similar pictorial informational aids should be used to develop this skill. I can only repeat that experimentation has demonstrated that the ability to read satisfactorily in one content area does not necessarily carry over to another area. Some commercially prepared materials can be obtained that give practice in using the study skills with different kinds of content.

2. *Select content material that presents no real meaning difficulties other than those on which practice is intended.* Students should be able to understand what is stated in the paragraphs; otherwise, they might experience interference with what they are trying to learn. Some teachers have found that practice materials chosen from selections the students have already read for other purposes are helpful. Thus, students will be reading familiar materials, and teachers can spend their time on the study skill instead of on word recognition or comprehension.

3. *Teach only one study skill in a lesson.* If students need to learn how to use a complex index, full attention should be given to that. This does not

preclude the teacher's inclusion of ample opportunities for them to practice what they have already learned.

4. *When a study skill consists of related smaller skills, teach these in sequence.* Before students are able to locate main ideas that are implied, they must be able to find those that are explicitly stated. One reason students fail to learn study skills is that steps in the learning sequence frequently are skipped or treated hurriedly. Equal time need not be allotted to each of the smaller skills; some may require only the briefest treatment while others demand lengthy consideration.

5. *For best results, teach a study skill when the need to know it arises.* What better opportunity is there for teaching students how to use the library card catalog, for example, than when they are trying to solve problems for which their textbooks do not provide the answers? Motives for learning vary from student to student, but recognized needs are springboards to successful achievement. A teacher will find numerous opportunities for teaching study skills in programs wherein students are active participants in the learning process.

SELECTION AND EVALUATION

Selection and evaluation consist largely of identifying important ideas and their related details in paragraphs and larger units of material. The ability to spot essential thoughts quickly is the mark of a good reader; the ability to recognize unessential information is equally important. If students are unable to identify important information, it is pointless to ask them to do so. They must be taught how to select it. Similarly, they must be taught how to distinguish between significant and unimportant details. These skills may be taught through a series of lessons that progress from the simple to the complex. Of course, not all students will require instruction on every phase of the skills; some effort to assess how well they can perform can be undertaken before work begins. (See Chapter 4 for a review of diagnostic surveys.)

Selecting the Main Idea in a Paragraph

If students do not understand the concept of a main idea, time should be taken to develop it. Teachers might refer to a newspaper headline and the information that follows it and then discuss the relationship between the two. The title of a "how to" book and its contents could serve a similar purpose. Or teachers might contrast the succinct message of a telegram with a rambling letter to point up highlighting important information.

A first step in teaching students how to select important ideas is to have them recognize what a passage is about, or in other words, its *subject*. The subject might be an object or place, a person or other living thing, an idea. Students and teacher should examine several paragraphs and decide what each one is about. All or most of the sentences should revolve around the same subject so that what the paragraph is about is clear. Choices of subjects might be provided and the sentences studied to determine if they pertain to them. These choices could be omitted as students learn to identify the subject.

> **EXERCISE: From the choices after the paragraph select its subject.**
> Balancing on his surfboard, a surfer rushes toward the shore, racing the wave crest that rises in a threatening arch over his head. A veil of spray is tossed high into the air by the churning water. The surfer swoops at an angle in front of the crest of the wave, a wake spreading behind him. The wave seems to speed up and to rise higher, as if gathering strength to overwhelm him.[1]
> The subject of the paragraph is
>   a. surfboard
>   b. surfer
>   c. wave

> **EXERCISE: State the subject of the following paragraph.**
> Earlier in this chapter you discovered that the noun phrase is made up of sentence parts such as *nouns,* determiners, and *pronouns.* Now you are ready to investigate the parts that make up the verb phrase. Look at the verb phrases in the following nine sentences. Note that the main verb *melt* appears as a part of each verb pharase.[2]

Once students can identify the *subject* of a paragraph, they are ready to proceed to the next step, which is to determine the *topic.* The topic tells what the subject is about.

Present a paragraph and have the students identify the subject. Then, offer some possible topics for students to consider. Discuss each one in order to determine if the paragraph concentrates on that topic. (All or most of the sentences should be centered around the topic.)

> **EXERCISE: Read this paragraph and identify its subject. Then, from the choices provided, select the topic of the paragraph.**
> The Age of Reason paved the way for a change from absolutism to democracy. Although the writings of the Encyclopedists and *Philosophes* were often burned, their works and views had vast influences. So influential did their works become that some absolute monarchs tried to study their ideas, and a few even tried to put them into practice, but the deeds of the so-called "benevolent" or "enlightened" despots fell far short of their good intentions. Since reform and revolution was not to come through the hands of the absolute kings, reform and revolution had to come through the hands of the people. Guiding those hands were the *Philosophes* of the Age of Reason. In days when newspapers were

1. *Investigating the Earth,* Earth Science Curriculum Project of the American Geological Institute (1967), p. 227. Reprinted with the permission of Houghton Mifflin Co.
2. John S. Hand and others, *Power in English: Experiences in Language* (1972), p. 242. Reprinted with the permission of Laidlaw Brothers, a division of Doubleday & Company, Inc.

few, and radio and televison did not exist, the Philosophes did much to encourage change and progress.[3]

The subject of the paragraph is _____ .

The topic of this paragraph is _____ .

    a. the ideas of absolute kings.

    b. political changes during the Age of Reason.

    c. beliefs of the *Philosophes.*

EXERCISE

REMINDER

If *t* represents the measure of an acute angle of a right triangle,

if *y* represents the measure of the side opposite the acute angle, and

if *x* represents the measure of the side adjacent to the acute angle, then you can use the formula $\tan t = \frac{y}{x}$ to find the tangent of the acute angle.[4]

The topic of this passage is _____ .

After students have learned to identify the topics of passages, they may proceed with the same and other materials to determine what important statement is made about the topic. This will be the passage's main idea.

LESSON: Selecting the main idea of a paragraph with the aid of choices.

Teacher: A well-written paragraph usually contains an important idea that is expressed in one or more of its sentences. This idea is supported by information in the form of details that explain or illustrate the important idea. For example, a paragraph that discusses the importance of a balanced diet contains much information, but one thought runs through the entire content — that is, the necessity of eating different kinds of foods. The details underscore the idea around which the paragraph is built by providing information about the topic.

Read this paragraph silently and then decide which of the ideas listed below makes the most generalized statement about the paragraph.

No two countries in Latin America are alike. The land is different. The products of the fields, forests and mines are different. And even in the same country there are many contrasts. There may be every kind of building from modern skyscrapers to palm-thatched huts. There may be both airplanes and burros for transportation, tractors and ox teams for farming. There may be fashions ranging from ancient Indian garb to Hollywood's latest.[5]

3. Gerald Leinwand, *The Pageant of World History* (1962), p. 318. Reprinted with the permission of Allyn and Bacon, publishers.

4. Henry Van Engen and others, *Seeing Through Mathematics*, Book 3, Part 1, p. 16. Copyright 1964 by Scott, Foresman and Company. Reprinted with the permission of the publisher.

5. J. G. Meyer, W. H. Gray, and R. Hancock, *Our American Neighbors* (1950), p. 6. Reprinted with the permission of Follett Publishing Co.

1. differences in methods of farming in Latin America
2. differences in means of transportation in Latin America
3. differences in buildings and clothing of Latin America
4. contrasts in the nature of Latin American countries

Teacher: Let us consider 1. Does this phrase make the most generalized statement about the paragraph? Does it include all the statements in the paragraph? Does it make a statement about the topic?
Students: [Will note that tractors and ox teams are mentioned in the paragraph but that nothing more is said about them. All agree that phrase 1 is not the generalized statement on which the paragraph rests.]
Teacher: What about phrase 2? Is this idea expansive and therefore inclusive of all the other ideas contained in the paragraph?
Students: [Same conclusion is reached for phrase 2 as for phrase 1 and for the same reasons.]
Teacher: Is it phrase 3? Does that meet our criterion of inclusiveness or generalization? Is it so important that more is said about it?
Students: [Phrase 3 is rejected for the same reasons.]
Teacher: That leaves 4. Does it tie the sentences of the paragraph together? Does it make a statement about the topic? Read the paragraph again to be sure the sentences are related directly to this idea, *contrasts in the nature of Latin American countries.*
Students: [Reread and conclude that phrase 4 is inclusive of the various ideas in the paragraph.]
Teacher: Contrasts in the nature of Latin American countries, then, is the main idea of the paragraph. It offers information about the topic.

ADDITIONAL EXERCISES

The lives of industrial workers have been bettered by laws passed by governments. The many people who moved to cities to work in factories asked for the right to vote. In most democratic countries they received it. In addition, workers formed labor parties in some countries. These labor parties often ran the government. Once workers could vote and had positions in government, they passed factory laws to protect themselves. These laws said that workers did not have to work more than a certain number of hours per week and must earn no less than a certain wage. In addition, governments passed laws to insure workers against sickness, old-age, and unemployment. Two new systems of government also grew out of the Industrial Revolution. These systems are socialism and communism.[6]

The main idea of this paragraph is _____

1. The workers in some countries formed labor parties that were elected to power.
2. Governments passed laws that benefited industrial workers.
3. Industrial workers earned the right to vote.
4. Industrial workers received insurance against sickness, old-age, and unemployment.

The Communist Party changed the political and economic system of Russia. A dictatorship was set up. All land, factories, mines, railroads,

6. Sol Holt and John R. O'Connor, *Exploring World History* (1969), pp. 413-417. Reprinted with the permission of the Globe Book Company.

banks, and other property were taken over by the government. This ended the private ownership of property in Russia. No one was allowed to run any business for profit. The farms, owned and run by the government, were worked by peasant workers who were paid by the government. The factories and mines were also owned and run by the government. Capitalism or the profit system was ended. And so czarist Russia became the Soviet Union.[7]

The main idea of this paragraph is _____ .
  1. taking over of all businesses by the Communist government.
  2. ending of private ownership of property in Russia.
  3. ending of the profit system in Russia.
  4. changing of the Russian political and economic systems by the Communist government.

As soon as the students have mastered the selection of the main idea when choices are provided, the teacher should give the students practice in perceiving relationships among sentences without such helpful hints. Again, the teacher should work with the students, as in the lesson below, until he feels they are ready to do similar exercises on their own.

LESSON 1: Selecting the main idea of a paragraph without aid to choices.
Teacher: You have learned how to determine the main idea of a paragraph for which several choices are given. Let's see if you can determine the main idea of paragraphs without the aid of choices. Read this paragraph and decide what idea binds the paragraph together.
The greater part of Palestine is hilly or mountainous. On either side of the Dead Sea depression, the land rises steeply. On the Palestine (western) side, the peaks that overlook the Dead Sea rise as high as 3,000 feet above sea level. Then the hilly land slopes gradually westward to the edge of the coastal plain. South of the Dead Sea, the triangle that extends to Al' Aqabah, known as the Negeb, is a desert.[8]

Teacher: What is the main idea of the paragraph?
Student: [An incorrect response: mountains of Palestine are rugged.]
Teacher: Let's see if that is the most important idea in the paragraph. How extensive is the information about mountains?
Students: [Mention steep rise and height.]
Teacher: What other information is given in the paragraph?
Students: Land slopes to coastal plain; desert.
Teacher: Obviously the paragraph discusses the mountains, plains, and deserts of Palestine. Is the reference to the mountains the overwhelming consideration in the paragraph? Is it the generalization on which the rest of the paragraph is based?
Students: [Agree that mountains of Palestine is not the main idea.]
Teacher: What single idea is inclusive of the entire paragraph?
Student: Surface features of Palestine are varied.
Teacher: Prove your choice.

7. Ibid., pp. 513-514. Reprinted with the permission of the Globe Book Company.
8. Preston James and Nelda Davis, *The Wide World*, pp. 320-321. Copyright © 1959 by Macmillan Publishing Co., Inc., and reprinted with their permission.

Student: [Lists topographical features.]
Teacher: Do we have the main idea now?
Students: [Agree.]
Teacher: Let's see what you can do with these paragraphs. Each one contains a main thought, and it's up to you to pick it out.

There are few heavy industries in Israel. The emphasis has been on the production of small valuable items that require great skill in manufacturing but which consume little in the way of raw materials. Israel's factories turn out optical instruments, precision tools, watches, cosmetics, pharmaceuticals, and many other valuable products. Many of the Jewish immigrants were skilled diamond cutters, and Tel Aviv is beginning to rival Amsterdam as a diamond center.[9]

The main idea is _____ .

The government is also taking many steps to improve the transportation system. An extensive road-building program is ending the isolation of many of the small rural villages, giving them access to the expanding urban market of Baghdad. The airfields at Basra and Baghdad have been enlarged and improved. These airfields are indeed busy; through them passes almost all the air traffic between Europe and southeast Asia and Australia.[10]

The main idea is _____ .

As soon as students are able to find the main idea of a paragraph by analyzing it, they can be taught to locate the sentence that expresses the main idea. This sentence — the key or topic sentence — may be found at the beginning, in the middle, or at the end of a paragraph. Students should first state the main idea in their own terms and then locate the sentence that states this idea.

EXERCISE: Finding the topic sentence.
You have already learned one cause of an overloaded circuit: Too many appliances are connected in the circuit at one time. So more current flows than the circuit is supposed to carry. Another cause is what is known as a short circuit. In this kind of overload, the current takes a short cut back to its source without first flowing through some electrical appliance that uses its energy. A short circuit has such a low resistance that a very large current flows. You can find out what a short circuit is by doing Experiment 5.[11]

The main idea of the paragraph is _____ .

The topic sentence is _____ .

9. Ibid., pp. 323-324. Copyright © 1959 by Macmillan Publishing Co., Inc., and reprinted with their permission.
10. Ibid., p. 306. Copyright © 1959 by Macmillan Publishing Co., Inc., and reprinted with their permission.
11. Wilbur Beauchamp, John Mayfield, and Joe West, *Science Problems*, Book 2, p. 281. Copyright 1952 by Scott, Foresman and Company. Reprinted with the permission of the publisher.

The teacher may then proceed to having the students select the main idea from a paragraph when it is expressed in two sentences. Procedure should in general be as that suggested earlier, but, now that a new element has been added, students may need considerable direction at first in spotting the two sentences that contain the main idea. In the following paragraph, the two sentences have been italicized.

EXERCISE: Selecting the main idea when it is expressed in two sentences.

One way in which seeds are often scattered is by the wind. You have surely seen the fluffy white head of a dandelion. This white head is made up of a great many seeds with a feathery parachute attached to each one. Other kinds of seeds have wings or long, silky hairs that help them float through the air. The seeds of elm, maple, cottonwood, linden, ash, thistle, and milkweed are good examples. The wind can blow such seeds for a long distance before they reach the ground. *Besides wind, moving water helps scatter seeds.* Bitter pecan, sycamore, and grass seeds float easily in water. They often fall into a stream or are washed into it by heavy rains. Then the moving water carries the seeds to a still place, where they are left and can begin to grow. Along the banks of streams or among the driftwood after heavy rains, you are likely to find many kinds of seeds that were carried there by moving water.[12]

The main idea is _____ .

The key sentences are _____ .

Some paragraphs contain a key idea but do not express it in a sentence. Even though they have mastered the extraction of main ideas from paragraphs, students may require help in formulating the key idea, and at the beginning of practice the teacher may have to provide them with a choice of suggested key statements. As similar paragraphs are studied and practice provided, students should come to recognize the implied key sentence for themselves.

EXAMPLE: Stating the key sentence of a paragraph when it is implied.

A few trucks and automobiles are run by electric motors that get their current from large storage batteries. Some locomotives in mines are driven by current from batteries they carry. Telephone exchanges and small power-plants have batteries to supply current when the generators are not running or when extra power is needed. Country homes often get electricity for their light from storage batteries that are charged by a generator run by a gasoline engine. Sometimes when they do not have electric lights, country people operate their radios with storage batteries that are kept charged by a small windmill.[13]
1. Electricity is stored in batteries.
2. Storage batteries have many uses.
3. Farmers use storage batteries to obtain their electric supply.

12. Ibid., p. 354. Copyright 1952 by Scott, Foresman and Company. Reprinted with the permission of the publisher.
13. Beauchamp et al., *Science Problems,* Book 3. Copyright 1946 by Scott, Foresman and Company. Reprinted with the permission of the publisher.

Selecting the Main Idea in Larger Units

If students are able to select key ideas in single paragraphs, they should have little difficulty dealing with a group of paragraphs that are bound together by a single thought. Practice should follow along much the same lines as before, with the teacher asking the students to select the key sentences of several paragraphs and to choose an all-embracing title for them. At first, it may be wise to have the teacher suggest possible choices from which the students choose the appropriate title.

EXERCISE: Obtaining the main idea from larger units of thought.

A drop of blood contains about 300 million red corpuscles. There are enough of them in the blood of a full-grown person to cover half an acre, or four average building lots. Each one is a single cell floating in the liquid part of the blood. In the red corpuscles is a colored compound called hemoglobin which makes them look red.

By looking a little more closely at the layer of blood under the microscope, perhaps you can see a smaller number of irregular clear specks. These are the white blood cells, or white corpuscles. A drop of blood usually contains from 300,000 to 500,000 white corpuscles. So there is only about one white corpuscle for every 600 or more red corpuscles in the blood.

Other corpuscles in the blood are called platelets. These are much smaller than either the red or white corpuscles. A drop of blood contains about three million platelets.

The red and white corpuscles and the platelets make up almost one-half of the blood. The rest consists of plasma in which these three kinds of corpuscles float. About 90 percent of the plasma is water and 9 percent is proteins. Dissolved fats and sugars, salts, minerals, and chemicals make up the rest of the plasma.[14]

Possible Titles

1. The blood contains red and white blood cells and platelets.
2. Plasma consists mainly of water and proteins.
3. Blood is composed of red and white corpuscles, platelets, and plasma.

Recognizing Irrelevant Material

While students practice selecting the main idea from a paragraph or group of paragraphs, they become increasingly aware of the extraneous information that may detract attention from it. Quite often the details are related to the topic but not to the specific idea on which the writer wishes the reader to concentrate. These kinds of details may provide additional information, but not the type students should consider relevant. Since students should be cognizant of unrelated details as they read, locating irrelevant sentences or details should be practiced if the teacher feels it is needed. The first passage points out which details are not related to the main idea; students should discuss why they could be ignored. The second passage also contains some irrelevant details that can be identified and discussed.

14. Beauchamp et al., *Science Problems*, Book 2, pp. 311-312. Copyright 1952 by Scott, Foresman and Company. Reprinted with the permission of the publisher.

EXERCISE: Noting irrelevant or unrelated details.

About one sixth of Cuba is covered with forests. The hardwoods are very valuable because they resist termites and other insects. Cedarwood is used for cigar boxes and pencils. Mahogany and ebony are among the island's exports. *The hugh mahogany logs are hauled to the sawmill on carts, drawn by several yoke of oxen. Most of the carts have only two wheels, but the wheels are eight feet high.*[15]

EXERCISE: What details are unrelated to the main idea?

The composition of water by weight. In 1895, an American chemist, Dr. Edward W. Morley (1838 - 1923), determined the composition of water by weighing measured volumes of hydrogen, oxygen, and water which resulted from their union. It took him about twelve years to perfect his apparatus, purify the gases, check temperatures and pressures, and devise various precautions to secure as accurate results as possible. As a result of his painstaking experiments, he concluded that *1.0000 part by weight of hydrogen unites with 7.9396 parts by weight of oxygen.* These quantities produce 8.9396 parts by weight of water. In elementary work these figures can be "rounded off" — *One part by weight of hydrogen unites with eight parts by weight of oxygen to form nine parts by weight of water.*[16]

Other types of exercises that teachers may wish to use in helping students develop selection and evaluation skill include:

matching headlines with short articles
providing headlines with short articles
determining the purpose of an experiment from its details
choosing alternative titles for poems or short stories.

For the first two types of lessons — matching headlines with short articles and providing headlines for short articles — materials may be taken directly from newspapers or magazines. To prepare the materials, the teacher need only remove the headlines from the articles and have students match the appropriate headline with its article and suggest headlines for the articles, respectively. The first lessons might require students to make gross distinctions while succeeding lessons could demand finer ones.

A series of steps in performing an experiment such as the one given below can be used as an exercise for developing insights into the relationship among ideas. The first group of experiments might be accompanied by jumbled purposes that students would match to the appropriate experiments: Later, students might provide their own purposes for the experiments.

Materials: two tin cans (one polished and the other painted black); ice cubes and water; two thermometers.

15. Meyer, Gray, and Hancock, *Our American Neighbors* (1950), p. 261. Reprinted with the permission of Follett Publishing Co.
16. H. Clark Metcalfe and others, *Modern Chemistry*, p. 135. Copyright ® 1974 by Holt, Rinehart and Winston, Publishers, and reprinted with their permission.

Procedure:
1. Fill cans with water of same temperature. Place thermometer in each and place both cans in sunshine.
2. Note temperature readings after one-half hour.
3. Remove water from cans and refill them with water of equal temperature.
4. Put ice cubes of equal number and size in each can and observe which ice cubes melt first.
5. Refill cans with hot water and note temperature after a period of time.

Purposes: (Select one)
1. to demonstrate heat conduction
2. to demonstrate absorption and radiation of heat
3. to demonstrate evaporation

Poems and short stories often contain titles whose origins are obscure. Discussing the reasons why authors chose them can be stimulating as well as informative. Students might select alternative titles from a group the teacher provides or might suggest others that they consider appropriate. The merits of each title should be discussed in terms of the selection's unifying thought or message. Insights about "big" ideas can be developed in this way.

Answering Questions

Practice in determining the significance of content will help students become selective in their search for answers to problems. Mature readers recognize the relative importance of different passages as they seek answers to general and specific questions and sort them according to their requirements. A series of topics such as those listed below might be prepared by the teacher from portions of a chapter or chapters:

1. neutrality
2. submarine warfare
3. Atlantic Charter
4. the threat of invasion
5. lend-lease policy

The aim of the exercise would be to have the students identify the portions of the text that were associated with each. The teacher might underscore selected passages which students would evaluate for their relevancy. Discussing the basis for selection would help students make judgments about the content's significance and its relation to students' purposes in reading it. This procedure might be reversed by presenting passages from a book and asking with what broad area each was concerned. Presenting of alternate topics with each selection would help students who were having difficulty evaluating its significance.

Most assignments in reading content materials require students to locate answers to specific questions. Some students have difficulty responding to questions that call for stated details and facts, while others fail to use the latter to reach answers based upon them. Each group of students requires assistance in reading for these purposes, but the nature of the lessons should vary with the group's deficiencies.

Students must be able to respond to questions whose answers are directly stated before they can be expected to answer questions whose answers must be inferred. If student performance is extremely poor, the questions may be worded in the way the passage states the information; later, the wording of the questions should vary from the text.

The ability to select and sift material appropriate to the readers' requirements is one that should not be assumed. Superficial reading is characteristic of many students and accounts for some of their failures. Teachers must make provisions for helping students overcome this weakness in the same way that they assist them in mastering content. It would not be unrealistic to suggest that better reading performances will assure greater mastery of the content with which subject-matter teachers are primarily concerned.

ORGANIZATION

Students frequently complain that they are unable to remember what they read, yet the act of studying implies retention of required information for immediate or future use. Research for a paper, preparing for a test, dozens of academic demands require that students do more than merely read materials. And they can be in command of this material if they are able to recognize the organizational plan that a writer follows, if they are able to organize their notes systematically, and if they are able to summarize what they have read. Moreover, if they can recognize the system by which the author relates his ideas, they can use the same system to record them. (See Chapter 7 for the different ways in which writers organize information.)

Outlining

When students are able to recognize main ideas and their significant details, they can then learn to organize the information according to levels of importance. Students must learn to see the distinction between one level and another, and this ability to outline levels of thought must be developed sequentially, just as the determination of main ideas was taught.

A practical way of helping students grasp the concept of different idea levels as well as providing a basis for understanding how an outline might be constructed is to examine a chapter or a section of it for the way in which the information is divided under main headings and subheadings. The main headings and subheadings can be used by the student as major topics and subtopics in his outline which he can then fill in with the important ideas. Here are the headings of two such sections of a chapter.[17]

17. Lewis P. Todd and Merle Curti, *Rise of the American Nation*, 2d ed. (New York: Harcourt, Brace and World, 1966), pp. 666-672. Copyright © 1966 by Harcourt Brace Jovanovich, Inc., and reprinted with their permission.

The Nation Undertakes a Great Experiment. (Chapter title)
1. The New Deal provides relief and work for the unemployed. (Main head)
        Direct relief (Subhead)
        Work relief (Subhead)
        Work for youth (Subhead)
        Evaluating the relief program (Subhead)
2. Recovery measures are launched to stimulate agriculture. (Main head)
        Saving the farmer's homes (Subhead)
        Higher incomes for farmers (Subhead)
        Limiting farm production (Subhead)
        Evaluating the agricultural program (Subhead)

The chapter contains three other main headings with their respective subheadings. Students should examine them to determine if the chapter is organized in a uniform way and how this organization can be used by them to record the information they need to learn.

Each textbook or reference source will adopt different typographical features to sharpen the differences between major headings and subheadings. The position on a page and the size and type of print will often indicate which ideas are subsumed under others. These features should be studied so that students have no difficulty recognizing an idea's importance and placement as indicated by such aids.

Some high school students already practice outlining skills and need no further teaching in this area, but many have never learned to outline efficiently. When main headings and subheadings are not provided in the materials or do not appear to be very useful, students will have to rely on their own resources to prepare their outlines. The teacher may use a pretest to determine which skills should receive special attention.

The following exercises suggest a natural progression in teaching outlining skills, and these may be used also to find out how well students can perform them. When an outline is drawn, sentences are reduced to topics or phrases so that important ideas are expressed in brief form while retaining their essentials — much as a letter could be reduced to a telegram. An efficient method of emphasizing this technique is to have the students eliminate unessential words in key and other sentences.

EXERCISE: Reducing key sentences to topics.
Now you have learned several ways in which rocks are broken up. Rocks exposed to air and water are changed by weathering. Water, oxygen, and carbon dioxide may change them chemically into softer materials. Expansion and contraction during changes of temperature and the freezing of water in cracks break the hardest rocks into pieces. Plants and animals also help change rocks. Another way in which rocks are broken up is by moving water, wind, and ice. Moving water and ice grind rocks together and wear them down. Wind-blown sand cuts rocks to pieces. In all these ways, rocks are constantly being broken up and worn away.[18]

18. Beauchamp et al., *Science Problems*, Book 2, p. 143. Copyright 1952 by Scott, Foresman and Company. Reprinted with the permission of the publisher.

The first sentence of this paragraph is the topic sentence, but the sentence contains words that need not be included in an outline. Teacher and students can decide which words are extraneous and eliminate them.

~~Now you have learned several~~ ways ~~in which~~ rocks are broken up.

Other sentences in the paragraph may be reduced in the same way:

~~Rocks exposed to air and water are changed by~~ weathering.
Plants and animals ~~also help~~ change rocks.
~~Another way in which rocks are broken up is by~~ moving water and ice.

Other sentences, however, must have the order of their words changed before they convey ideas clearly. In the sentence

India's independence led to startling results.

the order of the words is changed to

results of India's independence.

When students have had ample opportunity to reduce sentences that contain main thoughts to outline phrases, they may proceed to discriminating between major and subsidiary topics. A suggested procedure is to have the teacher select several topics from paragraphs and show how these may not be of equal importance.

EXERCISE: Distinguishing topics from subtopics.
Food Constituents
1. Vitamins
2. Proteins
3. Amino Acids
4. Minerals
5. Fats
6. Thiamine
7. Carbohydrates
8. Water

It is not difficult to demonstrate that "Amino Acids" and "Thiamine" are in a different class from the other items in the list and therefore are of lesser importance.

When students can make distinctions readily, the relationships of topics to subtopics can be taught. Subtopics that are grouped must possess common characteristics; if not, they have been misgrouped and belong under another heading. In this type of exercise, students select subtopics and place them under appropriate topics.

EXERCISE: Classifying subtopics under main headings.
economic aid
construction of roads
stimulus to services
efforts to maintain world peace
disarmament conferences
effects of automobile on America
development of new industries
international bodies

When students are able to classify similar ideas under appropriate headings, the teacher may present the formal outline. The use of Roman numerals should be introduced first. These are assigned to the most important ideas and all Roman numerals are of equal value.

It is helpful to provide a partial outline and show how it may be completed from the information in the selection being read.

EXERCISE: Learning the basic form of an outline.
Causes of the American Revolution
I. Economic Causes
II. Political Causes
III. _____

Introducing capital letters is the next step in teaching students to prepare an outline. Students are shown that capital letters are assigned to subtopics and that a subtopic under one main heading is on the same level as a subtopic under a second main heading. Using a partially completed outline will help students see the relationship between the topic assigned the Roman number and its subtopics. This type of skeleton may be prepared from chapters in the textbook and completed by the class with the help of the teacher.

Farming in the United States
I. North
   A. Dairying
   B. Poultry raising
   C. _____
II. South
   A. _____
   B. _____
   C. _____
III. West
   A. _____
   B. _____
   C. _____

If a student were to suggest that "oranges" should be A under II, attention would be drawn to A, B, and C under I. *Fruit growing* is the all-inclusive term, while "oranges" is merely an example of the kinds of fruit grown.

A three-step outline will ordinarily meet the needs of most high school students. The final phase is the assignment of Arabic numbers to details that fall within the subtopic. Present the partially completed outline of a section of the text and help the group complete it.

Title
I. (Filled in)
   A. (Filled in)
      1. (Filled in)
      2. _____
   B. (Filled in)
      1. _____
      2. _____

Students may read a section of the textbook and complete the skeleton outline presented by the teacher.

EXERCISE: Completing a skeleton outline.

Title

I. _____
   A. _____
   B. _____
   C. _____
      1. _____
      2. _____

II. _____
   A. _____
      1. _____
      2. _____
   B. _____
      1. _____
      2. _____
   C. _____

Preparing outlines of short and long selections is the final step in the process of learning to outline what is read. The skills involved in outlining have been developed through a series of graded lessons, and students have been taken through them step by step. Applying these skills to reading will reinforce the skills and enable students to study efficiently.

Summarizing

A student's ability to summarize the contents of a single paragraph or groups of paragraphs depends upon the skills that have been discussed so far in this section. He must be able to identify important ideas of the writer together with essential details, to omit irrelevant facts, and to place the information in some sensible order. One other skill is needed before he can compose a summary: succinct expression of the writer's ideas in his own words. The following types of exercises will help to develop this skill.

1. Choosing the best sentence that summarizes a paragraph.
2. Choosing the best statement that summarizes a longer selection.
3. Restating the author's idea in a single sentence.
4. Restating paragraphs by combining author's ideas into shorter statements.
5. Recognizing different types of paragraphs and their functions.

Here is a sample of the first type of lesson designed to teach students how to summarize. A paragraph is analyzed in order to determine which sentence contains the essential information to be remembered.

Teacher: We need to learn how to summarize paragraphs. When we state the main points of a paragraph in a brief but compact form we are summarizing it. Let's read a paragraph to obtain its important points.

Students: [Read a paragraph selected by teacher.]

Teacher: Let's list the important points of the paragraph on the board.

Students: [Suggest main points.]

Teacher: Here are four sentences that might summarize this paragraph. Let us see which one does the job best.

Teacher and students: [Consider each summary statement in relation to the main points they have listed and select the one that contains the essence of the paragraph.]

Lessons in which students analyze single paragraphs and prepare their own summary statements may follow exercises in which the summary statements are provided. The selection of each appropriate summary sentence should be discussed to help students understand why one is preferred to another.

These same kinds of exercises may be used with longer selections. Students might list the main points of each paragraph and select the statement that encompasses them. Discussing the reasons for preferring one statement to the others will help students understand the nature of summaries and their composition. When they have demonstrated that they are able to select the best summary statement for a series of paragraphs, they may prepare their own statements for other selections. It is a good idea for students to select samples from all their textbooks, because the style of writing in each is not identical. Social studies texts are more likely to contain longer explanations of concepts and the author's ideas than are science texts, and students must learn to separate these explanations from the essential material. Science content is usually presented in more compact form, and care must be taken not to overlook an important point that should be included in a summary of the material.

Students may have some difficulty combining all the important points into a single statement. They may find it easier to prepare two or three sentences first and then combine them in one sentence. This exercise naturally leads into one that requires students to reduce longer expository and narrative material into shorter statements by rewriting it. The identification of the author's major points will provide a guide for the students to follow as they prepare their summaries.

Exercises that provide practice in restating the important ideas in a single sentence help students to develop skill in preparing summaries. We may take a paragraph and groups of paragraphs and combine their information into a summary sentence.

Another desirable exercise is one in which students compare summaries which have been prepared by the teacher or the students and consider why one is preferred to the other. The worthiness of the summaries will depend on the degree to which the major points — main ideas and details — are highlighted or to what extent lesser ideas and details are emphasized. Notice how the following summaries are different, particularly in detail. Both are based upon the same content.

Millions of hungry people are found throughout the world. It is hard to realize how many people in the world face starvation since we have more food than we need. The supply of food is not keeping pace with the increase in the world's population.

Countries that produce a food surplus have been sending food to India and elsewhere. But we realize that a more permanent solution to this difficult problem must be found. The United States has helped India build a dam to provide power and water, taught its farmers modern farming methods, supplied agricuitural tools, and built schools and health centers.

OR

Hunger is one of the world's great problems. A majority of the world's population is facing starvation because its food supply has not kept pace with its numbers.

The United States and other countries are supplying hungry nations with food as well as helping them to produce more food and to improve their education and health.

We have pointed out the ways in which paragraphs are structured to serve an author's purposes. Knowing and recognizing these techniques will help students separate major points from lesser ones that may be omitted in their summaries. The content of introductory paragraphs may help readers understand new material, but it is not an essential part of the material. The content of illustrative paragraphs can be viewed similarly, although some examples may be included in summary statements. Transitional paragraphs signal a new or different idea that should probably be part of the summary. Concluding or summary paragraphs can be used by students to compare the content of their own summaries with the points the author believes he should restate. Such comparisons, will help students determine whether or not they have missed material that the author considers important enough to repeat or have included some that is incidental to the main points.

LOCATION OF INFORMATION

High school students do not depend on a single textbook as their source of information. They also read other texts, reference books, newspapers, encyclopedias, almanacs, and whatever else is available. Because they must often locate answers to specific questions, they need to be masters of study skills that will enable them to do so readily.

The ability to use the index of a book and to determine sources through a library card catalog are but two applications of the skills in locating information that many high school students never fully develop. Since these skills are needed in a variety of content fields, teachers may need to give practice in developing and using them by introducing them in order of difficulty.

Table of Contents

Most high school students will have less difficulty using a table of contents than they will have with other sources of information. However, students should understand that the table not only indicates what topics a book covers but also reveals how the author organizes the topics. Quite often, a table of contents lists the subheads of the chapters; students should study it to help them decide whether or not the book contains the kinds of information they seek.

Students who are not able to use a table of contents efficiently can be assigned to work on problems such as the following which will help them understand its purpose:

1. What topics does the author cover in the book?
2. Into how many major sections is the first chapter divided? Second chapter?
3. Of what chapters does the third unit consist?
4. What chapter is likely to contain information about _____?
5. Why are some chapters much longer than others?
6. On what pages does the author discuss _____?
7. How likely is it that this book will contain information about _____ _____?
8. Does the book contain graphic aids? A glossary?

Students will realize that they may have some questions about a book which cannot be answered by studying the table of contents. Students may have to turn to the index in order to decide just how much specific information on a topic the book contains or whether it offers any of the information they require.

The Index

Some indexes are more complex than others. The index of an encyclopedia, for example, contains many more entries and symbols than does the index of a typical textbook. Still, students should be able to use and understand the index of any book that they read.

Since topics are indexed in alphabetical order, students should be able to locate entries quickly. If they cannot, teachers should use the index to prepare lessons on alphabetical order and have the students apply what they learn to locating entries in it. (See Chapter 5 which contains exercises on alphabetization.)

A first step in studying how to use an index efficiently is to examine its structure. A teacher may use the following kinds of questions as guides for considering the way in which it is organized:

1. In what order are the entries listed? What other sources of information are organized in a similar way?
2. In what way are these two entries different?
   a. Shiloh, battle of
   b. Spoils system
   What is the natural order of the words in the first entry? Why is inverted order followed in the first entry but not the second?
3. In what way are the names of persons listed?
4. How is this entry different from others?
   PWA. *See* Public Works Administration
5. Why do commas separate page listings in some entries, and dashes in others?

In addition to these questions which apply to most indexes, teachers might have to devote some time to special features in the indexes that students use. For example, some indexes designate pages with pictures or maps by using the letters *p* or *m* along with the page number which is also in italics. Others may use boldfaced print for page numbers to indicate those on which a term is defined or *ff* after a page number to show on what page the discussion of a topic begins. Students must become familiar with the styles of indexes in order to use them in the ways intended.

The subentries of a good index will be placed under the topic in alphabetical order as in this excerpt:[19]

> Insects, *control* of, 89; *disease* spread by, 44; as *food* for plants, 22-23; *forests* damaged by, 89; *groups* of, 34-36; *migration* of, 33, 72; *reproduction* of, 27; *shelters* of, 18; *slavery* among, 44; *social* life of, 36

What the students need to understand about subentries is that they may contain descriptive words which may be placed in inverted positions and which are not considered when the subtopics are arranged in alphabetical order. Similarly, conjunctions and prepositions, when used in subentries, are often disregarded when alphabetizing.

Students may need additional help when trying to pinpoint specific information in subentries. Should they wish to know the parts of the eye, for example, they need to be able to determine if one of the subtopics under "eye" refers to that, and not look up all the pages listed under "eye."[20]

> Eye, adjustment of, 267; care of, 269-270; functioning of, 267-268; nerve cells in, 268, parts of, 266-267; structure of, 265-270.

When students seek answers to specific questions, they need to know the topic under which to look. In the question "Why are grapes grown in the Finger Lakes region?" either or both of the two important terms might appear in an index: grapes, Finger Lakes. The students should not only realize that the answer to the question might be found under either topic, but should be ready to seek a broader topic, such as fruit growing; this would be necessary in some indexes. When a topic does not appear in an index, the students must be able to substitute some possibility. They may need training to provide themselves with suitable substitutes. If, for example, they are trying to find out the life cycle of a termite, and *termite* is not an entry in the index, they may have to look under *insects.* This ability, of course, depends on the students' knowledge of the subject matter under consideration.

When students have been taught the skills they will use to locate information through an index, their ability to use an index is strengthened by

19. Gerald S. Craig and John Urban, *Facing Tomorrow with Science* (Science Today and Tomorrow series), pp. 352-353. Copyright © 1956 by Ginn and Company (Xerox Corp). Used with permission.
20. Ibid., p. 351. Copyright © 1956 by Ginn and Company (Xerox Corp). Used with permission.

practice in resolving real problems, which may be presented by the teacher. Content subjects should be taught in such a way that opportunities for finding information independently are present.

Other Sources of Information

If students are able to use an index with ease, they should have little trouble learning to locate a book, periodical, or other reference material in a library card catalog. They do need to become acquainted with the arrangement of cards in the files — that is, the guide letters on the outside of the card file drawers. They should know that for every publication in the library the card catalog contains (1) an author's card, (2) a title card, and (3) a subject card all filed in alphabetical order. They should know in what circumstances to seek one or another of the cards and should know the information that the cards contain; they should also be acquainted with the decimal system or other manner in which books are shelved, and they should know the location of these shelves.

The best place in which to teach students how to use the card catalog is the library itself. Immediately applying what has been learned always helps to make learning meaningful. The following questions may be used to help students generalize about the nature and organization of card catalogs:

1. Why are there separate subject, author, and title cards?
2. Why is the topic of a subject card placed across the top of the card?
3. What purpose do the numbers and letters in the upper left-hand corner of the cards serve?
4. What common information do each of the different types of cards contain?

Knowing the skills associated with using an index is needed when materials that contain specialized information are to be consulted. For example, *The World Almanac* contains an index located in the front of the book; *Who's Who in America* and *Readers' Guide to Periodical Literature* offer quite different types of information in alphabetical order. These reference materials and many others serve useful purposes, and all high school students should be familiar with them. Again, students will develop ability to use a variety of source materials properly when the teacher presents real problems to be solved with the aid of these sources.

Many students find the *Reader's Guide to Periodical Literature* a difficult reference source to use because it relies on abbreviations and an unusual format. It will be time well spent to examine the *Reader's Guide* much in the same way as other sources are studied so that students may see what all have in common and how the *Guide* is different from the others. Just as there is no need for students to memorize what sounds correspond to diacritical marks when they use the dictionary to pronounce unfamiliar words, so they don't need to memorize what each abbreviation in the *Guide* represents. They may refer to the key in the front of the *Guide* whenever they have to, and, with use they will easily learn to recognize what many of the abbreviated forms represent.

FOLLOWING DIRECTIONS

How many times does a high school teacher give directions only to find afterward that some students did not follow them? Whether the students had preconceived ideas of how to proceed, read too rapidly, or were unable to follow steps in order, the teacher chalks up the failure to carelessness in following directions. But carelessness is not the whole answer. Learning to read to follow directions is a study skill that must be taught, not taken for granted. Knowing the printed word does not assure accurate performance; teachers may find that they must train some students to follow directions carefully.

When initiating lessons in carrying out directions, the teacher should choose the content for the directions from the subject matter being taught. A science teacher, for example, can use an experiment demonstration, preparation of slides, or the drawing of charts as vehicles for teaching students to follow directions. A social-studies teacher may use map-making, oral and written reporting, and record-keeping.

Whatever the subject area, of course, lessons should begin with following simple directions and proceed to more complicated kinds. The sequence below is suggested for teaching students to follow directions:

1. Begin with one-step directions (underlining all adjectives, circling proper names, labeling pictures, numbering items).
2. Proceed to two-step directions (measuring ½ teaspoon of salt and 1 tablespoon of sugar, counting the number of books and recording the number in a specific place).
3. Introduce directions that consist of three or more simple steps (measuring out two ingredients and adding water, measuring the length and width of a room and calculating its square footage).
4. Finally, introduce directions for which the number of steps is not stated explicitly (classifying a number of items, arranging a scientific display, assembling a model).

A complicated set of directions requires careful reading and rereading. Students should be encouraged to recognize and understand the overall requirements of the task before tackling it. Each step of the process should be considered carefully before it is undertaken. Students who are trained to think through sets of directions are likely to carry them out successfully.

GRAPHIC AIDS

Although a special skill may be called for by some specific content area, most specialized study skills are common to more than one area. For example, map-reading is required in geography, history, and science. Charts, tables, graphs, and diagrams are found in texts on a variety of subjects. Each of these informational aids generally illustrates what the author is discussing or brings the reader additional information in pictorial form. Students can find the reading of these informational aids as rewarding as studying the text, but the value of these devices is limited by the extent to which the students are able to understand them.

Too many students are inclined to ignore the illustrations authors provide to accompany the text. This failure to use them may be due to the fact that many books do not make any special references to them, and students acquire the habit of skipping them. Illustrations are ordinarily intended to help make clear difficult and abstract ideas as well as to supplement them, and students should be encouraged to interrupt their reading to study the graphic materials that relate to the text. This "back and forth" reading can yield real dividends in increased understanding of the text.

A surprising number of high school students lack full ability to read maps, graphs, tables, or other pictorial representations of data. Each instructor, therefore, should also teach students how to interpret the graphic aids that are associated with his subject matter. If the specialized study skill being taught can be applied to another content area, so much the better. Direct instruction is likely to insure student transfer of learning from one field to another.

Reading Graphs, Tables, and Charts

For any student, to read a graph, table, or chart as an informational aid requires two major abilities: understanding what is stated directly and understanding what is implied. The first step in reading such a visual aid is to determine what information it conveys. The second is to seek deeper meanings: inferences, generalizations, and conclusions. The ability to perform this second reading act depends on the students' experiential background and their ability to use it. Through judicious questions, a teacher should be able to guide students' thinking so that they will begin to seek more than is apparent on the surface.

The reader must understand the mechanical aspects of a graph, table, or chart. Attention should be drawn to the *title, the values that are being compared,* and the *meaning of the symbols.* Questions whose answers are stated directly should precede questions whose answers require extrapolation. Bar and pictorial graphs are easier to read than line graphs, and all three are easier to understand than tables. Below are a series of questions that may be answered by studying the graph in Figure 8-1. Notice that the students must *make use* of information in the graph to answer the last few questions.

1. What percentage of all 14- to 17-year-olds was enrolled in 1900? What percentage was not enrolled in 1900?
2. What percentage of all 14- to 17-year-olds was enrolled in 1910? 1920? 1930? 1940? 1950?
3. What was the increase in percentage of enrollment between 1900 and 1910? Between 1900 and 1920? Between 1900 and 1950?
4. Between what two periods was there the largest percentage increase in enrollment?
5. Compare the enrollments in 1940 and 1950.
6. What generalizations can you make about the growth of high school enrollment?

Figure 8-1.   Growth in High School Enrollment

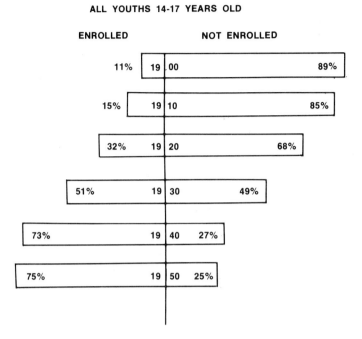

ALL YOUTHS 14-17 YEARS OLD

ENROLLED   **NOT ENROLLED**

11%	19 00	89%
15%	19 10	85%
32%	19 20	68%
51%	19 30	49%
73%	19 40	27%
75%	19 50	25%

Adapted from Leon Canfield and Howard Wilder, *The Making of Modern America* (Boston: Houghton Mifflin, 1958), p. 600. Used with the permission of the publisher.

7. If the trend in high school enrollment continues, what may we expect for 1960? 1970?

The line graph of Figure 8-2 seems simple enough but might confuse some students because of the multiple lines and the fact that they intersect. The author of this line graph assumes that the reader knows the elements represented by symbols and understands what the vertical axis represents. Even though the text refers to "solubility," one cannot assume that the concept will be understood in the context of the graph. It would be well for the teacher to read such graphs with students who do not seem to be able to extract information from them.

The reading of tables may be guided in the same way. The title and the items that are compared are studied first. The information that the table conveys is then considered. Suitable questions by the teacher will draw responses that will enable the students to see the relationships among items. The questions that apply to Figure 8-3 are both factual and inferential.

1. Which of the Southern states had the largest population in 1954?
2. Which state had the largest area in square miles?
3. Which state had the smallest population in 1954?
4. What is the area rank of Florida?

5. About how many times is the population of Texas greater than the population of North Carolina?
6. Which state has the greatest density of population? Why?

Reading Maps

Maps contain such common elements as legends, scales, and networks or lines. If students are to obtain all the information presented in a map, they must understand the functions of these elements. When students find map-reading difficult, the teacher can plan a series of lessons, making use of known concepts to develop new ones. For example,

Figure 8-2. Solubility Curves

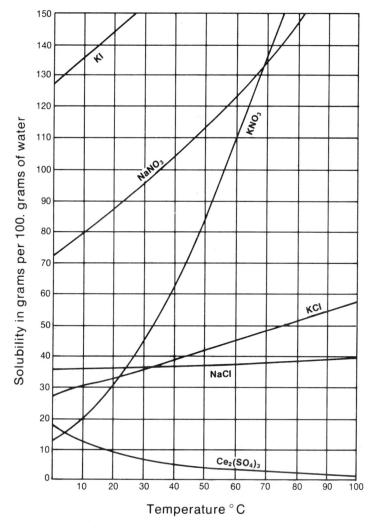

From H. Clark Metcalfe and others, *Modern Chemistry*, pp. 231-232. Copyright ©1974 by Holt, Rinehart and Winston, Publishers. Used with permission.

Figure 8-3.   Population and Area of the South

State	Population (1954 Estimates)	Population Rank in United States	Population per Square Mile (1954) Land Area	Area in Square Miles	Area Rank in United States
Texas	8,468,000	6	32.1	267,339	1
N. Carolina	4,250,000	10	86.6	52,712	27
Missouri	4,154,000	12	60.0	69,674	18
Georgia	3,660,000	13	62.6	58,876	20
Virginia	3,588,000	14	89.9	40,815	35
Florida	3,524,000	16	64.9	58,560	21
Tennessee	3,362,000	17	80.4	42,244	33
Alabama	3,121,000	18	61.1	51,609	28
Kentucky	2,995,000	20	75.0	40,395	36
Louisiana	2,924,000	21	64.7	48,523	30
Maryland	2,602,000	23	261.3	10,577	41
S. Carolina	2,238,000	26	73.8	31,055	39
Mississippi	2,204,000	28	46.6	47,716	31
W. Virginia	1,947,000	30	48.8	24,181	40
Arkansas	1,910,000	31	36.3	53,104	26

SOURCE: U.S. Bureau of the Census

From Norman Pounds and Edward Cooper, *World Geography* (Cincinnati: South-Western, 1957), p. 284. Reprinted with the special permission of the South-Western Publishing Co.

1. the concept of the starting point on maps: the Equator or Greenwich Observatory (comparison to a diagram of local streets)
2. the concept of directional lines: lines of latitude and longitude (comparison to sections of a cut-up orange)
3. the concept of degrees (comparison to a circle)
4. scale (comparison to a building plan)
5. legends (comparison to words)

Practice exercises in reading maps should be planned. Students might be asked to ascertain:

the distance and the shortest route between two places
the location of points of interest
the relation between one feature and another (amount of rainfall and productivity)
answers based on symbols.

Some types of maps are less common to one subject area than another. Fig. 8-4 represents a type of map found in earth science books, similar to other weather maps. Questions like the following, which involve literal and inferential meaning, will help make the map easier to understand:

1. Which areas of the world experience the greatest temperature changes?
2. Which areas experience the least temperature changes?
3. What do the areas that experience the least temperature changes have in common?

Figure 8-4.   Map of Annual Temperature (C) Ranges

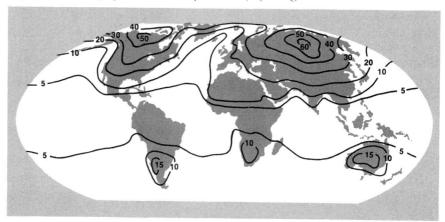

From *Investigating the Earth*, Earth Science Curriculum Project of the American Geological Institute, p. 155. Copyright ©1973 by Houghton Mifflin Co., and reproduced with their permission.

Fig. 8-5 is a type of map found in social studies books. As with the previous map, it can be read for literal and inferential meaning. It is not uncommon for such maps to contain insets which show one or more sections in greater detail. Students should understand the purpose of such insets and how their areas relate to the whole map.

Reading Pictures, Cartoons, and Diagrams

Most textbooks and reference sources use a variety of pictorial illustrations as aids to comprehension. The most common are photographs and diagrams, which are found in materials of almost all subject areas. Cartoons are typically placed in social studies books and, of course, in newspapers and magazines. As with other illustrations, they are intended to supplement and help explain the information in the text. Cartoons not only do these but also express a point of view. Captions with the illustrations facilitate comprehension of them.

Literal and inferential meanings can be drawn from these graphic aids. For example, Figure 8-6 is a picture which reveals more than words what happened to one segment of the American population in the 1930s. Students may be helped to infer, from the information that the picture alone reveals, the people's plight during this period. Figure 8-7 reveals the cartoonist's view of President Theodore Roosevelt's attitude toward monopolistic practices in business.

Figure 8-5.   Compromise of 1850 and Kansas-Nebraska Act of 1854.

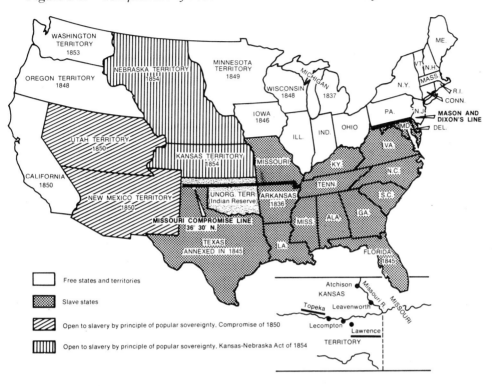

From Lewis P. Todd and Merle Curti, *Rise of the American Nation*, 2d ed., p. 357. Copyright ©1966 by Harcourt Brace Jovanovich, Inc., and reproduced with their permission.

The significance of the cartoon will be understood if students consider such questions as:

1. Why is Roosevelt pictured as a hunter?
2. What kinds of trusts did Roosevelt consider "bad"?
3. How was he able to control other trusts?
4. What is the cartoonist's point of view toward Roosevelt's actions?

The diagram in Figure 8-8 is intended merely to identify the parts of a dry cell and enable students to see its interior. But even from such a simple diagram, students can draw inferences (Why is a carbon rod used as a core? What reaction do the several chemicals produce?).

FLEXIBILITY AND SPEED IN READING

Obviously, students who can cover given amounts of material in less time than others have certain advantages. For one thing, they can read more — provided that they understand what they read.

Figure 8-6.   Dust Storm in Oklahoma

Photograph by Arthur Rothstein.

Efforts to increase student reading speed are being pushed from se-
eral directions. Originally, college students and adults were the ones wh-
were encouraged to leave the horse-and-buggy world of reading and ent-
the new era in which everything moved rapidly. Special courses were e-
tablished for them, and they attracted large numbers who wanted to rea-
rapidly. These same efforts now are extended to youth and even young chi-
dren. Commercial organizations advertise their courses in newspapers; a-
ticles in popular and trade magazines feature glowing accounts of the a-
complishments of individuals and groups; one newspaper reported that
fifth-grade pupil who started out by reading 308 words a minute achieved
rate of 20,250 words a minute after completing a speed-reading course.-
Those who plod along at a slower pace are not keeping up with the times, -
we are told.

Just how accurate are reports of students who achieve phenomen-
reading rates by taking a short course in rapid reading? Several years ag-
reports of a breakthrough in the speed reading barrier excited the interests-
reading specialists who were told that a new method for teaching students-

21. *New York Times*, Feb. 27, 1970.

Figure 8-7.   Taming the Trusts

Cartoon by Clifford Berryman.

reach reading speeds far beyond those attained heretofore had been developed.[22] Similar, but perhaps more modest, claims continue to appear in newspaper advertisements that guarantee results or "your money back."

Some investigators have cast doubts upon results that far exceed the reading performance of most students.[23] They question the feasibility of

22. Russell G. Stauffer, "A Magnificent Ambition," and Evelyn N. Wood, "A Breakthrough in Reading," *Reading Teacher* 14 (Nov. 1960): 74, 92; 115-117.
23. Stanford E. Taylor, "An Evaluation of Forty-one Trainees Who Had Recently Completed the Reading Dynamics Program," *College and Adult Reading*, 1st Annual Yearbook, North Central Reading Association, 1962, pp. 51-71; George D. Spache, "Is This a Breakthrough in Reading?," *Reading Teacher* 15 (Jan. 1962): 258-263; William Liddle, "An Initial Investigation of the Wood Reading Dynamics Method," doctoral diss., Univ. of Delaware, 1965; Allen Berger, "Speed Reading: Is the Present Emphasis Desirable?," pp. 45-84 in *Current Issues in Reading*, ed. Nila B. Smith (Newark, Del.: International Reading Association, 1969).

reading at rapid rates while maintaining levels of comprehension. Stated or implied is the idea that any reading style that allows students to read at exceedingly high rates — 1,500, 4,000, and 10,000 words or more per minute — is really nothing more than a form of skimming or scanning and not to be confused with continuous reading.

Figure 8-8.   Sectional View of a Dry Cell

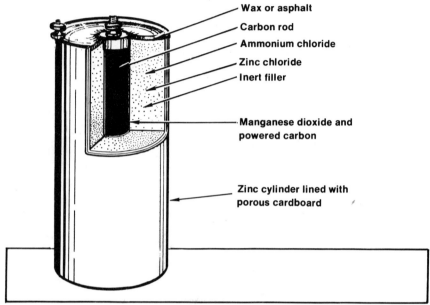

From H. Clark Metcalfe and others, *Modern Chemistry*, p. 231. Copyright ©1974 by Holt, Rinehart and Winston, Publishers. Used with permission.

According to estimates obtained by eye-movement photography, it appears that the maximum rate possible for continuous reading is under 1,000 words per minute if comprehension of material is taken into account. How, then, are the higher speeds attained? If you were to "cover" 20 pages of text consisting of 8,000 words in two minutes and have some impressions of its content, you would have "read" at the rate of 4,000 words per minute. Such reading is as valid as other kinds of reading if it serves one's purposes, but it is not to be confused with the kind of reading that is required for mastering unfamiliar, difficult information. Skimming or scanning is a useful technique when applied properly, but it is hardly one that can be recommended to meet all reading requirements.

Therefore, putting aside the possibility of incredible reading speeds, high school teachers should understand that with students it is not so much a matter of increased reading rate as it is the ability to adjust reading rate to different kinds of materials. A good reader knows how to shift gears when he reads, and he lets the nature of his materials and his purpose for reading control his speed. He does not read a treatise in philosophy as he would a newspaper article on baseball, nor does he read literature as he does a detective story.

Textbook reading is careful reading. Students may enjoy a light novel that they have read rapidly, but they read a biology or history textbook to master the information it contains. When they are held responsible for specific information, they cannot cover the ground rapidly. Imagine reading a series of unknown physics formulas quickly! What students need to know is how to tackle their reading assignments. Too often, those who flounder around are seeking an easy solution for difficult tasks.

Students should be encouraged to decide how they ought to read different types of materials. Teachers might have them compare selections from the same source and decide how each should be read. What students know about a topic, and how difficult the concepts are, are factors that could influence the way in which they would read them.

EXERCISE: Which of these passages seems difficult? How might you read each?

a. One of the striking differences between water plants and land plants is the root system. Water plants such as algae do not have absorbing roots. But structures for absorbing water and minerals from the soil are essential for land plants. Therefore, some sort of anchoring and absorbing structures must have developed in early land plants.[24]

b. Fig. 18-7 shows the main water-conducting structures in a tree. Note that some root cells have long, thin projections. These are the *root hairs.* Water and minerals in solution enter the cells through the root hairs. Water and minerals diffuse from the root hairs into other root cells and finally enter water-transport channels.[25]

c. Scientists believe that the primitive strands of cells shown in Figure 18-8 evolved into two types of channels. One channel, called the xylem (ZY-lem), transports water and minerals. The other channel, called the phloem (PLOH-em), transports food. The phloem is located nearer the outer bark of a tree, and the xylem, or woody tissue, is located closer to the center, or *pith,* of the tree trunk.[26]

Notice that the second passage refers the reader to an illustration. He is expected to stop reading the printed text and examine the diagram. Then he must return to the printed text and possibly study the diagram again. This kind of interrupted reading is essential if the student is to master the content. The student who reads in this way shows that he varies his reading with the requirements and is likely to be a more successful reader than another who is not as flexible in attacking his reading assignments and reads as though conditions are normal.

24. Claude A. Welch and others, *Biological Science: Molecules to Man,* rev. ed., Blue Version, p. 470. Copyright 1968, 1963 by the Regents of the Univ. of Colorado. Reprinted with the permission of Houghton Mifflin Co.
25. Ibid., pp. 471-472. Copyright 1968, 1963 by the Regents of the Univ. of Colorado. Reprinted with the permission of Houghton Mifflin Co.
26. Ibid., p. 472. Copyright 1968, 1963 by the Regents of the Univ. of Colorado. Reprinted with the permission of the Houghton Mifflin Co.

Purpose for reading will also determine the rate at which a high school student reads. If he seeks specific information from a source, he may be able to pass hurriedly over extraneous material or, if he wishes to determine the main point a writer is making and nothing more, he will read more quickly than when doing study-type reading.

Some observers have suggested that students should be trained to avoid rereading passages, since this slows down reading considerably. Certainly, however, any paragraph that is not understood needs to be read again. A phrase or an expression, although recognized, should be reread if it is not completely meaningful to the reader. And when a sentence that contains a beautifully stated thought or makes a profound observation is passed over quickly, the reader has suffered a distinct loss.

How rapidly do high school students read? Any answer, of course, depends on the materials involved, but it is safe to say that the typical student reads easy narrative material at between 200 and 300 words per minute. This is not a fast rate and may be increased with training. But evidence does support the conclusion that many students read all kinds of materials in the same way. Even when the content presents no problems in meaning, they will continue to read at a snail's pace. Time spent in helping these students adjust their rates of reading to materials at hand is time well spent.

Machines and Rate of Reading

Using mechanical devices to increase reading rate has achieved rather wide acceptance among teachers who conduct reading-improvement programs. Many high schools use different types of instruments, and some reading programs rest almost wholly upon them. Reports on the value of machines for increasing speed of comprehension are common, and one device or another has its enthusiastic supporters throughout the country, with large sums of money invested in each.

There are three basic types of instruments: flashmeters, pacers, and films. Some schools use all three in their reading programs while others rely on one or two. Financial considerations often dictate which shall be purchased.

The Flashmeter

A flashmeter is an overhead projector, known by the technical name of *tachistoscope*. It projects an image on a chalkboard or screen for a brief, measured period. The projection period is controlled by a manually set timing device and may be varied from one or two seconds to perhaps one-hundredth of a second, or less. Series of digits, individual words, phrases, sentences, and paragraphs are projected from glass slides that may be purchased from the manufacturer or prepared by the user.

The usual procedure is to initiate reading training with a series of three digits, for example, 467. The observer records the numbers he sees flashed on the screen at speeds varying from one-tenth to one-hundredth of a second.

The number of digits in the series is increased to four — 2590, 5041, 7982, and so on — until the observer recognizes these at the above-mentioned speeds. Some training programs continue this practice through twelve digits — 154647983842. Images of words, phrases, and then whole sentences are flashed in succession and the observer records what he sees each time.

Another type of tachistoscope is designed for individual use. The observer flashes a light (of predetermined duration) to illuminate a printed card that contains digits, words, phrases, or sentences similar to those used in the first program. Each observation is recorded and immediately verified by the observer. A third type uses films that flash these items on a screen with a specially-designed projector.

Flashmeter programs for increasing reading rates have grown out of studies on how the eyes move when an individual reads. When photographs of the eye movements of good and poor readers were compared, the good reader was seen to make fewer stops, or fixations, of shorter durations. Every time the eyes stop, a given amount of print is seen. Readers who require fewer stops to complete the reading of a line take in more with each stop than those who make more stops per line. Below are samples of the number of stops that two readers might make to complete the same line.

A — Another fac / tor in / the election / was / the intern / al splits.
B — Anot / her / factor / in the / electi / on / was / the / inter / nal splits.

Reader A requires fewer fixations to reach the end of the line than does reader B. If the duration of fixations are the same, A will complete the line in about half the time needed by B. Therefore, those studying the eye movements of readers reasoned that, if the width of a reader's perceptual span were to be increased, fewer fixations would occur in reading a line, and as a result the reader would be able to cover the line more quickly. Tachistoscopic drills are believed to be one way of achieving this end.

Critics of tachistoscopic programs insist that eye-movement films record what happens during reading but do not explain *why* eye movements happen. Reading is not dictated by eye movements but by thought processes controlled by the central nervous system. Results of controlled research seem to demonstrate that the use of tachistoscopic drills to increase reading speed is not as effective as other methods.

The Film Series

A second type of mechanical device designed to increase reading rate is the series of films that are designed to be used with 16-millimeter motion-picture projectors. Each film tells a story that is followed by a number of comprehension questions. The films are constructed so as to permit the observer to see portions of a line of text in succession; what has preceded and what follows are occluded. The rate at which each portion of text appears is built into the film, although the speed at which it is shown may be varied. The earlier films in the series divide the text into small units that are intended to represent the fixation or stops that the average person would make in reading the material. In later films, the units are increased in width to permit more text to appear on the screen as each portion of the line is shown.

The rationale for using films to improve reading rate is the same as for tachistoscopes: to increase the reader's span of perception so that, ultimately, he will be able to see more with each fixation and thereby be able to read more quickly. The same objections have been raised to the use of films as to the use of tachistoscopes. Investigators report gains in reading rate without the use of films equal or superior to those made with films.

The Pacer

A pacer is an instrument that contains a movable bar or screen under which a book may be placed.[27] The bar or screen is regulated to move down over the page at a predetermined rate of speed, for example, 350 words per minute. If the reader is able to keep pace with the descending bar or screen, he knows that his reading rate is equal to the speed at which the machine is set.

The reader's normal rate of reading is determined before he uses the pacer, and this speed becomes the basis for beginning training. One pacer program suggests that the reader increase the rate at which the bar or screen descends by 15 percent each time he is able to keep pace with it while maintaining a comprehension score of at least 70 percent.

Pacers come closer to duplicating natural reading situations than do other devices. Investigators report that pacers help some persons increase their reading speed. Reading specialists who do not place much confidence in other mechanical instruments have used pacers as training aids. I have employed pacers to convince adults that they can read narrative materials faster than they do without any corresponding loss in comprehension.

Natural Speeded Reading

Earlier, the point was made that the nature of materials and the purpose for reading them should determine how they are read. A student should have one speed for reading complex material packed with detail and another for easy narrative writing; possibly, he might have a third speed for reading newspapers and popular periodicals.

There is no question that a typical high school student can increase his reading rate, except for complex and difficult selections, without any appreciable loss in comprehension. He must, however, be free from weaknesses that interfere with rapid reading, such as difficulties in recognizing words readily and understanding the meaning of individual words and larger units of thought. He must be able to read without lip movement and vocalization, since silent reading may be done more rapidly than oral reading. (Some subvocalization is done by most readers but it need not interfere with silent reading.) Students who must pronounce each word or who does not recognize a word easily are not candidates for speeded reading training.

27. One pacer uses a line of light instead of a bar or screen.

Rapid Reading

Since a student's reading rate may not be separated from under-standing, the most effective way to increase reading rate is to improve ability to understand units of thought. Students can read only as rapidly as their grasp of ideas from printed materials permits. Lessons in extracting ideas from different kinds of material will lead to increasing their reading rate. Eliminating word-recognition, comprehension, and study-skills weaknesses is bound to produce an increase in reading rate.

Many high school students, however, are in the habit of reading slowly when there is no need for doing so. For these students, direct attention to improvement in their reading rate can be beneficial. One way for a teacher to help them overcome this shortcoming is to provide interesting but relatively easy materials and simply encourage students to read as quickly as possible.

Another technique that the teacher may use to increase the reading speed of narrative materials is the *timed exercise*. Students read short selections and the teacher records the time in intervals of ten or fifteen seconds. The students then answer the comprehension questions that accompany the selections, and record their total reading time. After substantial progress in reading rate has been achieved, longer selections may be introduced. In such timed exercises, students are competing against themselves and striving to better their previous performance.

In another version of timed exercise, the teacher uses narrative materials and a predetermined rate of reading. For example, a passage that contains 400 words is to be read at the rate of 300 words per minute — that is, reading must be completed in one minute and 20 seconds. A kitchen timer may be used to clock the time. The object is for students to complete the reading before the signal to stop is given.

The teacher may use short, timed exercises that require students to react quickly to ideas as a third possible way of increasing reading rate. These exercises may use individual words, phrases, sentences, or paragraphs, as in these sample exercises:

EXERCISE: **Underline the words in the series that are synonyms of the italicized word.**
infallible — certain, unreliable, unfailing
lethal — deadly, fatal, immortal

EXERCISE: **Circle the word or phrase that means the same as the italicized phrase.**
on the other hand — therefore, but, since
come to one's senses — make certain, see the light, feel well

EXERCISE: **Circle the word that does not belong with the other words in the series.**
dog, cat, bee, horse, pig
elm, maple, ash, cotton, oak

EXERCISE: **Each sentence contains one word that does not fit. Circle this word.**
The aircraft carrier sank in ten fathoms.
We nearly froze when the temperature rose to − 10° F.

Skimming and Scanning

Some reading specialists make a distinction between skimming and scanning. For them, *skimming* refers to the rapid reading the reader does when he is interested merely in gaining the author's intent or his important ideas. It may be compared to "skimming" the cream off the top of milk. *Scanning* refers to reading rapidly to locate such specific information as birth date, temperature range, location, and so forth.

Understandably, the reading rates for skimming or scanning are faster than any other rates in reading. In skimming, no attention is paid to anything except the ideas that the reader is seeking. As the reader scans a page for a specific word or group of words, he pays no heed to anything else; he is not reading conventionally and will remember little of the content. During scanning, the fastest kind of reading, the reader runs his eye over the words or down the page as rapidly as he can until he spots what he is seeking. If scanning is done properly, the reader will be unable to recall anything he read except the answer he sought.

A teacher can make up any number of lessons to develop his students' skill in scanning. After he has explained the purposes for scanning, he might begin by having students find a proper name, such as Saturn, on a page in their textbook. He should explain beforehand that the students are to sweep their eyes across the lines of text from left to right, and record the time it took them to find the word. When the exercise has been finished, the teacher does well to ask questions to see if any student picked up any other information from the page being scanned, because the students must understand that correct scanning ignores everything but the word being sought. In the illustration below, arrows indicate the paths that students should follow as they sweep their eyes across the line to locate the answer to the following question: *How is longitude measured?* They should read the sentence in which the term appears and, possibly, the sentence before and after it to verify the answer.

Points on the earth's surface are located by ordered pairs of numbers. Since the earth is a sphere, a straight line cannot be drawn on its surface. A circle and a half circle are chosen as the axes. Do you know what these axes on the earth are called? The equator is the circle axis and is midway between the two poles; the half-circle axis, called the prime meridian, extends from the North Pole through the city of Greenwich, England, to the South Pole. Latitude is measured in degrees north and south from the equator and longitude is measured in degrees east and west from the prime (Stop! Read the sentence in which longitude appears) meridian. The maximum number of degrees of latitude is 90 and the maximum degrees of longitude is 180. Any point on the earth can be located by specifying its latitude, north and south, and its longitude, east or west (two numbers and two directions).[28]

Practice locating single words rapidly should be followed by exercises in spotting short phrases. When students have developed this skill, they are ready to scan material for answers to questions. Once again, students must be told what to expect. The question contains the *clue* to the type of answer sought. To answer the question "How long is the Holland Tunnel?" students should be aware that feet or yards are involved and be on the lookout for a number. As soon as they locate one, they must read the sentence in which it appears to make certain it is relevant. Practice in finding answers to various sorts of factual questions will enable students to deal with the requirements of many situations.

Scanning to answer more generalized questions is also possible and may be taught to most average readers. One way is to scan materials for signpost words. The answer to "Why did Jefferson make the Louisiana Purchase?" may be introduced in the text by a signpost, such as *in the first place*, *in addition*, or *since*. Marginal headings may also provide clues for scanning. When either of these scanning aids is introduced to the students, practice should be provided to help students make use of them when scanning to answer generalized questions.

Some readers scan for specific information by directing their eyes to the center of the top line of a page and running down the middle of the lines of print. They depend greatly on their peripheral vision to view enough to locate an answer rapidly. Students may profit from practice exercises in this scanning technique. Textbooks that have a double-column format are especially suited to this kind of scanning and should be used during the early stages of training.

When students are reading rapidly to find the important ideas within a selection or the author's purpose for expressing them, they need to know how to use the techniques of skimming. Scanning techniques are not suitable, for no longer are they looking for a single word or group of words, but for ideas expressed in sentences and even paragraphs. Skimming implies a slower reading rate than scanning but a faster rate than when comparable materials are being read and studied.

When students are familiar with patterns of organization, they can quickly see whether to dwell on a paragraph or move on to the next. By reading the first couple of sentences of a paragraph, a student should be able to determine whether it contains what he needs to know. Selections that contain different kinds of paragraphs should be chosen by teachers giving training in skimming. Each should then be examined to determine its role in a writer's scheme of thought.

Rapidly reading the beginnings of paragraphs is all that is required for a student to know whether any one of them should be read carefully or

28. H. Vernon Price, Philip Peak, and Phillip S. Jones, *Mathematics: An Integrated Series*, Book 1 (New York: Harcourt, Brace and World, 1965), pp. 175-176. Copyright © 1965 by Harcourt Brace Jovanovich, Inc., and reprinted with their permission.

skipped. If the student wants to grasp the gist of a selection, he will read the first portion in this manner until he believes he has located the thought, hurriedly look over the paragraphs that follow to make certain he is on the right track, and then turn to the end of the selection where a restatement or summary might be found. By skimming in this manner, a student can cover a 5,000-word selection in a few minutes.

If a student seeks more than the essence of the material, rapid perusal will reveal the details. Once again, he will not read all paragraphs carefully. Practicing this kind of reading will enable students to develop a skimming skill that can be applied when it is needed — for example, when searching in the library for materials on some specific topic. Skimming is a helpful technique, but it is not a shortcut to real learning.

Hop-skip-and-jump-Reading

High school students who are good readers can be taught another way to skim for ideas. By skipping words that do not add much meaning to a sentence, the essence of a paragraph may be obtained quickly. For example, the student can read

Teaching   consistent   principles   learning   produce   results

and obtain the key idea of the sentence that reads in full:

Teaching which is consistent with known principles of learning is likely to produce good results.

This type of skimming has been called "reading with a hop, skip, and a jump." Prepositions, articles, and adjectives may be omitted, yet the sentence will retain its message. Selections for hop-skip-and-jump reading may be prepared by the teacher from available materials, but questions to check understanding of the ideas must accompany each selection. Here is a typical exercise:

EXERCISE: **Read this selection to discover what ideas the author is trying to convey. Unnecessary words have been omitted from the text. Read as rapidly as you can. Remember to read for ideas.**

Congress failed adopt items New Deal: repeal Taft-Hartley; creation valley authorities, similar TVA; approval St. Lawrence Seaway; admission Alaska, Hawaii, provision, federal aid education; universal military training; improved farm support; system health insurance. Congress showed independence overriding President's veto McCarran-Walter Act, Internal Security Act.

QUESTIONS:
1. Which acts did the President veto?
2. What kind of defense measure did the Congress oppose?
3. Under what banner were these different proposals made?

After students have developed skill in hop-skip-and-jump reading by such prepared exercises, the teacher may let them try whole selections in the same way. Their first efforts should be with fairly easy narrative materials of short length. Each student should be encouraged to read as rapidly as he can, and if the materials are of equal length and difficulty, the added factor of timing should help to speed up reading. Newspapers and magazine articles lend themselves to this type of reading. Proficient readers are able to cover much ground quickly and obtain the sense of what they read. Every exercise should, of course, be followed by oral or written comprehension checks. And students must understand that textbooks are not to be read in this way, except perhaps to survey some specific section.

The importance of knowing how to read under different conditions cannot be overemphasized. One student's rate of reading may be 200 words a minute and another's 500, but in situations that call for skimming or scanning, the speed at which both will read will far exceed these normal reading rates. Applying the skills of rapid reading to real situations in which students are involved will reinforce the principles that govern reading speed and will develop the flexibility that different kinds of reading require.

OTHER SKILLS

Certain study skills should be taught to high school students, not only by English teachers as discussed elsewhere in this book, but also by other teachers. Students should be trained to *survey materials quickly* before carefully reading them. Practice in using organizational devices found in textbooks, such as chapter headings, main subheadings, marginal and paragraph headings, introductory and summary sections, and different type faces, will give students an overview of the book's content and provide some information about the author's pattern of writing.

When training students to use these devices, teachers should base exercises on the subject-matter materials the students are reading. Exercises could ask students to

read chapter titles and review what is known of the subject
read introductions and summaries and formulate questions about the
content
note major subtopics and restate them in the form of questions
note the use of type to distinguish major and subsidiary topics.

An extension of the chapter or section survey is the study habit of reciting as soon as the material is read. Students might respond to the questions they have formulated by writing the answers or giving them orally. This procedure would be followed after reading each segment. Thoroughly reviewing the entire material could be done if it were necessary to do so.

High school students also need to be taught to *recognize signposts* provided by the author of a textbook. Some writers use such words as *in the first place, next,* and *last* to alert readers when an important point is being made. Words or phrases such as *however, on the other hand*, and *but* indicate that an opposing statement will follow. Anticipating what is to come helps students understand more of what they read. Paragraphs that contain these signposts may be found in textbooks or can be prepared by the teacher. Whichever is used for an exercise, teacher and students should analyze them carefully with a view of understanding their organization.

Knowing paragraph structure helps high school students in their studying. Practice in recognizing introductory, transitional (those that bridge the gap between one thought and another), illustrative, definitive (those that define or explain terms), and summary paragraphs will help students discern sections that contribute materially to their grasp of the content. They will also be able to identify the portions of the text that expand and reemphasize the important ideas and pass quickly over sections in which they may not be particularly interested. Moreover, recognizing that the author stresses relationships among ideas through such patterns as *enumeration, topics, time, comparison-contrast*, and *cause and effect* will help students follow their thoughts and comprehend them better. Recognizing paragraph structure may serve to alert students to material, much in the same way as do signposts.

SUMMARY

High school students must master study skills if they are to complete assignments in textbooks and other expository materials in any content area. The ability to study efficiently depends on several study skills: selecting and evaluating important ideas and related details; locating, organizing, and retaining information; following directions; comprehending graphic aids; and flexibility in reading.

Each study skill should be taught by the teacher in whose subject area its use is required. These reading skills may be developed by using the books that students are using, but the content of any exercise material should present no real meaning difficulties other than those being considered. It is a good idea to teach only one skill in each lesson, developing skills in sequence of difficulty. The learning needs of students will dictate the study skills on which teachers must concentrate.

There is no one single way to teach reading skills. Teaching methods are less important then the principles upon which the methods rest, and this chapter has presented sample lessons and exercises that are intended to serve as guides to teaching the study skills, not as formal demonstrations of methodology.

Additional Readings

The identification and/or teaching of study skills are covered in the following publications:

Lawrence Hafner, ed. *Improving Reading in Middle and Secondary Schools: Selected Readings,* 2d ed. New York: Macmillan Company, 1974, pp. 161-195, 253-273.

Harold L. Herber, ed. *Developing Study Skills in Secondary Schools,* Perspectives in Reading No. 4. Newark, Del.: International Reading Association, 1965.

Robert Karlin, ed. *Teaching Reading in High School: Selected Articles.* Indianapolis: Bobbs-Merrill, 1969, pp. 242-269.

James L. Laffey, ed. *Reading in the Content Areas.* Newark, Del. International Reading Association, 1972.

David L. Shepherd. *Comprehensive High School Reading Methods.* Columbus, Ohio: Charles E. Merrill Publishing Co., 1973, pp. 101-125.

Nila Banton Smith, ed. *Current Issues in Reading.* Vol. 13, Part 2 of the Proceedings of the Thirteenth Annual Convention, International Reading Association, 1969, pp. 45-84.

Russell G. Stauffer, ed. *Speed Reading: Practices and Procedures.* Proceedings of the Forty-fourth Annual Education Conference. University of Delaware, 1962.

Ellen Lamar Thomas and H. Alan Robinson. *Improving Reading in Every Class,* abridged ed. Boston: Allyn and Bacon, 1972, pp. 108-203.

CHAPTER 9

READING
for APPRECIATION
and ENJOYMENT

Problems for Study and Discussion

1 *What are the justifications for including the teaching of literature in a comprehensive reading program?*

2 *Why have "classics" turned many high school students away from reading?*

3 *What problems in appreciation does each genre of literature present?*

4 *What elements do typical adolescents seek in books? Which kinds of books meet their needs?*

5 *How might teachers identify the reading preferences of individual students?*

6 *What can all teachers do to promote an interest in books and foster the reading habit?*

READING AND LITERATURE

When a student reads a literary selection, he uses a variety of reading skills. He may first recognize word meanings, but these are quickly melded into thoughts and then ideas. From this phase of literal comprehension, he may move on to deeper meanings —inferring symbols and detecting ambiguities, for example. From here, he may proceed to critical reaction and evaluation according to his experiences with life and with reading. Finally, he may be moved to change his attitude or alter some aspect of his behavior, and we say that he has learned from his reading.

Many readers do not pass through each of these phases when reading literature. A large number may not pass beyond literal comprehension; as passive readers they get the story but not the message. It is the active readers with their repertory of skills who translate the message into action.

Can all students learn to appreciate literature? Yes, if the following conditions are met: the material must be on their instructional level, and they must have had experiences which they can relate to those about which they read. Thus, even slow learners can be led to see the beauty and truths that literature contains. To teach high school students how to "commune with the author" presents a real challenge; the closer the literary selections match the reading and maturity levels of students, the more likely the content will have an impact on their appreciation and enjoyment of it.

Literature can give readers many kinds of enjoyment. Students may delight in learning more about the world and the people in it. They may enjoy reading a good biography or find pleasure in relating the modern world with the past in an historical novel. The insights of the special view of the poet, the moral and ethical commentaries of the essayist, or the motives of characters in a short story may yield the satisfactions of understanding. To do any or all of these things, any reader, and in this case the high school students, must be equipped to enjoy the keen delights that literature can offer.

According to one English educator, to experience literature is to be freed "from the inherent shackles fastened upon us by our society." It permits us, in his words, "to shake off, when necessary, the emotional censors of society."[1] While literature can provide momentary escapes from reality, it does bring us face to face with the real world that we might not know but that others do. In this respect, we have an opportunity to "try out" experiences on ourselves, or at the very least to become aware of what might be in store for us should we have to cope with comparable conditions.

Literature helps us understand human beings, for it reflects their motivations which could be the same as or similar to ours and thereby allows us to explain ourselves. The characters are likely to represent each of us at one time or another; understanding how others are influenced and shaped may help us come to terms with ourselves.

Since literature is a reflection of people and their worlds, it deals with humanity's conflicts and problems. There are lessons that can be learned and solutions that can be applied to present issues upon which past ones bear. Literature does not offer proper answers to all of people's problems; it does come to grips with them and may contain clues to some strategies for dealing with them, even if failures are possible.

Literature is an illuminator of beauty and a source of pleasure. It sharpens our appreciation of the ordinary through the magic of language. What is the usual house becomes a comfortable haven and the common flower a brilliant jewel. What we take for granted changes into an object of wonder through a heightening of the senses. The lyricism of language and the content of literature join to make possible a memorable experience.

1. Dwight L. Burton, *Literature Study in the High School*, 3d ed. (New York: Holt, Rinehart and Winston, 1970), pp. 5, 6.

READING AND RESPONSIVENESS

Why is it that seventh graders enter junior high school reading comic books with such zeal? Dwight Burton[2] feels that teachers can learn much to help them guide students in their reading if they will examine the appeal that comics have for high school students. Comics are easy to read; they appeal immediately to more senses than does "straight" reading; the content of the comic fits the nature of early adolescence; the picture of life and underlying assumptions are acceptable to the immature mind. In the transition or "weaning" period between the comics and literature that is read for appreciation, Burton suggests that reading selections should

be easy to read
reflect experience close to that of the reader
lack the gross distortion of experience of the comics
have the magic ingredient of "punch"
be made as available as possible.

These simple suggestions are a first step toward developing readers who will learn to appreciate and enjoy literature. Another is not to overshoot or underestimate the maturity of students; we do have the tendency to do the former much more than the latter.

Many may remember the desperate efforts of well-intentioned teachers who tried to make Shakespeare a meaningful and stirring experience to a class that was not ready for him. Hours were spent deciphering the language of 400 years ago, and the whole situation appeared ludicrous and weird to the class who could not yet appreciate the mind behind the masterpiece or the poetry and characterizations of a *Hamlet.*

That maturity plays a great part in understanding literature is highlighted by a layman whose child was wrestling with *Silas Marner.* After observing that any "required reading" sends high school students into a sort of stupor (although they may be sufficiently alert to read the newspaper or a current best seller), one layman, who had reread *Silas,* pointed out why the young "scholar" may not be equally enthralled by it:

He does not appreciate long sentences. . . . The young scholar finds strange — not intriguing — the appearance of words such as orts, distrain, pettitoes and springe. He resents the intrusion of the author's occasional moral asides. *But one suspects that the trouble is not with dog-eared* Silas Marner *but with a tradition that says that it must be read by youngsters of 14 or 15* [italics added]. One needs to have lived longer than that to enjoy "Silas."[3]

The trouble, then, is not with *Silas Marner* but with the lack of communication between the author and fifteen-year-old students living today.

---

2. Dwight L. Burton, "Campaigning to Get Students to Read," in *Reading in the Secondary Schools,* ed. M. Jerry Weiss (New York: Odyssey, 1961).
3. "Topic of the Times," *New York Times,* April 24, 1957.

The adult has read more, experienced more, built a larger vocabulary, and developed more patience. An adult's sense of the past is certainly greater than that of a high school student.

The Classics and the Curriculum

No doubt Eliot's classic was quite enjoyable when father read it to the family around the hearth of a Victorian household, when a story could move slowly and had no competition from television and the movies. But in a jet-propelled age, even the serious young student often has trouble understanding Silas, Eppi, and George Eliot. This is not to say that classics should not be taught in high school. Only that the classics should contain flesh-and-blood characters and interesting story lines. Students need to understand that the language of 200 years ago is not the language of today, and they must likewise grasp the concept that social values change along with styles, environment, and language. This demands skillful teaching.

Too often high schools have a stereotyped image of the classics; students are required to read "old chestnuts" that were questionable examples of literature when they were first adopted. John Ciardi has bemoaned the fact that in many school systems "Evangeline still wends her dreary way" while the students are bored with the whole trip. *The Virginian* is probably pretty tame fare for today's students of TV westerns.

An alert English department, however, will periodically evaluate what it is doing. It will question whether some classics should be taught just because they have always been taught, and it will consider the best of modern writing. It will strike a balance between classic and modern literature and offer the students something of both, something they will be able to understand and enjoy. Is it unreasonable to accuse *Ivanhoe* of containing a ponderous, turgid style and to observe that inflicting such a book on a student who is average or below in reading skills is a subtle form of torture? There are other books that contain just as much excitement and history that the students can handle. Appeal to custom is small reason for retaining torture, and such reading assignments will kill the love of reading.

We should be grateful that modern anthologies have changed this state of affairs. They offer themes that boys and girls can understand and a balance between the old and the new. If, in many cases, the staunch conservatives have been deferred to, it is encouraging, at least, to see the barnacles disappearing from high school literature texts. In the final analysis, however, thinking teachers must be responsible for exposing students to literature which they will want to read because it is meaningful to them.

READING AND CREATIVITY

Perhaps the most important appreciation skill that teachers can foster on students is "set of awareness" before any reading begins. If students are to derive maximum appreciation from reading literature, they must be alert to the author's purpose and style and be ready to muster their analytical talents. The "set of awareness" is the decision to be active and sensitive toward the upcoming experience with the printed page. Appreciative readers summon the best of their thinking powers and their experiences and focus them on the task at hand. They prepare to read with feeling and energy. If a book is considered literature, it must be of the best that books have to offer. If the author has given his best, so must the readers commit themselves, at least until they have given the book, story, or poem a fair trial to determine if it is indeed literature. They will involve themselves with all their powers to co-create with the author.

Once he begins to read, the *question* lies at the heart of the reader's awareness. What coal is to fire, questions are to his comprehension. The beginning of any piece of literature must be read slowly, analytically, intensively. Question after question should enter the reader's mind as he reads line after line. Who? What? Why? When? Where? How? The beginning of a novel, poem, or story is an orientation. To have a context in which events can happen, there has to be a beginning. The reader must know who characters are and how they are related. He must know what part setting plays in the story. The tone of the story must be felt. The problems of the characters must be understood. The author's point of view must be sensed.

Literature authors did not sit down without a purpose or a plan in mind. They had something to say about life. They had something to interpret. It is the job of the reader to "creep into the author's mind" as reading progresses — to follow the path of the mind behind the story or poem or essay. Identifying with the author makes reading the author's work a satisfaction. Gradually his theme, or philosophy — what he has to say about life — will unfold before the alert reader. The clues, subtle or obvious, that he provides for the reader through characters, imagery, events, asides, and other devices add up to a rich picture — a total impact. Ideas emerge; the reader must be aware of them and sensitive to them.

The mature reader becomes a part of the book he reads, hearing what is said and seeing what is described. He projects himself into the lives of the characters. He reacts to what they experience. Everyone has read writing so engrossing that it has made him unaware of the outside world and aware only of the web of reality woven by the writer. This plunge into another world is prepared for by the "set of awareness" — calling upon the reader's powers to appreciate the best that has been written. As long as teachers are aware of the need for this "set of awareness," they will probably have their own ways of inculcating in students those skills that will let them, as readers, co-create with authors.

Literature Skills

Just as over-analysis in the name of understanding can kill any interest students might have for reading literature, so can its use for teaching basic reading skills deaden any appreciation for it. The purpose of teaching literature is to heighten students' enjoyment of it. Students will not realize this objective if they have to spend their time learning how to analyze its words and pronounce them, learning how to perceive relationships in its sentences and paragraphs, or inferring ideas from them. They do have to apply their reading skills as they read imaginative writing, but the focus of teaching is upon the ways in which authors use language to convey ideas and moods and create effects through the use of different forms. The enjoyment of literature is bound to be enhanced by added appreciation of it through mastery of the following abilities: recognizing imagery and understanding figurative language and allusions; seeing how language conveys tone and mood; noticing the effects of word order and rhythm in prose and poetry; recognizing the generic qualities of literary forms; distinguishing between surface and underlying themes; and evaluating the quality of writing.

TEACHING APPRECIATION

Students learn to appreciate literature over a long period of time. No one develops "literary taste" in five minutes and no one stops developing literary taste until he dies — that is, if he reads. Many people have become concerned over the decline of the reading habit and the prevalence of capsule reading in the digest magazines. If reading becomes distasteful over the years as the students proceed through high school, then they will not develop the lifetime habit that supposedly is the business of English and reading teachers to develop. It is the job of the teacher to help students enjoy literature — not to kill their interest in it — and developmental lessons must therefore be rewarding and enjoyable experiences.

According to some critics,[4] a sure-fire way to dampen student desires for good reading is to require rote recall to answer literal-level questions with books closed; have the whole class read aloud, student by student, and interrupt to correct pronunciation; refuse to allow the reading of best sellers; don't ever tell them a word they don't know and have them stop reading to look up the word; don't give students the chance to tell what they think about a book; make a "federal case" when you catch a student reading by hiding a book or magazine in the textbook; use the library to house detention classes. While these conditions might be exaggerations of what occurs in most classrooms, there can be no doubt that some students have been turned away from books and reading by comparable practices.

Each type of literature presents a special set of appreciation problems and each specific selection within a type has its special set of problems too. Some of these will be gone into shortly. In the last analysis, the teacher must realize that, while the various types of literature possess common characteristics, teaching a specific novel, poem, or essay is an exercise in appreciation that applies mostly to that particular piece. He can only hope that there will be a transfer of learning from one selection to the next one that the students read. Behind all exercises must be the ultimate objective: encouraging students to read more examples of the best that the literary heritage offers, in order to develop their literary tastes.

4. Dorothy Pierce and Michael Obrenovich, "If Kids Don't Hate to Read by the Time They Get to High School, Here Are Some Suggestions to Help Them (Hate to Read, That Is)," *Journal of Reading* 16 (Jan. 1973): 305-309.

To teach a specific selection well, the teacher must know it well. He must construct intelligent, stimulating questions that students will use as guides while reading an assignment. These questions should be springboards to class discussion. They should pique the curiosity of the students. Finding the answers should yield the students a feeling of satisfaction. Often, questions should have open-ended answers to provoke thought and interest in the reading. To form such questions demands careful preparation on the part of the teacher, yet a stimulating and rewarding class can be the result.

The enthusiasm of the teacher is frequently a key to greater interest. If students observe that the person leading the class is excited over a book, they may wonder what all the fuss is about. Certainly, if a teacher thinks a work is dull, his feeling will come through to the class, no matter how he tries to mask it. Enthusiasm can be contagious and can lead to the motivation that will make the difference between an ordeal and a pleasure.

Enthusiasm, coupled with artful questioning, can make reading a rewarding experience for the students. After a class discussion, application of what students have derived from the work is in order. This should not be "busy" work. An essay on the theme of a novel can be interesting to write or it can be dull — depending on what the teacher requires. If the teacher uses imagination, assignments that avoid the hackneyed "book report" and allow students to express themselves can be developed.

True literature teaching involves inducing students to experience novels, plays, essays, and biographies; to "live into" poetry, as John Ciardi puts it, and to come away a slightly different person. If teaching takes root, then the student will perhaps some day switch off the television and take down a book he has always intended to read; perhaps, this will be because of a faintly remembered class about Dickens or Conrad or Hemingway that was tremendously interesting.

Each type of literature has some characteristics common to other types. Yet, novels have characteristics that poems lack; an essay differs from a play. One specific novel presents a set of problems different from those in the next specific novel; *Brave New World* is a long way from *The Mill on the Floss*. There are, however, some general things that can be said about each form of literature from which students may profit.

The Short Story

The writer of a short story is "economy-minded." He does not have the latitude that a novelist has. There are usually fewer characters, fewer settings, and fewer incidents in the short stories, even if they are unusually long. Students must infer what happened in a character's life before the story begins. In a few opening paragraphs, the writer must create an interesting situation that will hold the reader. Often, the main character is presented with a problem. Looking for that problem in the first paragraphs of a story helps the students to become oriented. The rest of the story is then concerned with how the problem is solved. This problem often makes the roots upon which the tree of suspense grows.

Conflict of one sort or another ordinarily creates interest in short stories. Without some sort of conflict or problem, there would be no interest. A story about a man and a dog crossing a stretch of snow and arriving at their destination promises to be dull. But when a man and a dog cross a stretch of snow and the man begins to freeze and must build a fire or die, the story becomes interesting and you have a classic: "To Build a Fire" by Jack London. Conflict may be between characters, between a character and the environment, or within a character. Without it, there would be few short stories, novels, or plays.

Students must learn to notice even minor clues in a short story. Since there is so little time to tell the story, the author must make almost every word count. Most short stories move, with suspense, toward a *crisis*, which is the turning point in the story that leads to a resolution. If students look for the problem that a character faces, the conflict, and the crisis, it will help their reading of the story. There may also be a *theme* — or message that the author has intended to transmit through telling the story. This comment on human nature can frequently be inferred from the story. Sometimes it is directly stated.

It can be profitable for students to think about the title of a story, both before and after reading it, if they wish to draw a conclusion about the title. It may be ironical, or it may be a statement of the main point of the story. Usually, too little attention is paid to the title of a story, a novel, an essay, and, especially, a poem.

Students should be able to sum up the plot, or sequence of events in a story, in a few lines. But the life of the story lies in the interaction of the characters, the reality of the tale it presents, and the author's style. A good short story is an experience that rings true. It is distilled life presented in an imaginative way.

Novels

It takes the author more time to say what he has to say through a novel. Its characters change more than do those in the story and may be more numerous. The theme may be more complex, and there may be more than one theme. Students get to know characters better in a good novel than in a short story. They should notice how characters change from the beginning to the end of a novel. Any reader should first look for problems facing the main characters, for these create interest. There may be several problems facing characters throughout the book. Conflict is as important an element in a novel as in a short story.

A historical novel can tell students much about the past. *The King Must Die* by Mary Renault is the myth of Theseus retold. It tells the reader about the ancient Minoan civilization while engrossing him in the problems of Theseus as the book proceeds to a climax. *A Tale of Two Cities* takes the reader to the France of the revolution. The novel emphasizes social change, and the hero must eventually make the decision to die for another or save himself. *The Once and Future King* by T. H. White retells the legend of King Arthur, and it contains a rich amount of history plus a wealth of humor and satire. The eternal problem of a love triangle occupies the latter half of the book, yet this is treated in an unusual way, seeming to say that problems of love, war, and mankind in general do not differ greatly from century to century.

There are many techniques a writer may use. The "stream-of-consciousness" technique made famous by James Joyce is radically different from the narrative technique of Robert Louis Stevenson in *Treasure Island.* John Dos Passos attempts to give us a comprehensive view of a period of time in his trilogy *U. S. A.*, which some mature high school students may read. The "camera-eye" presents a montage of events that attempts a *gestalt* that will give the reader a sense of the time he was writing about.

Writers vary in their purposes. Orwell writes devastating satire in *Animal Farm*, where the government of the animals by a dictator hog illustrates the dangers of a totalitarian society. *For Whom the Bell Tolls*, on the other hand, shows the courage of people fighting for an ideal in the face of certain failure. Novelists may use symbolism to enrich, and sometimes to obscure, their message. A great novel is a large comment on human nature, and readers who have used their powers to the fullest finish *War and Peace* with the feeling that they have lived through an era and have learned much about people.

"Literature is news that STAYS news," Ezra Pound has said, in *ABC of Reading*. The word *novel* means "news." What a great novel has to say will be fresh for generations, for the great novelist is concerned with the minds and hearts of us all.

The Essay

The essay is a flexible form of literature. It covers a wide variety of writing and many a parcel of prose hangs together in the name of the essay. A formal essay may be thousands of words long and read like a scientific article. A personal essay may be a few hundred words in length and concern itself with apparent trivia. Generally, essays are thought of as devices through which authors present opinions in an interesting way.

The main task of the students is to discover the author's purpose for writing the essay. Sometimes this purpose is stated openly; sometimes it is implied. Authors may be direct in their approach, or they may use satire, wit, or humor to put their points across. Students who can sense patterns of organization can read an essay with more ease. Some authors will inductively build up to a point, whereas others will make an assertion and illustrate their points with examples.

William Hazlitt, one of the great essayists of the early nineteenth century, begins "On Going a Journey," with this assertion: "One of the pleasantest things in the world is going a journey; but I like to go by myself. I can enjoy society in a room; but out of doors, nature is company enough for me. I am then never less alone than when alone." Later he says, "The soul of a journey is liberty, perfect liberty, to think, feel, do, just as one pleases. We go a journey chiefly to be free of all impediments and of all inconveniences; to leave ourselves behind, much more to get rid of others."

G. K. Chesterton uses irony with great skill in "On Running After One's Hat," where he argues that "An adventure is only an inconvenience rightly considered. An inconvenience is only an adventure wrongly considered." Why should not running after one's hat become an adventure?

Essays demand style and personality if they are to be great. In the personal essay, the writer often writes as if he were chatting with the reader and saying, "Here are some of my very best thoughts. Read on and see if you don't agree with me." Alert students will follow the essayist's line of thought with a questioning mind, examining his logic and resisting the temptation to be captivated by his style. Many people, for example, enjoy "going a journey" with a friend. They enjoy companionship when seeing new sights, and nature may be a dull companion. The reader who is beguiled by Hazlitt's style may have difficulty disagreeing with him while reading the essay, but in the cool atmosphere of reflection may pull up short and say, "But I don't agree with that nonsense at all!"

An essay that is literature is often the best thinking on a limited topic, beautifully expressed. Reading a fine essay can be a rich experience.

Biography and Autobiography

Any reader will probably get more truth from a biography than from an autobiography. Though the biographer suffers from the disadvantage of distance in time and usually from not knowing the subject, he has the advantages of greater objectivity and wider perspective. It is difficult, if not impossible, for a person to write about himself objectively. This is not to say that a biographer is completely objective. Usually, he takes a position on his subject; he either likes him or dislikes him, consciously or unconsciously, and his feelings are reflected in the book. Even with the most objective biographer, the selection or rejection of material reflects his attitudes.

A biography can be an excellent method for viewing a period of history from the standpoint of an individual. It gives the reader a special look in detail at an aspect of the past.

Biographies are usually written as narratives, much as a traditional novel is written. The biographer, like the novelist, selects those interesting and significant parts of a person's life that move the story forward. Unlike the autobiography, the biography uses the opinions of others about the subject so that a many-faceted portrait can emerge. In such a biography as Boswell's *Life of Johnson*, both the character of Samuel Johnson and the literate style of Boswell make the book a classic. It is interesting to compare Boswell's *Journals* with the *Life of Johnson* to see how autobiographical material and biographical material can differ.

Students should be aware of the fact that biographers have a great responsibility for honesty which might not always be realized. They should look for the problems the subject faced and how these were resolved, if at all. They should also ask what made the person worth writing about. Reading biographies and autobiographies can enrich students' understanding of the past and add to their appreciation of human nature.

Drama

Plays are usually written to be seen and heard, not read. For this reason, the playwright leaves much to the imagination of the reader. The nature of a play's prose differs greatly from that of a novel or a short story. Speech, or dialogue, is the essence of drama, while description is at a minimum. Ordinarily, every speech in a play moves the play forward and conflict is the element on which interest in the play rests. There are usually several crises in a play. One major crisis appears toward the end, which leads to a resolution of the major problem the characters face. In a comedy, the problems are ordinarily solved happily; in a tragedy, the hero generally is defeated by forces that he cannot master.

Plays can be read with enjoyment by students who understand the problems involved. In general, it is better to see a play than to read it. A good example is seeing an excellent Shakespearean production after trying to cope with the prose of Shakespeare's day. A teacher will notice how students react to and understand nuances in a stage production, a television production, or a screen play that would never come across in reading.

As students become more familiar with the way in which plays are produced and constructed, reading plays becomes more enjoyable to them. For beginners, it is a good idea to start with simple one-act plays, after which they can build up to more complex dramas.

Poetry

Teaching the appreciation of poetry is a delicate art. It is so easy for the teacher to become starry-eyed and consequently fatuous in the eyes of students. With adolescents, the job is made difficult from the beginning because of the prejudices that boys have built up against a "feminine art." Many boys feel that poets are wavy-haired sissies, and one way for the teacher to eliminate this stereotype at the outset is to cite examples of some of the more famous masculine poets. One might ask if the football captain would have liked to have tangled with Hemingway in his younger days or with Jesse Stuart. Usually, students will realize that one can be sensitive to beauty and be tough at the same moment. Forcing students to read dull "chestnuts" will probably kill their interest in reading poetry even faster than the other forms of literature. It is little wonder that students who have had to read "Evangeline," "The Courtship of Miles Standish," and "Idylls of the King" find poetry indigestible and detest it.

Perhaps the first appreciation technique a teacher should use is the stimulation of interest through simple, enjoyable poetry. Humor is one of the most effective ways to win students' hearts and make them see that all verse is not deadly and dull.

Another way to have an enjoyable time with poetry is to take obviously dull and badly written verse and show students why it is not considered good. "The Day of Doom" by Michael Wigglesworth or anything by Felicia T. Hemans would be starters. Much of the popular Victorian poetry contains a wealth of unctuous, even bizarre, examples.

Still another approach is to use ballads to show that stories can be told economically and beautifully through poetry. The relationship of ballads to music, though it would seem apparent, comes as a surprise to many students. There are many folk ballads on records, and students enjoy hearing and discussing them. Popular interest in folk music works in the teacher's favor.

Teachers can move from simple poetry to more complex poetry in slow stages. If they select poems to which students can relate, teaching poetry can be a valuable experience for both students and teacher. John Ciardi has said: "Above all else, poetry is a performance." He objects to killing interest in poetry that some secondary teachers have seemed able to effect so well. "The concern is not to arrive at a definition and close the book, but to arrive at an experience."[5] Good ways to kill interest in poetry are to emphasize technicalities from the outset, to place poets on pedestals or in ivory towers, and to talk about poetry at the expense of reading it. Teachers who recognize that a goal of teaching poetry is to help students enjoy it should be able to tell from student reactions when they are succeeding or boring them to death.

Oral Reading

There is no question that students have less need for oral reading than silent reading. But there are occasions in and out of school when oral reading is required. It is not uncommon for people to share what they have read in a newspaper or magazine by orally reading excerpts to others who are interested in the content. If someone wished to make or prove a point, he might find evidence to support his views and read it orally.

Certainly, there is a place for oral reading in studying literature. We all have enjoyed listening to others read selections from prose and poetry. In fact, many poems are intended to be read orally so that the rhythm and sounds of words may be appreciated. Plays are generally better understood and enjoyed when heard than read.

One of the requirements of oral reading is the presence of an audience. There is little justification for having students read orally if no one is listening to them. Another requirement is the ability to read well enough so that the interest of the listeners is maintained. There is hardly a more worthless and boring undertaking than having a captive audience listen to poor readers.

Effective oral reading requires that the reader have a real understanding of the author's intentions and ideas. Otherwise, he will not be able to convey, through proper emphasis, tone, rate, and pauses, the full meaning, both stated and implied. Therefore, before students are expected to read orally, they should have the opportunity to examine the material so that they can unravel its difficulties and establish a purpose for reading it.

Good oral reading is characterized by proper articulation of words; flexibility in rate, volume, and tone; adequate phrasing; effective use of pauses; and appropriate bodily movements. Teachers who read well can serve as models for students. They can alert students to listen to the ways in

5. John Ciardi, *How Does a Poem Mean?* (Boston: Houghton Mifflin, 1960), p. 666.

which they read selected portions in order to convey specified meanings. Recordings of fine literature by professionals may be introduced to demonstrate how special effects are employed to convey a variety of feelings and hold the listener's interest. Students may analyze their own oral reading through tape recordings, suggest changes for improvement, and then compare the original reading with a subsequent rendering.

THE INTEREST TO READ

Apparently, many high school students do not turn to reading as a leisure activity and apparently this disinterest continues into college and later life.[6] However, in a national survey on student attitudes toward reading and the extent of their reading, 98 percent of the thirteen-year-olds and 95 percent of the seventeen-year-olds reported that they read on their own.[7] This survey, which is part of the National Assessment of Educational Progress, indicated that girls read more than boys, whites more than blacks, people in the suburbs more than those in the cities, and people whose parents had higher education more than others whose parents' education was less. Interestingly enough, fewer than one in ten said they read great literature because they enjoyed it. This might be a clue as to why some students prefer to spend their leisure time in activities other than reading.

Whichever data are more accurate (and there is reason to question the results of studies which *ask* students about the extent of their reading), teachers can do much to foster an interest in recreational reading in all students, particularly those who have been "turned off" by the reading diets offered in some schools. A brief look at today's adolescents and what they want can provide teachers with the information they need to promote more and better reading among all students.

Adolescents and Their World

Adolescents suffer from an understandable sense of insecurity. How true this is can be underscored by quotations from the poetry and prose of six thirteen-year-old students. In a poem called "Epilogue," envisioning life after a nuclear war, one wrote:

> . . . *There is nothing here to bury*
> *No, there is nothing human here.*
> *Mankind lies crumbled, melted.*
> *Torn and burned beyond recognition,*
> *Fused inseparable with the lifeless heaps of pebbles and sand.*

6. Naomi C. Chase, "Lifetime Reading Habits," in *Development of Lifetime Reading Habits,* ed. Dorothy Dietrich and Virginia Mathews (Newark, Del.: International Reading Association, 1968), p. 46.
7. Simon S. Johnson, "How Students Feel About Literature," *American Education* April 1974, pp. 6-10.

> *. . . Swift as a dying candle, the moon has slipped*
> *Behind a leaden cloud.*
> *And endless velvet folds of darkness,*
> *Envelop the hate-cold planet.*

Another found the world

> . . . one of frequent beauty — yet there is much that is ugly. Even the glories of spring cannot disguise the many tensions, born from the ruin of World War II and the Korean War — tensions which found nourishment in the fears and doubts of anxiety-ridden people.

An eighth grader ended a poem call "Realization" with

> *. . . Trees sans buds,*
> *Existence sans happiness,*
> *Children burdened with clothing,*
> *Elders troubled with cares.*
> *Winter is the core of life — winter is Truth.*

while another said

> I wonder about the world around me. Our parents try to instill in us sound moral principles and a good sense of values. At the same time, graft and corruption are rampant among high government officials, the entertainment world, and in big business.

A ninth-grader wrote a poem called "The Pile":

> *I once dreamt a dream, when I was young,*
> *About a pile of men.*
> *And at the bottom, they were black,*
> *And at the top, they were white.*
> *And every one was trying to push down his neighbor,*
> *To reach the top.*
> *And then the plane flew overhead and dropped a bomb,*
> *And the pile was dust.*
> *And the dust at the top was the same*
> *As the dust at the bottom.*
> *But I was young then, and did not understand.*

And another said:

> The word *teenager* has taken on a special meaning. They are either to be ignored, watched over constantly, or treated with kid gloves while growing out of still another stage. Perhaps the young adult should be recognized for what he is himself rather than prejudged on the basis of the false standards set by a misguided few. . . .

Some people have called such thoughts of young people "soft-minded pessimism," but they are the honest interpretations of young, bright adolescents who have observed closely and who feel intensely the life going on about them. Multiply this general uneasiness a millionfold and you have the feelings of a large group in our society who may be less articulate than some other minorities but who feel just as deeply. Its members are not delirious with gaiety; for many of them, a dismal crystal ball with the possible vision of a large mushroom cloud has replaced the bowl of cherries that life used to be.

Parents sometimes are puzzled by teen-aged introspection and will ask "Why are they all so serious?" One answer can be found by scrutinizing the front page of any daily newspaper and thinking about the effects the news has on young and old alike. Life is not as it was on Sunnybrook Farm. But the thoughts of youth are still long, long thoughts, and the "boy's will is still the wind's will" — with a difference. Today's young people would not be a bit surprised to see a scientifically manufactured tornado sweeping down on them.

Most boys and girls in junior high school have entered upon the period of early adolescence, and the girls are likely to have surpassed the boys in physical and emotional development. Girls in senior high school are well on their way to physical maturity, and most boys have begun to undergo the physical changes whose influences on behavior are so strongly felt. Almost without exception, they will hold attitudes toward self and others far different from those held just a short time earlier. In this they are no different from the young people of earlier periods. Youths who go through puberty and adolescence have always faced a maze of physical, emotional, and social problems, for adolescence is basically a phrase characterized by conflicts. Yet as every secondary school teacher knows, this stage between childhood and maturity can be a time of charm and beauty as well as of awkwardness and apathy and rebellion. When least expected, students can come up with astounding work, and such experiences more than offset the teacher's maddening moments.

Physical development, emotional involvement, social standing, the home, the future, and other aspects of a world that may threaten to overwhelm them — these, then, are some of the problems young "child-adults" face. They are in the throes of learning that some kinds of behavior are rewarded and some rejected in our culture and that behavior which was acceptable at age twelve is no longer so at seventeen. Adolescents need the approval of their group and the approval of the "bosses" — parents and teachers. They also need to learn to be independent individuals; they need to experience success; and they must give and receive affection. To live successfully, they must learn to meet these needs, yet all the while they show a mounting resentment toward authority and a blossoming independence — to the dismay of the parents and teachers who have to live with them. At the same time, while protesting their ability to handle themselves and their problems, adolescents secretly appreciate meaningful guidance.

An equally disturbing element is the fact that youths are torn by conflict. They love their parents, yet reject many of their values. As they learn about the effects of modern technology on the environment and society, they cannot help but question the desirability of material rewards as a prime motivator of most activity. They may wonder why it is necessary to accumulate goods, to have more than anyone could possibly enjoy. At the same time, they see feeble efforts to eradicate massive poverty and despair.

They have learned to distrust adults. "Do as I say and not as I do" they believe is the adult creed. They can point to countless examples of violations of moral and religious ethics. It is no small wonder that youths have expressed their unhappiness through the dress, mores, and causes they embrace. How effectively can teachers deal with the young who are disenchanted?

There is another group who is no less disenchanted. It is the culturally different and disadvantaged youths — black, Puerto Rican, American Indian, and Americans of Mexican origin. They resent middle-class efforts to make them over in their own images; they reject ideals which they feel they never can match; the American dream of success in the face of adversity is for others but not for them. They know reality from their earliest years, and school and books seem so far removed from truth. We represent both and perhaps we, too, in their eyes "are not for real." At the very least, we might examine our goals to determine their appropriateness for all youth. That differences exist among individuals, we acknowledge; perhaps one way to accept the individuality of youths is to respect them and at the same time be a model that they might wish to become.

Books Students Prefer

When Mary L. Smith and Isabel V. Eno[8] asked 510 Iowa students in grades seven through twelve "If you could have an author write a story to order for you, what would you have him put in it?" junior-high-school boys wanted mystery, sports, science fiction, adventure, animals, and sea stories and 65 percent of the girls wanted romance; the rest wanted mystery, career, and comedy. In senior high school, the boys preferred adventure stories but also liked mystery, sea stories, comedy, historical tales, and science fiction; 66 percent of the girls wanted romance and also liked career stories, mystery, adventure, and comedy. The leading characters should be young (from fifteen to nineteen years old for junior-high and twenty to twenty-four for senior-high readers), attractive, kind, intelligent, physically strong, good-natured with a sense of humor, and popular.

High school students, as has been said, are often in a period of rebellion, groping for independence and individuality. While they enjoy identifying with characters they recognize, they often resent books that have been especially written for them and want books that grapple with adult problems. David Russell[9] quoted from the opinions collected by a California teacher from an "average" ninth-grade class that had been asked about books labeled for "teen age":

8. Mary L. Smith and Isabel V. Eno, "What Do They Really Want to Read?," *English Journal* 50 (May 1961): 343-345.
9. David Russell, "Impact of Reading on the Personal Development of Young People," *New Frontiers in Reading*, International Reading Association Conference *Proceedings* 5 (1960): 77-82.

1. I'd like more realism, not so much fairy stuff, with phony living happily ever after.
2. Books which present the ordinary teenager and his problems, so we can see how some are solved.
3. Teen-agers cuss and know cuss words, but the books I read sound as if they were written for ten-year-olds.
4. I'd like a book which would show how hard it is for a high school girl to get to know the boy she likes. Parents always tell you that you should go with someone else.
5. A book which shows us what life is like when you grow up.
6. Most teen-age books are too childish and not real enough. Most of them sound like a little 8- or 9-year-old wrote them.
7. Authors must think that teen-agers are awfully innocent.
8. Life isn't like what you find in books. Life is hard and people are cruel and don't think of others. It's dog eat dog, and an eye for an eye, and a tooth for a tooth.

If these remarks are typical of ninth graders, we seem to have underestimated the students' maturity of tastes, especially if we are concerned about providing for average and below-average students, while challenging the able and above-average. (Intelligence and reading ability do not appear to be factors in reading choices of adolescents.) Students in the National Assessment of Educational Progress survey cited earlier also preferred adult popular fiction to novels written for them. In the average high school class, teachers are likely to find students who prefer books intended for adults, others who prefer teen-age books, and still others who favor magazines and newspapers.[10] Obviously, all sorts of reading materials should be available to students, and they should be permitted to select those they wish to read.

Another indication of student preferences for adult literature are their responses to questions regarding subjects they wish to read about. When a group of high school students were asked to indicate what books influenced them, an analysis of their responses indicated they were interested in these areas: their search "to find themselves" through ideas of great minds, their growth, and philosophy; social problems, responsibility, and a concern for the world; and a determination to become involved if only to be better informed.[11]

What books, then, have students preferred to read? These two lists give some indication, and offer wide choices for teachers who are looking for books to recommend to their students. The first list contains titles which represent some of the rebellion of the sixties:[12]

10. Arthur V. Olson and Carl L. Rosen, "A Comparison of Reading Interests of Two Populations of Ninth Grade Students," pp. 365-369 in *Teaching Reading Skills in Secondary Schools: Readings,* ed. Arthur V. Olson and Wilbur S. Ames (Scranton, Pa.: International Textbook, 1970).
11. Helen Wilmott, "YASD Asks the Young Adult," *Top of the News,* Jan. 1965, pp. 143-147.
12. Peter Marvin, "Tripping the Heavy Fantastic," *New York Times Book Review,* Part 2, Feb. 21, 1971.

Cat's Cradle, Kurt Vonnegut
Stranger in a Strange Land, Robert A. Heinlein
Steppenwolf, Hermann Hesse
Dune, Frank Herbert
The Lord of the Rings, J. R. R. Tolkien
Do It!, Jerry Rubin
Revolution for the Hell of It, Abbie Hoffman
Soul on Ice, Eldridge Cleaver
The Autobiography of Malcolm X
Quotations From Chairman Mao Tse-tung

The second list, according to researchers, contains titles which suggest that young people are looking "for heroes worth modeling after, values worth upholding, and a sense of hope:"[13]

A Sporting Proposition, James Aldridge
The Memory of Old Jack, Wendell Berry
The Thirteenth Trick, Russell Braddon
Journey to Ixtlan, Carlos Casteneda
A Hero Ain't Nothin' But a Sandwich, Alice Childress
The Chocolate War, Robert Cormier
Kingdom Come, Gwen Davis
Dutch Uncle, Marilyn Durham
The Falling Man, Warren Forma
Joshua, Son of None, Nancy Freedman
Ward 402, Ronald Glasser
The Taking of Pelham One Two Three, John Godey
The Princess Bride, William Goldman
The Honorary Consul, Graham Greene
The Gift, Peter Hamill
Christie Malry's Own Double-Entry, B. S. Johnson
The Son of Someone Famous, M. E. Kerr
Serpico, Peter Maas
I'm Somebody Important, George Mitchell
Revolutionary Suicide, Huey Newton
Theodore Jonathan Wainwright Is Going to Bomb the Pentagon, Louis
    Phillips
Loophole or 'How to Rob a Bank', Robert Pollock
Alive, Piers Paul Reed
As We Are Now, May Sarton
Fairy Tale, Eric Segal
Richie, Thomas Thompson
Theophilus North, Thornton Wilder
The Summer Before, Patricia Windsor
Uncle Herschel, Dr. Padilsky and the Evil Eye, I. S. Young
Let Me Hear You Whisper, Paul Zindel

By contrast, compare the types of books students prefer with those that eighteen critics of books for adolescents reviewed and ranked as the best

13. G. Robert Carlsen and others, "Honor Listing, Books for Young Adults," Univ. of Iowa, 1975.

written books for young people. They are arranged by order of number of votes cast.

Johnny Tremain, Esther Forbes
The Yearling, Marjorie K. Rawlings
Seventeenth Summer, Maureen Daly
My Friend Flicka, Mary O'Hara
Goodbye, My Lady, James Street
Lassie Come Home, Eric Knight
Winter Wheat, Mildred Walker
Swiftwater, Paul Annixter
Caddie Woodlawn, Carol Brink
Loon Feather, Iola Fuller
The Ark, Margot Benary-Isbert
Ready or Not, Mary Stolz
Adam of the Road, Elizabeth J. Gray
Banner in the Sky, James R. Ullman
Light in the Forest, Conrad Richter
Old Yeller, Fred Gipson
Smoky, the Cowhorse, Will James
Patterns on the Wall, Elizabeth Yates
Sarah, Marguerite Bro
Banners at Shenandoah, Bruce Catton
Innocent Wayfaring, Marchette Chute
Santiago, Anne Nolan Clark
Trumpeter of Krakow, Eric Kelly
And Now Miguel, Joseph Krumgold
Thunderhead, Mary O'Hara

If a survey of what books teenagers are reading today were made, there is no doubt that the list would include some of the adult best sellers as well as those previously chosen. Although authors continue to write for adolescent boys and girls, it would appear that many prefer to read what their parents choose rather than opt for books whose characters and events involve youth.

A number of surveys made by groups of librarians and teachers included the following adult books recommended for the high school reader:[14]

A Death in the Family, James Agee
Go Tell It on the Mountain, James Baldwin
Wuthering Heights, Emily Brontë
The Stranger, Albert Camus
The Old Man and the Sea, Ernest Hemingway
Hiroshima, John Hersey
The Lonely Crowd, David Riesman
The American Presidency, Clinton Rossiter
Walden, Henry David Thoreau
The Organization Man, William H. Whyte

14. G. Robert Carlsen, *Books and the Teen-Age Reader* (New York: Bantam Books, 1967), pp. 201-206.

The preference for adult books by some students can create a touchy situation. Keeping adult books out of teen-age libraries certainly seems foolish, for current best-sellers often have strong appeal and are one of the best springboards to encourage a lifetime habit of reading. Generally speaking, teachers should employ any reasonable device for encouraging more and better reading. When some modern literature can compare well with anything that has been written earlier, students deserve to enjoy it.

Edward Gordon, who directed the Master of Arts in Teaching program at Yale University, has remarked that if we exclude books that contain love-making and vulgar language from our booklists, most of the great books written in the past and in the present would be excluded. Good novelists and short-story writers present life as they see and interpret it, and they are honest about it. Understandably, some mothers would object to placing *Lolita* and *Lady Chatterley's Lover* on a seventh-grade reading list. What teachers and librarians are to do about modern novels with accents on sex and vivid realism is a problem. *The Catcher in the Rye* by J. D. Salinger, which has been mentioned before, is a good example. Clifton Fadiman called this novel a "modern classic"; furors have arisen because of its language. Although it requires a mature reader, students seem to fall in love with the book and what it has to say about growing up, because most sensitive readers find something of themselves in the "crazy mixed-up kid" who is its hero.

If students are actually reading books that deal with the raw facts of life, what should the role of the teacher and the high school be in providing such books and encouraging their reading? Some students will read adult books solely for prurient effects; if the author's purpose is to be salacious, those books should be excluded. In most cases, however, the answer must be made individually, depending on the title and the student. Such a problem again emphasizes the need for the teacher to provide individual analysis and attention. Teachers must consider the students, the parents, and the communities in which they teach. They must be forthright; nothing will lose the respect of a student sooner than shilly-shallying about reasons for objecting to a book. If students are too immature to read it, say so.

Books and the Needs of Youth

Part of the responsibility a teacher shoulders when he enters his first classroom is to help students understand their environment and culture. The teacher, presumably, has been trained to present to students methods of attacking problems that will meet in high school and society. Though teachers may use nonprint media as instructional materials, books remain the basic source through which students can be stimulated and educated.

In books there are many characters who face the same problems that high school students do today, characters with whom they may identify. Through books, they can learn of others who have feared what they fear, loved what they love, and survived. It students have difficulty achieving proper relationships with peers of either sex, they can learn what others like them did in similar situations. No matter what the issue, books are likely to contain identical or comparable situations from which adolescents can take comfort. Although emotional problems may interfere with reading achievement, it is possible that reading books may have therapeutic effects that can be of great help for successful reading. While *bibliotherapy*, the technique of helping people to solve their emotional problems through reading, is not to be considered a science, evidence suggests that reading and discussion books whose characters and events are timely and identifiable may lessen tensions and anxieties.[15]

The realization that others are beset by feelings that trouble youth is comforting, but for the teacher to provide the right book for the student's need demands skill and understanding and a wide reading background. If the teacher sees that almost every adolescent boy finds something of himself in Holden Caulfield in *The Catcher in the Rye* or that girls find their problems resemble those of Julie in *The Divided Heart*, he could steer students toward these books. From these and other real-life characters, high school boys and girls can learn that growing up can be accompanied by doubts and anxieties, and they may also develop insights into their own behavior.

IDENTIFYING READING INTERESTS

The titles of favorite books, previously cited, give some clues as to the general preferences of high school boys and girls. Teachers can also learn much about the interests of individual students in their classes from interest inventories and their own observations.

To discover the reading interests of students, teachers can administer inventories to identify attitudes toward reading and reading habits. If the inventories are administered orally, teachers have an opportunity to probe into responses and reveal motivations and behaviors that might not otherwise be uncovered. Students could write their responses and meet individually with teachers to discuss them. A sample inventory is shown here:

THE INDIVIDUAL INTEREST INVENTORY

Name _____Class_____Date _____
    1. Do you like to read? Check one answer.
       a little _____ a lot _____ not at all _____ an average amount _____
    2. Did you know how to read before you started school? _____
    3. Did someone read to you before you started school? _____

15. Caroline Shrodes, "Bibliotherapy," *Reading Teacher*, Oct. 1955, pp. 24-29, reprinted in *The Reading Teacher's Reader*, ed. Oscar Causey (New York: Ronald, 1959). See also Eunice S. Newton, "Bibliotherapy in the Development of Minority Group Self-Concept," *Journal of Negro Education* 38 (Summer 1969): 257-265; "Bibliotherapy," *Library Trends* 11 (Oct. 1962): 97-228; Viola Kantrowitz, "Bibliotherapy with Retarded Readers," *Journal of Reading* 11 (Dec. 1967): 205-212; Harold A. Moses and Joseph S. Zaccaria, "Bibliotherapy in Educational Context: Rationale and Principles," *High School Journal* 52 (April 1969): 401-411.

4. How many comic books do you read every week? ____
   What are your favorite comics? 1. _____
   2. _____ 3. _____

5. What are your favorite comic strips in the newspapers?
   1. _____ 2. _____ 3. _____

6. What newspapers do you read? 1. _____
   2. _____ 3. _____

7. What magazines do you like best? 1. _____
   2. _____ 3. _____

8. What do you like about them? _____
   _____

9. What three living men do you admire most in the world?
   1. _____ 2. _____ 3. _____

10. What three living women do you admire most?
    1. _____ 2. _____ 3. _____

11. Who are your favorite heroes (men or women) from the past? ____
    _____

12. What hobbies do you have? _____

13. What are your favorite TV programs? _____

14. How many hours (average) do you watch TV each day? _____
    _____

15. Do you listen to radio? If so, what programs?
    _____

16. List your three favorite movies of all time.
    1. _____ 2. _____ 3. _____

17. Who are your favorite movie stars?
    _____

18. What are the three best novels you ever read?
    1. _____ 2. _____ 3. _____

19. What are the three best nonfiction books you ever read?
    1. _____ 2. _____ 3. _____

20. What men or boys from fiction or nonfiction do you remember
    best ? _____
    _____

21. What women or girls from fiction or nonfiction do you remember
    best? _____
    _____

22. Check the kinds of things you like to read about (as many as you
    wish).
    love stories_____
    baseball_____
    criminals_____
    war stories_____
    murder mysteries_____
    famous people_____
    mathematics
    historical tales_____
    mythology_____
    true life adventure_____
    poetry_____
    movie stars_____
    essays_____

how to make things_____
football_____
teen-agers' problems_____
nature stories_____
scientific experiments_____
basketball_____
dictionaries_____
horses_____
space travel_____
cowboy stories_____
travel articles_____
encyclopedias_____
politics_____

23. If you could buy as many books as you wanted, which kinds would you buy? _____

_____

24. What do teen-agers read about? _____

_____

25. If you wanted to write a book, what would its title be? _____

_____

26. How would others in your class like it? What do you think they would like about it? _____

_____

27. What books have you read that you disliked very much? Why? _____

The answers that students give to the questions of an inventory can be used as a basis for suggesting books they might wish to read. For example, if a student responds that she is interested in politics, a book such as *The Making of the President* by Theodore White might be recommended. Another student might be interested in sports; Muhammad Ali's *The Greatest* could appeal to him. For those who wish to read about war, Hemingway's *For Whom the Bells Toll* or *A Farewell to Arms* would be possibilities. There is no dearth of books for students, regardless of their tastes and levels of reading achievement. Careful study of interest inventory responses combined with teacher evaluations become a basis for providing and recommending books for students to read.

DEVELOPING AND EXTENDING READING INTERESTS

The influence that teachers can have upon the reading habits of students is considerable. Wulliam S. Gray summed it up neatly when he said:

Inquiries made among mature readers revealed two very illuminating facts. They indicated, first, that the crucial point in the development of permanent reading interests was when reading began to inspire, to bring convictions, to make changes in the reader's core of values, and to open up new vistas.

> The second is the very great influence of a teacher who is a lover of good books and who has the capacity to open up to children and youth the appreciations and other rewards inherent in reading.[16]

Teacher attitude can make a real difference in student reading habits. As was noted earlier, students soon sense when a teacher is bored or when enthusiasm is strained and insincere. Those teachers who truly love what they espouse do not have to worry about enthusiasm; it springs forth from their actions, tone of voice, and more subtle forms of communication. If teachers expect students to read more, they must read more. Just as poetry is literature that is "caught, not taught," so can interest in reading be cultivated. Moreover, interests are not fixed but can be shaped and extended.

Sources of Good Books

It is obvious that if teachers are to advise students what books to read, they should be acquainted with them. If their reading background is skimpy, they are limited in the amount of help they can give students. Teachers do not need to be familiar with every book that has been written, but a balanced reading background is invaluable when recommending authors. Skimming various books can give a teacher some idea of their tone and quality. The fine art of browsing in a library or a bookstore is still as popular and as satisfying as it ever was, and a few minutes spent in browsing may some day have a lasting effect when the teacher puts the right book into a student's hand at the right time.

School librarians and public librarians can be very helpful. Most of them are eager to help with any problem concerning books, and often they will prepare special shelves for school classes and search for books to fit the need of a specific group of students. Librarians are the unsung heroes and heroines of the "reading battle," on the firing line day after day, and sustained by the desire to promote the love of books in the hearts of children and adults.

Many booklists classify titles according to subject and include brief statements about stories along with interest levels, names of publishers, and prices. Some of these lists provide all this information and add each book's level of difficulty as determined by a readability formula. They can be extremely useful to a teacher who wishes to prepare a booklist for his class or who wants to widen his scope of knowledge about available books. If a teacher discovers a good booklist for his purposes, he will do well to check the library to see what books are available on the shelves. This may seem unnecessary, but many a booklist has contained books not readily available. Here are several good booklists for two categories of students: normally progressing readers and poor readers.

16. William S. Gray, "Providing Reading Materials Appropriate to Interest and Maturity Levels," International Reading Association Conference *Proceedings* 5 (1960): 22.

Booklists for Normally Progressing Readers

AASA Science Book List for Young Adults. American Association for the
    Advancement of Science, Washington, D. C.
A Basic Book Collection for Junior High Schools. American Library Associa-
    tion, Chicago.
A Basic Book Collection for High Schools. American Library Association,
    Chicago.
Best Books for Children. New York: R. R. Bowker Co.
Book Bait: Detailed Notes on Adult Books Popular with Young People.
    American Library Association, Chicago.
Books for the Teen-Age. New York Public Library.
Combined Book Exhibit. The Combined Book Exhibit, New York.
Crosby, Muriel. *Reading Ladders for Human Relations.* American Council on
    Education, Washington, D. C.
Current Books, Senior Booklist. National Association of Independent Schools,
    Boston.
Paperbound Book Guide for High Schools, R. R. Bowker Co.
Paperbound Books in Print. R. R. Bowker Co.
Reader's Choice of Selected Paperbooks for Schools and Libraries. Scholastic
    Book Services. Englewood Cliffs, N. J.
Standard Catalog for High School Libraries. H. W. Wilson Co., New York.
Strang, Ruth. *Gateways to Readable Books.* H. W. Wilson Co.
The Negro: A List of Significant Books. New York Public Library.

Booklists for Poor Readers

Blair, Glenn M. "Reading Materials for Pupils with Reading Disabilities,"
    High School Journal, 39 (October 1955), pp. 14-21.
Dunn, Anita and others. *Fare for the Reluctant Reader.* Albany: State Uni-
    versity of New York, 1964.
"Easy Adult Books for Slow High School Readers." *Top Of the News,* 17
    (December 1960), pp. 19-21.
Emery, Raymond and Houshower, Margaret. *High Interest-Easy Reading for
    Junior and Senior High School Reluctant Readers.* Champaign, Ill.:
    National Council of Teachers of English, 1965.
Hunt, Jacob T. "Easy and Interesting Fiction for the Handicapped Reader."
    High School Journal, 39 (April 1956), pp. 378-385.
Lundeen, Alma and Prendergrass, Margaret. "Books for Retarded Readers."
    Illinois Library, 43 (April 1961), pp. 271-287.
Rollins, Charlemae. *We Build Together.* Champaign, Ill.: National Council of
    Teachers of English, 1967.
Selected Lists of Children's Books and Recordings. Washington: Office of
    Economic Opportunity, 1966.
Spache, George. *Good Reading for Poor Readers* (Fifth Ed.). Champaign,
    Ill.: Garrard Publishing Co., 1968.
Your Reading. Champaign, Ill.: National Council of Teachers of English,
    1966.

In addition to these lists, individual publishers periodically issue lists.
There is a special paperback summary in the Sunday edition of the *New
York Times.* Professional journals, such as *Language Arts* and the
English Journal, often summarize new books that appeal to children. The

New York Times prints annual summaries of children's books that have appeared during the year. The *Scholastic Book Services* issues a monthly newsletter for each of its clubs (Arrow, TAB, Campus, etc.,) that contains descriptions of books which are interesting to average and poor readers. *Publisher's Weekly* is a good source of recent book reviews.

Other excellent sources of information about books for adolescents are Daniel Fader and Elton MacNeil's *Hooked on Books: Program and Proof* and G. Robert Carlsen's *Books and the Teen-age Reader.* Two other publications sponsored by the National Council of Teachers of English are also very useful: *Books for You* and *High Interest-Easy Reading.*

Motivational Devices in the Classroom

A classroom atmosphere that will foster reading can be created by teachers. As always, teachers must be the stimulators for good reading, and their love of books must be evident to students. Here are several strategies that teachers may adopt to promote interest in books and reading.

First, the classroom should be bright and cheerful. As has been said before, surrounding the students with books heightens the probabilities that they will pick them up and read. Classroom libraries, to be mentioned later, should make books readily available. In some classes, students loan several of their own books to the classroom for one term or the school year. Posters and sayings about reading and pictures of authors and of people reading create an image of the reading act as something people like to do and add to an environment conducive to reading.

Connected with browsing is allowing time in class for free reading. Teachers may forget that students are usually tremendously busy people. If they expect students to read, they should go part way by providing them with the *time* to read. Too many adults avoid books by saying that they have no time to read. Probably, most students could truthfully say the same thing. Teachers should certainly not feel guilty about allowing students time for books.

Reading a few good stories aloud to students and then suggesting others that are similar is a useful technique for gaining their interest in reading. Group approval is a powerful influence here. If a student realizes that his classmates are caught by the magic of a story, he may feel that he should join the crowd. To achieve this, the teacher must select "sure-fire" material. Then, if he can read aloud reasonably well and has a gripping tale, the effect can be productive and pleasing to both students and teachers.

Sometimes when teachers read part of a book and stop with the comment that the students would enjoy reading the rest on their own, students are motivated to read alone. "Auctioning off" books by reading the first few paragraphs in one book and offering it to the most interested student and repeating the procedure with paragraphs from the next, and so on, can be an excellent way of using the competitive spirit to "sell" reading.

Another possibility is forming a *reading club,* where interested students can share their experiences with others. When a club is well organized, meetings will not degenerate into conversational sessions. Sometimes authors in the school area will come to these meetings, or field trips can be taken to interesting places associated with authors or books. Whatever the activity, it must be well planned by the teacher.

Book fairs can be organized to aid a school cause. Students enjoy the work that goes into planning such a major activity. Bookstores are usually eager to cooperate with such projects. Fairs can provoke more interest in books and can be profitable for the school.

Pride in personally owning books can be fostered by providing ways in which students can build their own libraries. Now that paperback books are popular and inexpensive, few students are deprived of buying personal books. Commercial companies such as Scholastic Books Services offer package arrangements and easy procedures for ordering books. The corner drugstore also has a wide variety of them. Whatever the source, building a personal library is a worthwhile part of the design a teacher should have in mind for teaching his students.

Using topical devices that are close to the students' experiences is still another technique. A "Hit Parade of Books," "A Reading Diet," or other imaginative aids can stimulate reading. Ellen Lamar Thomas has written of using "reading rainbows" in the classroom.[17] Colorful book record slips — with each type of book represented by a slip of paper of a different color — are placed in book pockets on a bulletin board. Students complete the color spectrum by reading types of books they have not read before. Such devices may encourage balanced book selection and help break the student of the compulsion to read one sort of book only.

The foregoing suggestions are only a few of the devices that might be used in a classroom. Imaginative teachers will think of many more ways to develop student interest. Focusing attention on how to generate enthusiasm for books is half the battle.

The Classroom Library

Each year, school systems spend thousands of dollars for books. In the past, principals would have scoffed at the idea of ordering any but durable hardbound books, but there are indications that the age of the paperback may be upon the school classroom. Paperbacks are far better produced and bound today than they used to be and, although they are not as durable as hardbound books, they often cost much less. They allow teachers much more variety in assigning reading; they are light for the students to carry; and much up-to-date material (for instance in the rapidly changing field of science) can be read. The content quality of paperbacks is also far superior to what it was when they first came on the market.

Young people seem to prefer paperbacks to hardcover books. It isn't uncommon to see paperbacks protruding from the pockets of jeans or being carried in handbags. They are smaller and lighter to carry than hardbacks. One author tells how he was able to stimulate reading among delinquent boys through paperbacks. Many high schools have introduced racks of pa-

17. Ellen Lamar Thomas, "Reading Rainbows," *English Journal*, Nov. 1961, pp. 558-560.

perbacks which students may purchase, and they report brisk sales. It is estimated that more than 400 million paperbacks were sold in 1976.

It is certainly feasible for a teacher to provide a wide variety of reading through a paperback classroom library. I know one teacher who convinced a principal that such an idea would be productive. Ten teachers ordered as many books as they wanted for their classrooms; one teacher ordered 300. The total bill was roughly $500 which is not a tremendous sum in education budgets. The books also held up very well. If teachers impress on their students that they must care for the books, the books will not fall apart quickly.

School or town libraries can also be tapped for hardcover books for the classroom library. Most librarians will gladly help a teacher assemble a group of books for a long-term loan. It takes but a little time and energy for the benefits gained.

Whether the book be bound in paper or cloth, the factor of quick availability in the classroom is a powerful one. Students who will not visit the school library one flight upstairs may check out books if they are within easy reach. The convenience of a classroom library can go a long way toward exciting students' desire to read and helping form good reading habits.

Making Book Reports Meaningful

Once students have read a book, they often are faced with the prospect of a "book report," which requires that they pick the bones of what they have just read. Teachers are *not* promoting the cause of reading if they ask students for a dreary, involved analysis of books that have been an enjoyable experience. The trouble with most book reports is that they are *dull*, both for the student and the teacher. It is true that students can gain satisfaction from reflecting on what they have read and drawing conclusions. Immediately using what they have done and reward from their teacher is consistent with the concept of responsive environment. But for a student to feel rewarded and his book report to be meaningful, he must put his ideas to uses that at least seem productive. When a book report is a boring ritual and is negatively reinforcing, students may feel that they are being punished.

For teachers who are interested in an imaginative approach to book reports, Jerome Carlin has suggested a number of possibilities.[18]

1. A report on the book as it would be given by a man of the future.
2. The diary of a major character.
3. A letter written in the role of a book character.
4. Describing the characters.
5. Written analysis from a specific standpoint (such as supplying a topic sentence, i.e. "Like people in life, the characters in a book sometimes make us ashamed of the human race).
6. Formal book review (using a newspaper model).
7. The scholarly critical paper.

18. Jerome Carlin, "Your Next Book Report," *English Journal,* Jan. 1961, pp. 16-22.

8. Round-table discussion under a student chairman.
9. Conversation (with each student expressing curiosity about the other's book).
10. Oral reading and discussion of brief excerpts.
11. Significant incident or anecdote (as a speaker on a TV program whose job is to interest the audience through the use of an incident or anecdote).
12. Dramatization.
13. Group performance in the style of "This Is Your Life."
14. Reporter at the scene.
15. The trial of a major character.
16. Interview by a reporter of a major character or of the author.
17. The author meets the critics (Dickens might defend *The Tale of Two Cities*).
18. Quiz program.
19. Monologue (speaking as the main character).
20. Dialogue (between two students who have read the same book).
21. Counseling by experts (such as a character explaining his crucial problem to several social workers).
22. Sales talk (a salesman attempting to sell the book to a class).
23. Presentation to a publisher (where a student has to face a selection committee).
24. Discussion of proposed production conducted by a "playwright" and a "producer."
25. Outline of a TV or motion-picture version.
26. Ceremonies for Recognition Day (where the author is to receive an award or a character in a biography is to receive an award).
27. Dinner meeting of the Social Welfare Club (used when the class has read biographies and the new members of the club must tell how they will be assets to the club).
28. Preview of coming attractions.
29. Art and other creative work (book jackets, advertising blurbs, scenes from the story, posters, etc.).

The teacher could distribute this or a similar list to the class and let students decide for themselves the form they wished to use for their next book reports. The teacher can also ask for a brief, pleasantly written report instead of a long, tedious one, or he can ask for no report at all.

High School youths, not unlike adults, prefer to discuss and talk about books rather than write about them. If teachers feel they must have some way of knowing whether or not students are reading and what they are reading, they can easily obtain this information by talking with them. There is little justification for insisting on a written report, which can be completed without reading a book, when more can be accomplished in a natural way — encouraging students to share their reading with others. Generally speaking, teachers should try to make book reports a pleasure and not a chore for students. A dull and senseless requirement says something about the teacher who imposes it.

Instead of a book report *per se*, the teacher might make use of the personal record. A student who keeps a record of what he reads with a brief analysis of his reactions may, in later years, appreciate the habit if it is formed. Justice Holmes found most satisfying the reading record he kept for many years. Such a habit might also help to balance a student's reading and encourage him as he watches his own growth.

Using Mass Media

Once, long ago, the average person needed only to understand the special language of conversation and personal contact while the privileged one needed also the special language of print. Today's "Everyman" must grasp the special "grammars" of radio, television, cartoons, newspapers, films, magazines, recordings, and other forms of communication. In the modern world, many more demands are made on receivers of communication than were made on the serf working for his lord. We are so involved in this sort of world that we do not realize how much we have learned to adjust to receiving and understanding these special languages, or how great an impact they have had on us.

The meaning that these changes have had for teachers of reading is summarized by Edmund Carpenter, noted Canadian anthropologist:

> First, it requires that we accept the fact that the book format is a unique language with its own grammar, its own biases; that we also accept the fact that English is changing as rapidly as our culture changes. Changes in English in the last forty years have probably been as great as those from Chaucer's day to Shakespeare's. When a student is instructed to read *Moby Dick* without any warning that it is written in another language, addressed to another society, expressing values alien to him, he ends up understanding the words, but not hearing the music.[19]

Whether teachers like it or not, reading has apparently lost ground to the other "grammars" which can provide experiences that reading cannot. If it is true that we tend to follow the path of least resistance, no teacher should be surprised that students are attracted by the temptations of television, which demand much less effort than reading and a more passive attitude. Jane Austen would await eagerly books that arrived by post from the lending library in London, or borrow from the personal libraries of friends. Conversation in her late eighteenth-century manor-house culture was a true, refined art, for the gentry had to amuse each other with words and ideas often derived from their reading. Today, although reading is still a status symbol and books are still important to about 10 percent of our population, the other 90 percent often yield to less demanding pleasures. If there is a surfeit of communicative "honey" to attract a population that can behave more like drones than "busy bees," we can blame our dynamic advances in technology — our irresponsible "progress."

Arthur S. McDonald reported that the high achiever in a survey of 1,650 students in tenth, eleventh, and twelfth grades watched television eight

19. Edmund Carpenter, "Effects of New Media on Current English Speech," in *Reading in a Changing Society*, International Reading Association Conference *Proceedings* 4 (1959): 16-17.

and one-half hours per week; the low achiever spent nineteen hours watching television.[20] More recently, Paul Witty reported that since he began his study of high school students in 1949, their TV viewing had declined hardly at all.[21] From an average of 12 to 14 hours a week, they were now watching television on the average of 12 hours a week. According to Witty, the first comic books appeared in 1936. Twenty years later, roughly, 500 different comics were being published by twenty-one companies and monthly circulation had reached 100,000,000 copies. In Great Britain the situation was comparable. Some psychiatrists feel that comic books contribute to juvenile delinquency, and the Dodd Committee investigated the implications of violence in television programming. Complaints from various groups and individuals center on the increasingly lurid movies with their emphasis on sex and violence. To put it succinctly, mass media has generally been criticized for pandering to sensational and immature weaknesses in the public character that tend to increase sales. One harmful by-product may be the deleterious effect on the youth of the country.

Instead of emphasizing the negative aspects of mass media, however, teachers need to use the positive side of the coin. An awareness of the different types of language today's students have unconsciously learned to receive — and to prefer at times over reading — is a "must" for today's teacher of reading. Besides understanding that most students are not panting to read more when vicarious experiences can be had in a much easier way, teachers must realize that reading can no longer be isolated from the other forms of communication. Using a McGuffey *Reader* or *Pilgrim's Progress*, the nineteenth-century schoolmaster had little communications competition and a birch rod or the dunce cap for persuasion. If today's students understand Madison Avenue techniques better than other methods of persuasion, teachers perhaps can use a multi-media approach to "sell" their students on reading.

Paul Wagner has reported how he used a film on *Men and Oil* to promote the reading of *Cimmaron* by a class of reluctant readers. Alfred Holman has described how the newspaper is used daily as a textbook at Trenton State College. Patrick and Mary Hazard have shown how paperbacks, television, films, and recordings might be integrated in a multi-media lesson.[22] Using the paperback edition of Walter Van Tilburg Clark's *The Oxbow Incident*, the teacher might compare the book with the motion picture. Then an above-average television "western" might also be compared, after which the students could include in their study the art of Frederick Remington, folk songs of the West on records, and a picture history of today's cowboys.

Such imaginative integration of different "grammars" certainly will make any topic more interesting to the students — and more meaningful.

20. Arthur S. McDonald, "Television, School, and Marks," *Journal of Developmental Reading*, Autumn 1959, pp. 27-34.
21. Paul Witty and L. Melis, "A 1964 Study of TV: Comparison and Comments," *Elementary English* 42 (Feb. 1965): 134-141.
22. Patrick Hazard and Mary Hazard, "Multi-media Literacy," *English Journal*, Feb. 1961, pp. 132-133.

Reading is not an island in but part of the mainstream of communication in today's world. Comics need not necessarily be bad for the student. Some of the satire in comics can be fine, correlated springboards to Swift and Fielding. Movies and television shows often are excellent springboards to the reading of the original book or play, although, as one student said, "Never judge a book by its movie." Teachers who use imagination and are not snobs about technological advances will find a variety of ways to lead students from the living room screen to the pleasures of print. And a teacher can learn how to interest students by studying the appeal that comics have for them, especially in the early high school years.

SUMMARY

Literature teachers are reading teachers in the sense that their responsibility is to instill a love of quality reading in their students. To do this involves guiding students through the various types of literature while keeping in mind that the examples used must serve as samples of the whole field. Teachers must beware of killing the students' interest by requiring them to read materials that are beyond their capacities for understanding and enjoying, or that are not sufficiently challenging.

By cultivating students' "set of awareness" before they read, teachers will help students increase their sensitivity and understanding. Encouraging students to form questions as they read selections will aid comprehension.

The short story, the novel, the essay, the biography, drama, and poetry — each requires special sets of appreciation skills. Developing the students' sense of the structure of each of these types of literature is one objective for the teacher. Two others are to teach students to understand that each specific novel, poem, or story dictates its own set of problems, and that experiences with examples of literature serve as maturing influences and add to the understanding of human nature as well as reading ability.

In a sense, no one can teach literature. A teacher can teach about examples of literature that show what reading literature can do for the reader. A teacher can motivate, inspire, and guide students toward literature, but it is the student who will form a lifetime habit of reading quality works — who will want to develop his taste for good books. Perhaps it is the real job of the teacher to make classes as exciting as possible through artful questioning and discussions of books that really reach the student. If the teacher will serve as an example of the incorrigible, enthusiastic, constant reader, the contagious enthusiasm may infect his students.

Knowing about student interests, and, in particular, the books that interest them, can help teachers promote the reading habit. If teachers love to read and create a classroom atmosphere that encourages reading, reading will flourish. With each book that students sample and enjoy, positive attitudes toward reading grow. As the saying goes, "The more you read, the more you learn; the more you learn, the more you understand what you read; the more you understand, the more you like to read; and the more you like to read, the more you read."

Additional Readings

There are a number of publications on the teaching of literature:

Dwight L. Burton. *Literature Study in the High Schools,* 3d ed. New York: Holt, Rinehart and Winston, 1970.

Deborah Elkins. *Teaching Literature: Designs for Cognitive Development.* Columbus, Ohio: Charles E. Merrill, 1976.

Wilfred Guerin and others. *A Handbook of Critical Approaches to Literature.* New York: Harper and Row, 1966.

Louise Rosenblatt. *Literature as Exploration,* rev. ed. New York: Noble and Noble, 1968.

James R. Squire, ed. *Response to Literature.* Dartmouth Seminar Monograph. Champaign, Ill.: National Council of Teachers of English, 1968.

Extended treatments of the teaching of literature will be found in anthologies on teaching English in high school:

Dwight L. Burton and John S. Simmons, eds. *Teaching English in Today's High Schools.* New York: Holt, Rinehart and Winston, 1965, pp. 25-165.

Lois S. Josephs and Erwin R. Steinberg, eds. *English Education Today.* New York: Noble and Noble, 1970, pp. 305-386; 473-514; 637-672.

Of special interest to teachers who seek to provide effective reading guidance in meeting adolescents' needs are:

G. Robert Carlsen. *Books and the Teen-age Reader.* New York: Bantam, 1971.

Daniel Fader and Elton MacNeil. *Hooked on Books: Program and Proof.* New York: Berkeley, 1968.

Helen W. Painter, ed. *Reaching Children and Young People through Literature.* Newark, Del.: International Reading Association, 1971.

Alan C. Purvis and Richard Beach. *Literature and the Reader: Research in Response to Literature, Reading Interests, and the Teaching of Literature.* Urbana, Ill.: National Council of Teachers of English, 1972.

Harold Tanyzer and Jean Karl, eds. *Reading, Children's Books, and Our Pluralistic Society.* Newark, Del.: International Reading Association, 1972.

CHAPTER 10

INDIVIDUALIZING READING INSTRUCTION in CONTENT AREAS

Problems for Study and Discussion

1 *What does individualizing reading instruction entail?*
2 *How might the student-teacher conference associated with individualized reading be used by subject teachers to promote content mastery through reading?*
3 *What are the advantages of offering individual instruction to students?· What safeguards should be built into individual learning programs?*
4 *How might subject teachers allow for differences in student reading ability? What other measures might they adopt to reduce students' frustration caused by reading deficiencies?*
5 *Grouping for instruction is a means of meeting individual differences. How might grouping be used to advantage in subject and reading classes?*

THE PROBLEM OF MEETING INDIVIDUAL NEEDS

Examining the reading achievement scores for a grade in almost any junior and senior high school will reveal marked differences in attainment levels. The range between the achievement level of the poorest and of the best readers can be as much as eight years. In some high schools, students who are reading as well as college freshmen and sophomores are to be found in the same class with those who are not able to read at the second and third grade levels. And in almost any school, students can be found who are classified as "nonreaders" or "near nonreaders." As a rule, these students are unable to identify words readily, yet many of them are quite intelligent and could comprehend the content if they were able to recognize the words easily.

Added to the differences in reading-achievement levels in any one grade are the differences in development of reading skills. Two students at approximately the same instructional level may be weak in some reading skill, but not necessarily the same skill. Consequently, their reading needs are completely different. Whatever the causes of these differences, meeting all the different reading needs that exist in any given class or grade presents a very real problem. It is probably the most troublesome problem that reading teachers in high school must face. Individual differences *increase* as students reach higher grades, so the problem in junior and senior high schools is, if anything, more difficult. However, some of the elementary school plans that have proved useful may be adapted by junior and senior high schools to overcome the differences in reading achievement of their students.

To eliminate at the outset any confusion over the *means* of meeting individual needs for reading achievement, I would point out that this is more a matter of organization than of methodology. Methods of teaching reading skills do not change just because students in a given group do not have the same reading needs. What is affected are the provisions for these students to receive the required instruction. Instead of having all students read the same selections, learn the same skills, or do identical exercises, the instructional program is varied to account for some of the students' differences in reading ability.

Theoretically, individual instruction is the preferred means of providing for differences in learning ability and achievement. The benefits derived from using teaching machines have been expressed in terms of individualization; the earlier Dalton and Winnetka plans, as reactions against the rigid teaching practices of their time, attempted to individualize instruction. Considering time and resource limitations, practicality has led many educators to advocate a combination of individual and group instruction as the means to meeting individual differences in reading needs. The sections that follow describe both individual and group plans for teaching reading. Subject specialists might adjust their teaching styles to accommodate one or more of these plans or adapt them to fit their requirements. Teachers who conduct reading classes might combine individual and group instruction to meet the requirements of their students.

INDIVIDUALIZED READING

A strong movement in some quarters has been advocating the complete or almost complete individualization of reading instruction in the elementary school. Known as "Individualized Reading," this organizational program has yet to be introduced into very many secondary school reading programs, but more high school teachers may be expected to experiment with it. As explained by one of its chief advocates,[1] individualized reading is based on the principles of self-interest, self-selection, and self-pacing, which are put into practice through an organizational program whereby each pupil is taught reading on an individual basis.

If an individualized reading program were conducted in, say, a tenth grade, the classroom would be provided with a large collection of books, including a range of titles, such as those in some of the reading lists in Chapter 9, to satisfy the varied interests of boys and girls of this age. Books would also be selected on the basis of student reading abilities, with "easier" books being available for those students with low reading ability. Each student would select a book for personal reading, his choice being determined by his own interests and needs—one that he wants to read. The teacher might guide the selection but would not dictate what the student should read. Multiple copies of titles would be included in the collection so that several boys and girls could read the same title.

An important feature of individualized reading is the conference that each student holds with the teacher after the student has read a book. During this conference, the teacher should become acquainted with the student's reading ability and reading tastes. Several activities may be carried on during this meeting. Teacher and student may discuss the author and the work. Selected portions of the work may be read orally by the student. The teacher may pose questions that probe beneath the surface of the selection and may also initiate follow-up activities related to the reading. The teacher may also deal with specific difficulties that the student has experienced while reading independently or working with him. If other students are known to have similar problems, the teacher might delay instruction until a time when a group of such students could be assembled. It is claimed that the individual conference between student and teacher is of inestimable value in that it gives the participants the opportunity for enjoying a one-to-one relationship impossible under ordinary conditions. It serves further to give importance to the individual and his requirements.

At times, students would be treated as a class. During such sessions books would be introduced by the teacher or the students who had read them and discussed and shared as in any other reading program. The teacher might also use this time to teach a reading skill in which a number of students were deficient. He might devote one or more group sessions to any reading activity that called for group participation.

Supporters of individualized reading make several assumptions. One is that each classroom contains a large number of books on different topics and at different levels of difficulty, perhaps as many as ten per student. This is not an unrealistic assumption, if adequate funds are available. A second is that teachers are sufficiently familiar with the content of these books to be able to discuss all of them with students. This requirement can be met by those teachers who are willing to do or have done extensive reading. A third assumption is that teachers are able to teach students the needed reading

1. May Lazar, "Individualized Reading: A Dynamic Approach," *Reading Teacher*, Dec. 1957, pp. 75-83.

skills during specified sessions — which a well-trained and experienced teacher could do without advance preparation. A fourth assumption is that the principles of self-interest, self-selection, and self-pacing are such strong motivations that they overcome the effects of possible weaknesses in the program. On the basis of present knowledge, no definitive conclusion about this assumption can be reached.

Studies of individualized reading have been limited mainly to elementary schools,[2] and most of them merely describe what happened to a specific group of children. Many teachers who experimented with the individualized-reading programs report that expected gains in reading achievement resulted and that a love of reading developed. But the findings are mixed, and no conclusions regarding the superiority of individualized reading to other forms of reading organization may be reasonably drawn.[3]

It is certainly possible that an individualized reading program might work for some groups of students and for teaching certain reading skills. It is also possible that some teachers may feel very comfortable in this kind of organization while others might not. Individualized reading offers possibilities for meeting the special reading needs of high school students, but I do not feel that it would meet all their different reading need, particularly those associated with study-type reading.

INDIVIDUALIZED INSTRUCTION

It would seem that better results in reading should be realized through individual instruction than through group instruction. While this might not always be the case,[4] efforts to create individual instruction systems are likely to increase. Individually prescribed instruction, computer-assisted instruction, and programmed instruction are examples of these systems.

Individually Prescribed Instruction

This plan was developed at the Learning Research and Development Center of the University of Pittsburgh, in cooperation with the staff of a local

2. In a 1967 study by Bruce C. Appleby, "The Effects of Individualized Reading on Certain Aspects of Literature Study with High School Seniors" (Univ. of Iowa, *Diss. Abstracts* 28, No. 7: 2592), high school seniors who participated in a one-semester program developed greater ability to understand the purposes and meaning of literature and seemed to enjoy fiction more.
3. Patrick Groff, "Comparisons of Individualized (IR) and Ability Grouping (AG) Approaches as to Reading Achievement," *Elementary English* 40 (March 1963): 258-264,276; Yvonne Lofthouse, "Individualized Reading: Significant Research," *Reading Teacher* 16 (Sept. 1962): 35-37; Harry W. Sartain, "The Research Base for Individualizing Reading Instruction," pp. 523-530 in *Reading and Realism, Proceedings of the Annual Convention*, Vol. 13, Part 1, ed. J. Allen Figuerel (Newark, Del.: International Reading Association, 1969).
4. John V. Galatto, "The Comparative Effectiveness of Individual Reading Therapy and Group Reading Therapy," New York University, *Diss. Abstracts* 22, No. 3. (1961): 801. Lawrence Gold, "Comparative Study of Group and Individualized Reading Instruction with High School Students," New York University, *Diss. Abstracts* 25, No. 2 (1963): 1042-1043.

public school system. In the plan, individual lessons are assigned to students on the basis of pretests and observations by teachers. Each student accomplishes individual assignments which have been cataloged so that they can be located easily. Each assignment is checked by the teacher before the student goes on to the next lesson. Teachers rely heavily on commercially prepared materials which fulfill the lesson requirements. These are drawn from reading textbooks, boxed and programmed practice exercises, tapes, workbooks, and so forth. Occasionally, teachers conduct group sessions during which problems students have are discussed and some instruction is offered.

If individually prescribed instruction is to be effective, there must be careful planning and preparation of appropriate lessons for different students. Otherwise it can deteriorate into a "shotgun" or busy-type program. If the lessons do not provide instruction as well as practice, students will not be able to complete exercises for which they lack the skills. Teachers might prepare a series of self-instructional lessons on a given skill intended for students who read at a certain level. Then, these lessons could be duplicated and filed for future use. In this way, suitable instructional and practice materials could be compiled for use with students whose reading achievement and skill development vary. Individually prescribed instruction can be an efficient system to meet individual differences if it offers adequate instruction to those who need it and opportunities to practice what has been learned.

Computer-Assisted Instruction

Although sophisticated computer systems have been developed for industry and government, they are still in their infancy insofar as reading instruction is concerned. The main problem is not with the computer but with the "software" that must be fed into it. Computer programs have been developed for teaching reading skills and offering practice in them. These programs deal largely with beginning reading skills and, as yet, have not concentrated on higher level skills, for the reason that the latter seem to be more difficult to program.

Simpler computer programs merely require students to respond to typed items by pushing the proper keys. If a student makes the correct response, the next item in the sequence appears on the typewriter.

Highly sophisticated systems combine visual with auditory presentations. Lessons are projected on a screen and a recorded voice explains what the student is expected to do. Students respond to instructions by pressing keys or indicating answers directly on the screen with sensitized light pens. If the response is incorrect, the voice tells the student to try again; otherwise, the next item appears on the screen.

Undoubtedly, basic reading skills *can* be taught through such systems. It is not unlikely that more computer programs will be introduced in schools if the costs can be controlled and the "software" improved. Nevertheless, some critics have raised questions about the effects of impersonal treatments on students and the wisdom of expecting computer programs to assume a major role in the reading curriculum.

Programmed Instruction

The underlying principles of programmed instruction are *sequential learning* and *immediate reinforcement.* Programmed materials consist of a series of frames or steps which become progressively difficult. Students verify their responses to each item before moving ahead to the next one. Presumably, when the program has been completed, the student has mastered whatever it covered. There are some programs that are designed to teach vocabulary, main ideas, reference skills, and some aspects of inferential reading.[5]

If a process is broken down into its components, the process is more likely to be learned. This principle has been established and applied in treating skills throughout this textbook. The difference between programmed materials and these skills lessons is the degree to which a learning unit is divided into segments. A programmed lesson on main ideas might consist of dozens of frames, each of which requires a separate response by the learner. Repetition is built into the program to reduce possible retrogression.

Advocates of programmed instruction believe that it is an ideal way to make individualized instruction possible. Programmed instructional materials are unlike others in that they offer instruction and not merely practice in reading. It has been pointed out, however, that most reading programs are linear, that is, all students must go through the entire program without any deviations. There are no provisions for students who do not need all of the exposures, although each proceeds at his own rate. Few, if any, programs direct students to skip portions or provide more than one set of exposures if required.

As with other individualized plans, programmed instruction should be judged on its own merits. Although its principles are sound, their translation through materials might be poor. But programmed materials have the potential for helping teachers individualize their work, particularly for the small group of poorer students who seem to profit from carefully sequenced presentations.

Differentiated Reading

All students do not have to be taught the same reading skills, nor do they have to read the same materials at the same time. This is why publishers have provided multilevel packaged materials such as workbooks.[6] These materials may be used by students according to their own reading requirements and learning rates. Several materials provide for self-correction so that teacher involvement may be kept to a minimum.

---

5. *Lessons in Self-Instruction in the Basic Skills* (California Test Bureau); *Programmed Reading* (Globe Publishing Co.); and *Programmed Reading* (McGraw-Hill).
6. Some examples of these materials are *It's Your World* (Continental Press); *Study Skills Library* (Educational Developmental Laboratories); *Reading Skills Lab* (Houghton Mifflin Co.); *Be a Better Reader* (Prentice-Hall); and *Reading Laboratory and Reading for Understanding* (Science Research Associates).

It is important to realize that most of these materials offer little or no instruction; their greatest value is the *practice* they offer students. Wise teachers will not indiscriminately assign these materials to students without determining that they can do the exercises and that they need the practice that the exercises offer. These materials can best be used after teachers have offered whatever guidance students need to master specified aspects of the reading curriculum.

There are other ways in which teachers can differentiate reading instruction. One way is to vary the purposes for which students read the same materials. For example, one group of students might read for literal ideas if the materials are quite difficult for them. A second group might concentrate on meanings that are not clearly expressed, if they are capable of doing so. A third group might seek applications of the ideas gained through reading.

A second way to differentiate reading instruction is to limit the *length* of the reading assignments required by different groups of students. Poorer readers normally need more time to complete an assignment than superior readers. For example, if the assignment were to cover eight to ten pages, the best readers could be responsible for reading all of them and the poorest readers perhaps four or five.

A third way to differentiate reading is to provide materials covering the same general area but intended for less mature students. Information on the nature of electricity or the Industrial Revolution, for example, could be found in textbooks intended for fifth grade, eighth grade, and high school students. Students would than be assigned reading in whichever sources were appropriate. Additionally, there are numerous nonfiction "trade" or library books on these and other subjects with which librarians are familiar and can recommend for students of varying reading ability. Whichever plan (or combination of plans) is adopted, any concepts or important ideas that some students have not gained through reading can be obtained from class discussions, reports, demonstrations, and so forth.

You will recall how the processes guides and content guides (Chapter 5) enable students to read with greater understanding. Each may be used to individualize instruction. The process guide may be general in nature and call the reader's attention to a variety of reading skills he should use, or it may focus attention on one specific group of skills of which the reader needs to be aware. Differentiation through the use of content guides can be achieved by grading the questions to fit the reading ability of different students and directing their attention to larger sections or smaller units of the text.

GROUPING IN READING

By the time students reach seventh grade, reading differences among them are marked; these grow even greater in senior high school. Various group instruction plans to lessen these differences have been suggested, each with some good features. As with other efforts to provide suitable instructional programs, much of their success rests on the teachers who administer them.

Grouping for instruction, however it is done, is not a perfect means of dealing with reading ability differences. It is an organizational device that permits teachers to provide for differences in ways that would not be possible in a class where all students were taught at the same time. Grouping approaches individualized instruction, since the needs of the group are narrowed and teachers are geared to cope with them. However, the emphasis that is actually given to individual needs depends on how well the teacher functions within the group setting.

Limited Intra-Class Grouping

One "grouping for instruction" plan to meet reading needs is intra-class grouping. Within a class, teachers may organize group reading instruction based on the students' instructional levels, their specific reading weaknesses, or a combination of the two. Teachers who have had little or no experience with grouping are likely to find that group instruction proceeds more smoothly when organized around instructional levels. After this experience, they are better able later to organize and teach groups composed of students with similar needs who are reading on different levels.

Although it is almost impossible to form a homogeneous reading class, it *is* possible to reduce the range of reading levels within a single class by grouping at the instructional level. Thus, instead of a span of eight or more years in reading achievement, differences would be, perhaps, four or five years. This class organization plan is more feasible in schools with larger populations.

The number of reading groups in a class should be determined by the teacher's ability to provide for them; the greater the number of groups, the greater the likelihood that the reading needs of students will be met. However, good teaching demands that teachers should not be expected to plan for and instruct a large number of groups without adequate help such as teacher aides. The team approach, therefore, *does* permit many small groups to function at the same time, but high school teachers cannot give differentiated instruction without preparation.

I would recommend that a teacher organize his class into two groups. As soon as he feels secure in that plan, he can extend his instruction to three groups. How far he should go beyond that he must decide for himself. Teaching quality should never be sacrificed for the sake of group instruction. Group instruction per se does not insure learning; grouping can help learning only if teachers are able to meet its demands.

Classroom Management

Before undertaking group instruction, teachers should be familiar with certain details of classroom management. Many students who enter high school have had experience with some form of grouping, but it is helpful for everyone concerned to review and reemphasize procedures. If everyone knows what is expected, the atmosphere of a "three-ring circus" can be avoided.

Since each group might use a different set of materials for instruction, certain members of each group should be given the responsibility for distributing and collecting the materials. These should be stored in places that are accessible to students, thereby obviating the need for the teacher to devote time to such details. Availability of supplies should be considered; students should be permitted to take what they need without interrupting the teacher. Students are quite able to assume such responsibilities.

Grouping may require shifting students and, possibly, tables and chairs within the classroom. Students who are accustomed to the typical classroom setting may need help adjusting to the new arrangement; some groups may require more time than others to learn what is expected of them. If there is understanding between teacher and students, however, the amount of noise can be kept to a minimum.

Discipline problems can exist in any classroom, regardless of how it is conducted. These are likely to occur in groups that have not developed a sense of self-discipline. However, if no unreasonable demands are made on them, students who are not working with the teacher will not often seek opportunities to cause disruptions. There is no reason why one student should not consult a classmate provided the student has valid reason and does not disturb others; if the student obtains help from a neighbor, the teacher's work is not interfered with. Teacher can further reduce the number of interruptions by making certain that group members with which the teacher is not working know what they have to do and how to do it. A glance from the teacher may be all that is needed when a student misbehaves.

Mechanics of Grouping

Standardized test scores may be used when the level of achievement is the criterion for group placement, although the level of instruction may have to be adjusted for each group since reading test scores often do not coincide with actual reading performance. Figure 10-1 shows a possible distribution of reading test scores for a class of ninth-grade students who have been placed together with the view of narrowing their range in reading ability. If it is assumed that this class is divided into two groups, the eleven students whose test scores fall between 7.1 and 9.0 may form one group while the rest constitute the other. If three groups were formed, Group 1 could consist of the students whose test scores fell between 7.1 and 8.5, Group II between 8.6 and 10.0 and Group III between 10.1 and 11.0. Since the difference between the final limits of one distribution and the beginning of the next one is very small — that is, the difference between 9.9 and 10.1 — it is possible to shift students between groups to effect a more suitable distribution.

If informal inventories were administered to the same students and instructional levels determined for them, the distribution would probably approximate that in Figure 10-2. The make-up of each group, in a two-group plan based upon such testing, would be a bit different from that obtained through conventional testing. Group I might consist of those whose instructional levels were sixth and seventh grades and Group II all the others. A three-group plan might be organized as follows:

Group I — students of sixth-grade level
Group II — students of seventh- and eighth-grade levels
Group III — students of ninth- and tenth-grade levels.

Figure 10-1.   Frequency Distribution of Ninth-Grade Standard Test Scores

Grade Placement	Frequency	Cumulative Total
10.6-11.0	2	32
10.1-10.5	4	30
9.6-10.0	6	26
11	9	20
8.6- 9.0	4	11
8.1- 8.5	4	7
7.6- 8.0	2	3
7.1- 7.5	1	1

N = 32

Figure 10.2.   Frequency Distribution of Ninth-Grade Informal Test Scores

Instructional Level by Grades	Frequency	Cumulative Total
10	4	32
9	12	28
8	9	16
7	5	7
6	2	2

N = 32

Regardless of the means by which students are divided into groups, upward and downward adjustments are usually necessary after instruction begins.

After distribution is completed, teachers must decide what level of materials will be appropriate to each group. If any group consists of students on more than one level, it is necessary to find the point at which all the students in the group can operate. Thus, for students in Group II of the three-group plan based on informal testing, materials of eighth-grade level difficulty might be used. Students whose reading level was beginning seventh grade would probably have some difficulty with the material, but the problem is not insurmountable if the teacher provides the extra help they may need. Materials of eighth-grade difficulty may be used with a group of students whose reading abilities range between seventh and ninth grades (as in a group of eleven students whose standardized test scores fell between 7.1 and 9.0).

When *specific reading weaknesses* are the criteria for intraclass groupings, groups may be formed solely on the basis of need, or they may be organized within the existing groups that were established through grade-placement scores. In the latter case, the original groups are maintained but all students who are weak in a specific reading skill — say, selection and evaluation — are brought together for this specific instruction, then returned to their original groups. If the class is not organized around instructional levels, students with similar reading weaknesses are brought together for instruction. Since participants may be reading on different levels, the teacher must use instructional materials that can be managed by each student and provide practice on the level at which each can perform. In this kind of grouping, group composition does not remain the same, because a group is formed whenever a number of students have a common problem. A student may join seven other classmates to learn how to divide words into syllables, but leave them when instruction turns to phonics if he does not need help in phonics.

Regardless of the basis on which students are grouped, teachers must plan lessons so that the group or groups with which they are not working can engage in meaningful activity. Students who are not under their direct supervision must be able to work independently. Two teaching schedules are given in figures 10-3 and 10-4. Provisions for recreational reading are incorporated in both.

With a two-group plan, the teacher is able to work with both groups every day; with a three-group plan, he may not work with all groups each day, although it may be possible when teaching schedules consist of blocks of time, rather than the usual forty- or fifty-minute periods. However, it is not absolutely necessary that teachers present a formal reading lesson to each group every time the class meets.

A typical instructional program could consist of study techniques and directed reading lessons (see Chapter 5), specific lessons in reading skills (see chapters 6 through 8) and recreational reading. Independent activities, based on what the teacher covers, follow the lessons. If students were deficient in a reading skill, the teacher would provide ample practice material for them to work independently after they gave some assurance that they could do so. On some days, students receive instruction and proceed to independent work. They continue this independent work on the following day; when it is completed, they read books that they prefer. When the teacher returns to the group, the independent work is checked and discussion of the books encouraged. A new lesson may follow or grow out of these discussions.

There is little justification for not conducting classwide reading activities, and teachers may plan for these in the schedule or suspend group work whenever this seems desirable. Dramatizing a play, reading poetry, or discussing books can be situations in which everyone in the class participates. Many students can listen to readings that they are unable to manage by themselves. Group teaching is reserved for occasions when the needs of learners cannot be met by treating the class as a unit.

Advance planning is essential to teaching in a group setting; most teachers will find that they can operate more effectively if the lessons are planned on a weekly rather than on a daily basis. Care in selecting practice materials and avoiding conflicts in teaching schedules are factors in successful group work.

Figure 10-3.   Two-Group Plan for Teaching Reading

Group I	Group II

Monday
Teaching——→* Independent Work   Recreational Reading——→Teaching

Tuesday
Independent Work——→Recreational Reading——→Teaching   Teaching——→Independent Work

Wednesday
Teaching——→Independent Work   Independent work——→Recreational Reading——→Teaching

Thursday
Independent Work——→Recreational Reading——→Teaching   Teaching——→Independent Work

Friday
Teach Class as a Unit

*The arrow in each case indicates the activity to which the preceding activity leads. Thus on Monday, Group I has independent work to complete after the teacher has met with it. Group II works with the teacher after having recreational reading. The term *Teaching* means that the teacher works with group.

Figure 10-4. Three-Group Plan for Teaching Reading

	Group I	**Group II**	**Group III**
Monday	Recreational Reading⟶Teaching	Teaching⟶Individual Work	Individual Work⟶Recreational Reading
Tuesday	Individual Work	Recreational Reading⟶Teaching	Teaching⟶Individual Work
Wednesday		Teach Class as a Unit	Recreational Reading⟶Teaching
Thursday	Teaching⟶Individual Work	Individual Work⟶Recreational Reading	Independent Work
Friday	Recreational Reading⟶Teaching	Teaching⟶Independent Work	

Multiple Intra-Class Grouping

Team learning has been tried in the intermediate grades with some degree of success.[7] Although emphasis in this specific experimental reading program was on improving reading ability through team study of content subjects, students used reading textbooks several days a week and completed team assignments following the reading lesson.

During team learning, groups of two or three students are organized on the basis of reading ability. After the teacher has taught a lesson, members of a team work together on materials that have been prepared for them. Although teachers are available to work with the teams or individual members, students are expected to help each other with the assigned work.

There is no doubt that some students can improve their reading skills with the help of other students. In some cases, older, poor readers have successfully taught younger readers who also had reading difficulties. If multiple intraclass grouping is done in moderation, some benefits may accrue to learners. However, except for conducting routine assignments and correcting limited responses, it is doubtful that students can assume the responsibilities of mature teachers. But introducing self-instructional materials could reduce problems that might arise. An additional limitation is the number of team assignments that the teacher must prepare; in a class of thirty students, she might have as many as ten or twelve teams. Whether or not a teacher will find such a task too burdensome without some help and reliance upon commercially prepared exercises has not been explored fully.

Any program of individualization is no better than the teacher who supervises it. Some teachers may find the student-team approach to meeting individual needs a workable structure; others may feel less comfortable with it and prefer an arrangement in which no more than two, three, or four groups are functioning at the same time. Whatever the pattern, the teacher must be able to administer it and teaching must not degenerate to mere distribution and correction of assignments.

Inter-Class Grouping

Some schools advocate a type of differentiated instruction in which several teachers participate. This pattern is particularly suited to departmentalized teaching. Students are grouped on the basis of reading achievement and assigned to one of several sections in reading, all of which meet at the same time. If such a program were conducted in a junior high school, students from the seventh grade might meet for reading instruction with students from the eighth and ninth grades. Grade lines disappear since each reading section is assigned students whose reading ability falls within a given range.

The greater the number of teachers who participate in the program, the narrower the reading range in each group. If three teachers were partici-

7. Donald Durrell, "Evaluating Pupil Team Learning in Intermediate Grades," *New Frontiers in Reading*, International Reading Association Conference *Proceedings* 5 (1969): 112-115.

pating, each section might contain students whose reading-achievement levels varied two and three years; if the number of teachers were doubled, the spread in reading levels would be halved.

The effectiveness of interclass grouping is increased by further grouping within sections whenever that is required. The need for additional grouping becomes evident when the reading performances of students with identical reading levels are compared. Grouping on the basis of reading deficiencies usually improves the results of a teaching program in reading.

A variation of interclass grouping is the program in which a group of teachers forms a subunit within the school organization and works only with an assigned number of students. One teacher in the subunit is responsible for the language arts classes in which reading is taught, a second for the science classes, a third the social studies classes, a fourth the mathematics classes, and so forth. For each learning experience, students in the subunit are grouped with those of similar abilities. The teachers work as a team in planning the reading activities of all the groups and integrate them into their subject areas. This teacher-team approach helps when forming new groups and when shifting students from one group to another. Close cooperation between reading teachers and content teachers is also made possible.

The homogeneity of such subunits is, of course, theoretical. Although students in these groups have common needs that may be met by teaching them as a class, they are likely to progress more rapidly if less gross measures are taken. Further grouping is recommended for teaching reading skills in which only some members of the unit are weak.

With team teaching, it is possible to form many more learning groups than is the case otherwise. If one teacher was able to work with two or more groups of students, a team of teachers could manage several. This means that the learning needs of students could be met more readily and instruction differentiated even though some groups might be larger than usual. If one teacher were to lead a reading lesson for all the students, the remaining teachers could circulate freely and offer individual help to students who needed it.

SUMMARY

The problem of providing for individual differences in reading is similar to problems found in other learning areas. The need for differentiated instruction becomes progressively greater as students move into the upper grades. Elementary schools have been using several different methods of class organization for reading instruction that may be adapted by junior and senior high schools.

The most common method of providing for individual reading differences is to group students in any one class on the basis of reading achievement and reading needs, two or three groups being thus formed. While the teacher works with one group, the other student groups engage in independent activities that are outgrowths of the previous lesson. Recreational reading is provided for in the schedule. The teacher moves from group to group as time permits; if there are more than two groups, the teacher may not present a lesson to each group every day. Intraclass grouping is reserved for situations that require differentiation; there will be occasions when the students are brought together and taught as a class.

Student teams consisting of two or three members may work on common reading problems. Job sheets must be prepared for each group and materials made available to carry out the assignments. Self-direction is a key to this form of organization.

Interclass grouping is followed in some schools. In this plan, students from different classes are assigned to sections on the basis of reading achievement. Further grouping within these sections is often desirable. Variations of this organization are seen in programs that use teams of teachers to integrate the work of one or more grades and subjects.

Individualized reading is a form of organization in which each student selects the books he wants to read. The student than meets periodically with the teacher to discuss the books, raise questions, and receive help. Some group instruction may be incorporated in this plan.

Individual prescribed instruction, computer-assisted instruction, and programmed instruction offer additional possibilities for differentiating teaching on the basis of students' abilities and requirements. Using multilevel materials and adopting instructional adjustments also further this objective.

Additional Readings

The problem of individualizing reading instruction and ways to resolve them are discussed in the following publications:

Donald C. Cleland and Elaine E. Vilscek, eds. *Individualizing Reading Instruction.* Report of the Twentieth Annual Conference on the Twentieth Annual Conference on Reading. Pittsburgh: University of Pittsburgh Press, 1964.

Larry A. Harris and Carl B. Smith, eds. *Individualizing Reading Instruction: A Reader.* New York: Holt, Rinehart and Winston, 1972.

Vergil M. Howes, ed. *Individualizing Instruction in Reading and Social Studies.* New York: Macmillan Co., 1970.

Wallace C. Ramsey, ed. *Organizing for Individual Differences.* Perspectives in Reading No. 9, Newark, Del.: International Reading Association, 1967.

H. Alan Robinson, ed. *Meeting Individual Differences in Reading.* Supplementary Educational Monographs, No. 94. Chicago: University of Chicago Press, 1964.

See also these related publications:

Nelson B. Henry, ed. *Individualizing Instruction,* 61st Yearbook of the National Society for the Study of Education, Part 1. Chicago; University of Chicago Press, 1962.

Phil C. Lange, ed. *Programed Instruction* 66th Yearbook of the National Society for the Study of Education, Part 2. Chicago: University of Chicago Press, 1967.

Judson T. Shaplin and Henry F. Olds, Jr., eds. *Team Teaching.* New York: Harper and Row, 1964.

Ralph C. Voight. *Invitation to Learning: The Learning Center Handbook.* Washington, D.C.: Acropolis Books, 1971.

Robert A. Weisberger, *Developmental Efforts in Individualized Learning.* Itasca, Ill.: F. E. Peacock, 1971.

CHAPTER 11

OVERCOMING READING DIFFICULTIES in CONTENT AREAS

Problems for Study and Discussion

1   To what extent may reading difficulties be attributed to single factors?
2   What justification is there for questioning the assumed relationship between nonstandard speech and reading disability?
3   What educational factors might account for some reading failures?
4   How might poor readers and their needs be identified?
5   Why might the principles on which "developmental" reading instruction is based be applicable to instruction for disabled readers of diverse backgrounds?

POSSIBLE CAUSES OF READING DIFFICULTIES

Linda stood before her American history class, reading from the report she had prepared. Her source materials had been carefully chosen, and her facts had been marshaled in interesting order, but she stumbled miserably through a quotation she had included and burst into tears. "What," wondered her teacher, "is causing Linda to make such mispronunciations? Can it be that Linda needs glasses, or is this a symptom of some emotional problem?"

In another classroom, the biology teacher looked despairingly at Dan, who had failed on a review test. "Didn't you read the questions?" the teacher asked. The teacher was puzzled because Dan's past records gave no clue to his poor performance. Was Dan letting his after-school job undermine his health, and did he just need sleep? Did the boy have worries in addition to those about money? Was it possible that there was a reading problem hitherto unsuspected because Dan had been promoted year after year?

Whatever the answer in these two cases, Dan's reading difficulty did not stem from the same cause as did Linda's — or that of Suzie or Mike or Camillo or any of the thousands of other high school students who have reading problems. Generalizations from one student to another simply cannot be made.

Until recently, the tendency among educators was to regard *all* reading failures as the product of a single cause — the cause varying with the discipline making the "authoritative" answer. For example, since some children who were known to be emotionally disturbed had reading problems, all children with reading problems were, for a time, said to be emotionally disturbed — a most unwarranted conclusion. Fortunately, the validity of these "one-cause" explanations was challenged by those close to the students with reading difficulties, and teachers themselves began to suggest other reasons for reading weaknesses. Today, teachers know that there is no identical explanation for all reading failures, and they seek a specific explanation for each individual case. Unhappily, as teachers know, there are many causes.

The percentage of secondary school students who have serious reading difficulties varies from school to school and community to community. In some schools, no more than 5 to 10 percent of students would be considered disabled readers.[1] In other schools, the percentage of students who are disabled readers is considerably higher. A student whose reading ability is significantly below the average reading level for his age falls into this category. On standardized reading tests, such a student will achieve scores equivalent to several years below those attained by average readers of the same grade. (Students whose mental ages are significantly higher than their reading achievement levels could be considered "disabled" too.)

In one way or another, some disabled readers manage to satisfy school requirements, although their achievements are minimal. Teachers in many secondary schools are aware of disabled readers and sometimes attribute their inability to achieve more to low intelligence and lack of interest. Others who are capable of surpassing present performance remain undetected since they complete their work satisfactorily.

Truly disabled readers cannot cope with the materials they are expected to study. A large number cannot pronounce many of the words in these materials and, as a result, fail to understand much of what they try to read. Many of these students are also weak in comprehension skills and the combination of these difficulties is just too much for them to overcome. They are utterly frustrated when they have to acquire information through reading.

In previous years, most of the research into reading difficulties has centered on three major areas of growth: physical, intellectual, and emotional. Many investigators made real contributions to improved understanding of the nature of reading failures. More recent studies have sought to penetrate these areas in greater depth and add new dimensions to their scope. In addi-

1. Some reading specialists use the term "retarded readers," but others are reluctant to do so since this term often is confused with "mentally retarded pupils." Consequently this book will use the term "disabled readers."

tion, explorations into the ways in which language is acquired, the nature of the reading process, and the relation between language development and reading have opened new avenues for studying reading weaknesses. Moreover, investigations into cultural and economic factors and their influences on personal and reading development have yielded additional insight into reading problems.

Although the results of some research suggest the possibility that the nature and quality of reading instruction could account for a share of the reading failures, this aspect of the environment and how it might contribute to poor reading has not been studied carefully. In fact, only three investigations that touch on this question are reported by Artley and Strang. Therefore, considerable attention will be paid this area later in the chapter.[2]

One thing is certain. The majority of disabled readers in secondary schools have long histories of failure. Their reading difficulties appeared in the early grades and, with each passing year, became more severe as reading demands increased. Failure feeds on failure, so we ought not to be surprised that some students have been unable to overcome their problems in reading. Whatever the causes for reading failures, schools must accept responsibility for reducing tensions that accompany reading disabilities and make suitable provisions for helping students progress in reading.

Physical Factors

The earliest investigations into the causes of reading difficulties were mainly concerned with physical development, with emphasis on handedness and visual and auditory handicaps. Later studies sought to explore other possibilities, such as the effects of mental and emotional status on reading. Some recent research has again centered around physical factors, including handedness, maturation influences, and body chemistry.

Vision and Hearing

The study of visual and auditory defects in relation to reading ability has received wide attention. Children who are unable to hear normal speech or see what is written or printed are obviously in serious trouble, but few are sightless or without hearing. Some do suffer to a degree from visual and auditory defects. To what extent do these influence reading ability? The findings of many investigators are not in agreement. Explanations for the diverse conclusions possibly may be found in the differences of populations, criteria of hearing and seeing, and methods of treating the data.

Helen Robinson of the University of Chicago investigated the importance of visual defects in cases of reading failure. She reported that, while defects existed in 50 percent of the cases studied, not all could be said to contribute to reading failures. Paul Witty and David Kopel, Thomas Eames, and others found little relationship between visual acuity and reading achievement. Paul Fendrick, however, reported that he was able to distinguish

2. References that contain information about research on the causes of reading difficulties appear in the "Additional Readings" at the end of this chapter.

between poor and good readers in terms of visual acuity. There is greater consistency among the results of studies of eye coordination than among those of visual acuity. Several investigators reported significantly more cases of eye imbalances among reading failures than in normally developing readers.

Equally contrary findings have been reported in hearing studies. Sybil Henry and Helen Robinson found little relationship between hearing acuity and reading ability, while Emmet Betts and Guy Bond reported positive findings. More general agreement is seen among the investigations that measured auditory discrimination. Bond, W. Franklin Jones, and Marion Monroe concluded that positive relations exist between the ability to discriminate between like and different sounds and reading ability.[3]

It appears that visual and auditory discrimination are important factors in reading. Thomas Barrett, who reviewed the literature on visual discrimination, reported that ability to discern likenesses and differences among words is tied to reading progress.[4] Insofar as auditory perception is concerned, investigators found relative independence between hearing acuity and ability to discriminate sounds within words. Robert Dykstra concluded that auditory discrimination is significantly related to reading achievement.[5] While many children "outgrow" visual and auditory discrimination weaknesses, adults who are virtually illiterate often suffer from such inadequacies. Training in auditory and visual discrimination as related to reading, has been shown to be of help in overcoming reading weaknesses in children and adults.

Any summary of the research in the area of vision, hearing, and reading could safely conclude that *in most cases* reading achievement is not directly related to vision and hearing, but that *in some cases* specific defects of vision and hearing may be contributing factors to reading disability. These physical defects may be sources of irritation and discomfort and may interfere with learning. Surely, no one would question the desirability of removing them wherever possible.

Health

While no direct relationship appears to exist between reading failure and general physical condition, some evidence supports the conclusion that poor health can interfere with learning to read. Children who suffer from prolonged illnesses, malnutrition, and other equally serious health disturbances have additional burdens with which to cope and are not free to concentrate upon a difficult learning task.

3. Specific references for investigators cited above who studied the relationships between visual and auditory defects and reading ability will be found in Marjorie Johnson, "Factors Related to Disability in Reading," *Journal of Experimental Education* 26 (Sept. 1957): 1-26.
4. Thomas C. Barrett, "The Relationship Between Measures of Pre-reading Visual Discrimination and First-Grade Reading Achievements: A Review of the Literature," *Reading Research Quarterly* 1 (Fall 1965): 51-76.
5. Robert Dykstra, "Auditory Discrimination Abilities and Beginning Reading Achievement," *Reading Research Quarterly* 1 (Spring 1966): 5-34.

Some clinicians have reported the effects of treatment for endocrine dysfunction on reading progress. Children who received thyroid medication showed great improvement not only in their reading but also in other school activities. Improvement in their ability to deal with social situations was also noted. Donald Smith has advanced the theory that reading disability is related to body chemistry and the ductless glands. His major hypothesis suggests that an imbalance between cholinesterase and acetylcholine affects the way in which nerve impulses in the brain are transmitted and that perception of word symbols is controlled to the extent that these two substances are in a balance or imbalance.[6] While the evidence is inconclusive, Smith's hypothesis draws attention to an apparent interdependence of body chemistry and learning ability. It is possible that some of the children who give every indication of restlessness and inattention and who find it almost impossible to attend to their daily assignments are the ones who desperately need medical assistance. Even where reading achievement cannot be traced to these physical conditions, remedies for these conditions should be sought.

There is some evidence that drugs can reduce distractability and thereby make students more amenable to learning. Ruth Strang refers to the reports of several investigators who found that medication increased perception and reading efficiency.[7] However, two investigators were not successful in improving reading performance with the drug *deanol*. It is entirely possible that future studies will show positive results as more knowledge about body chemistry and its relation to learning is acquired. Reports of the ability of scientists to reproduce learned behaviors in untrained rats by injecting their brains with a chemical drawn from the brains of trained rats suggest the future role that chemistry might have in memory and learning.

Physical Maturation

Hypotheses connecting physical growth or maturity with reading progress have been formulated by a few investigators. Willard Olson studied fifty-six boys and girls who attended the Laboratory School of the University of Michigan and charted their various growth indexes, expressing them in equivalent age units: mental, educational, and physical. He combined these measures into one which he called *organismic age*.[8] Olson found that most of the underachievers in reading were likewise underachievers in other growth aspects. Some questions have been raised about the validity of translating these several measures into equal age units. I, for one, studied a similar problem but treated the data differently from the manner in which Olson treated it. In the population that I studied, I found a small but definite relationship between skeletal development (an index of physical maturation) and reading ability.

6. Donald E. P. Smith and Patricia M. Carrigan, *The Nature of Reading Disability* (New York: Harcourt, Brace and World, 1959).
7. Ruth Strang, *Reading Diagnosis and Remediation*, ERIC/CRIER Reading Review Series (Newark, Del.: International Reading Association, 1968), p. 146.
8. Willard C. Olson, *Child Development*, 2d ed. (Boston: D. C. Heath, 1959), p. 165.

Of course, it would be unrealistic to explain reading failures at the secondary level purely in these terms. Surely by the time most boys and girls reach junior high school they are ready to learn. Some of them will be maturing at less rapid rates than others, but the slower maturing students will still be able to profit from instruction. However, if the slow growers do not receive the attention they need, they seem to fall farther behind each year, taking on the characteristics of chronic failures.

Sex

The fact that boy failures outnumber girl failures in reading by about four to one has led investigators to considerable speculation. Studies at junior and senior high school levels show that there are no basic differences between the reading performances of boys and girls. Then why do more boys than girls seem to have trouble with reading? No one is certain, but several reasons have been suggested. In our society, to read is not considered the most suitable way boys ought to spend their time. Instead, they should be more interested in physical activities. Some people believe that this attitude toward males "rubs off" from adults and causes boys to assume a similar posture. Others say that the content of materials used for teaching reading, and used by schools generally, favors the interests of girls rather than boys. Therefore, boys are "turned off" by these materials. Still others believe that boy failures do not really exceed girl failures by such seemingly wide margins; boys are just more visible than girls.

Whether or not sex is a significant factor in reading achievement has yet to be determined. But it seems that environmental influences might be responsible for some of the differences that could exist. In this connection, one report concluded that in Germany there was a higher incidence of reading failures among girls than boys. Perhaps the attitudes toward women's role in that society — one that stresses the female's responsibility for the home with a corresponding deemphasis upon formal education — possibly accounted for the differences in reading performance of boys and girls.

Dominance

Early investigations sought to find out if hand or eye preferences were related to reading disability, but no clear-cut conclusions could be drawn since the results were mixed and often challenged. Similarly, when she summarized more recent findings, Marjorie Johnson declared that "the evidence available on the significance of the relationships between hand and eye preferences and reading disability is inconclusive."[9]

Some investigators claim a connection between confused or mixed dominance and reading failure. The child who prefers to use the left or right hand and the opposite foot (say, in kicking) or favors the eye that is on the side opposite the preferred hand or foot may be one who suffers interference as he tries to perceive word symbols. Some theorists have explained such

9. Marjorie Johnson, "Factors Related to Disability in Reading," *Journal of Experimental Education,* Sept. 1957, p. 10.

confusion in neurological terms; it may be possible that some learners are so influenced.

William Barger and his associates have reemphasized the factor of mixed dominance and reversal tendencies as revealed by reading words such as *saw* and *was* as *on* and *no*, and their importance to reading.[10] In an uncontrolled study of poor readers with mixed lateral dominance in which a mirror was used, some reading growth was achieved. It was theorized that using the mirror helped these children adjust to the confusion arising from the mixed laterality. However, in a carefully designed study that tested this hypothesis, the use of the mirror was found not to contribute to the reading achievement of such children.

The findings of more recent investigations on the relationship of laterality and poor reading appear to rule out mixed dominance as a factor. However, Albert Harris, who developed dominance tests and reported positive findings, believes that weaknesses in the research on laterality account for conflicting and inconclusive results.[11] Furthermore, he maintains that directional confusion or failure to know left from right occurs frequently in poor readers with mixed dominance. This confusion might be due to faulty or incomplete neurological maturation and can interfere with reading progress. Harris does acknowledge the possibility that directional confusion might have origins other than physiological, that it is often outgrown, and that reading failures with mixed dominance complicated by neurological or emotional problems are quite a small group when all reading disability cases are considered. Considering all the known facts about the former group, many reading specialists would discount the importance of both mixed dominance and directional confusion in reading difficulties.

Brain Damage and Learning Disability

The subject of brain damage and its relation to reading has challenged the thinking of many researchers. Physicians, psychologists, and others agree that structural weaknesses in the brain may account for reading disability. Soldiers who suffered brain injuries have been known to lose their power to read. In such cases the letters of words tend to become fused and blend into the background, with the result that difficulty in distinguishing one word from another interferes with reading. Some students known to have suffered brain injury at birth or in subsequent accidents also have had this difficulty. Brain-damaged children frequently suffer from hyperactivity, which is an additional obstacle they must overcome. Their attention span is short, and they are unable to concentrate on learning tasks that demand extended periods of steady effort.

Brain damage is not easily detected, and classroom teachers should not be overly concerned with its possible existence unless definite information from a competent authority points in this direction. I am familiar with cases

10. William C. Barger, *The Mirror Technique for Difficult Readers* (Great Neck, N.Y.: Robert L. Barclay, 1960).
11. Albert Harris and Edward R. Sipay, *How to Increase Reading Ability*, 6th ed. (New York: David McKay, 1975), pp. 274–279.

who were misdiagnosed as "word blind" and were trained to read under normal conditions.

Children who fail to respond to repeated efforts to teach them to recognize words are sometimes said to suffer from minimal brain damage, from specific learning disabilities, or from dyslexia. Implied in each designation is the belief that physiological factors are responsible even though they cannot be pinpointed. Those who believe there is such a "disease" as dyslexia attribute it to minimal brain damage or a lag in neurological development.

Some observers have referred to the "learning disability epidemic." Many students have been classified as learning disabled because of reading and other learning difficulties which are believed to arise from dysfunction of the central nervous system. Proponents of this point of view advocate assessing perceptual and motor abilities, abilities involving auditory and visual processing, language facility, and memory. Some learning disability specialists maintain that remediation of any deficiencies in these areas must occur before progress in teaching children with learning problems can be achieved. Recommended treatments for overcoming reading deficits in the area of word recognition draw on procedures long familiar to reading specialists. Some are believed to be useful while others are of questionable value.

Since evidence to support the belief that reading failures are constitutional in origin is yet to be demonstrated, appropriate measures must be taken to help children with learning problems. I personally believe that programs based on good principles of learning and teaching can be effective in working with children who have severe learning problems. These principles were discussed and illustrated in Chapter 3.

Intellectual Factors

Many studies have been made about intelligence and general learning ability, including the ability to learn to read, but intelligence is not the only intellectual factor that teachers should consider. Another is language development, which has been receiving attention in recent surveys.

Intelligence

There is no one given mental age at which reading success can be guaranteed. However, sufficient evidence supports the conclusion that a significant relationship exists between intelligence as measured by existing instruments and growth in reading.

Teachers may expect students who profit from academic work to be achievers in reading. Conversely, they may expect the students whose mental age is below expected levels not to achieve equal success in reading over the same period of time. The more gifted child ordinarily will outdistance the less well-endowed one. The less-gifted child often has not reached his maximum reading level, and suitable instruction can lead to real growth with accompanying satisfactions. If he is reading as well as he can but has not reached the achievement levels of his age peers, experience has shown that he can be pushed beyond his present capacities. Such ill-advised efforts should be avoided, because they can lead to serious disturbances, dislocations, and frustrations that will express themselves in resentment against authority, withdrawal from activities, and even overt rejection of parents and teachers.

Teachers must understand that a large percentage of students with serious reading problems are of normal or superior intelligence. These students simply are not keeping pace with their intellectual development, and the causes of reading failure must be sought elsewhere than in low mental age. Unfortunately, the widespread use of group verbal intelligence tests has led teachers to draw improper inferences about the learning abilities of their students. If a student is deficient in reading ability he is bound to do poorly on a group verbal test. Many parts of intelligence tests really measure reading ability; even individual intelligence tests are not completely free of verbal influences.

Teachers should also consider another possible effect on the results of intelligence tests. Many psychologists regard the ability to reproduce material that has been presented visually and aurally as one measure of intelligence, and sections of some intelligence tests require students to recall from memory series of designs, sentences, and numbers that are shown or read to them. The extent to which students are able to respond to these presentations is known as memory span. Reading consists of recognizing language symbols and associating meaning with these symbols. Auditory and visual weaknesses in memory span for these language symbols can have adverse influences upon reading growth and will be reflected in intelligence test scores.

Before they draw hard and fast conclusions about student learning abilities, teachers should understand that some performance tests are better indicators of present intellectual status than are the intelligence tests ordinarily used in schools. Also, they should realize that evidences of thoughtful reasoning in learning situations other than reading are real indications that students have the ability to achieve in school. To ignore these signs that are present in person-to-person contacts and accept test results as final arbiters of learning ability in the face of all we know about their inadequacies seems foolish.

Students of reading have speculated about reasons why many children who have the capacity to learn do not have nearly the same difficulties with arithmetic and other tool subjects as they do with reading. Perhaps there is something in the very process of learning to read that is very different from that which controls mastery over the others. According to Anne McKillop,[12] reading is the most personal and least structured form of communication. She believes that one's feelings and desires to communicate with others affects the ways that the person responds to printed symbols. Some students might reject reading because achievement represents growing up which they

12. Anne McKillop, "Why Many Children and Youth Are Retarded in Reading," pp. 52-59 in *Improving Reading in Secondary Schools, Selected Readings*, ed. Lawrence E. Hafner (New York: Macmillan, 1967).

don't want to do. Since our society considers reading as possibly the most important skill and conveys this feeling to children, fear of failure to master it leads to undue learning difficulties. Anne McKillop reminds us that we should not look for single explanations for complex problems.

Language Development and Experiential Background

Another intellectual factor associated with reading difficulties is language development, which is likely to carry with it a limited experiential background.

The ability to use speech has some bearing on the ability to obtain meaning from such abstract symbols as printed words. Listening and speaking precede reading on the language continuum, and students whose verbal ability has been slow in maturing are likely to experience difficulty in interpreting printed ideas. The converse, however, is not necessarily true: some students with superior language facility can have a reading ability decidedly below the level of the ability of their peers.

Students who come from homes in which a foreign language is spoken may not become proficient in English and may possibly feel the effects of this in reading. Some of our larger cities have been receiving numbers of people who do not speak English but whose children attend local schools. As a result, New York City, with its large increase in Spanish-speaking Puerto Ricans, and some other cities, have had to set up special programs to help these students overcome language barriers. Teachers would be unrealistic to expect such children to master printed symbols before spoken ones; in these special programs the emphasis has been on spoken English, with reading instruction paralleling the language instruction.

Language problems of students from non-English-speaking families are compounded by meager experiential backgrounds. This lack of experiences must also be taken into consideration with children who come from low socioeconomic groups. Since intelligence tests contain items that are removed from their experiences, the responses they make to these tests are not wholly satisfactory. Again, it is inaccurate to interpret the outcomes of intelligence tests as indicators of potential ability. The results, however, do confirm the belief that these children will have difficulty meeting the same academic demands that are being made on others unless special assistance is given to help them overcome deficiencies in background and language.

An experimental program in which efforts were made to overcome student weaknesses in background and language proved highly successful in New York City. Children who rarely left their immediate neighborhoods were taken on tours of factories, museums, art galleries, concert halls, parks, and theaters. Films and lectures supplemented classroom work, and personalities in the arts and sciences met with the groups. Pupils were thus exposed to a world that few knew existed. Language activities grew out of active participation and stimulating discoveries. The benefits pupils obtained justified the expense of these enriching experiences, for improvement both in speech and writing and in reading were measurable outcomes.

There are other groups of students — blacks, the Spanish speaking, American Indians, rural whites — who speak a nonstandard English with grammatical forms that vary from those commonly found in standard English. As a group, these students do not achieve in reading to the extent that comparable speakers of standard English do; some educators have sought to link this difference in achievement with language differences.[13] They maintain that the language patterns of nonstandard English are quite different from those found in printed materials and that the unfamiliar structures are obstacles difficult to overcome. There have been suggestions that these unfamiliar language patterns must first be converted into familiar ones before they can be understood, much in the same way a beginning student translates a foreign language into his own. A review of the research suggests virtually no relationship between language differences and reading achievement of black children.[14] Kenneth Goodman believes that they understand standard English but that teachers' negative attitudes toward the dialects the students speak interferes with learning.[15] In related studies with diverse students, the rewriting of content materials to conform to their language patterns did not appear to increase reading comprehension.[16] Until additional data become available, explanations for reading failures must be sought elsewhere. These will be considered in the next section on socioeconomic factors.

Socioeconomic Factors

Most reports show that children from low socioeconomic environments as a group do not read as well as children from higher socioeconomic levels. In a summary of environmental and cultural factors in reading achievement, Sterl Artley reported on three studies whose findings were quite in agreement on this matter.[17] In one of these studies, low socioeconomic status, family mobility, and family stability were cited among others as factors in poor reading achievement. In another study, children from homes in which fathers were absent did less well than children whose fathers were present. Similar findings with regard to the influence of social class, home conditions, and the education and economic status of parents have been reported from Canada, England, Sweden and other countries. Of course, none of these studies shows a *causal* link between reading failure, low socioeconomic status, and poor home conditions. But there is little doubt that their influ-

13. Joan Baratz and Roger Shuy, eds., *Teaching Black Children to Read* (Washington, D.C.: Center for Applied Linguistics, 1969).

14. Vernon C. Hall and Ralph R. Turner, "The Validity of the 'Different Language Explanation' for Poor Scholastic Performance by Black Students," *Review of Educational Research* 44 (Winter 1974): 69-81.

15. Kenneth S. Goodman, "Dialect Barriers to Reading Comprehension Revisited," *Reading Teacher* 27 (Oct. 1973): 6-12.

16. Daniel R. Hittleman and H. Alan Robinson, *Readability of High School Text Passages Before and After Revision*, Final Report, Project No. I-B-025 (Washington, D. C.: U.S. Office of Education, Jan. 1973); Fillmore K. Peltz, "Using Students' Writing Patterns to Repattern Reading Material," pp. 47-56 in *Teachers, Tangibles, Techniques — Comprehension of Content in Reading*, ed. Bonnie Smith Schulwitz (Newark, Del.: International Reading Association, 1975), pp. 47-56.

17. A. Sterl Artley, *Trends and Practices in Secondary School Reading* (Newark, Del.: International Reading Association, 1968), pp. 21-25.

ences have some bearing on other conditions such as interest in learning and expectations of success, which can affect reading progress.

Many culturally different students who speak nonstandard English and experience reading failure share another condition: poverty. According to those who have focused their attentions on poor black students, environmental factors interfere with developing the positive attitudes toward learning to read which are generally common among children from middle-class homes. Additionally, they believe that poverty prevents these students from enjoying experiences that reinforce those the schools offer. These hypotheses could be extended to include other populations who have to utilize their energies in ways that will enable them to survive. Families who dwell in poverty must satisfy economic and personal needs before any others, and education suffers.

Emotional Factors

Perhaps more has been written about emotional problems and reading failure than about any other type of reading disturbance. Inferences about the role of personality in learning have been drawn, with several writers declaring that personality disturbances can interfere with the ability to attend to a learning task. Specific studies have concluded that disabled readers were more handicapped by deviations in personality development than were advanced readers, and some investigators have found psychogenic factors — anxiety and guilt feelings, sadistic fantasies, and efforts to suppress these fantasies — common to all the disabled readers they studied. From available evidence, teachers can safely conclude that some students are not able to achieve because of learning interference resulting from emotional upset.

Students who are thought to be disturbed by major fears and anxieties should be referred to persons qualified to help them. No matter how many courses a teacher has taken, he is not a trained physician or psychologist; no matter how good his intentions, dabbling in amateur psychiatry is extremely dangerous. The results of clinical studies suggest that dislike for reading can stem from feelings of hostility toward parents and teachers or from feelings of dependency and insecurity, and disturbed children who were disabled readers have improved when given psychotherapeutic treatment. This is completely outside the province of the classroom teacher.

Reference was made earlier to the relation between expectations for success and reading progress. Students with long histories of reading failure have been found to think less well of themselves than students whose reading progress is satisfactory. In a review of the literature, F. K. Schwyhart found that there was quite a bit of evidence to show that self-concept and reading success are related.[18] Children with low self-concepts tend to do more poorly in reading than children with higher self-concepts. This tendency was found to hold in the elementary through college years.

Students with low self-esteem do not believe that they can succeed in difficult tasks. They stop trying as soon as they meet obstacles and often lack

18. F. K. Schwyhart, "Exploration of the Self-Concept of Retarded Readers in Relation to Reading Achievement," doctoral diss., Univ. of Arizona, 1967.

the motivation to undertake or persist in a task. Many give up before they start. Poor reading achievement may lead to low self-esteem and low self-esteem to poor achievement. Each seems to feed on the other.

Some evidence supports the view that emotional upsets are perhaps caused by reading failure. Failure of any kind affects the way each of us regards himself, and it would be unreasonable to assume that reading failure would have no effect on a student. Support for this view may be found in studies in which disturbed children responded to reading instruction. One investigator found that disturbed children who received remedial reading help showed greater gains in emotional adjustment than did children who were treated for personality maladjustments. Reports from reading clinics give further support to these views. Since most disabled readers are unknown before they enter school, it is difficult to determine whether they brought their personality problems with them or developed some after experiencing school failures. Cause may be confused with effect.

Existing evidence points to no clear-cut explanations of the relationship between reading difficulties and personality maladjustment. Insofar as teachers are concerned, they must work in the area of academic weakness, while providing a healthy classroom climate. Should a student manifest symptoms of serious emotional disturbance, referral to competent agencies is obligatory. Teachers must be ready to refer students to specially trained persons, such as reading consultants, school psychologists, guidance counselors, and school nurses and doctors if conditions beyond their own ken are suspected. When a school lacks a staff of specialists, teachers and supervisors should turn to local and regional agencies. Many universities offer clinical services to area schools; parallel services may be obtained from public and private welfare, health, and educational agencies.

Educational Factors

When teachers realize that reading difficulties are not generally the result of a single cause, they will not rule out the possibility that factors other than those already discussed might be behind the difficulties. They must pay at least as much attention to educational influences and their effects on reading success as they do to other possible contributing factors. Even in cases where it is necessary to correct a physical defect or to provide treatment for maladjusted behavior, schools are administering an instructional program for students. Supervisory and teaching personnel must seek to identify the possible educational factors that may be contributing to reading failure and adopt measures to deal with them.

Of all the possible causes of reading difficulties, none has received so little attention in the literature as those related to school influences. Despite several intemperate attacks by uniformed persons on schools and their practices in teaching reading, no one, so far as I know, has made a careful and thorough study of educational factors and their relations to students' lack of reading ability. (Many years ago, however, a reading specialist claimed that school conditions contributed to the reading failures of seventy-six out of eighty-three cases studied.)

Without hard data, one can only infer from existing conditions the extent that school inadequacies have contributed to reading failures.[19] The resurging interest in individualizing reading has been attributed by educators to an unjustifiably high incidence of poor reading at all school levels. What, then, are some educational factors that could influence the progress students make in reading?

Inadequate Teaching of Reading

Formal reading instruction normally begins in the first grade. Since children are generally assigned to first grade on the basis of chronological age, some will lack one or more of the essentials for reading success, such as language facility, experiential background, mental maturity, and perceptual development. *Poor teaching of reading in the first grade* (and in the later early grades) can lead to failure. These children are destined to almost certain failure unless the teacher can supply some of the essentials that they need in order to learn to read. Slower-maturing children must not be faced with tasks that are presently beyond them, while children able to learn should not be bored with so-called "reading readiness" activities for which they have no further need. Instructional programs must be modified to meet both needs. Failure to provide for such individual differences will put some children in untenable positions and will lead to reading disabilities.

In junior and senior high school, this same disregard for individual differences can lead to similar results. As students move through the grades, the range of reading ability widens, and some students are bound to develop serious reading weaknesses if individual differences are not taken into account and provided for. I have visited classrooms in which the same book was used as the text for all students in the class, even when it was obvious that many could not read the book well enough to comprehend the material. It was equally obvious that teachers did not know how to handle the problem, because they merely divided the class into groups and used the same materials and lessons for each. Many principals would provide these teachers with more appropriate texts at a different level for use with the students who were unable to cope adequately with the classroom text.

Emphasis on only one reading skill can also lead to reading failures. An almost complete emphasis on the oral reading skill can frequently lead to weaknesses in thinking and study skills, as well as to losing interest in reading. Having students stand up and take turns reading aloud is not teaching them how to read, yet there is still a large number of schools where students read from basic readers, social studies, and science books in just this way — and are deemed good readers if they pronounce the words and answer matter-of-fact questions. When too much emphasis is put on the word-recognition skill, students fail to learn to read for meaning. Too often, skills that involve selecting relevant information and its application to pertinent

19. There has been reported in the press the filing of a lawsuit by an eighteen-year-old who asserted that he graduated from high school with the reading ability of an average fifth-grade pupil. On the grounds that his reading deficiency is being overcome through private tutoring, monetary damages were sought from the school system for its failure to teach him to read better.

problems have been neglected; so too have been the skills tied to interpretation and critical reaction. Even in this day and age, too few teachers realize that there is more to reading than merely recognizing words.

Is it surprising, then, that some students, upon reaching high school, cannot cope with the demands made on them by their teachers?

Indiscriminate use of reading materials has also left its mark on some students. Teachers can use some materials profitably to develop reading skills, but if they depend on them to do what only the teacher can do, they are bound to produce reading failures. Most materials are designed to be used as practice exercises after the teacher has taught a specific reading skill; they are of little value to the student who has not yet learned how to perform that skill. Assigning such material without proper application to real reading tasks is another example of improper use. Emphasis upon isolated drill does not stimulate interest in learning to read. Teachers who require the completion of every exercise without regarding student weaknesses and strengths fail to offer a sound instructional program in reading.

No teacher can teach reading adequately if he or she has been inadequately prepared to do so. Summarizing the free responses to a questionnaire asking teachers to identify the professional areas in which they felt a need for graduate study, Constance Burns reported that more than 80 percent of these experienced teachers indicated that teaching reading was a major concern and that they felt uneasy about this important area of their professional tasks.[20]

Other teachers express the same concerns. Responding to a questionnaire, secondary school reading teachers rated themselves as adequate or very adequate in only four of twenty-five identified tasks in teaching reading.[21] They felt the greatest confidence in teaching phonics, the use of the dictionary, and word meanings, and the least confidence in constructing tests, diagnosing reading difficulties, and remedying reading problems. Content teachers expressed confidence in their ability to reach key vocabulary and ask stimulating questions to guide discussion but found the greatest amount of difficulty in individualizing instruction and improving reading rates. For solutions to reading problems, they gave the greatest weight to training content teachers to teach reading skills. The investigator attributed both groups' shortcomings and the students' reported weaknesses in reading to low-level or no training. This conclusion is supported by the results of another study that showed that many subject teachers are unaware of the skills that students need to read in their subject areas.[22]

Mary Austin and her colleagues at Harvard University undertook a

20. Constance Burns, "How Can We Give Teachers Better Preparation for the Teaching of Reading?," *Reading in Action*, International Reading Association Conference *Proceedings* 2 (1957): 151-153.
21. Wallace Z. Ramsey, "The New Secondary Reading Teacher: Problems and Concerns," pp. 57-63 in *Reading R$_x$: Better Teachers, Better Supervisors, Better Programs*, ed. Joseph S. Nemeth (Newark, Del.: International Reading Association, 1975), pp. 59-63.
22. Leonard S. Braam and James E. Walker, "Subject Teachers' Awareness of Reading Skills," *Journal of Reading* 16 (May 1973): 608-611.

study to find out how institutions of higher learning were preparing teachers of reading.[23] They conducted personal interviews with faculty members and administrative personnel of seventy-four colleges throughout the United States and received answers to questionnaires from 371 additional colleges, or 70 percent of the colleges engaged in teacher training. Colleges and practice-teaching classes were observed; college catalogs, outlines, and facilities were examined. After summarizing their findings, the investigators presented twenty-two recommendations having to do with instructors of reading courses, nature and content of these courses, and relationship of these courses to practice teaching. Throughout the report runs the belief that better preparation of good teachers will lead to quality programs in reading. Recommendation 9 urges a basic reading course for *all* prospective secondary school teachers.

Preservice teacher preparation has ordinarily not included intensive study in the teaching of reading. Too many teachers have had to rely almost entirely on the teaching manuals that accompany most reading series. While these manuals contain useful information, they cannot replace the insights that are developed through adequate training and practice. Secondary school teachers have had to face reading problems with the same lack of preparation. Reading is the third aspect of the language continuum, yet few teachers have had an opportunity to study its processes.

A number of surveys of high school teachers in the field reveal how few of them have had any training in teaching reading.[24] In one survey, less than 10 percent of 570 secondary school teachers claimed to have any preparation for teaching reading. In another, which sampled 127 high schools, only one school reported it had a qualified reading teacher. A third survey deplores the fact that very few prospective secondary school teachers elect to take any courses in how to teach reading, and of those who do about three out of four prepare to teach English.

Two other surveys cite lack of preparation as reasons why secondary school teachers cannot provide the help in reading that students need, and one suggests that some average and borderline readers suffer serious setbacks when they enter junior high school. It is not surprising — if these data are representative of the country as a whole — that relatively few high schools offer comprehensive reading programs, or that much of the instruction is of inferior quality.

23. Mary Austin and others, *The Torch Lighters* (Cambridge, Mass.: Harvard Univ. Graduate School of Education, 1961), pp. 146-147. See also Mary Austin and Coleman Morrison, *The First R: The Harvard Report on Reading in the Elementary School* (New York: Macmillan, 1963), pp. 181-191.
24. Dorothy McGinnis, "The Preparation and Responsibility of Secondary Teachers in the Field of Reading," *Reading Teacher* 15 (Nov. 1961): 98-101; John S. Simmons, "Who Is Responsible? The Need for Qualified Supervision of Reading Programs," *English Journal* 52 (Feb. 1963): 86-88; Richard W. Burnett, "Reading in the Secondary School: Issues and Innovations," *Journal of Reading* 9 (April 1966): 322-328; Barbara F. Freed, "Secondary Reading — State of the Art," *Journal of Reading* 17 (Dec. 1973): 195-201; and Harold H. and Marcia A. Roeder, "1,000,000 Reasons for Improving Preparation of Secondary Teachers," *Journal of Reading* 17 (May 1974): 604-607.

Today, more and more colleges and universities are recognizing the importance of training *all* teachers to help in developing reading skills and fostering more and better reading in their students. These institutions are aware that high school classes include students whose reading ability is poor, and that many of their teachers are not ready to give adequate help. Accordingly, they offer courses for secondary teachers in the improvement of reading, in the diagnosis and remediation of reading difficulties, and in reading in content areas. First-hand experiences that include working under supervision with students whose reading problems are typical of those found in schools are judged by teachers to be of greatest value. Simulation, micro-teaching, and conferences with reading experts are rated next in importance.

School Deficiencies

Deficiencies in administrative practices and policies over which teachers don't have much control have been known to contribute to reading problems. Among these are the failure to provide varied and adequate materials, adopt systemwide reading programs, and remedy conditions that interfere with effective teaching.

Some students have to be enticed into wanting to learn to read well, and the presence of a wide selection of all kinds of reading materials can arouse sufficient intellectual curiosity to accomplish this. Yet, on professional visits, I have seen classrooms where a dearth of reading materials, such as reference books, magazines, newspapers, and trade books, was all too evident. No teacher can expect students to become interested in reading when the school provides so little to read. Schools that show such a lack of interest can contribute to reading failures.

Many schools provide no formal reading instruction after fourth grade. This lack of continuity is difficult to understand, but an explanation may rest in the way in which the school regards the reading process. Skill in word-calling can be developed in young children, and if it is the school program, rather than the individual teacher, that is putting total emphasis on this ability, no wonder reading instruction is discontinued once this skill has been achieved by the students. Inability to teach the more advanced reading skills may be another reason for this neglect. Learning to read is an ongoing process, and schools must continue to provide opportunities for growth. It is nonsense to believe that all the complex reading skills have been mastered by students who are ten or eleven years old. Surely every junior and senior high school teacher has sufficient evidence to prove that this is just not so.

In a comprehensive survey of the literature on the status of high school reading, Margaret Early found that few schools had programs of any sort — often attributed to lack of qualified personnel — and most programs were of the remedial type.[25] Her summary of Squire's findings is particularly discon-

25. Margaret J. Early, "What Does Research in Reading Reveal About Successful Reading Programs?," *What We Know About High School Reading*, A Research Bulletin of the National Conference on Research in English (Champaign, Ill.: National Council of Teachers of English, 1969), pp. 40-53.

certing: in only 10 percent of the classrooms of 158 high schools with excellent reputations for preparing college-bound students was anything being done about reading instruction. More than half of the schools made no, or ineffective, efforts to teach reading as a skill. Early concluded that the status of high school reading was "dismal" and that improvement depended upon better administration, more useful instructional materials, and particularly upon motivated and skillful teachers who know how to teach students to read and study in their subjects.

No one knows what is the optimum class size for teaching reading, but teachers of large classes report that they are unable to spend enough time helping individual pupils overcome specific reading difficulties. When school districts fail to provide enough space and staff for their schools, the entire community is responsible for those pupils who fall victim to school inadequacies.

Despite all the inadequacies which reading surveys identify, we are making progress in ameliorating them. Schools which never had reading programs are establishing them; ongoing programs are being studied by schools to improve them. Teachers are participating in in-service training and are joining local, regional, and national groups whose primary interest is improving reading instruction. The rapid growth of the International Reading Association with its affiliated councils and the increased attention to reading improvement by the National Council of Teachers of English and other professional associations attest to the importance that teachers and administrators everywhere are placing upon reading. All these efforts should have a positive effect on the reading progress that students make.

IDENTIFYING DISABLED READERS

Classroom teachers do not have to be reading specialists to determine whether students are poor readers. Examining reading test scores is a gross but quick way of identifying some students with serious reading problems. If their partial or total grade placement or percentile scores are well below expected scores, there is a good possibility that they need to be treated differently from those whose scores are closer to expected scores. For example, ninth-grade students whose reading performances place them at fourth- or fifth-grade levels or in the tenth to twentieth percentile are likely to be quite weak in one or more reading skills that the tests measure and possibly others that the tests do not cover. Such test-score examinations, however, will not identify highly capable students whose reading ability merely approaches or is equal to expected performance levels.

Teachers may identify poor readers by having students read orally a few brief passages from materials they will be using and asking them to "tell in their own words" what they read. Frequent errors in word recognition accompanied by limited comprehension are signs of low reading ability. Some students may not read orally without errors but still manage to understand. Others will not seem to have much trouble recognizing words but will fail to grasp the meaning. Both groups are candidates for further study and help.

These procedures can be used for screening students for possible referral to reading specialists who will examine them with more refined instruments, such as those described in Chapter 4.

Some reading specialists use a rule-of-thumb guide to identify disabled readers. They compare student reading performances to reading potential as measured by mental ability or listening tests, and if the latter are two or more years above the former, students so described are regarded as disabled.[26] Naturally, a discrepancy of two years suggests a less severe problem for those of average ability than one of four or more years. Moreover, regardless of the degree of discrepancy between reading performance and reading potential, students whose reading performances are quite low will not be able to read typical subject materials with much success.

DIAGNOSING READING DIFFICULTIES

Experience shows that poor readers can make reading progress if instruction is specifically designed to overcome given deficiencies. The more severe the difficulties, the greater is the need to identify both the gross problems and precise weaknesses. For example, some of the poorest readers are weak in phonic skills. If phonic skills are mastered, it will enable them to pronounce many unfamiliar words. To institute phonics instruction without determining their knowledge of specific letter-sound associations within words, their ability to combine sounds to form words, and how well they recognize syllables in words is to work in the dark.

Other poor readers may be weak in comprehension. Shall instruction be focused on building vocabulary by studying word parts, context clues, words with multiple meanings, and figurative language? If the word parts study is indicated, shall emphasis be placed on compound words, prefixes and suffixes (which ones?), or roots within words? The more accurately such questions are answered, the greater the likelihood that instruction will produce results.

Subject teachers may be able to obtain diagnostic information as they work with and observe students and confer with the students themselves. From student responses based on what they have read, it is possible to analyze difficulties. For example, teachers might be led to believe that some students fail to recognize cause and effect relationships when not explicitly stated, while other students seem to confuse the importance of relevant details and illustrations of them. To confirm their observations, teachers might select passages that represent such relationships and have students identify

26. A formula commonly used to determine reading potential or expectancy age is, $2MA + CA/3$, where MA equals mental age and CA equals chronological age expressed in years and tenths of years. The reading expectancy age of a 15.2-year-old student with a mental age of 15.7 years is 15.5 + years. If 5.2 years is subtracted from 15.5 + years, we obtain a corresponding grade equivalent of 10.3 + years. Thus a student with a reading grade-placement score of 6.1 years and an expected reading grade-placement score of 10.3 + will be considered more disabled than another student with the same expected reading score but with an actual reading score of 7.8.

them. A similar procedure could be followed for assessing other skills that teachers have tentatively identified as requiring attention.

How intensively subject teachers diagnose student reading will depend on their students' needs, the teachers' ability to use diagnostic tools and interpret the results, and how much time they might devote to reading. Teachers should be able to refer students to the school's reading specialists who have the knowledge and resources to do as thorough a reading evaluation as is required.

There is one point to remember. Poor readers often need help in different skills areas. While it is useful to know what they are, it is not necessary to accumulate every bit of information about them before beginning instruction. Alert teachers will obtain valuable data on specific aspects of reading during their work with students. Testing will accompany teaching, and hypotheses about student strengths and weaknesses will be confirmed. Formal evaluations will be brief and cover areas that can be attended to. There is no real justification for gathering information that will not be used.

HELPING DISABLED READERS

What teaching strategies should be used with poor readers? Are special methods required? Partial answers to these questions will be found in one's attitudes regarding developmental and remedial instruction, and the nature of the population requiring help. Although some people think of remedial reading as an entity in itself and say that they teach it, my view on the subject is quite different.

Remedial instruction is intended to correct deficiencies in students. It hardly matters if these deficiencies exist despite earlier instruction or if they are present because of the lack of instruction. In a sense, *all* instruction is corrective since it is intended to produce changes in the behavior of learners. Schools refer to developmental reading programs and remedial reading programs, the former for students who are progressing satisfactorily and the latter for those who are not. This distinction suggests major differences in the methods and materials used in each. In reality, there are no basic differences; any that exist are differences in degree and not in kind.[27]

Poor or disabled readers do not respond very well to incidental teaching. This could be one of the reasons why they have fallen behind. While some students might not be adversely affected by instruction with vague objectives, others cannot compensate for them. Moreover, they require more skillful teaching than that they typically experience in classrooms. Perhaps this explains why some people have said that "regular" teaching methods have failed poor readers and that different ones must be substituted for them. Unfortunately, "different" methods — most are for overcoming weaknesses in word identification — violate the principles on which sound

27. It is possible that disabled readers with organic problems associated with the central nervous system might require treatments different from those which are recommended. However, there isn't much evidence which shows that the former produce results superior to the latter.

practices rest. They tend to illustrate learning in isolation, which is hardly recommended for any student.

Teaching strategies described in this textbook apply generally accepted principles of learning. While conditions other than teaching practices also influence learning, *the more the latter are consistent with principles of learning the greater are the chances for successful learning.* Disabled readers need the best help that concerned and supportive teachers can provide. We should not strive for anything less on the justification that 'I tried it and it works.' Such a rationale might seem reasonable, but it is rather weak when evaluated in professional terms. There is no procedure that can guarantee success in overcoming reading difficulties, but experience shows that better results can be anticipated from some practices than others. Those based upon defensible principles are the ones teachers should try to implement. There is enough evidence that strategies which translate conditions conducive to learning are beneficial to all and particularly to those who experience difficulties in reading. These principles, expressed as guidelines to teaching, are:

1. Offer instruction that meets students' immediate needs rather than long-term goals.
2. Prepare students for undertaking learning tasks so that their chances for success are enhanced.
3. Provide students with meaningful, rather than rote and isolated, learning experiences.
4. Direct student learning to avoid them having to depend on trial-and-error learning.
5. Introduce experiences sequentially and pace instruction to reduce interference with learning.
6. Help students recognize growth, however small, whenever it occurs. This will encourage them to strive to achieve.

While instructional materials should "fit" all students, it is essential that poor readers not be frustrated by them. If teachers err in selecting materials, it best be with materials that are too easy. Teachers cannot expect much success if materials interfere with learning. For example, you might be working with students on using context clues for word meaning. If they don't recognize most of the words, their attention will be drawn away from the lesson's objective as they struggle to pronounce the words. Instead, they should be able to "read" the words easily so that they might concentrate on context clues.

Providing materials whose content appeals to poor readers can be a problem. Many are too difficult, even though they contain high-interest selections. One solution is to use textbook and reference materials intended for lower levels but which cover topics that other students study. Another is to obtain "library" books on sports, science, biography, "how-to," and so forth — with subjects which appeal to older students but written in a simpler style. A third source are materials written especially for poor readers. These are fiction and nonfiction books, some of which could be used with adolescents.[28]

28. See George D. Spache, comp., *Sources of Good Books for Poor Readers* (Newark, Del.: International Reading Association, 1969).

Examples of such materials are found in the *American Adventure Series* (Harper and Row), *Checkered Flag Series* (Field Educational Publications), *Childhood of Famous Americans Series* (Bobbs-Merrill), *Deep-Sea Adventure Series* (Field Educational Publications), *Everyreader Series* (Webster), *Landmark Books* (Random House), *Pilot Libraries* (Science Research Associates), *Simplified Classics* (Scott, Foresman), *Teen-Age Tales* (D. C. Health).

The very poorest readers can be taught with materials that they themselves create. If they are able, they can write about themselves or what interests them; otherwise, they can dictate their "stories" which are transcribed and used to develop sight vocabularies and reading skills.[29] This procedure has been used successfully with older students and adults, even though it was developed for beginning readers.

READING FOR CULTURALLY DIFFERENT STUDENTS

How should the poor readers among black students, Chicano students, American Indian students, rural Appalachian students be treated? Many people have written on the subject and suggested guidelines for teaching them. The following ones are fairly representative of those that they offer.

> To begin the instructional program, teachers should first discover their pupils' present performance levels and immediate needs. . . . When this is done a plan must be developed that will provide for daily instruction in the deficient areas.
> The bases of the instruction must be materials and activities that are immediately interesting and useful to the students. . . .[30]

How are these recommendations different from those intended for other poor readers? Apparently, they are not different. Some of the ways in which they have been *implemented* have varied. The methods and materials used in programs considered successful have not been the same. For example, there are some with a language-experience orientation that teach reading skills through materials students develop. Other programs also stress the motivational aspects of instructional materials and favor those with content to which students can relate.[31] Still others suggest using literature that explores diverse values to which students can respond and presents characters with whom they can identify. Unfortunately, a number of the materials

29. Russell G. Stauffer, *The Language-Experience Approach to the Teaching of Reading* (New York: Harper and Row, 1970).
30. James L. Kinneavy and William L. Rutherford, "Junior High School Level," in *Reading for the Disadvantaged: Problems of Linguistically Different Learners*, ed. Thomas D. Horn (New York: Harcourt, Brace and World, 1970), p. 203.
31. Among these are the *ACE Program* (Scott, Foresman); *Action Series* (Houghton Mifflin); *Crossroads* (Noble and Noble); *Gateway Series* (Macmillan); *Hip Readers* (Book-Lab); *Impact* (Holt, Rinehart and Winston); *Living City Adventures* (Globe); *Scope* (Scholastic); *Springboards* (Great Society); *The Way It Is* (Xerox); and *Voices of Man* (Addison-Wesley).

of high interest are too difficult for many poor readers and cannot be used to develop reading skills.

Not unlike programs for other disabled readers, typical materials in the form of workbooks, packaged skills and literature units, and audio-visual materials are recommended.[32] Many of the materials are the same ones suggested for overcoming weaknesses in word-attack skills, comprehension, and reading-study skills and are not designed for any particular cultural group. These materials ought to be evaluated in the same way as materials intended for any readers.

There is much to learn about how to improve the reading ability of students of diverse cultural backgrounds. It is possible that some practices are more suitable for one group than for another. Nevertheless, schools have been able to achieve some successes with such groups. Observers who studied schools where programs were more successful noted qualities shared by them which were absent in others:[33]

1. administrators respected by teachers and students who took personal interest in the reading program.
2. high expectations for student progress with efforts to match them.
3. availability, in each classroom, of large quantities and varieties of books and other materials.
4. trained reading personnel who worked with teachers to upgrade the program.
5. reliance upon no single approach or sets of materials.
6. individualization through small groups and special reading sessions.

These characteristics do not appear to be unique; they represent conditions that ought to be present in all schools, regardless of their populations. Perhaps their presence in schools with diverse student bodies is more crucial than in others with students who meet expectations.

SUMMARY

Before teachers can help students who are reading poorly or not as well as they might, they need to have some idea of the possible causes of the reading weaknesses. These may be some physical defects; possibly intelligence factors including inadequate experiences and language backgrounds; emotional problems that are characterized by anxiety and low self-esteem; socioeconomic conditions that lead to lack of motivation for learning and interest in reading; educational factors that include lack of trained teachers who know what reading skills are needed by students and how to teach them; and limited instructional programs. No one single cause may explain all reading failures, and some students might be experiencing several that interfere with their progress.

32. See S. Alan Cohen, *Teach Them All to Read* (New York: Random House, 1969), pp. 278-318.
33. *New York Times*, Oct. 31, 1971; May 28, 1973; and Nov. 18, 1973.

Informal and standardized screening devices suitable for classroom and clinical use will identify students in need of special help. Any evaluation should provide information about levels of performance and specific reading strengths and weaknesses. Corrective instruction should be directed at problem areas which have been noted. Continuous evaluation will accompany instruction whose methodologies are consistent with principles of learning. Skillful teaching is a basic ingredient for overcoming reading difficulties.

Students from culturally diverse backgrounds who are also poor readers have the same needs as other poor readers. An effort should be made to provide them with instructional materials whose content interests them. However, suitability should be judged not on relevance alone, but also on difficulty. As with other disabled readers, reliance upon single approaches cannot be expected to produce results comparable to those flowing from sound but eclectic procedures.

Additional Readings

Information on the causes and treatment of reading difficulties will be found in these sources:

A. Sterl Artley. *Trends and Practices in Secondary Reading.* Newark, Del.: International Reading Association, 1968, Ch. 2.

Guy L. Bond and Miles A. Tinker. *Reading Difficulties: Their Diagnosis and Correction,* 3d ed. Englewood Cliffs, N.J.: Prentice-Hall, 1973.

Albert J. Harris and Edward R. Sipay. *How to Increase Reading Ability,* 6th ed. New York: David McKay Co., 1975.

George D. Spache. *Investigating the Issues of Reading Disabilities.* Boston: Allyn and Bacon, 1976.

————. *Diagnosing and Correcting Reading Disabilities.* Boston: Allyn and Bacon, 1976.

Ruth Strang. *Reading Diagnosis and Remediation.* Newark, Del.: International Reading Association, 1968, Ch. 2.

Robert M. Wilson. *Diagnostic and Remedial Reading for Classroom and Clinic,* 2d ed. Columbus, Ohio: Charles E. Merrill, 1972.

Problems associated with students of culturally diverse groups with reading difficulties are discussed in:

S. Alan Cohen. *Teach Them All to Read.* New York: Random House, 1969.

J. Allen Figurel, ed. *Reading Goals for the Disadvantaged.* Newark, Del.: International Reading Association, 1970.

Thomas D. Horn, ed. *Reading for the Disadvantaged: Problems of Linguistically Different Learners.* New York: Harcourt, Brace and World, 1970.

Kenneth Johnson. *Teaching the Culturally Disadvantaged.* Chicago: Science Research Associates, 1970.

Hy Ruchlis. *Guidelines to Education of Nonreaders.* Brooklyn, N.Y.: Book-Lab, 1973.

BIBLIOGRAPHY

CHAPTER 1

Marilyn Birkley. "Effecting Reading Improvement in the Classroom through Teacher Self-Improvement Programs." *Journal of Reading* 14 (Nov. 1970): 94-100.

Leonard S. Braam and James E. Walker. "Subject Teachers' Awareness of Reading Skills." *Journal of Reading* 16 (May 1973): 608-611.

Margaret Early. "Taking Stock: Secondary School Reading in the 70s." *Journal of Reading* 16 (Feb. 1973): 364-373.

Thomas H. Estes and Dorothy Piercey. "Secondary Reading Requirements: Report on the States." *Journal of Reading* 17 (Oct. 1973): 20-24.

E. C. Frederick. "Will the Real Reading Teacher Please Stand Up." *English Journal* 63 (Nov. 1974): 45-47.

J. T. Hunt. "The Refinement of High School Reading Skills." *High School Journal* 49 (April 1966): 307-313.

S. D. Marani. "What's Really Going On in Junior High School Reading Programs." *NASSP Bulletin* 58 (April 1974): 78-81.

Arthur V. Olson. "Attitude of High School Content Area Teachers Toward the Teaching of Reading." *Multidisciplinary Aspects of College-Adult Reading.* 17th Yearbook of the National Reading Conference, 1968, pp. 162-166.

James R. Squire. "Preparing for Future Shock in Reading and English Education." *New England Reading Association Journal* 10, 1 (1975): 10-13, 58-63.

CHAPTER 2

A. Sterl Artley. "Implementing a Developmental Reading Program on the Secondary Level." *Reading Instruction in Secondary Schools,* Perspectives in Reading No. 2. Newark, Del.: International Reading Association, 1964, pp. 1-16.

Jerome Axelrod. "Some Flaws in Commercial Comprehension Materials." *Journal of Reading* 17 (March 1974): 474-479.

Sally C. Berkey. "A Successful High School Developmental Reading Program." *Journal of Reading* 10 (April 1967): 442-447, 456.

Sally Berkey and Irwin H. Fields. "Reading and Study Skills Program." *Journal of Secondary Education* 36 (April 1966): 197-202.

Susan Boyle. "Trends in Florida High School Reading Programs." *Journal of Reading* 14 (Feb. 1971): 299-302.

N. P. Criscuolo. "Seven Creative Reading Programs for the Secondary Schools." *English Journal* 64 (Feb. 1975): pp. 76-80.

Margaret J. Early. "Reading: In and Out of the English Curriculum." *Bulletin of the National Association of Secondary School Principals* 51 (April 1967): 47-59.

Karl D. Hesse and others. "Content Teachers Consider the Role of the Reading Consultant." *Journal of Reading* 17 (Dec. 1973): 210-215.

Lloyd W. Kline. "Five Sites in Search of the World, Part 2." *Journal of Reading* 17 (Feb. 1974): 383-387.

J. N. Mangieri and H. D. Olsen. "Five-phase Task Force Technique." *NASSP Bulletin* 58 (Oct. 1974): 66-70.

Lorraine Schottenfeld and Florence Lang. "Reading Resource Center: Programs and Personnel in Modular Scheduling." *Journal of Reading* 17 (Nov. 1973): 104-107.

Nathaniel Shapiro and Noel Kriftcher. "Combatting the Lower and Higher Illiteracies." *Journal of Reading* 19 (Feb. 1976): 381-386.

Richard J. Smith and others. "Teaching Reading in the Content Areas — an Inservice Model." *Journal of Reading* 13 (March 1970): 421-428.

Thom Swiss. "Right to Read/Modular Programs." *Journal of Reading* 19 (Oct. 1975): 89, 91, 93.

CHAPTER 3

Kenneth M. Ahrendt and Donald S. Mosedale. "Eye Movement Photography and the Reading Process." *Journal of the Reading Specialist* 10 (March 1971): 149-157.

John S. Barlow. "Brain Information Processing During Reading." *Diseases of the Nervous System* 32 (Oct. 1971): 668-672.

R. D. Chester. "Psychology of Reading." *Journal of Educational Research* 67 (May 1974): 403-411.

Charles R. Cooper and Anthony R. Petrosky. "Reading Strategies and Teaching Implications from the Psycholinguistic Model of the Reading Process." *High School Journal* 59 (Nov. 1975): 91-102.

R. T. Green and R. Way. "Reading as an Existential Act." *Journal of Reading* 18 (Jan. 1975): 301-307.

Robert J. Havighurst. "Social Factors that Influence Learning and Reading." *Journal of the Reading Specialist* 5 (Oct. 1965): 18-25.

Marion D. Jenkinson. "Sources of Knowledge for Theories of Reading." *Journal of Reading Behavior* 1 (Winter 1969): 11-29.

William S. Palmer. "Reading — A Thought and Language Process." *High School Journal* 59 (Nov. 1975): 50-59.

R. A. Silverston and J. W. Deichmann. "Sense Modality Research and the Acquisition of Reading Skills." *Review of Educational Research* 45 (Winter 1975): 149-172.

Wendell Weaver. "On the Psychology of Reading." *New Concepts in College-Adult Reading.* 13th Yearbook of the National Reading Conferences, 1964, pp. 64-74.

Joanna P. Williams. "Learning to Read: A Review of Theories and Models." *Reading Research Quarterly* 8 (Winter 1973): 121-146.

CHAPTER 4

Emery P. Bliesmer. "Assessing Vocabulary and Word-Attack Skills." *University of Pittsburgh Conference Proceedings*, No. 18, 1962, pp. 121-130.

John R. Bormuth. "Readability: A New Approach." *Reading Research Quarterly* 1 (Spring 1966): 79-132.

J. Culhane. "Cloze Procedures and Comprehension." *The Reading Teacher* 23 (Feb. 1970): 410-413.

Mary M. Dupuis. "Diagnostic Teaching for Every Teacher." *High School Journal* 59 (Nov. 1975): 65-76.

Marvin Glock. "How the Classroom Teacher Can Use a Knowledge of Tests and Measurements." In *Diagnostic Viewpoints in Reading*, ed., Robert E. Leibert. Newark, Del.: International Reading Association, 1971, pp. 31-40.

Kenneth S. Goodman. "Psycholinguistics of Reading: Insights from Miscue Analysis." *English Journal* 63 (Nov. 1974): 61-64.

S. K. Hollander. "Why's a Busy Teacher Like You Giving an Informal Reading Inventory?" *Elementary English* 51 (Sept. 1974): 905-907.

H. F. Livingston. "What the Reading Test Doesn't Test — Reading." *Journal of Reading* 15 (March 1972): 402-410.

Walter H. MacGinitie. "Testing Reading Achievement in Urban Schools." *The Reading Teacher* 27 (Oct. 1973): 13-21.

G. McNinch and M. Carmichael. "Word Analysis Assessment Inventory." *Reading Improvement* 10 (Spring 1973): 45-53.

William R. Powell. "The Validity of the Instructional Reading Level." In *Diagnostic Viewpoints in Reading*, ed. Robert E. Leibert. Newark, Del.: International Reading Association, 1971, pp. 121-133.

Edwin Smith and others. "Informal Reading Inventories for the Content Areas: Science and Mathematics." *Elementary English* 49 (May 1972): 659-666.

Ruth Strang. "Diagnostic Teaching of Reading in High School." *Journal of Reading* 8 (January, 1965): 147-154.

W. J. Valmont. "Creating Questions for Informal Reading Inventories." *The Reading Teacher* 25 (March 1972): 509-512.

Carol K. Winkley, "What do Diagnostic Reading Tests Really Diagnose." In *Diagnostic Viewpoints in Reading*, ed. Robert E. Leibert. Newark, Del.: International Reading Association, 1971, pp. 64-80.

CHAPTER 5

Ira E. Aaron. "Reading in Mathematics." *Journal of Reading* 8 (May 1965): 391-395, 401.

Larry Andrews. "Reading Comprehension and Three Modes of Prereading Assistance." *Journal of Reading Behavior* 4 (Fall 1972): 237-241.

Peter Edwards. "Panorama: A Study Technique." *Journal of Reading* 17 (Nov. 1973): 132-135.

Thomas H. Estes. "Teaching Effective Study Reading." *Reading Improvement* 8 (Spring 1971): 11-12, 20.

T. Stevenson Hansell. "Increasing Understanding in Content Reading." *Journal of Reading* 19 (Jan. 1976): 307-310.

Laura S. Johnson. "The Newspaper: A New Textbook Every Day." *Journal of Reading* 13 (Nov. 1969): 107-112, 164; (Dec.): 203-206, 240-245.

L. D. Kennedy. "Textbook Usage in the Intermediate-Upper Grades." *The Reading Teacher* 24 (May 1971): 723-729.

Donald S. Leeds. "Summary of Research Related to Reading in the Content Areas: Science and Mathematics"; "Summary of Research Related to Reading in the Content Areas: English and Social Studies." *Journal of the Reading Specialist* 10 (Dec. 1970): 88-95; 11 (March 1971): 175-186.

Anthony Manzo. "The ReQuest Procedure." *Journal of Reading* 13 (Nov. 1969): 123-126, 163.

R. B. Shuman. "School-Wide Attack on Reading Problems." *Clearing House* 49 (Oct. 1975): 76-80.

CHAPTER 6

R. Barr. "Processes Underlying the Learning of Printed Words." *Elementary School Journal* 75 (Jan. 1975): 258-268.

Morton Botel. "Strategies for Teaching Letter-Sound Relationships." *Vistas in Reading*. Proceedings of the International Reading Association Annual Convention, 1967, pp. 156-159.

Lou E. Burmeister. "Usefulness of Phonic Generalizations." *The Reading Teacher* 21 (Jan. 1968): 349-356, 360.

Kathleen Clayton. "Word Recognition for the Junior High School." *Forging Ahead in Reading*. Proceedings of the Annual Convention of the International Reading Association, 1968, pp. 59-62.

K. L. Dulin. "Using Context Clues in Word Recognition." *The Reading Teacher* 23 (Feb. 1970): 440-445, 469.

Patrick Groff. "Dictionary Syllabication — How Useful?" *Elementary School Journal* 72 (Dec. 1971): 107-117.

M. Hardif and others. "Word Attack: How Do They 'Figure Them Out?'" *Elementary English* 50 (Jan. 1973): 99-102.

Charles E. Railsback. "Consonant Substitution in Word Attack." *The Reading Teacher* 23 (Feb. 1970): 432-435.

M. K. Shapiro. "Simplified Diacritical Marking System as a Remedial Tool." *Reading Improvement* 11 (Winter 1974): 12-16.

Harry Singer. "Teaching Word Recognition Skills." In *Handbook for the Volunteer Tutor*, ed. Sidney J. Rauch. Newark, Del.: International Reading Association, 1969, pp. 46-59.

Ronald Wardhaugh. "A Linguist Looks at Phonics." *Elementary English* 48 (Jan. 1971): 61-66.

CHAPTER 7

Wilbur S. Ames. "The Development of a Classification Scheme of Contextual Aids." *Reading Research Quarterly* 2 (Fall 1966): 57-82.

David Cooper. "Concepts from Semantics as Avenues to Reading Improvement." *English Journal* 53 (Feb. 1964): 85-90.

Ronald L. Cramer. "Setting Purposes and Making Predictions: Essential to Critical Reading." *Journal of Reading* 13 (Jan. 1970): pp. 259-262, 300.

W. J. Culhane. "Cloze Procedure and Comprehension." *The Reading Teacher* 26 (Feb. 1973): 410-413.

R. C. O'Donnell and F. J. King. "Exploration of Deep Structure Recovery and Comprehension Reading Skills." *Research in the Teaching of English* 8 (Winter 1974): 327-338.

Charles Duke and Anne Powers. "Reading in the Content Area." *Clearing House* 47 (Dec. 1973): 221-226.

Morris Finder. "Teaching to Comprehend." *Journal of Reading* 13 (May 1970): 581-586, 633-637.

James M. McCallister. "Understanding Paragraph Clues as Aids to Understanding." *Journal of Reading* 8 (Oct. 1964): 11-16.

A. V. Manzo and J. K. Sherk. "Some Generalizations and Strategies for Guiding Vocabulary Learning." *Journal of Reading Behavior* 4 (Winter 1971-1972): 78-89.

Leo Schell. "Promising Possibilities for Improving Comprehension." *Journal of Reading* 15 (March 1972): 415-423.

Russell G. Stauffer. "Reading as a Cognitive Process." *Elementary English* 44 (April 1967): 342-348.

Judy Stephen. "The Semantics of Reading." *English Journal* 63 (Nov. 1974): 7-8.

CHAPTER 8

Clara F. Alexander. "Strategies for Finding the Main Idea." *Journal of Reading* 19 (Jan. 1976): 299-301.

Allen Berger. "Are Machines Needed to Increase Reading Rate?" *Educational Technology* 9 (August 1969): 59-60.

———"Increasing Reading Rate with Paperbacks." *Reading Improvement* 4 (Fall 1967): 47-53, 57.

G. A. Blossom. "Tolleson School Reading Project: Use of Glossaries." *Reading Improvement* 10 (Winter 1973): 31-32.

Jane H. Catterson. "Successful Study Skills Programs." *Developing Study Skills in Secondary Schools*, Perspectives in Reading No. 4. Newark, Del.: International Reading Association, 1965, pp. 159-169.

James A. Fleming. "Skimming: Neglected in Research and Teaching." *Journal of Reading* 12 (Dec. 1968): pp. 211-214, 218.

W. Frinsco and G. Drew. "Look It Up! But Can They?" *Elementary English* 49 (Jan. 1972): 74-76.

M. Buckley Hanf. "Mapping: A Technique for Translating Reading into Thinking." *Journal of Reading* 14 (Jan. 1971): 225-230, 270.

J. William McKay. "The Nature and Extent of Work-Study Skills." *Proceedings* of the University of Pittsburgh Annual Conference on Reading, 1966, pp. 53-63.

G. Harry McLaughlin. "Reading at Impossible Speeds." *Journal of Reading* 12 (March 1969): 449-454, 502-510.

John R. O'Connor. "Reading Skills in the Social Studies." *Social Education* 31 (Feb. 1967): 104-107.

CHAPTER 9

Cecilia Algra and James Fillbrandt. "Book Selection Patterns among High School Students." *Journal of Reading* 14 (Dec. 1970): 157-162.

A. Sterl Artley. "Oral Reading as a Communication Process." *The Reading Teacher* 26 (Oct. 1972): 46-51.

Saul Bachner. "Teaching Literature and Reading to the Disadvantaged." *Journal of Reading* 18 (March 1975): 480-485.

Frances M. Beck. "Fostering Interest in Reading in Grades Nine Through Fourteen." In *Reading: Seventy-five Years of Progress*, ed. H. Alan Robinson. Supplementary Educational Monographs, No. 96, Chicago: University of Chicago Press, 1966, pp. 115-119.

Daniel J. Dieterich. "Black Literature in the English Classroom." *English Journal* 62 (Jan. 1973): 149-155.

Dan Donlon. "Developing a Reading Participation Guide for a Novel." *Journal of Reading* 17 (March 1974): 439-444.

Thomas H. Estes. "A Scale for Measuring Attitudes toward Reading." *Journal of Reading* 15 (Nov. 1971): 135-138.

Morris Finder. "Teaching to Comprehend Literary Texts — Drama and Fiction." *Journal of Reading* 17 (Jan. 1974): 272-278.

Daniel Fishco. "Paperbacks and the Reading Program." *The Wide World of Reading Instruction.* Lehigh University Conference on Reading, Vol. 5, 1966, pp. 161-168.

Susan Hinton. "Teen-agers are for Real." *New York Times Book Review*, Aug. 27, 1967, pp. 26-29.

Sister Nancy Hynes. "Learning to Read Short Stories." *Journal of Reading* 13 (March 1970): 429-432, 473.

Media and Methods 5 (Jan. 1969), "Bibliotherapy" (entire issue).

Ronald G. Noland and Lynda H. Craft. "Methods to Motivate the Reluctant Reader." *Journal of Reading* 19 (Feb. 1976): 387-391.

Emerita S. Schulte. "Resources for Adolescent Literature: A Selected Bibliography." *Journal of Reading* 19 (Nov. 1975): 117-120.

CHAPTER 10

A. Bailey and G. Housekeeper. "Does Individualized Reading Affect Other Subject Areas?" *Elementary English* 49 (Jan. 1972): 37-43.

Larry L. Chance. "Using a Learning Stations Approach to Vocabulary Practice." *Journal of Reading* 18 (Dec. 1974): 244-246.

Stevan Devan and others. "Priming — A Method to Equalize Differences between High and Low Achievement Students." *Journal of Reading* 19 (Nov. 1975): 143-146.

Richard A. Earle and Richard Morley. "The Half-Open Classroom: Controlled Options in Reading." *Journal of Reading* 18 (Nov. 1974): 131-135.

Richard A. Earle and Peter L. Sanders. "Individualizing Reading Assignments." *Journal of Reading* 16 (April 1973): 550-555.

Betty Elza and Diana Owatt. "Turning to Individualized Instruction." *Journal of Reading* 19 (Nov. 1975): 125-127.

David L. Shepherd. "Individualizing Reading Instruction for High School Students." *High School Journal* 59 (Nov. 1975): 77-82.

Alan Tepilitsky. "Simulation: Individualizing in Context." *English Journal* 62 (May 1973): 800-806.

James E. Twining. "Reading and Literature: The Heterogeneous Class." *Journal of Reading* 18 (March 1975): 475-480.

William J. Underwood. "Effective Grouping in Junior High School." In *Reading and Inquiry.* Proceedings of the International Reading Association Annual Convention, 1965, pp. 136-139.

Jerry L. Walker. "Conducting an Individualized Reading Program in High School." *Journal of Reading* 8 (April 1965): 291-295.

CHAPTER 11

Morton Botel. "Dyslexia: Is There Such a Thing?" In *Current Issues in Reading*, ed. Nila B. Smith. Proceedings of the International Reading Association Annual Convention, 1969, pp. 357-371.

R. H. Bradfield and others. "Project B.E.A.M.: An Experiment in Intervention." *Journal of Negro Education* 44 (Winter 1975): 34-41.

G. Cohen. "How one Middle School Helped Its Worst Readers." *NAASP Bulletin* 59 (April 1975): 94-97.

B. M. Gillespie. "Classroom Experiment in Last Chance Reading." *Journal of Reading* 18 (Feb. 1975): 391-394.

W. John Harker. "Materials for Problem Readers: Why Aren't They Working?" *Journal of Reading* 18 (March 1975): 451-454.

William Labov and Clarence Robins. "A Note on the Relation of Reading Failure to Peer-Group Status in Urban Ghettos." *Teachers College Record*, 70 (Feb. 1969): 395-405.

J. R. Levin. "Inducing Comprehension in Poor Readers: A Test of a Recent Model." *Journal of Educational Psychology* 65 (August 1973): 19-24.

Ruby W. Martin. "Realities and Fallacies of Teaching Reading to Black High School Students." *Journal of Reading* 18 (March 1975): 445-450.

J. P. Mulligan. "Using Language Experience with Potential High School Dropouts." *Journal of Reading* 18 (Dec. 1974): 206-211.

S. Jay Samuels. "Success and Failure in Learning to Read: A Critique of the Research." *Reading Research Quarterly* 8 (Winter 1973): 200-239.

Morton Wiener and Ward Cromer. "Reading and Reading Difficulty: A Conceptual Analysis." *Harvard Educational Review* 37 (Fall 1967): 620-643.

READING TESTS

HIGH SCHOOL READING AND STUDY SKILLS TESTS

Burnett Reading Series: Survey Test. Advanced (Grades 7.0-9.9, 10.0-12.9) Bensenville, Ill.: Scholastic Testing Service.

California Achievement Tests: Reading. Level 4 (Grades 6-9), Level 5 (Grades 9-12). Monterey, Calif.: California Test Bureau/McGraw-Hill.

Cooperative Reading Comprehension Test. Forms 1A (for typical students in grades 13-14 and superior students in grade 12) and 2A (for typical students in grades 9, 10, 11, 12). Princeton, N.J.: Cooperative Test Division, Educational Testing Service.

Davis Reading Test. Series 1 (Grades 11-13), Series 2 (Grades 8-11). New York: Psychological Corp.

Diagnostic Reading Tests: Upper Level (Grade 7-College Freshman Year). Mountain Home, N.C.: The Committee on Diagnostic Tests.

Gates-MacGinitie Reading Tests. Survey E (Grades 7-9), Survey F (Grades 10-12). New York: Teachers College Press.

Iowa Every Pupil Test of Basic Skills, Test A. Silent Reading Comprehension, Advanced (Grades 6-8). Boston: Houghton Mifflin.

Iowa Every Pupil Test of Basic Skills, Test B, Work-Study Skills, Advanced (Grades 6-8). Boston: Houghton Mifflin.

Iowa Silent Reading Tests. Level I (Grades 6-9), Level II (Grades 9-12), Level III (Grades 11-14). New York: Harcourt Brace Jovanovich.

Kelley-Greene Reading Comprehension Test (Grades 9-13). New York: Harcourt Brace Jovanovich.

Metropolitan Achievement Tests: Reading. Advanced (Grades 7-9). New York: Harcourt Brace Jovanovich.

Nelson-Denny Reading Test (Grades 9-16). Boston: Houghton Mifflin.

Sequential Tests of Educational Progress, Reading. Forms 2B (Grades 10-12), 3B (Grades 7-9). Princeton: Cooperative Test Division, Educational Testing Service.

Spitzer Study Skills Test (Grades 9-13). New York: Harcourt Brace Jovanovich.

SRA Achievement Series: Reading (Grades 4-9). Chicago: Science Research Associates.

Stanford Achievement Test: High School Reading (Grades 9-12). New York: Harcourt Brace Jovanovich.

Stanford Diagnostic Reading Test. Level II (Grades 4.5-8.5), Level III (Grades 9-12). New York: Harcourt Brace Jovanovich.

ELEMENTARY LEVEL READING TESTS
(For Students with Reading Disabilities)

Burnett Reading Series: Survey Test. Primary 1 (Grades 1. 5-2. 4), Primary 2 (Grades 2.5-3.9), Intermediate (Grades 4.0-6.9). Bensenville Ill.: Scholastic Testing Service.

California Achievement Tests: Reading. Level 1 (Grades 1.5-2), Level 2 (Grades 2-4), Level 3 (Grades 4-6). Monterey, Calif.: California Test Bureau/McGraw Hill.

Diagnostic Reading Tests. Lower Level (Grades 4-6). Mountain Home, N.C.: Committee on Diagnostic Tests.

Gates-MacGinitie Reading Tests. Primary A (Grade 1), Primary B (Grade 2), Primary C (Grade 3), Primary Cs (Grades 2-3), Survey D (Grades 4-6). New York: Bureau of Publications, Teachers College, Columbia University.

Gilmore Oral Reading Test (Grades 1-8). New York: Harcourt Brace Jovanovich.

Gray Standardized Oral Reading Paragraphs (Grades 1-8). Indianapolis: Bobbs-Merrill.

Iowa Every Pupil Test of Basic Skills. Test A, Elementary (Grades 4-8). New York: Harcourt Brace Jovanovich.

Iowa Silent Reading Test. Elementary (Grades 4-8). New York: Harcourt Brace Jovanovich.

Metropolitan Reading Test. Primary (Grades 2-3), Elementary (Grades 3-4), Intermediate (Grades 5-6). New York: Harcourt Brace Jovanovich.

Stanford Achievement Tests: Reading. Primary (Grades 1-3), Elementary (Grades 3-4), Intermediate (Grades 5-6). New York: Harcourt Brace Jovanovich.

Stanford Diagnostic Reading Test. Level 1 (Grades 2.5-4.5), Level 2 (Grades 4.5-8.5). New York: Harcourt Brace Jovanovich.

MATERIALS for TEACHING READING

Action Reading System, Scholastic Book Services.
Advanced Skills in Reading, Macmillan.
Basic Reading Skills in Junior High School, Scott, Foresman.
Basic Reading Skills for High School, Scott, Foresman.
Basic Skills System, McGraw-Hill.
Be a Better Reader Series, Prentice-Hall.
Better Reading, Globe Book.
Corrective Reading Program, Science Research Associates.
Critical Reading and Listening Skills Program, Instructional/Communications Technology.
Design for Good Reading, Harcourt Brace Jovanovich.
Developmental Reading, Paul S. Amadon.
EDL's Learning 100, Educational Developmental Laboratories.
EDL Word Clues, Educational Developmental Laboratories.
Learning Word Series, Oxford Book.
Programmed Study Techniques, American Guidance Service.
Programmed Vocabulary, Appleton-Century-Crofts.
Reading for Achievement, Holt, Rinehart and Winston.
Reading for Concepts, McGraw-Hill.
Reading for Meaning Series, J. B. Lippincott.
Reading in High Gear, Science Research Associates.
Reading Skills File, Reading Laboratory.
Reading Skillbook, American Book.
Reading-Thinking Skills Program, Continental.
Really Reading!, Charles E. Merrill.
Scope/Skills, Scholastic Book Services.
Skill File, Reading Laboratory.
Skill at a Time Series, Jamestown.
Sports Action Skills Kits, Troll.
SRA Reading Laboratories, Science Research Associates.
Steps to Better Reading, Harcourt Brace Jovanovich.
Student Reading Improvement Series, Science Research Associates.
Study Techniques for Academic Subjects, Baldridge.
Success in Reading, Silver Burdett.
Success with Words, Scholastic Book Services.
Tactics in Reading III, Scott, Foresman.
Turner-Livingstone Reading Series, Follett.
Vocabulary for the High School Student, Amsco.
World of Vocabulary, Book 3, Globe Book.

INDEX OF NAMES

SUBJECT INDEX